From Holland with Love.

Virginie

&

Leo

December 2018

The Netherlands
at its best Frans Lemmens

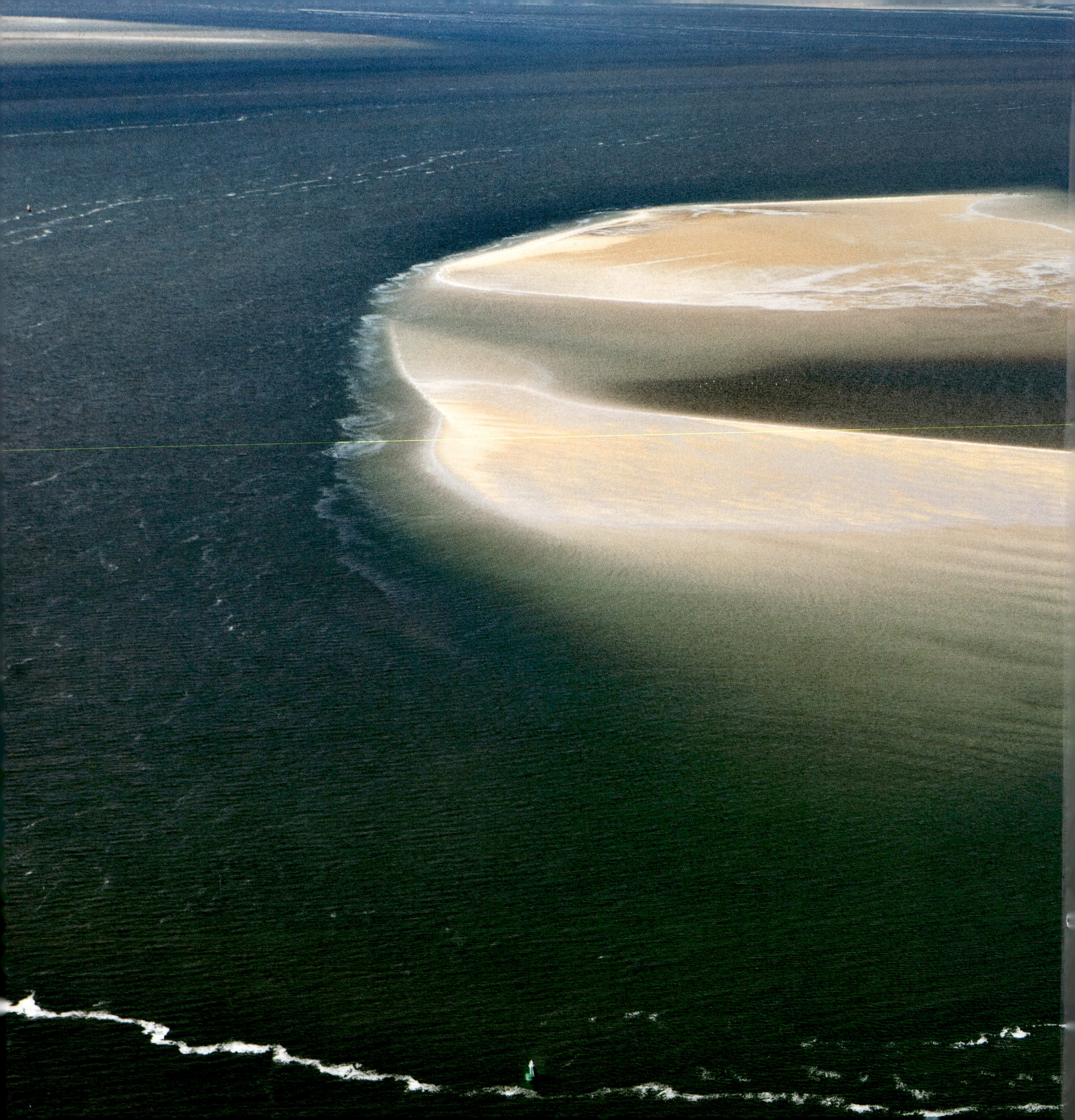

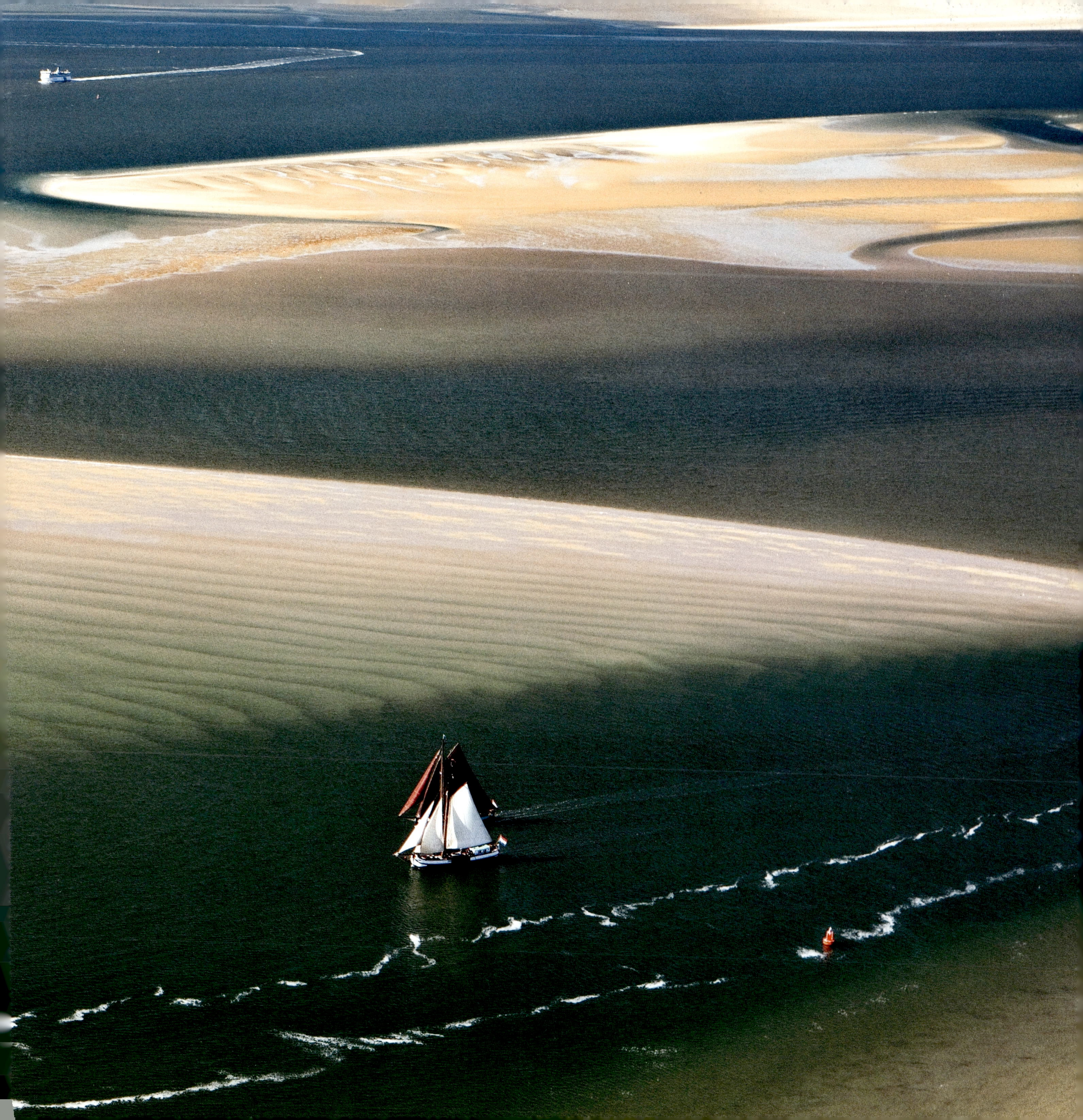

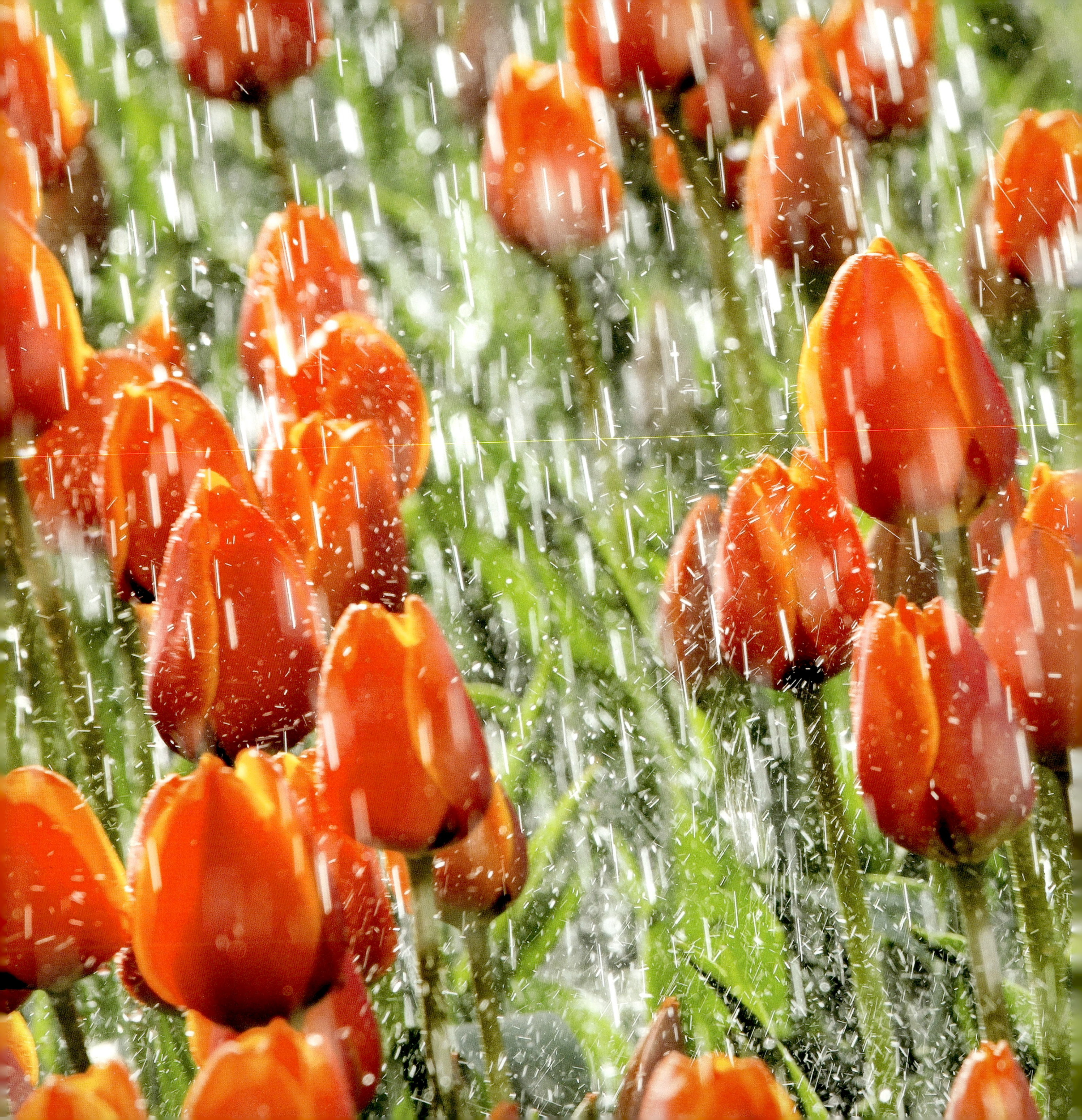

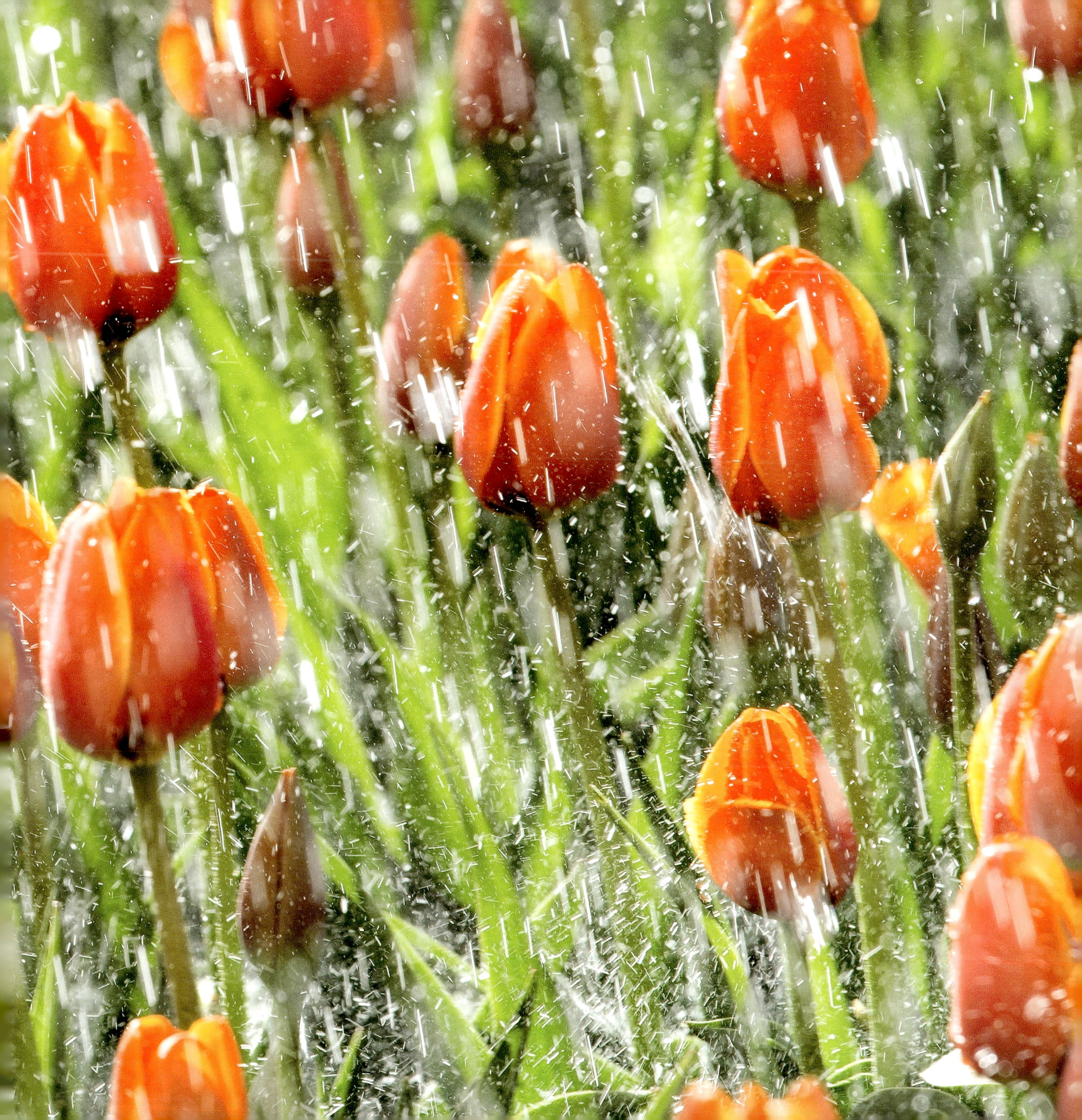

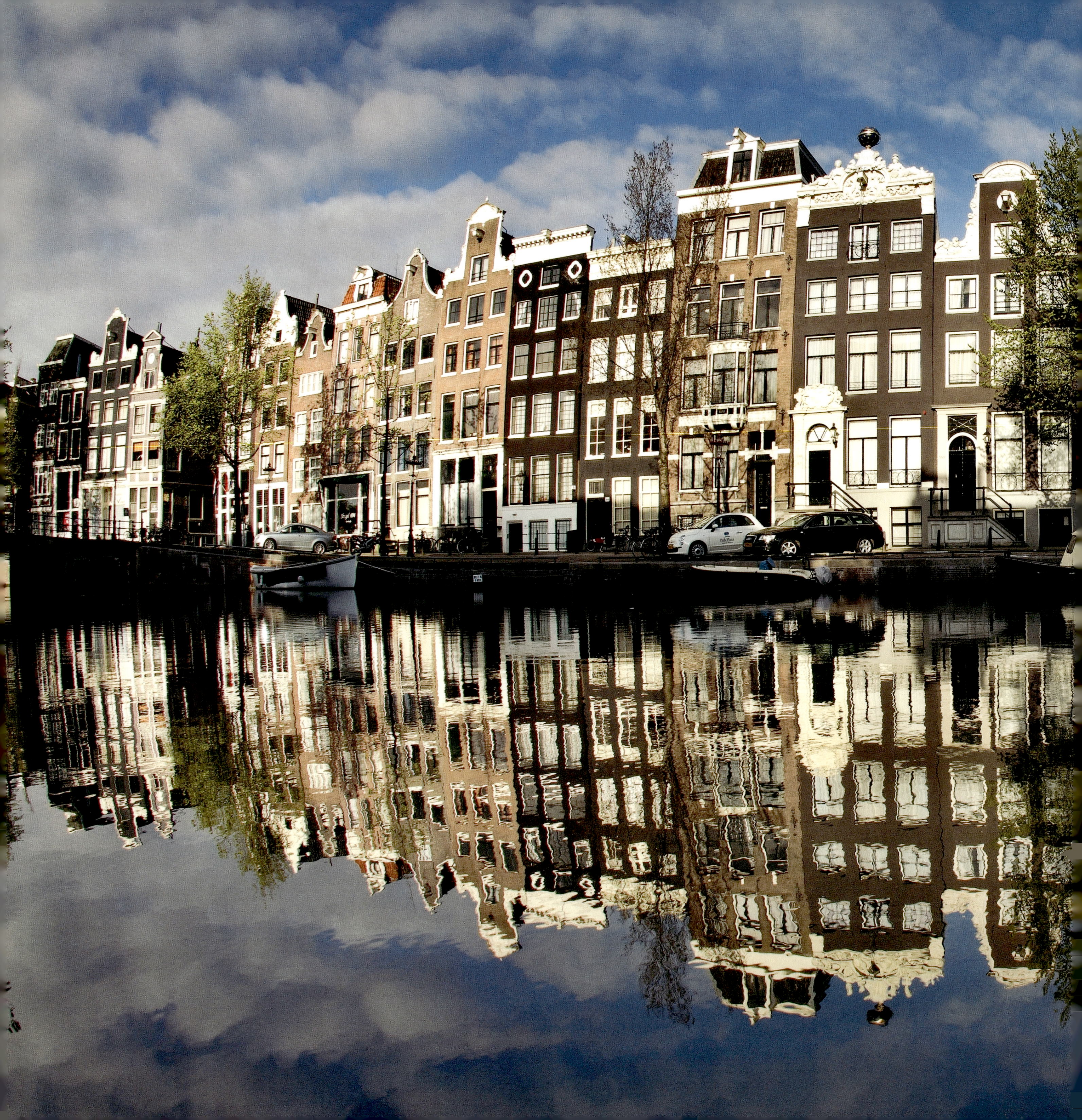

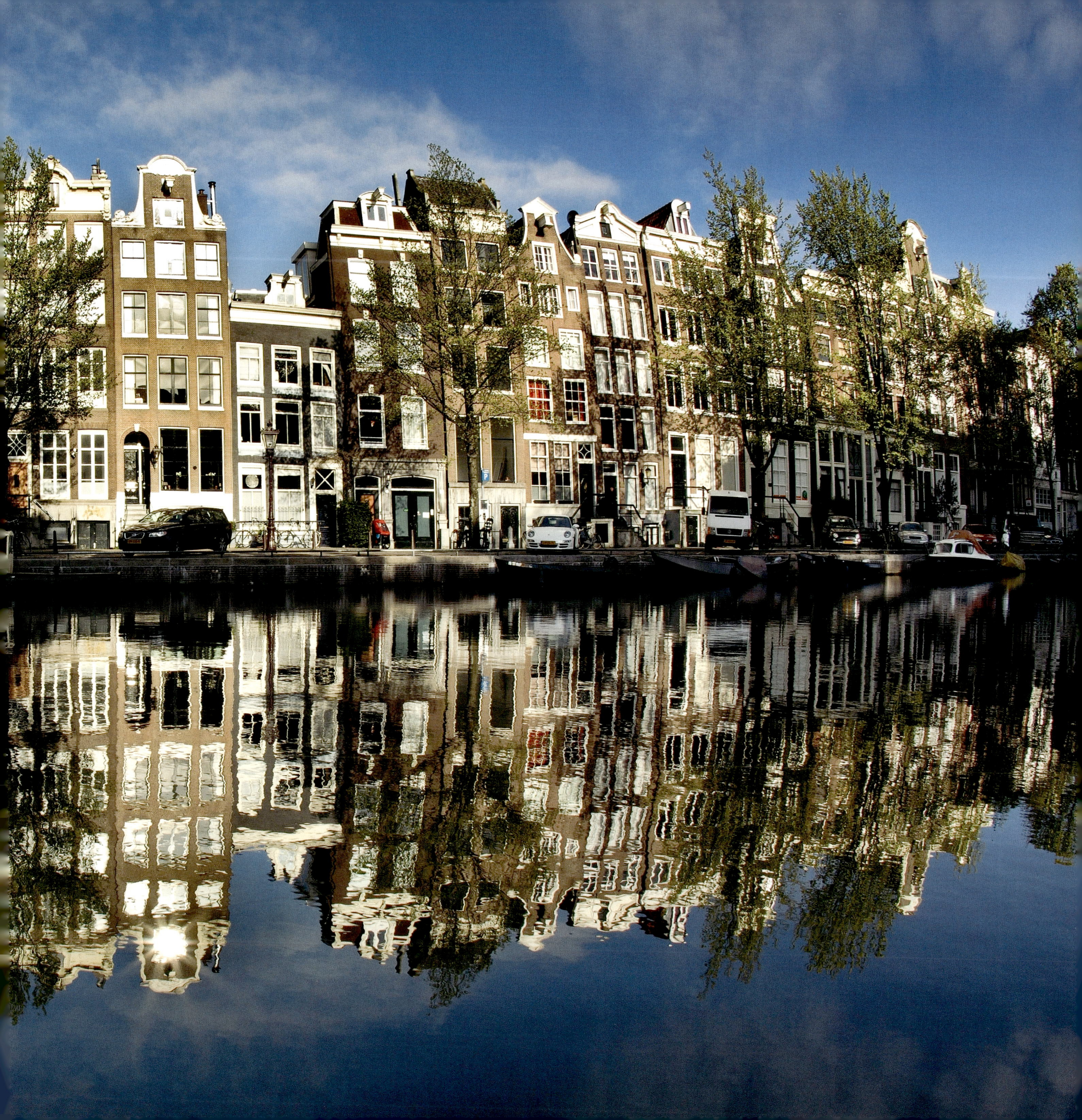

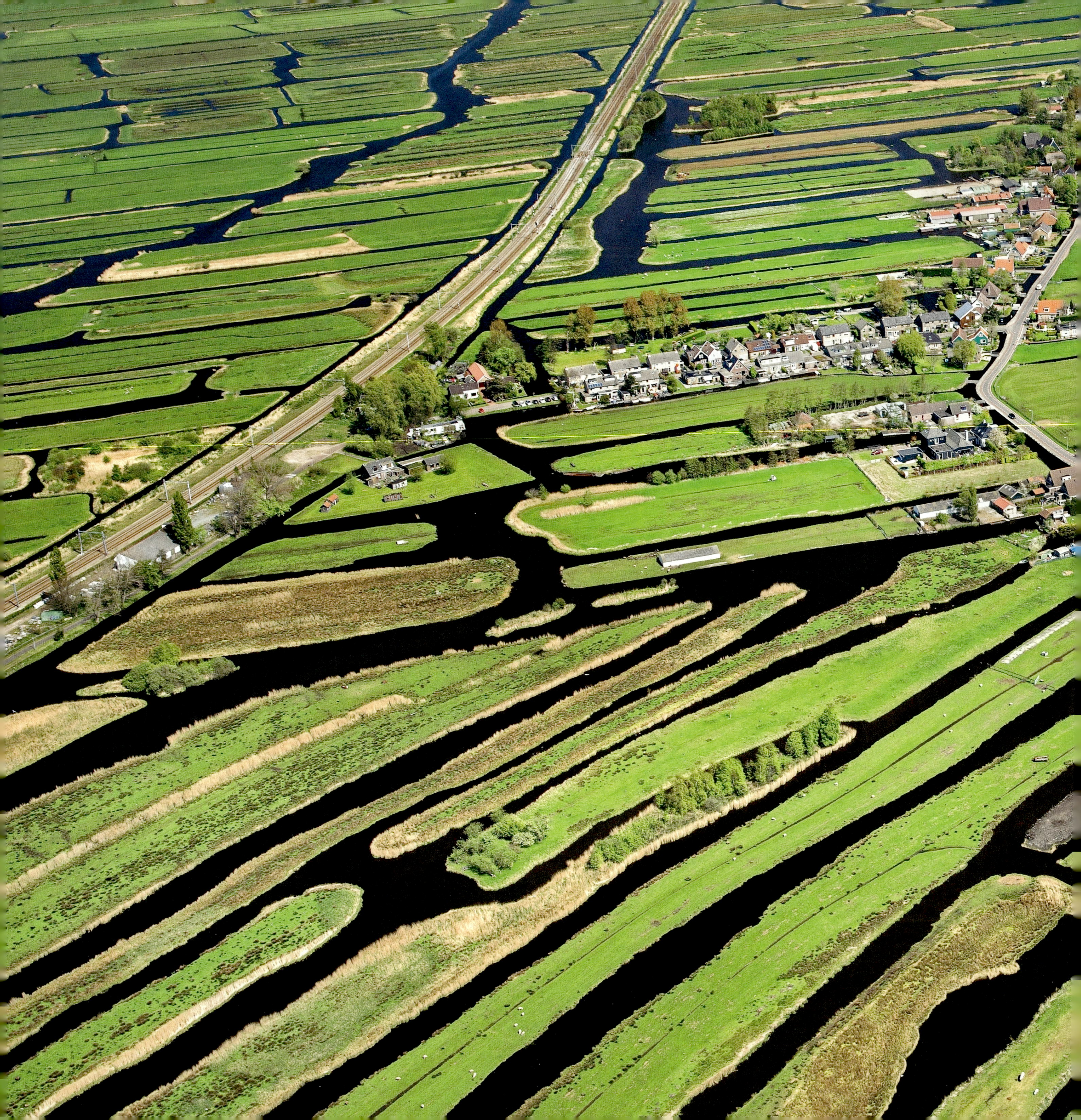

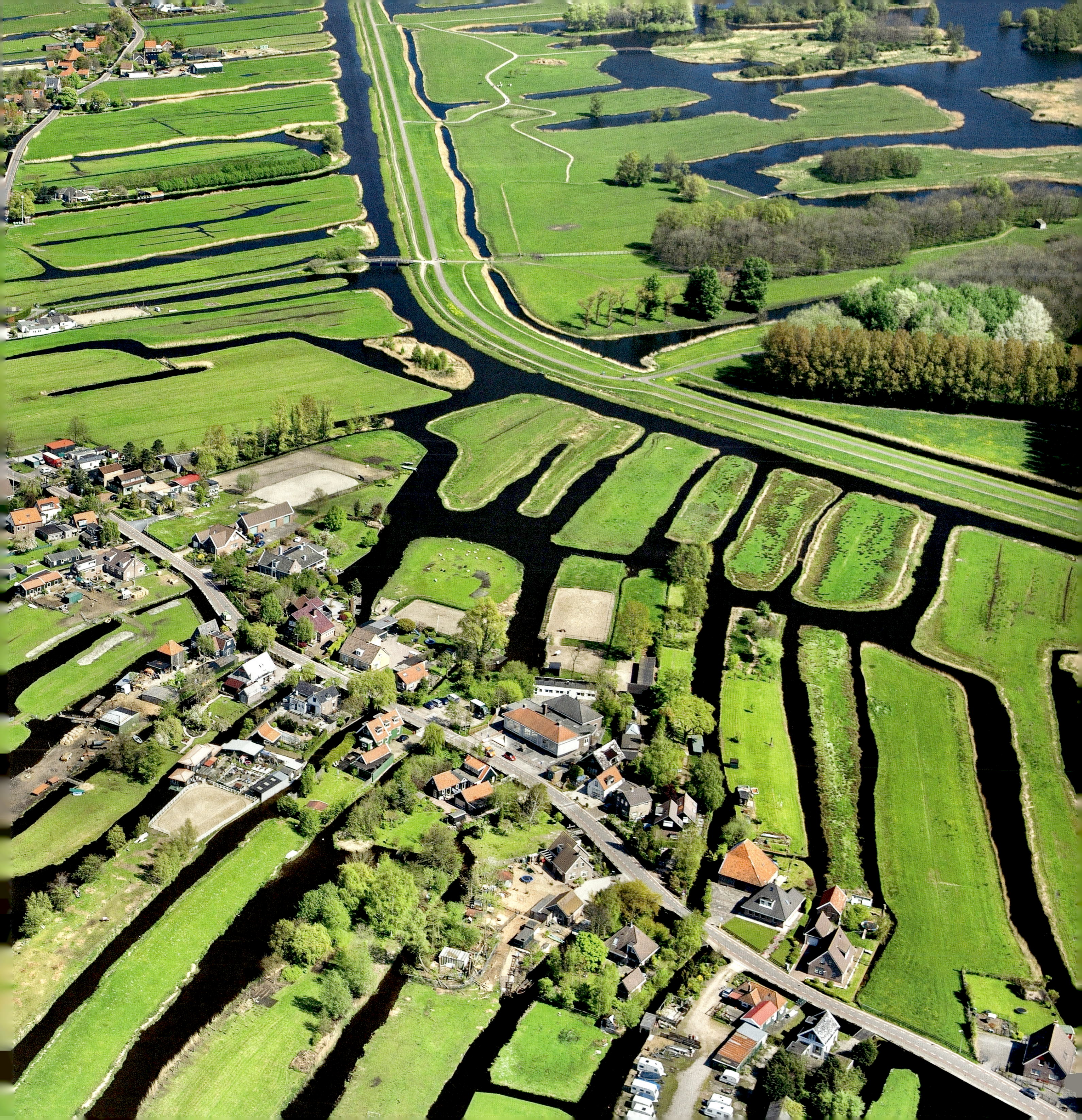

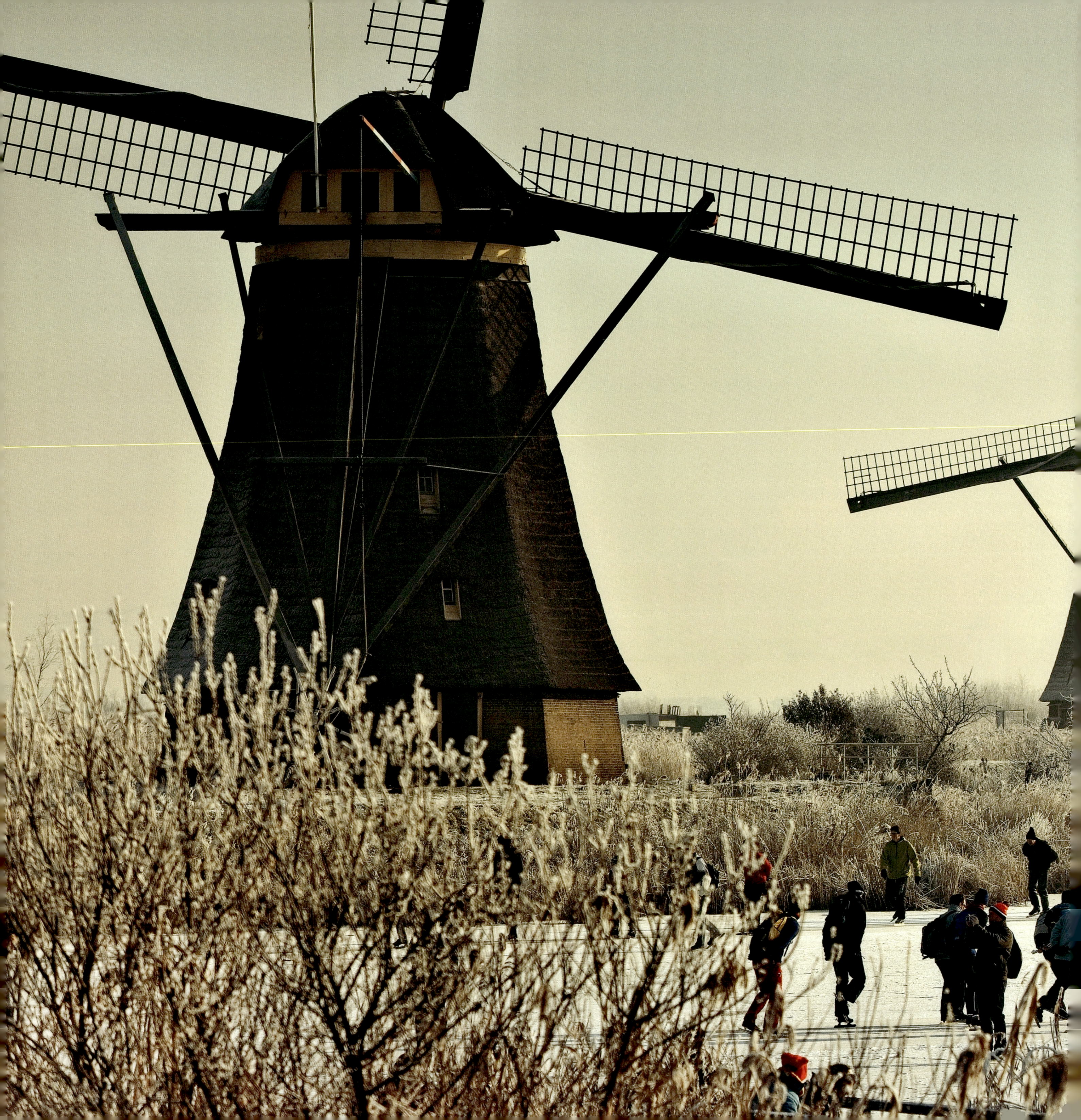

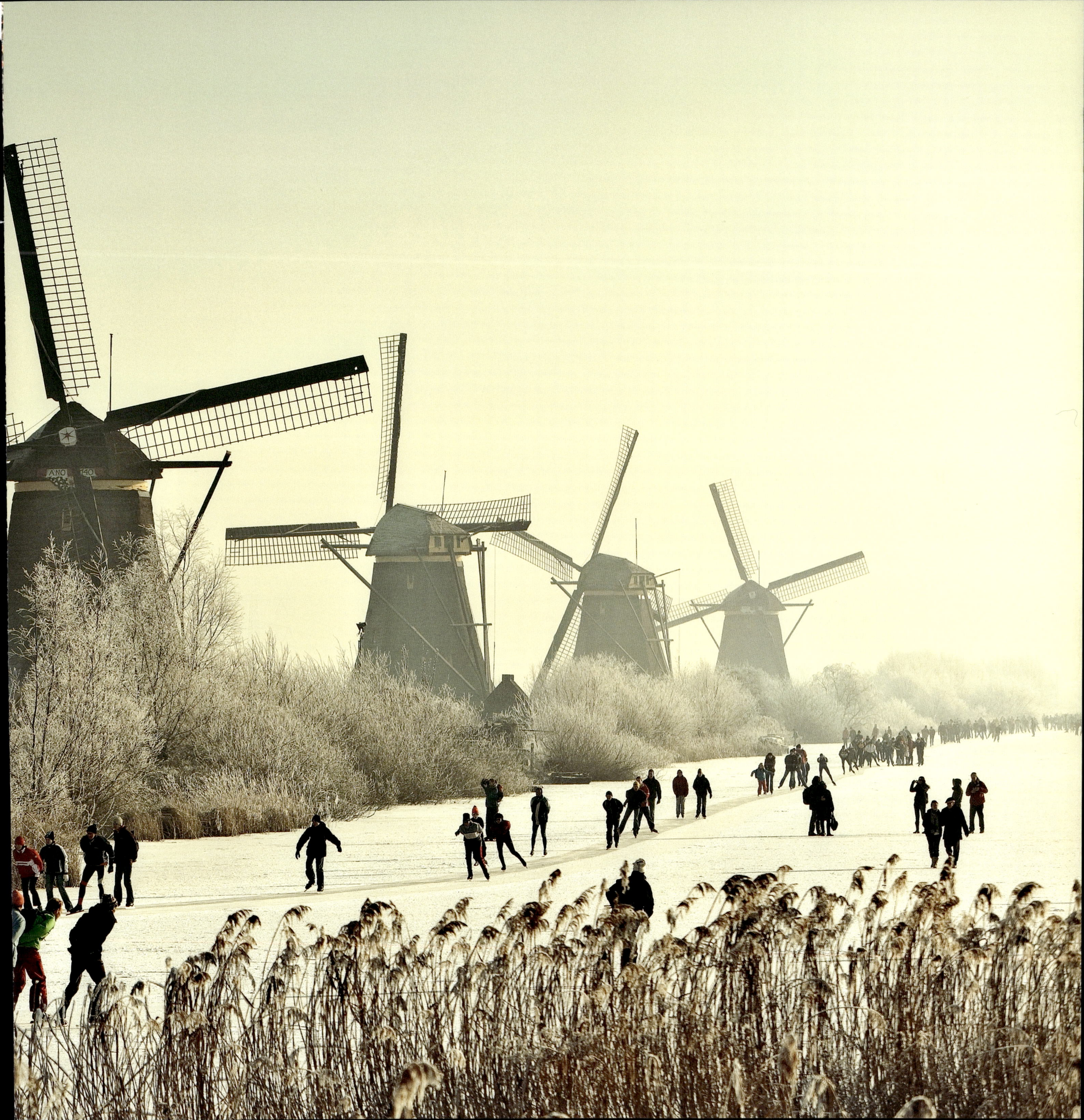

NATIONAL GEOGRAPHIC

The National Geographic Society is one of the largest scientific and educational non-profit organisations in the world. The Society was founded in 1888 to increase and diffuse geographical knowledge, and it illustrates the world through its magazines, books, maps, and interactive media. *National Geographic Magazine*, the official journal of the Society, is published in 29 languages and is read each month by forty million people in all countries of the world. The National Geographic Channel reaches 290 million households in 27 languages in 164 countries. The Society has funded more than nine thousand research projects. Visit the website of the National Geographic Society at www.nationalgeographic.com or visit the Dutch website at www.nationalgeographic.nl.

Cover: Aerial view of flower fields in Lisse, Zuid-Holland province.

- Pages 2-3: The Wadden Sea near Terschelling.
- Pages 4-5: Watering tulips near Espel in Flevoland.
- Pages 6-7: Canal houses on the Singel in Amsterdam.
- Pages 8-9: Aerial view of Oostzaan and the polder of the same name in the province of Noord-Holland.
- Pages 10-11: Skaters by the windmills of Kinderdijk.

The Netherlands
at its best Frans Lemmens

NATIONAL GEOGRAPHIC

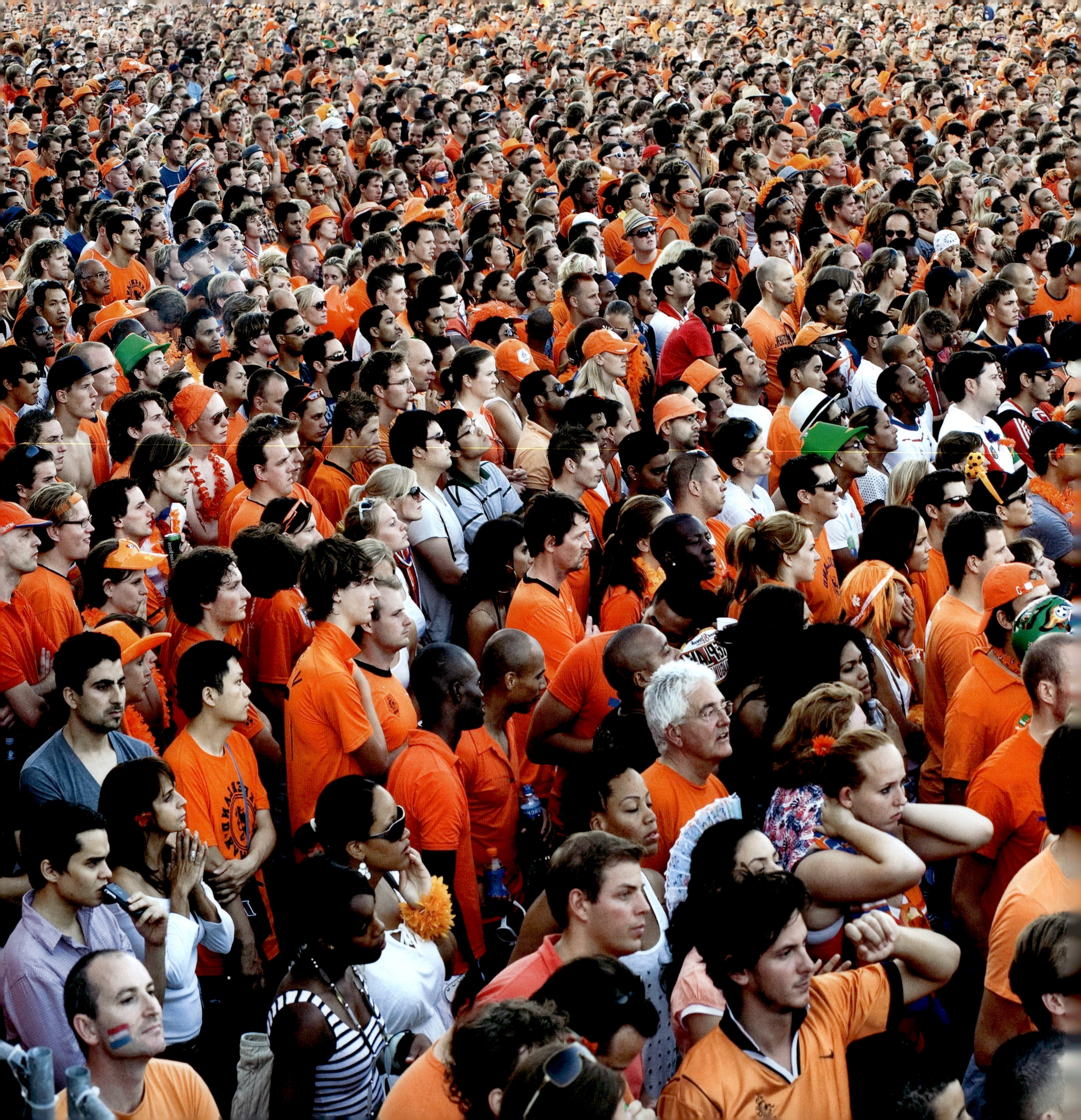

PREFACE

Try to think of a few themes that represent the core of the last thousand years of history in the Netherlands, and you'll come up with trade, water, survival, tolerance and cooperation.
For instance, there has been the struggle against the water, the oldest and greatest enemy, which early on made the inhabitants of the Low Countries a determined, obstinate, inventive and cooperative people. And while elsewhere in Europe feudal systems still had free rein, there arose in the swampy river deltas, born out of necessity, early forms of democratic governing bodies. The tolerance of dissent – opportunistic in origin though it often was – was much greater in the seventeenth-century Dutch Republic than in the rest of Europe. From that time on, the economy went from strength to strength, largely due to trade and shipping, but also helped by fishing, industry and agriculture. The country's location on the North Sea and at the mouth of three major rivers came in useful here.
All those aspects of the Netherlands are still visible in our country. And that's what this book is about: what makes the Netherlands so typically Dutch. We not only look backwards, but forwards, and when we do so we focus on economic activity and innovation. Our country can boast a number of top economic sectors that enjoy a great deal of international prestige. To maintain such top positions, or to strengthen them, the Dutch government invests extra money in these sectors. Examples of such top sectors include new technologies to protect the land from water, or to improve cultivation processes in greenhouse horticulture. For us, it was a wonderful challenge to illustrate that aspect of the Netherlands as well as the others. *The Netherlands at its best* shows how versatile, sparkling and dynamic the Netherlands is.

Marjolijn van Steeden and Frans Lemmens

Left: Amsterdam, Football World Cup. Thousands of fans gather on the Museumplein to watch the Dutch team perform, on large screens. No matter how many colours there are in Dutch society, orange is the colour for all of us.

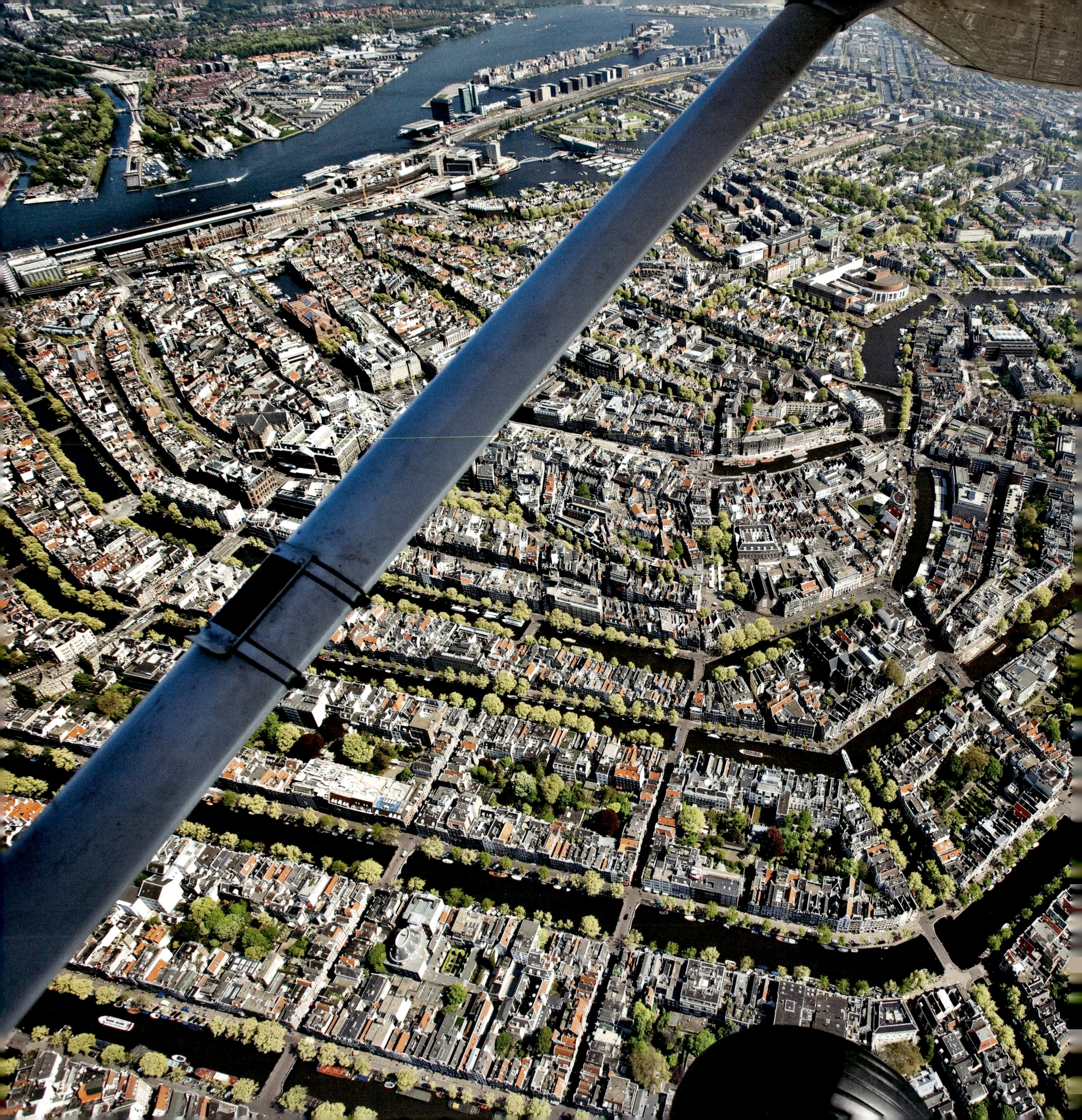

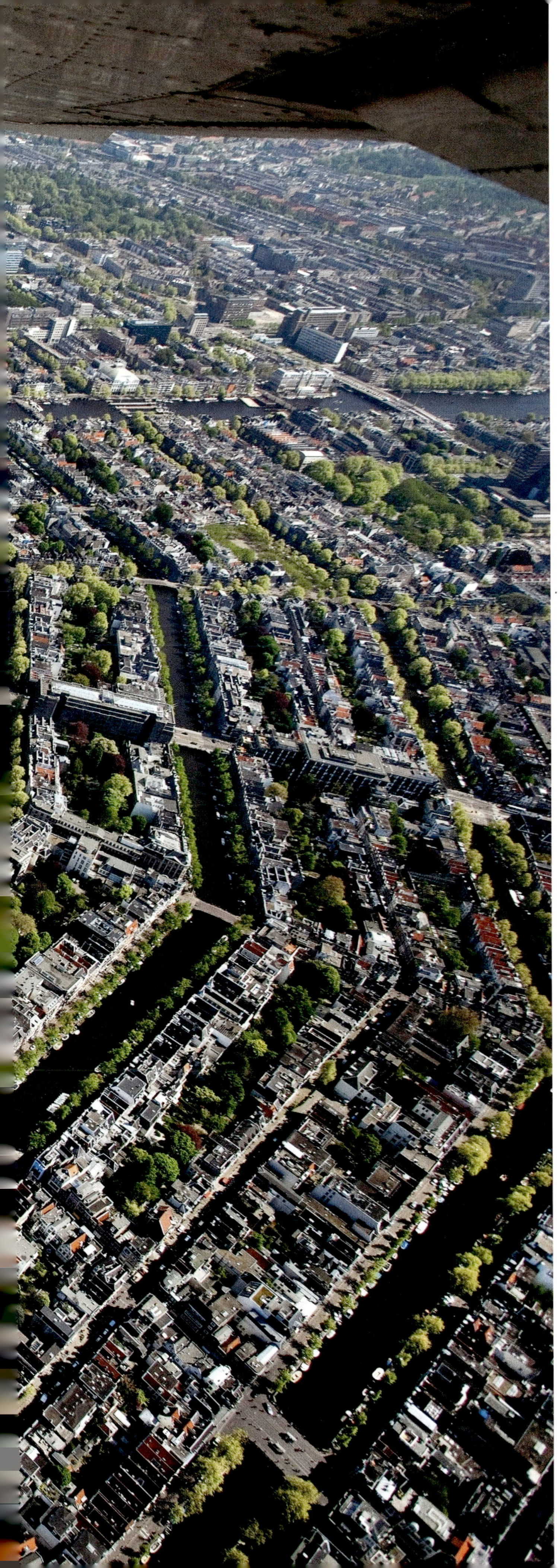

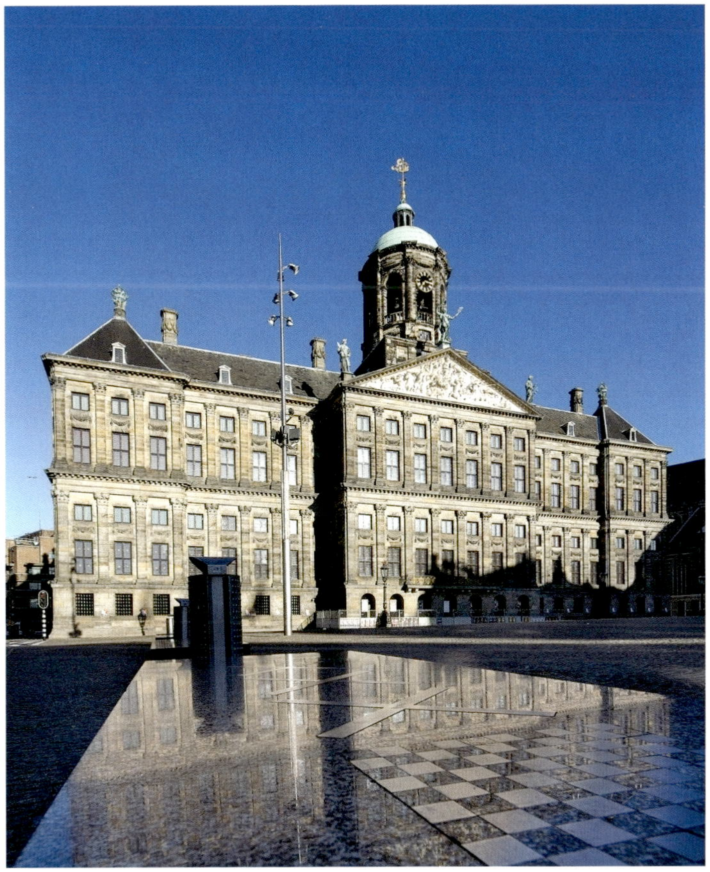

Amsterdam

Amsterdam old town oozes history. The seventeenth-century canal ring has been on the UNESCO World Heritage List since 2010. To understand the emergence of this ring of canals, we must take a step back in time.

Amsterdam was once no more than a simple agricultural settlement around a dam in the river Amstel. It did not take long to burgeon into a town surrounded by a canal, dug in 1425, which was reinforced in the late fifteenth century with a city wall. To protect Amsterdam from attacks, a new, broader city wall was built, allowing space for a significant expansion of the city. Between 1585 and 1680, the city was expanded in four phases with ramparts and moats that were extended down to the river Amstel. Thus arose the characteristic crescent shape of the city, which it kept for two centuries, until the city was further expanded. The seventeenth-century enhancements ensured that within half a century, Amsterdam became the third city of Europe, with a population of 220,000.

Left: This aerial photograph well shows the scale and shape of central Amsterdam.

Top: The Royal Palace on Dam Square is situated in the heart of the old town and was built between 1648 and 1655. In the seventeenth century, this palace, which then was still City Hall, was the largest secular building in the world, something that underscored the freethinking character of the city.

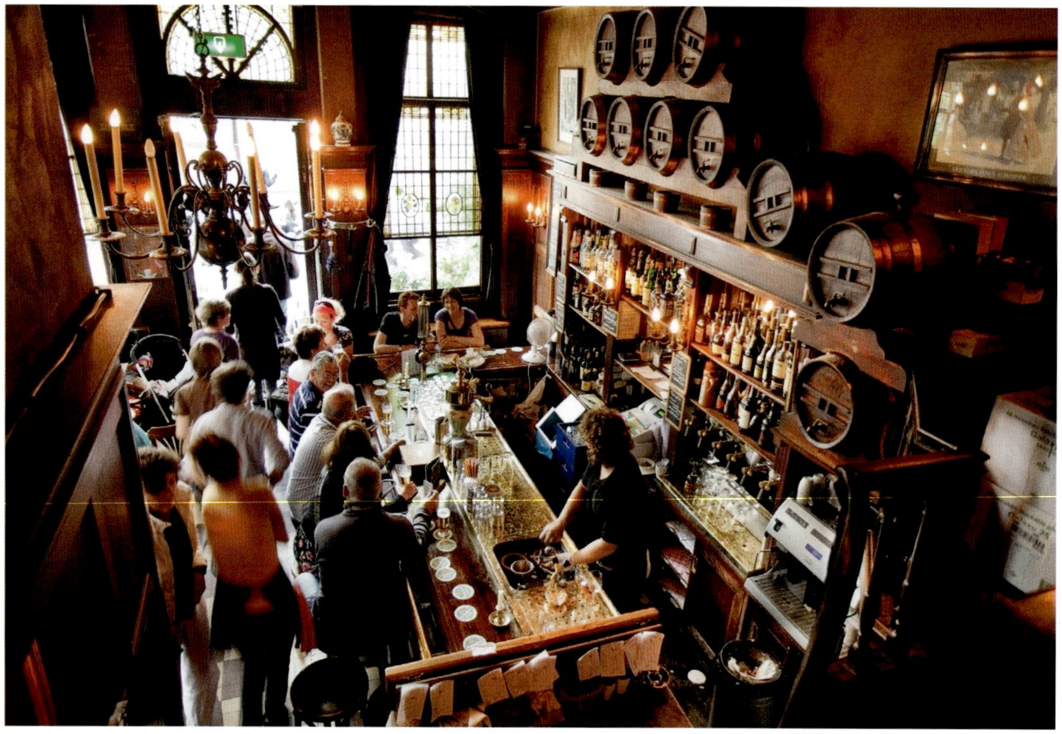

The Amsterdam canal belt is characterized by historic facades – very typical of the Golden Age. The reason why many canal houses are so narrow and deep is that tax was calculated at the time on the width of the facade. Horse and stagecoach might have been replaced by bicycles and cars since then, but the gables are still as beautiful as they were.

Top: Café Het Smalle, one of the many 'brown bars'.

Right: Crossroads of the Keizersgracht and the narrower Leidsegracht at dusk.

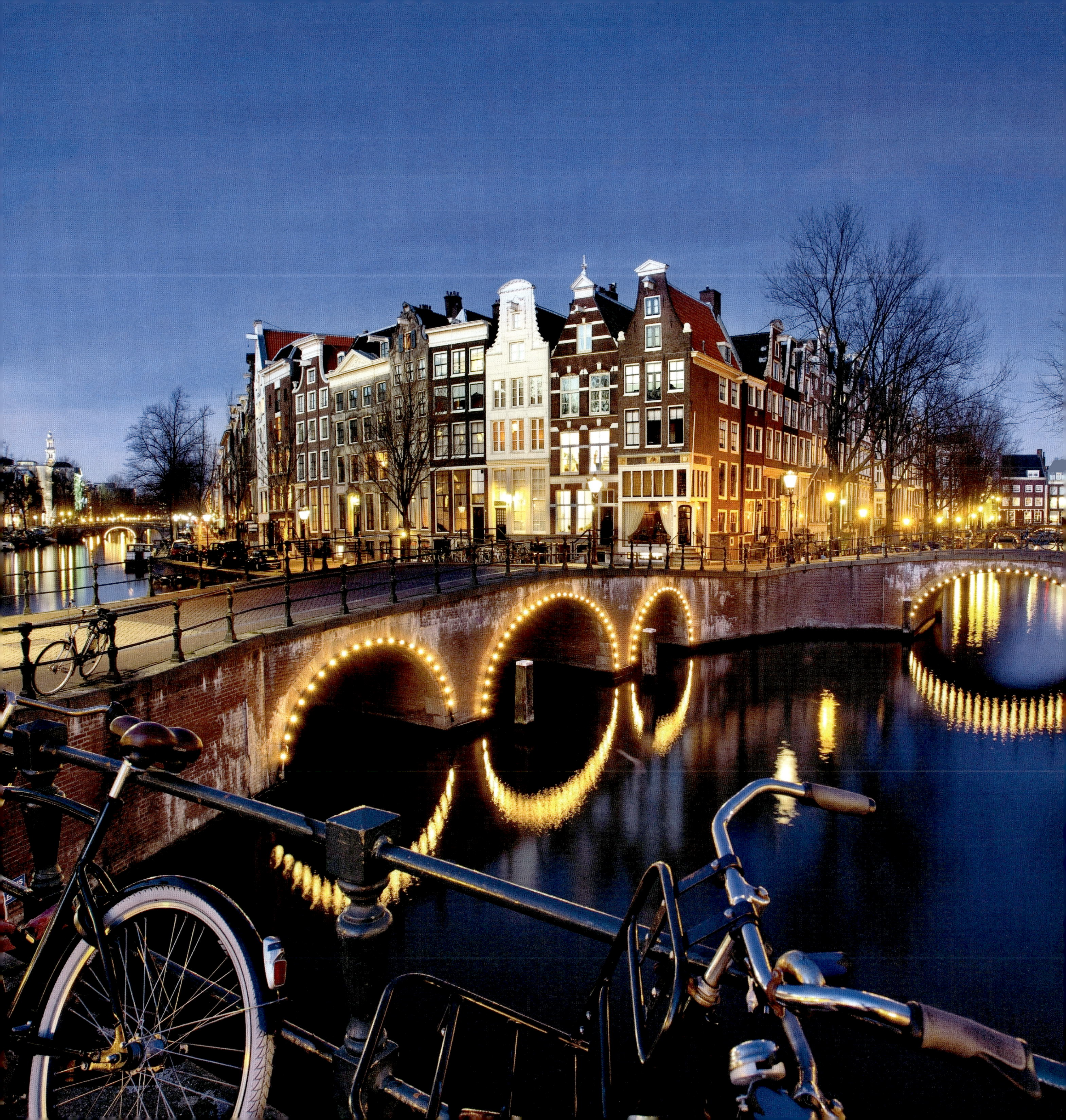

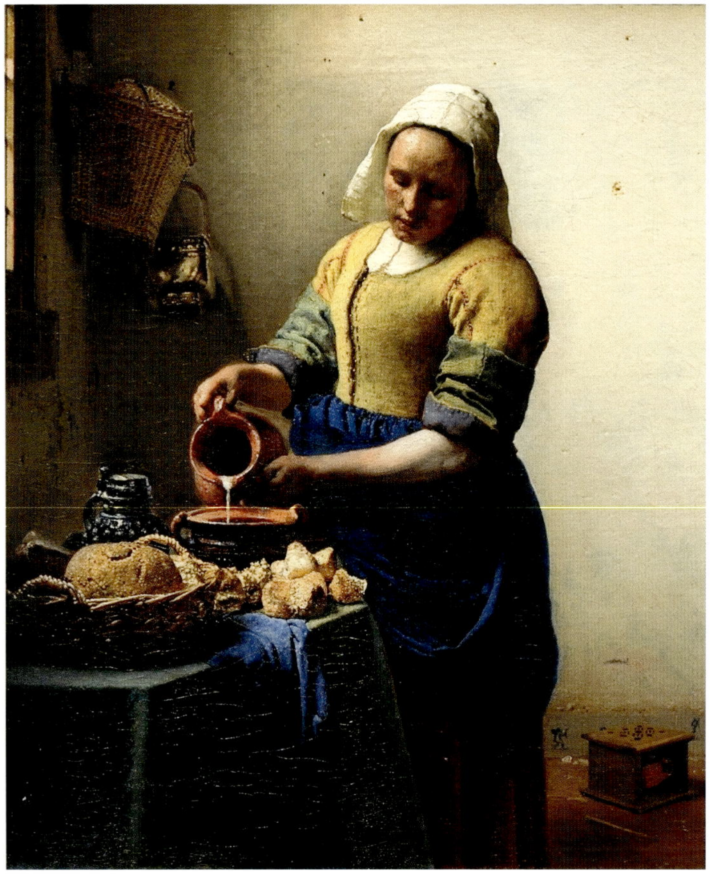

A visit to the Rijksmuseum is one of the best ways to get to know something about Dutch history, especially the Golden Age. The highlight of the museum is of course the Gallery of Honour, containing famous paintings like *The Milkmaid* by Johannes Vermeer, painted around 1660 (top), and *The Night Watch* by Rembrandt van Rijn from 1642 (right).

Following pages: The Magere Brug (Skinny Bridge) over the Amstel, its sides decorated with reflective artwork by Titia Ex entitled *Appears in Amsterdam*, during the Amsterdam Light Festival.

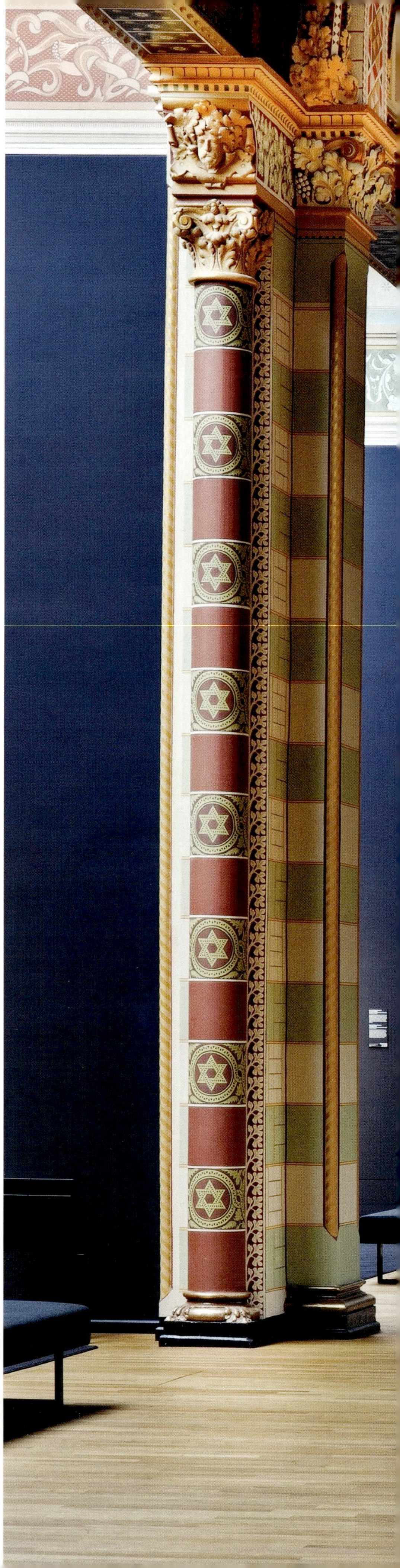

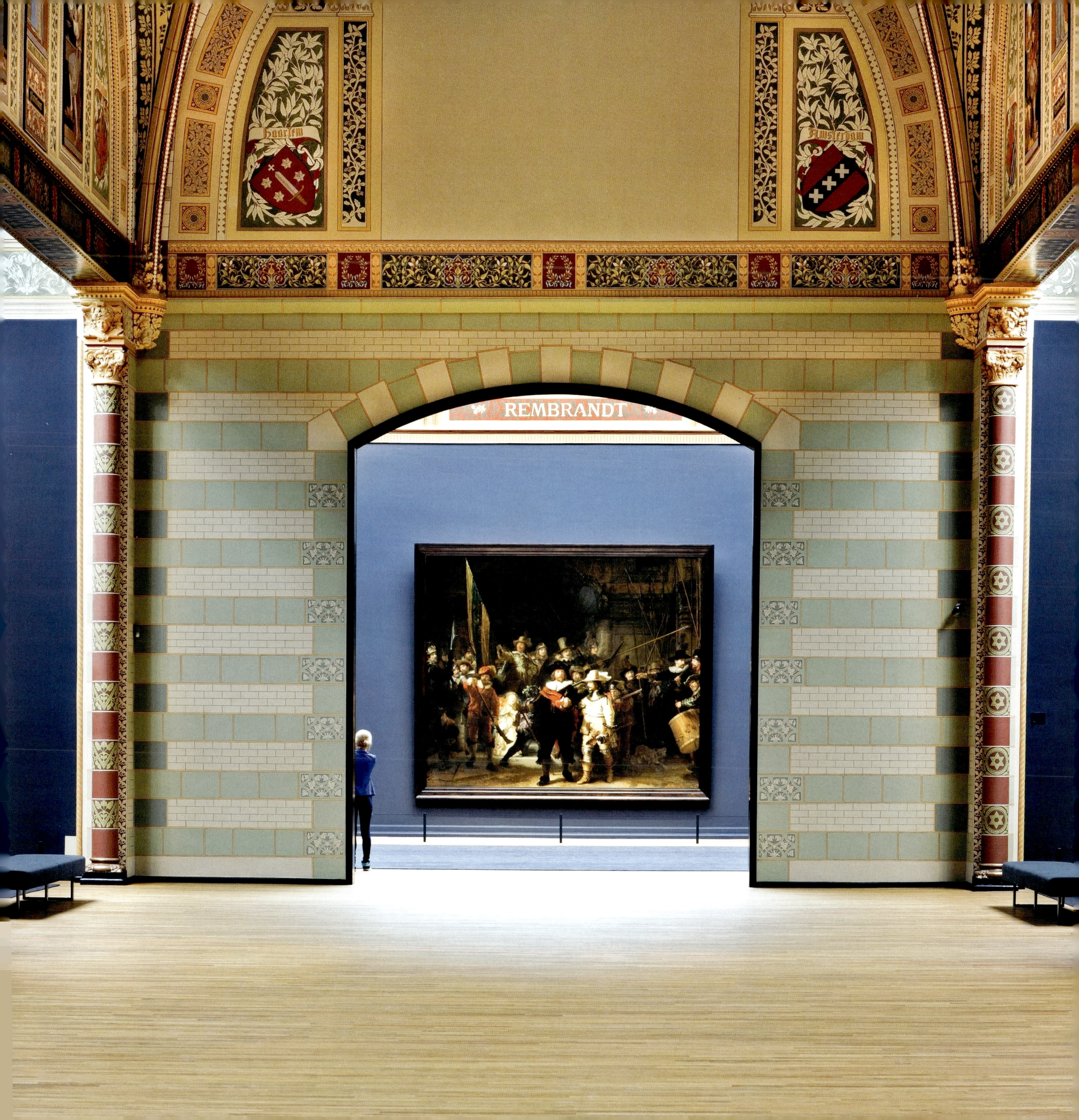
REMBRANDT

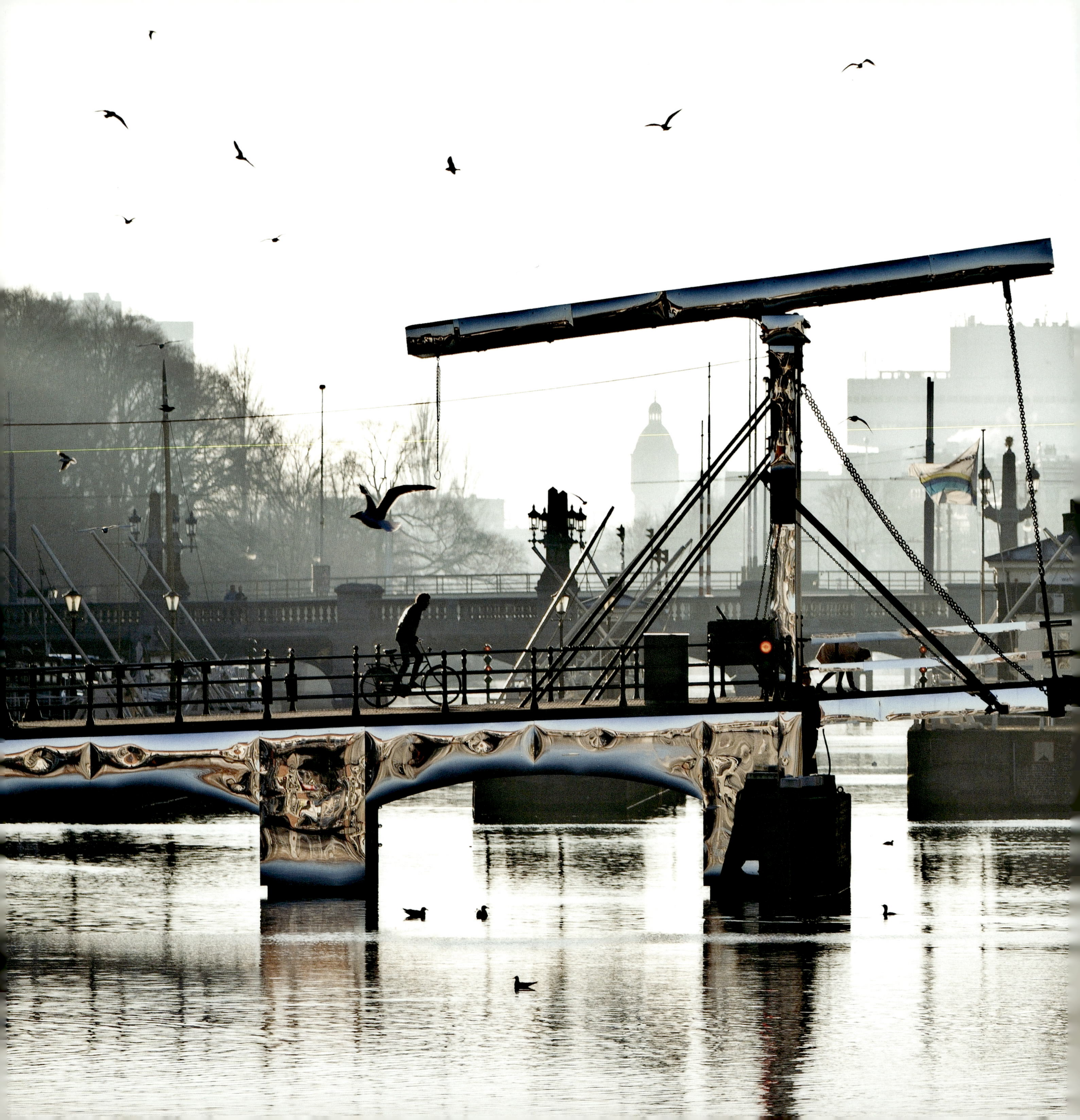

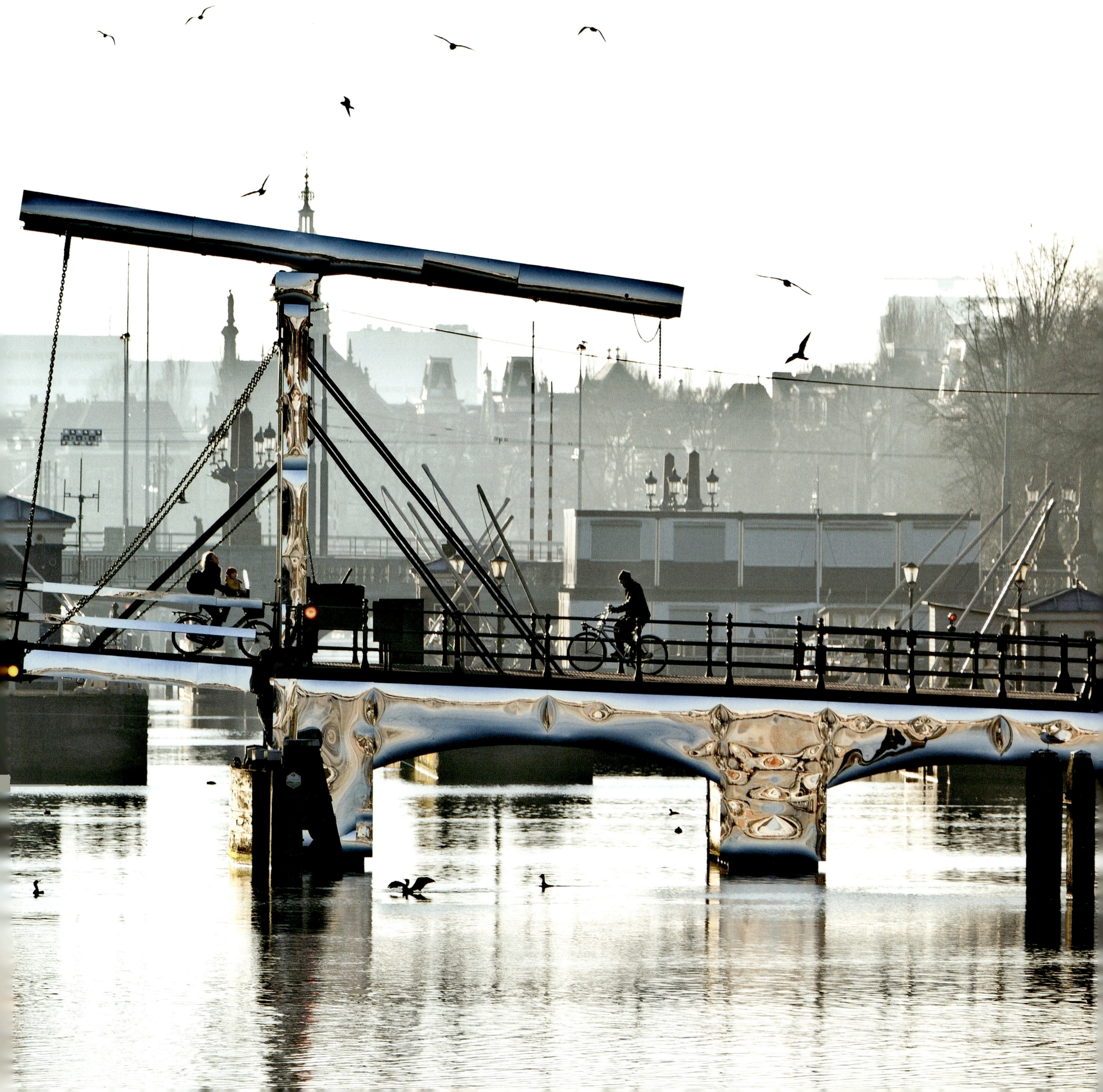

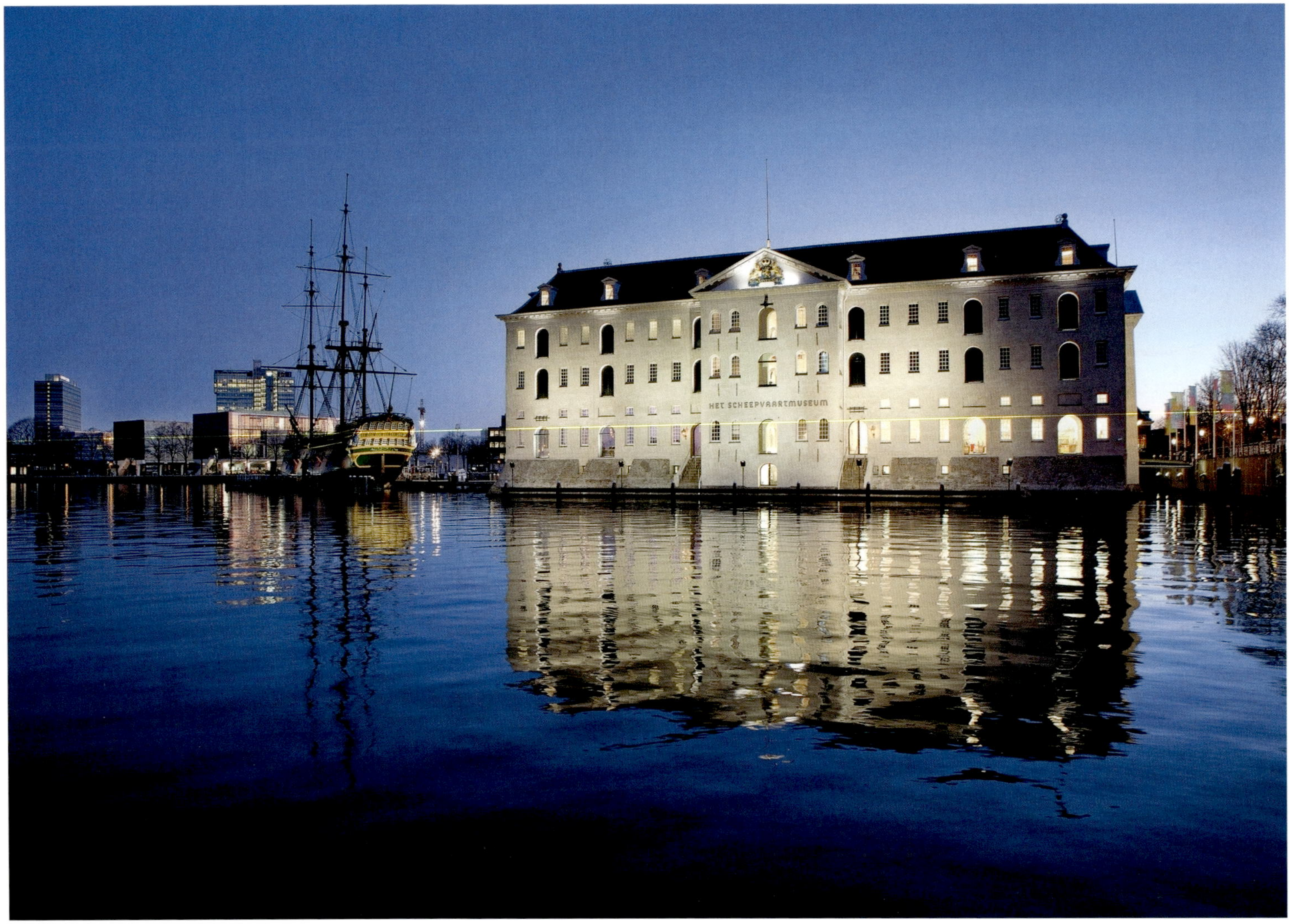

Top: The Museumplein plays host to famous museums such as the Rijksmuseum, the Van Gogh Museum and the Stedelijk Museum. But Amsterdam has much more than this one square to offer in terms of museums. Illustrated is the Maritime Museum, whose displays explain how the sea has shaped Dutch culture.

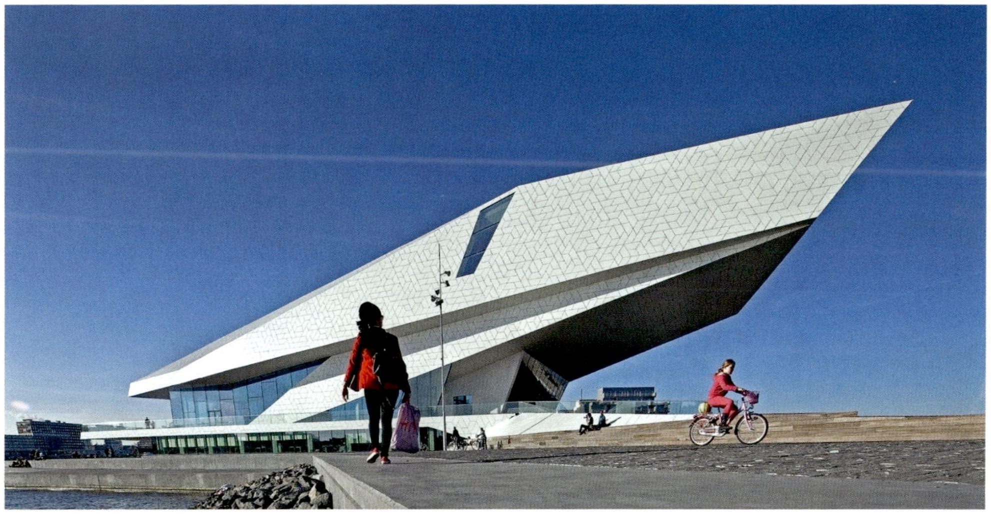

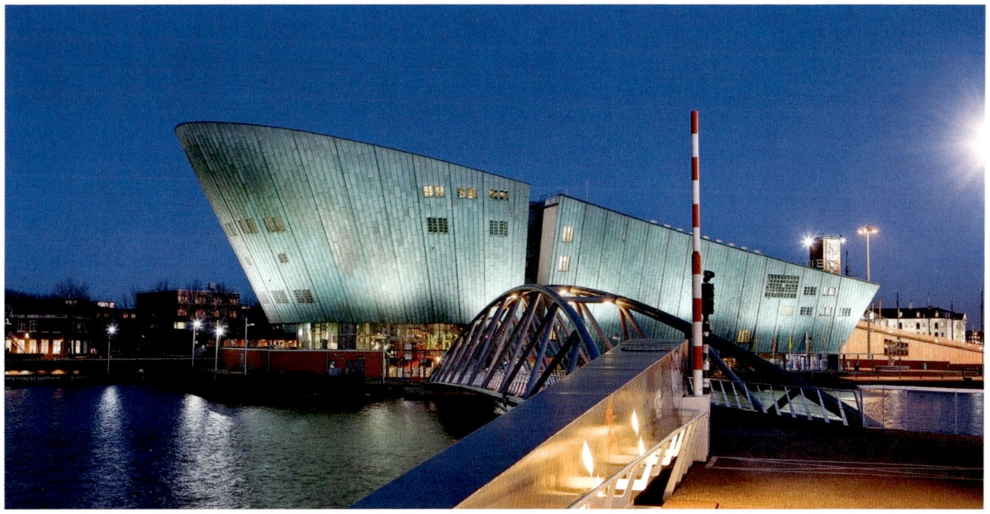

Top: EYE Film Institute, the leading centre for cinematography in the Netherlands.

Bottom: At NEMO Technology Museum, visitors can playfully get to grips with the world of science and technology.

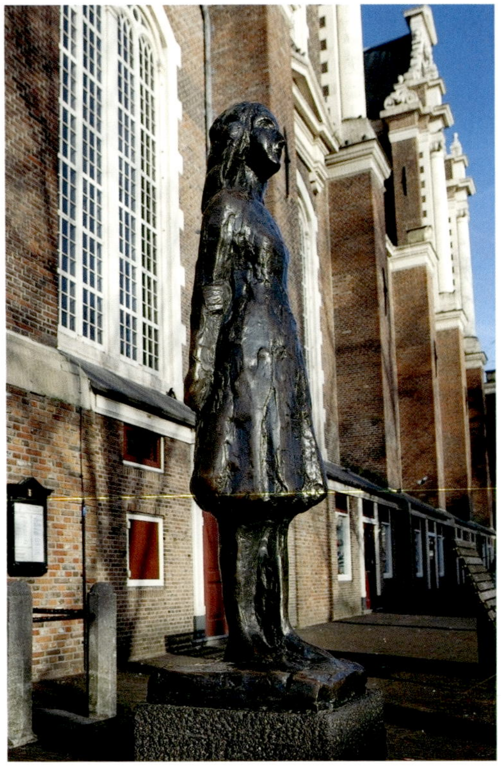

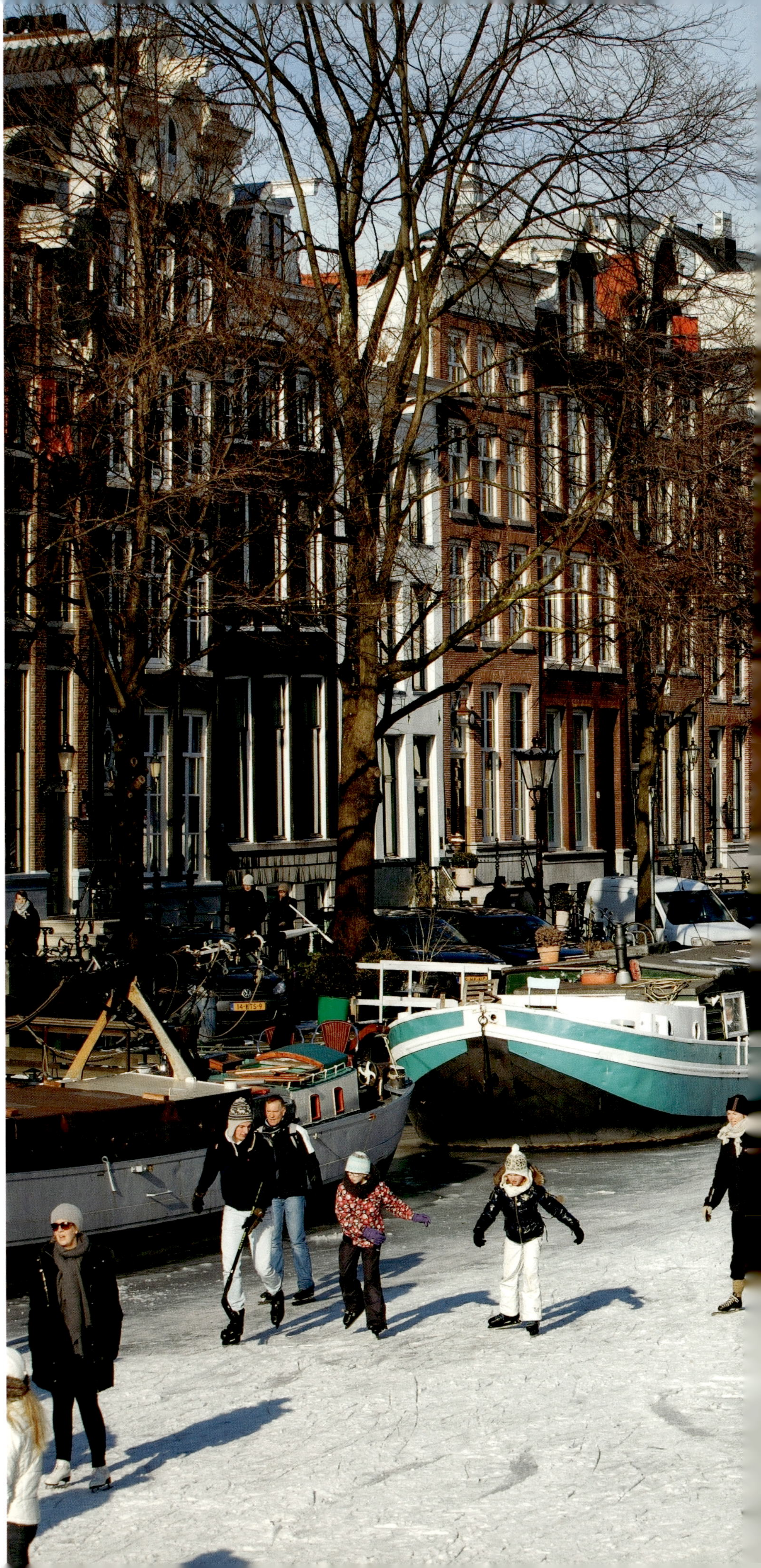

Top: Anne Frank was a Jewish girl of German origin who became world-famous through the diary she wrote during her period in hiding during World War II. Her diary was published posthumously and translated into many languages. Photo: Statue of Anne Frank at the Westerkerk, and the Anne Frank Museum.

Right: Skating on the Keizersgracht.

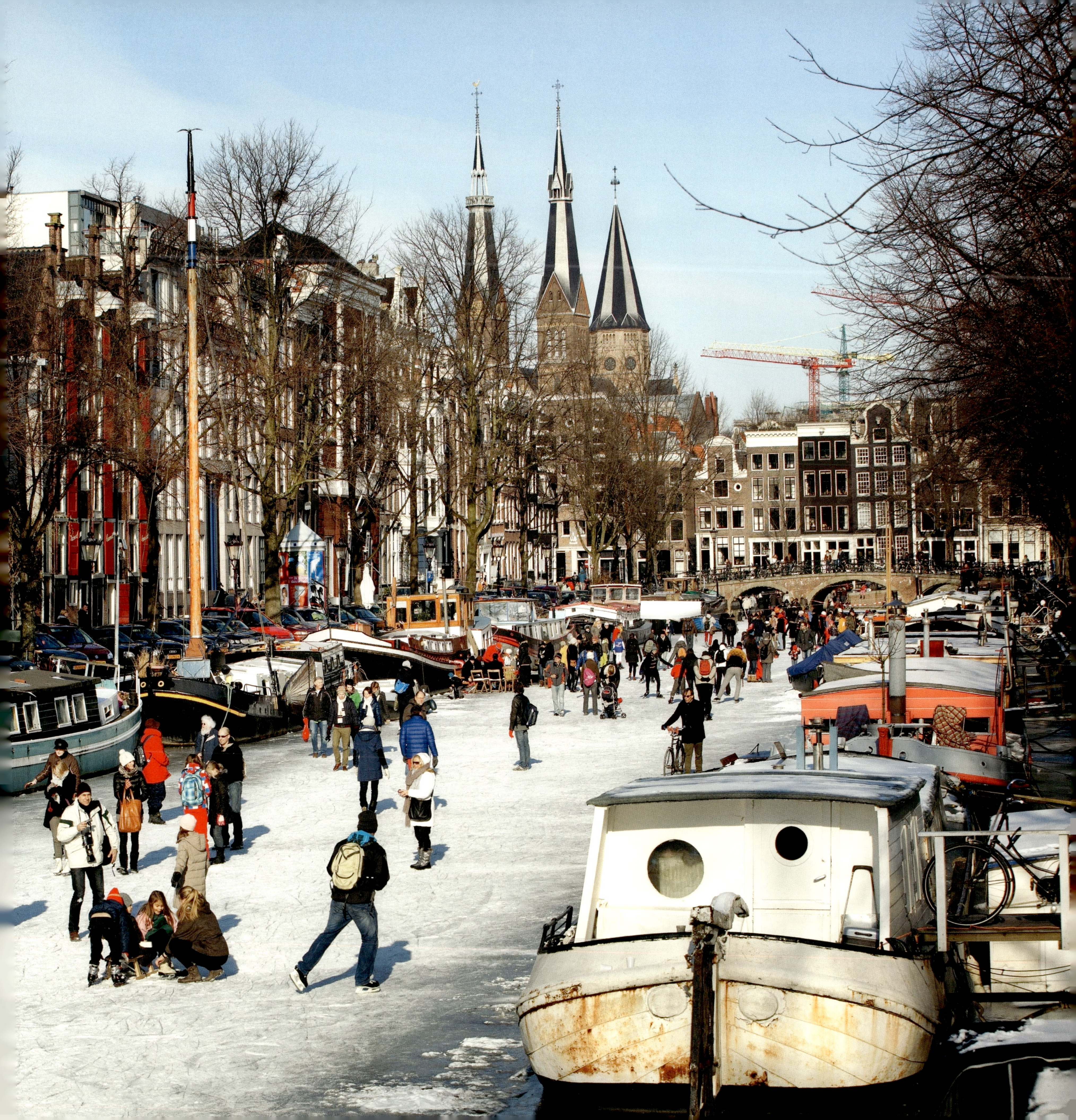

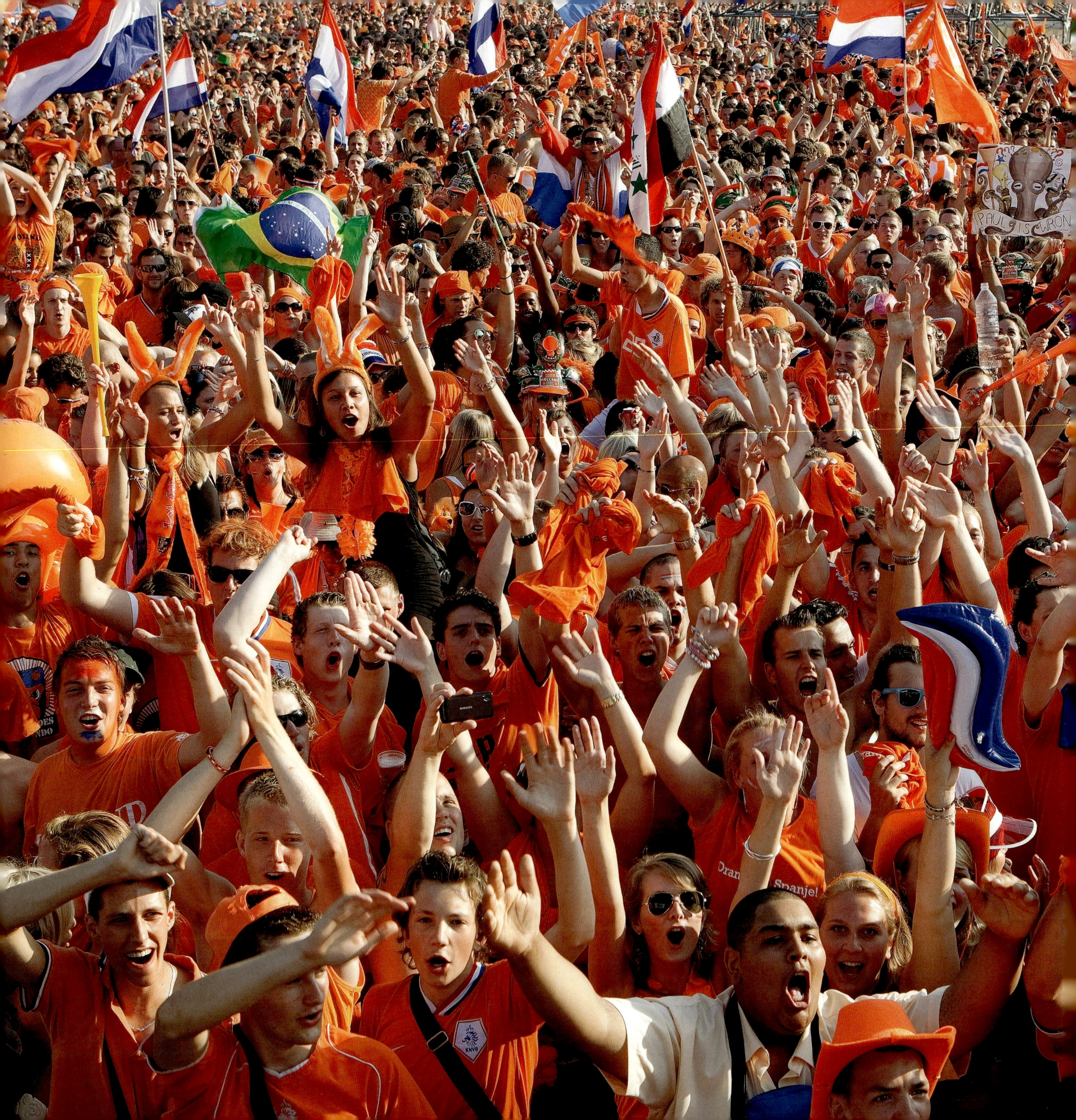
Spanje!

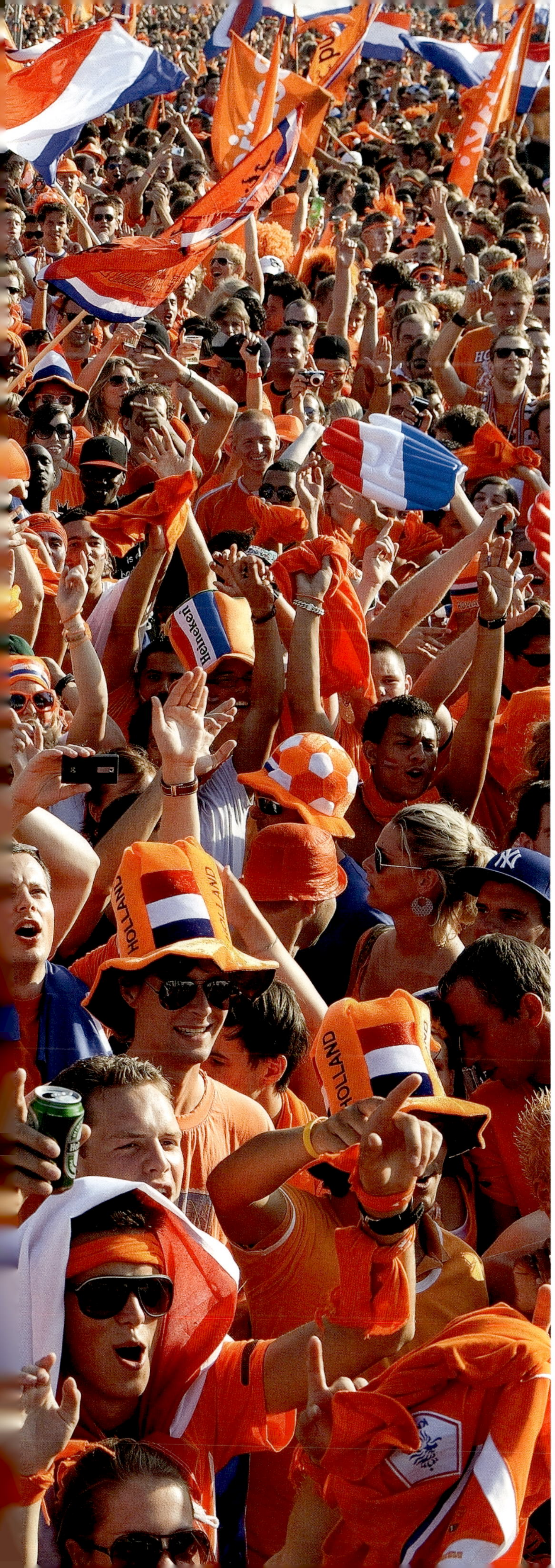

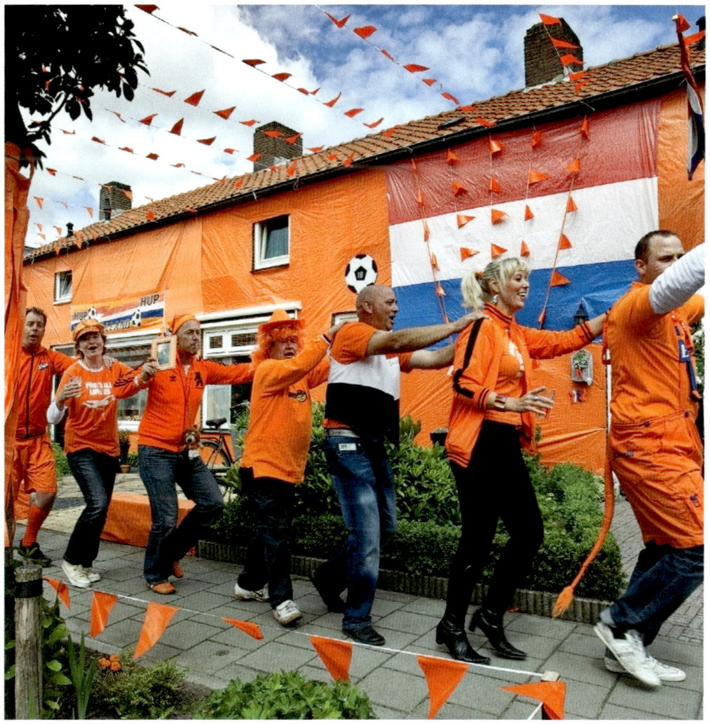

Left: Orange fever reaches its greatest heights when the Dutch football team is playing: tens of thousands of spectators watching the performance of the Dutch national team on large video screens at the Museumplein in Amsterdam.

Above: Residents of Irene Street in Goirle celebrate a win by the Dutch national football team.

Following pages: A pleasure boat, sailing down the River Vecht, passes by the stately home of Rupelmonde.

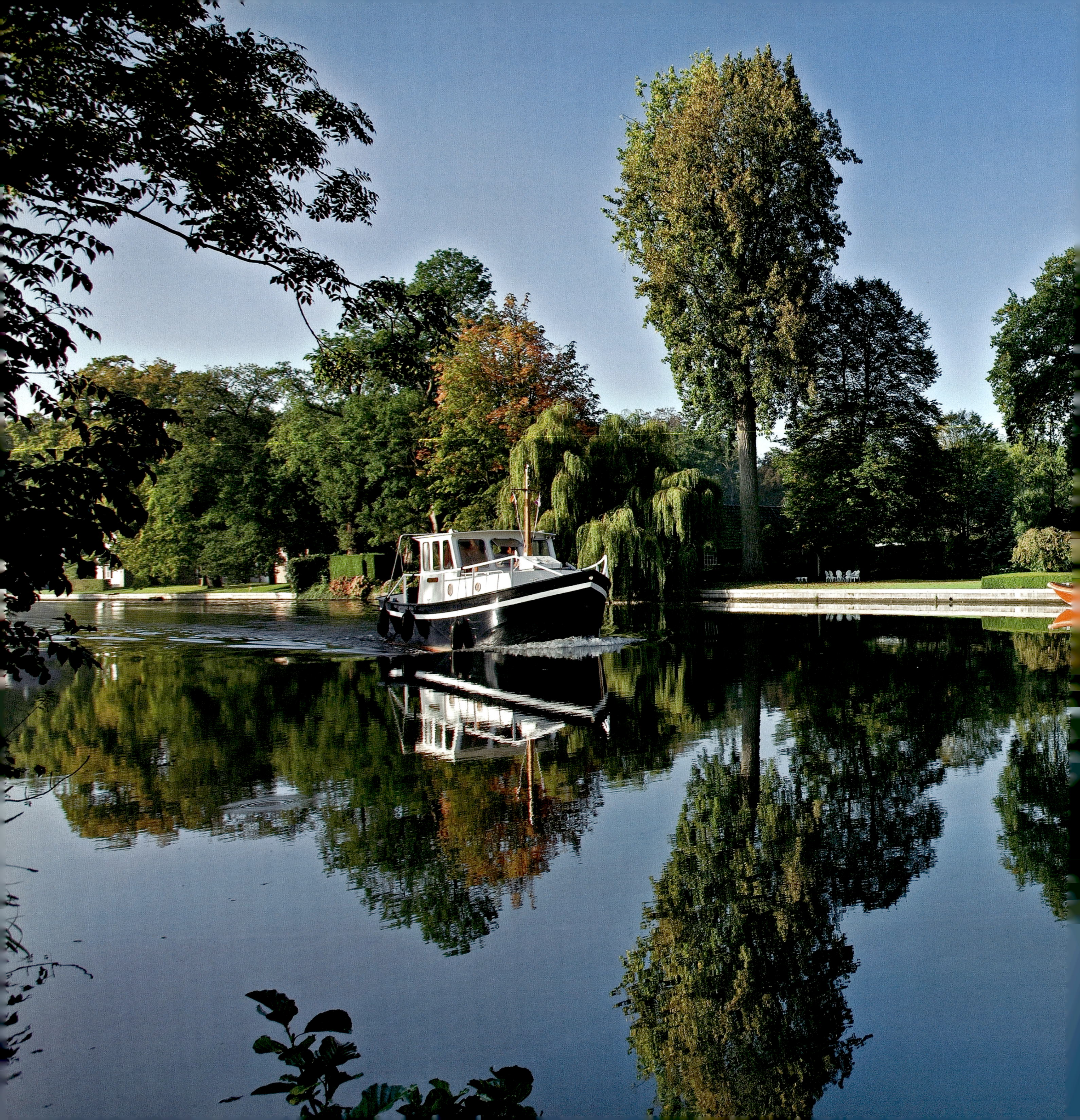

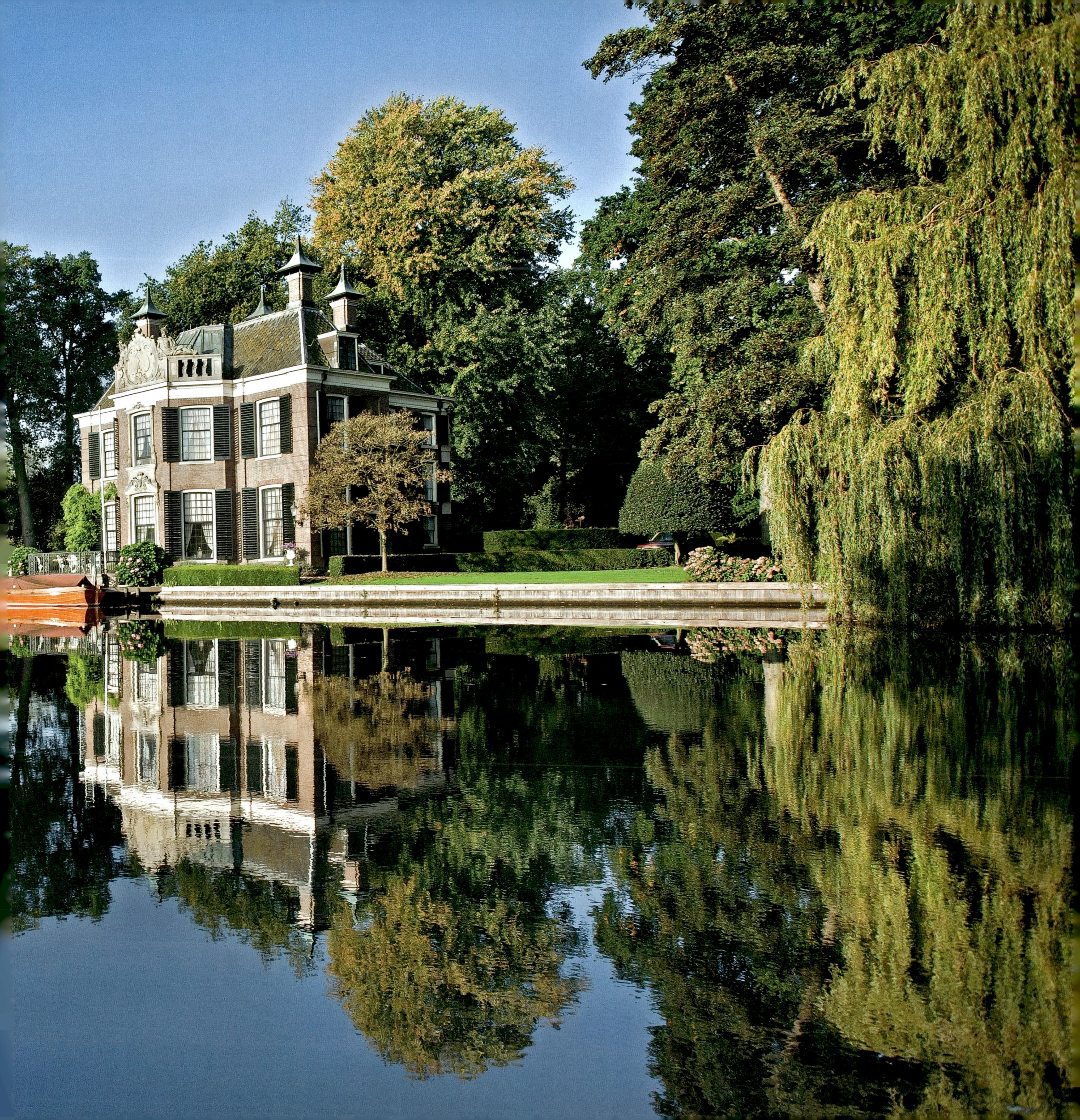

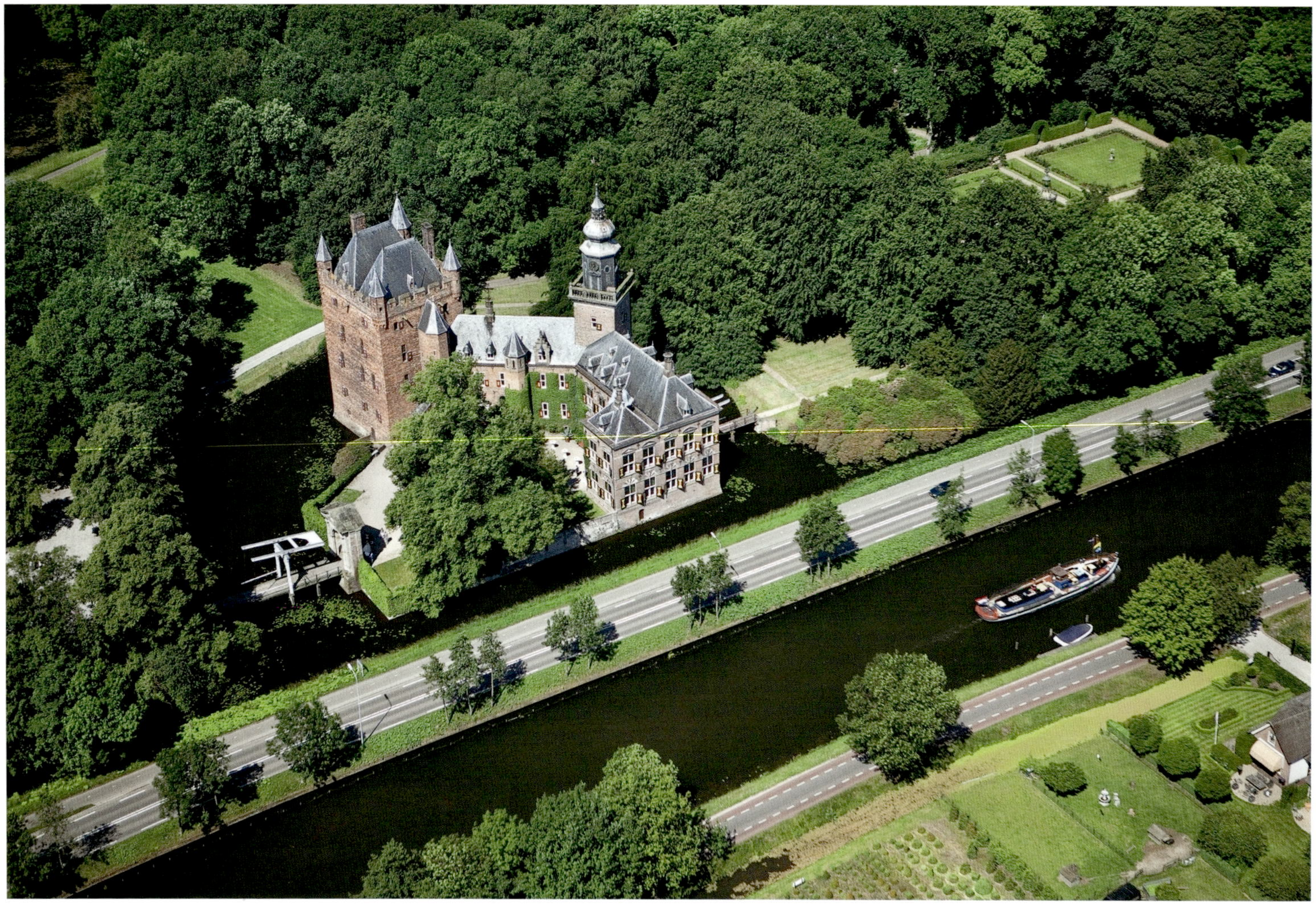

The Gooi and Vecht district is typified by its many country estates, mostly built by wealthy Amsterdam merchants in the seventeenth and eighteenth centuries. In the adjacent former fenlands, turf were dug or dredged up for peats, then the main fuel, from the sixteenth century until well into the nineteenth.

Top: Nyenrode Castle by the River Vecht, now home to Nyenrode Business University.

Right: Ponds in Breukelen, created by the dredging of fenland for peats. The peat-drying strips of land ('legakkers') that remained are nowadays often used for holiday homes.

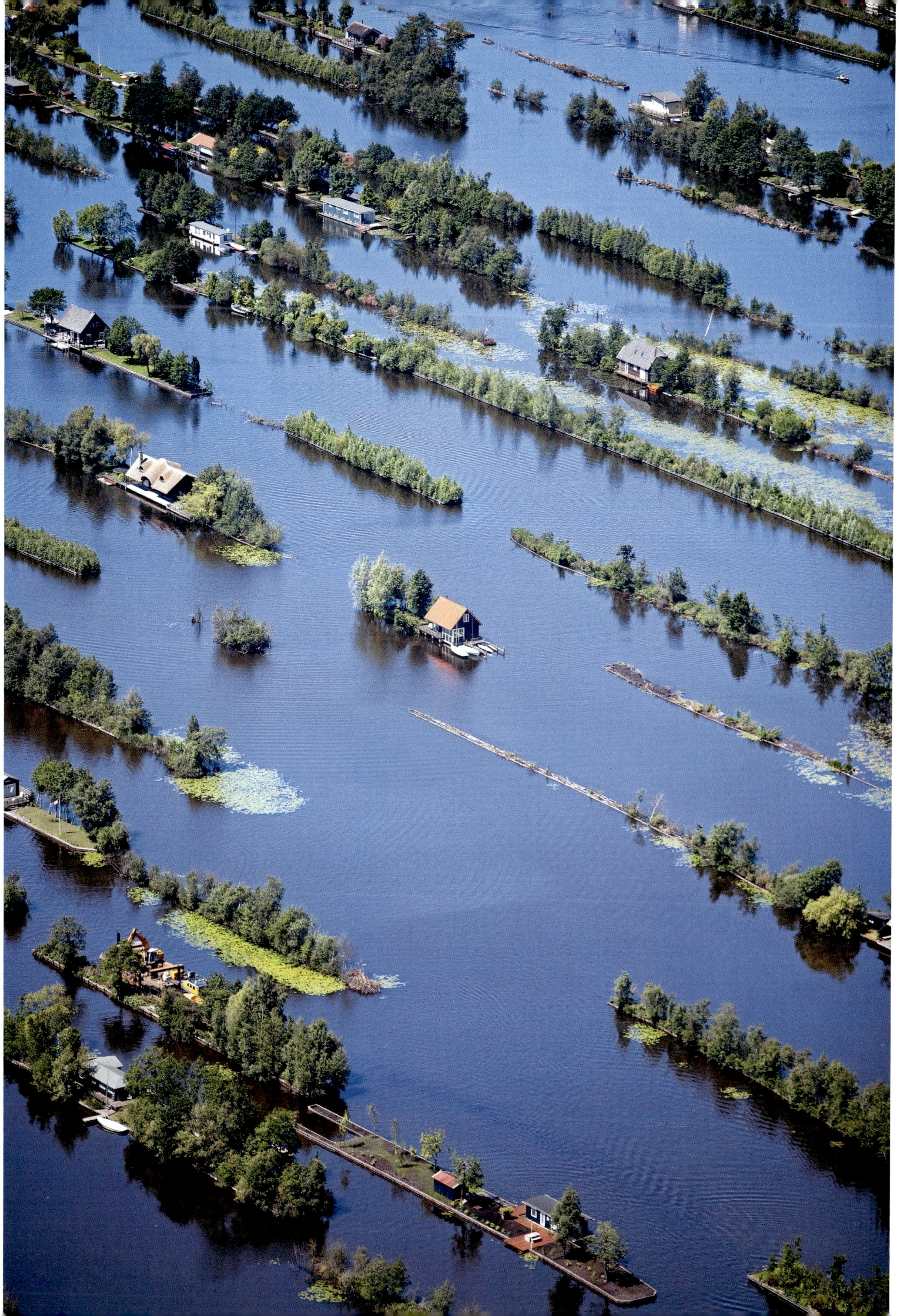

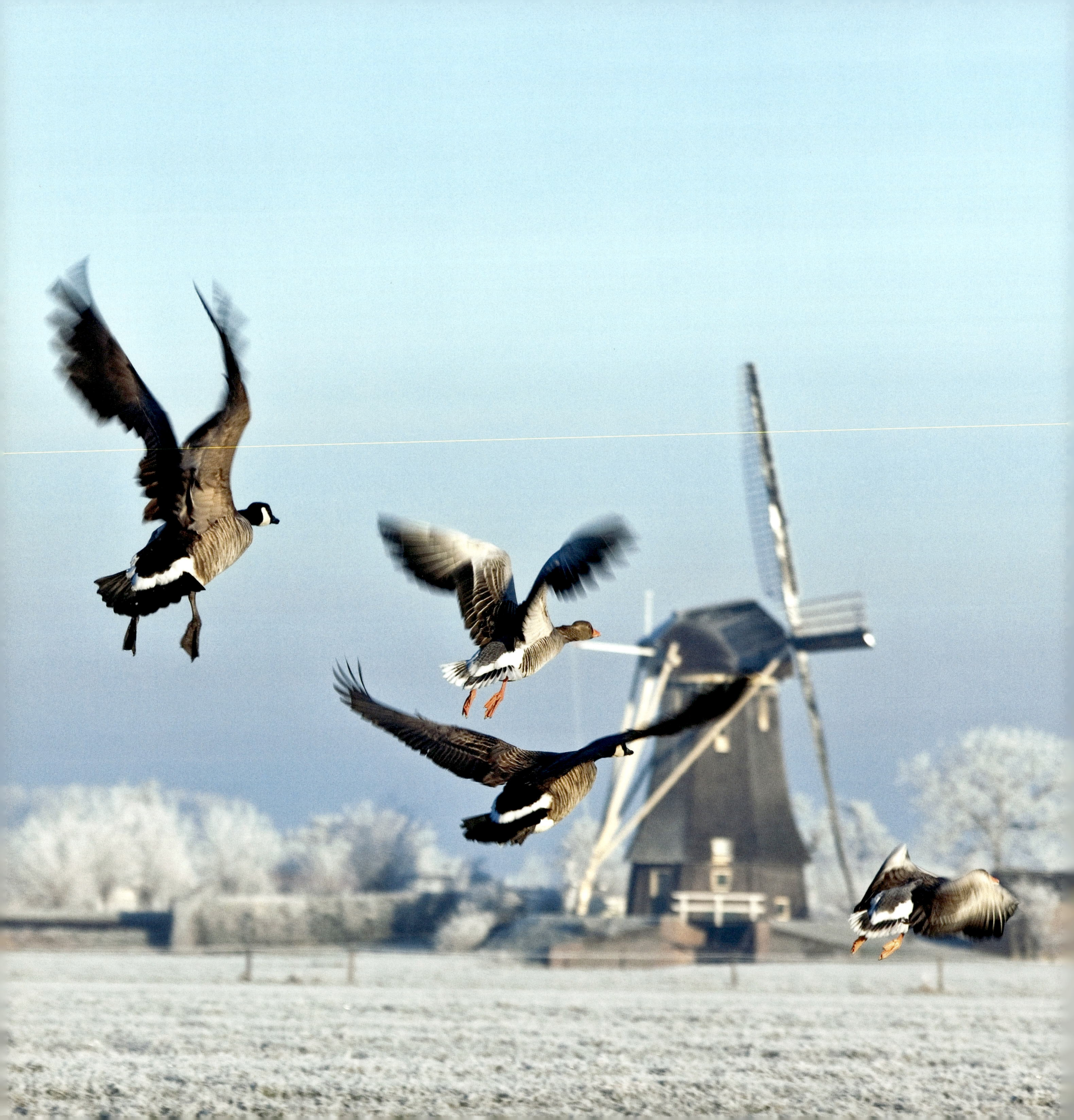

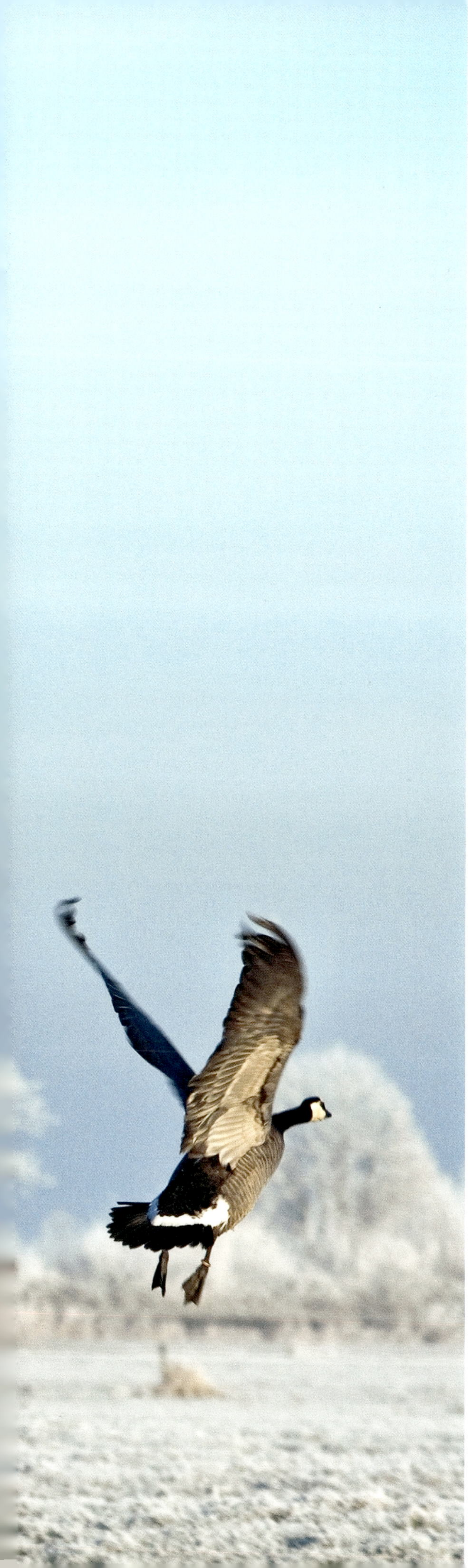

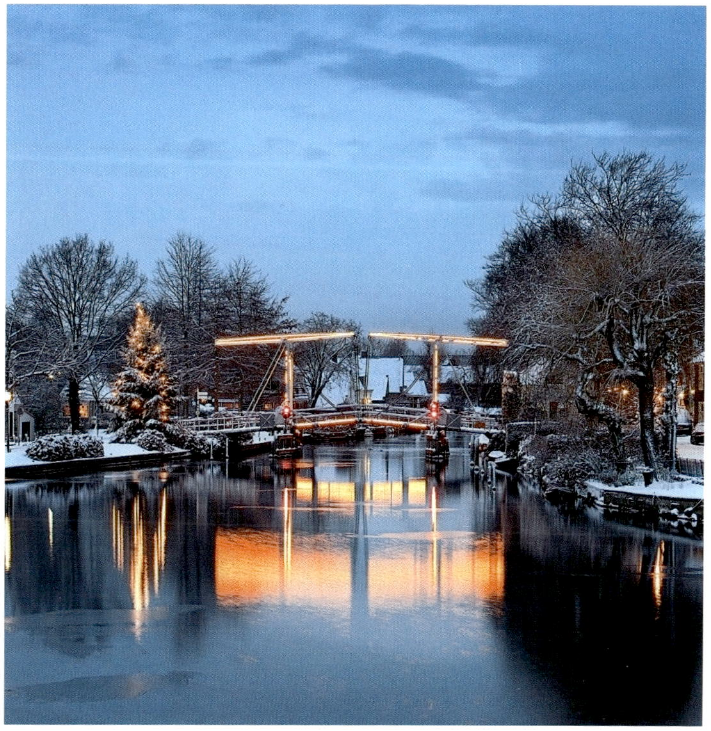

Left: A rare sight within living memory: Canadian geese taking off at Nigtevecht. Nowadays, more and more of these geese are breeding in this country.

Top: Lit drawbridge over the River Vecht in Vreeland.

Right: Cows grazing in a meadow near Maarssen.

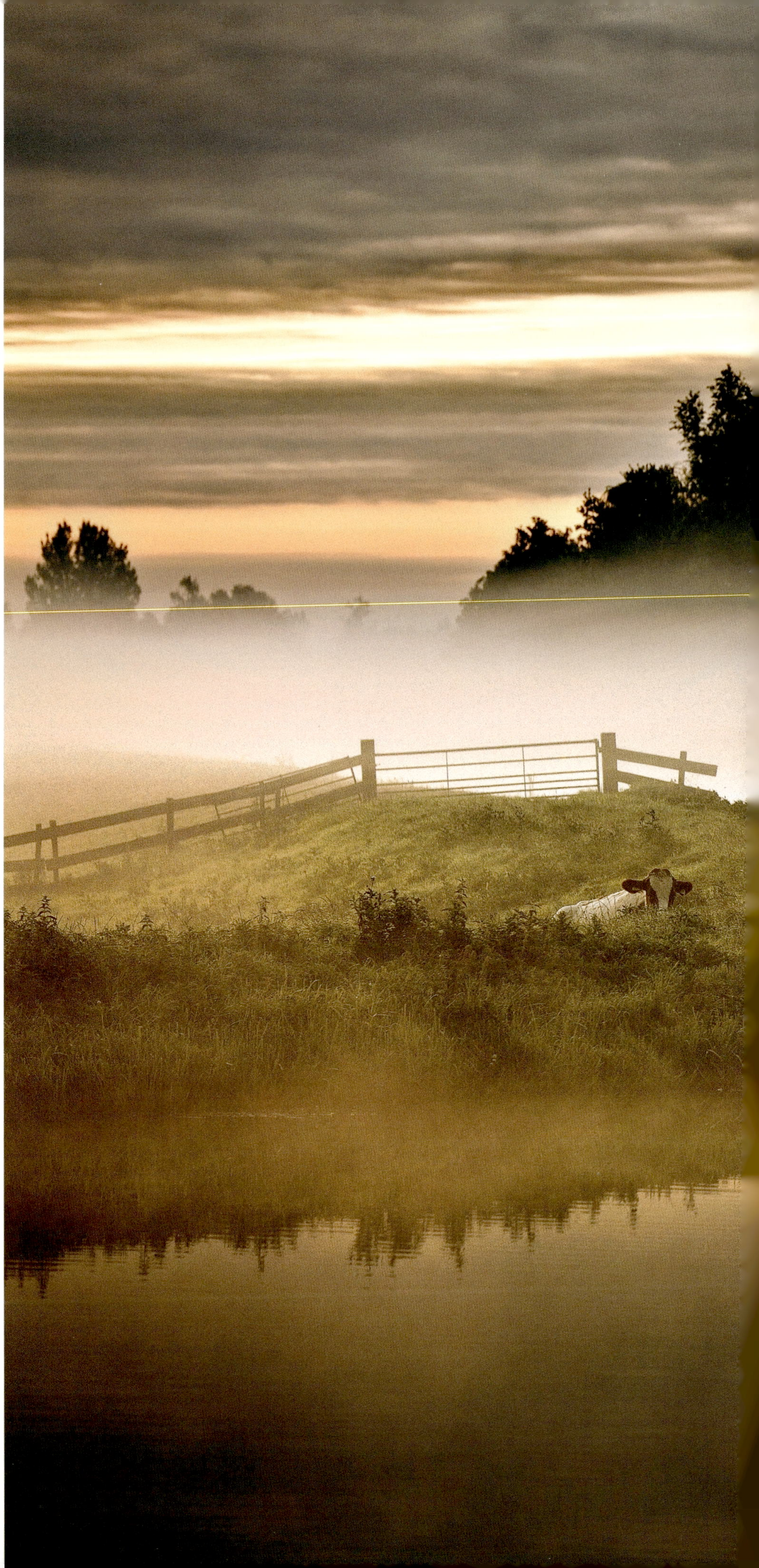

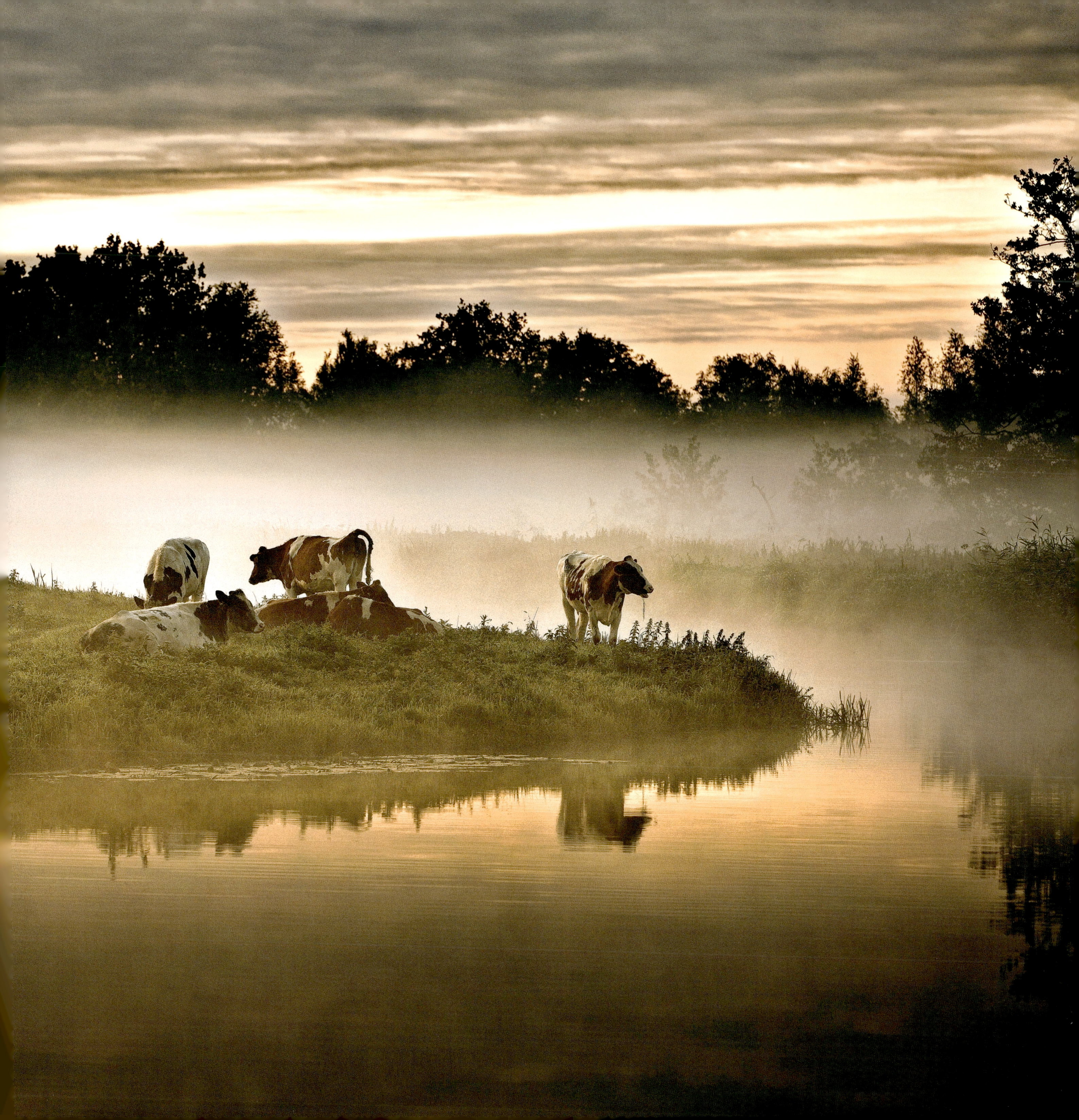

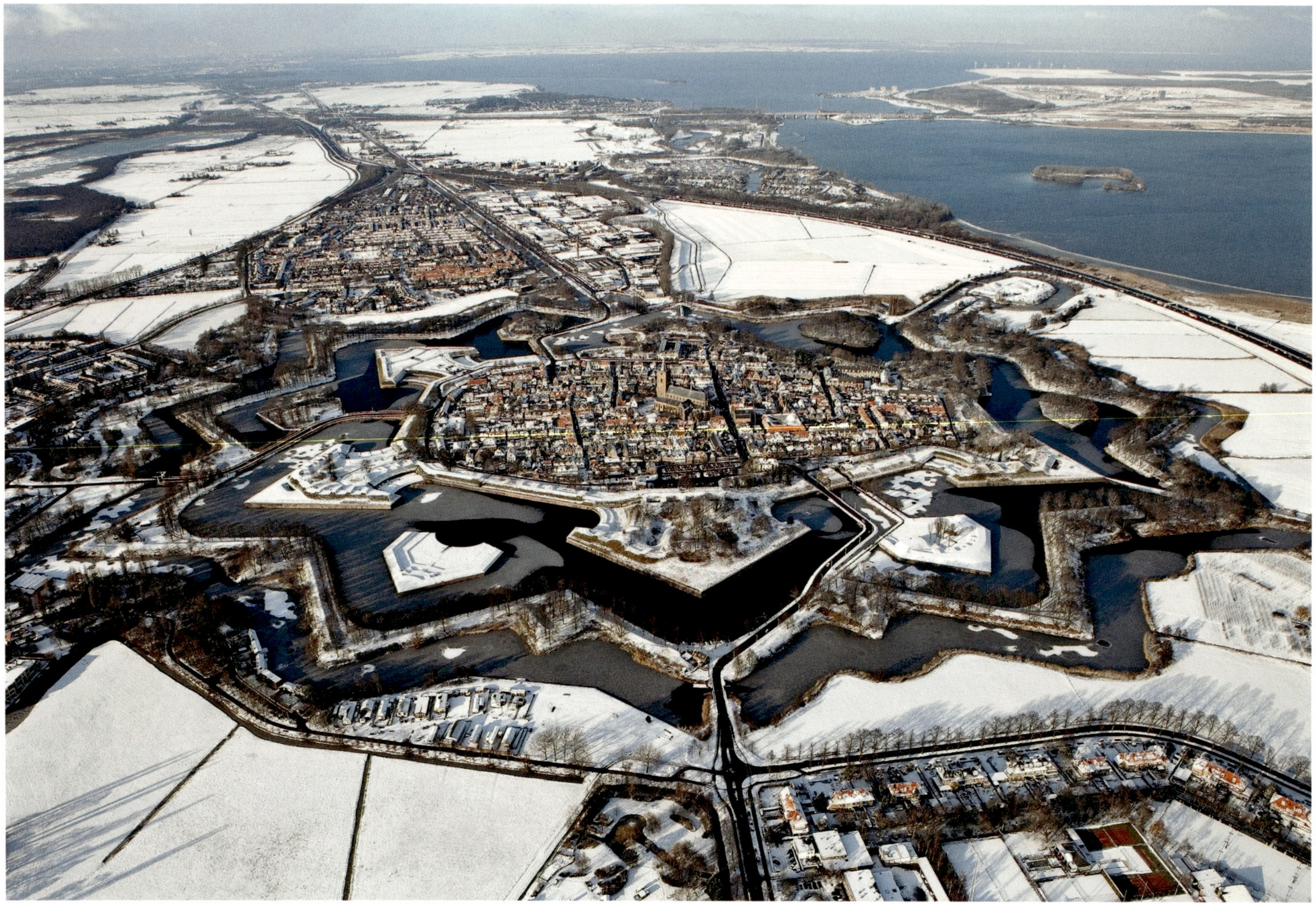

Above and right: Winter and summer views of the star-shaped Naarden Fortress. The fortress is strategically located on a spur of the Utrecht Hill Range and has since the seventeenth century formed part of the defensive Dutch Water Line.

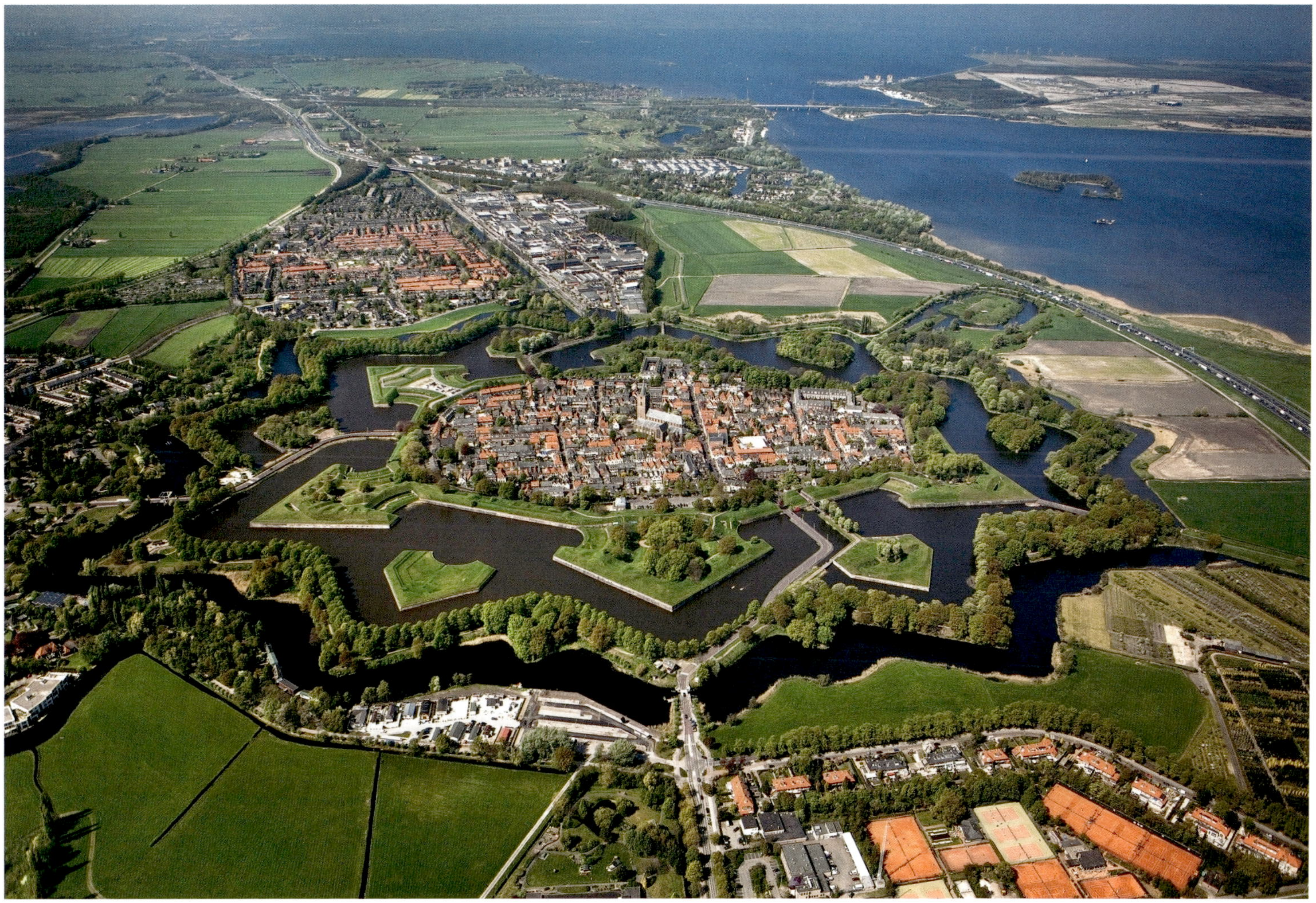

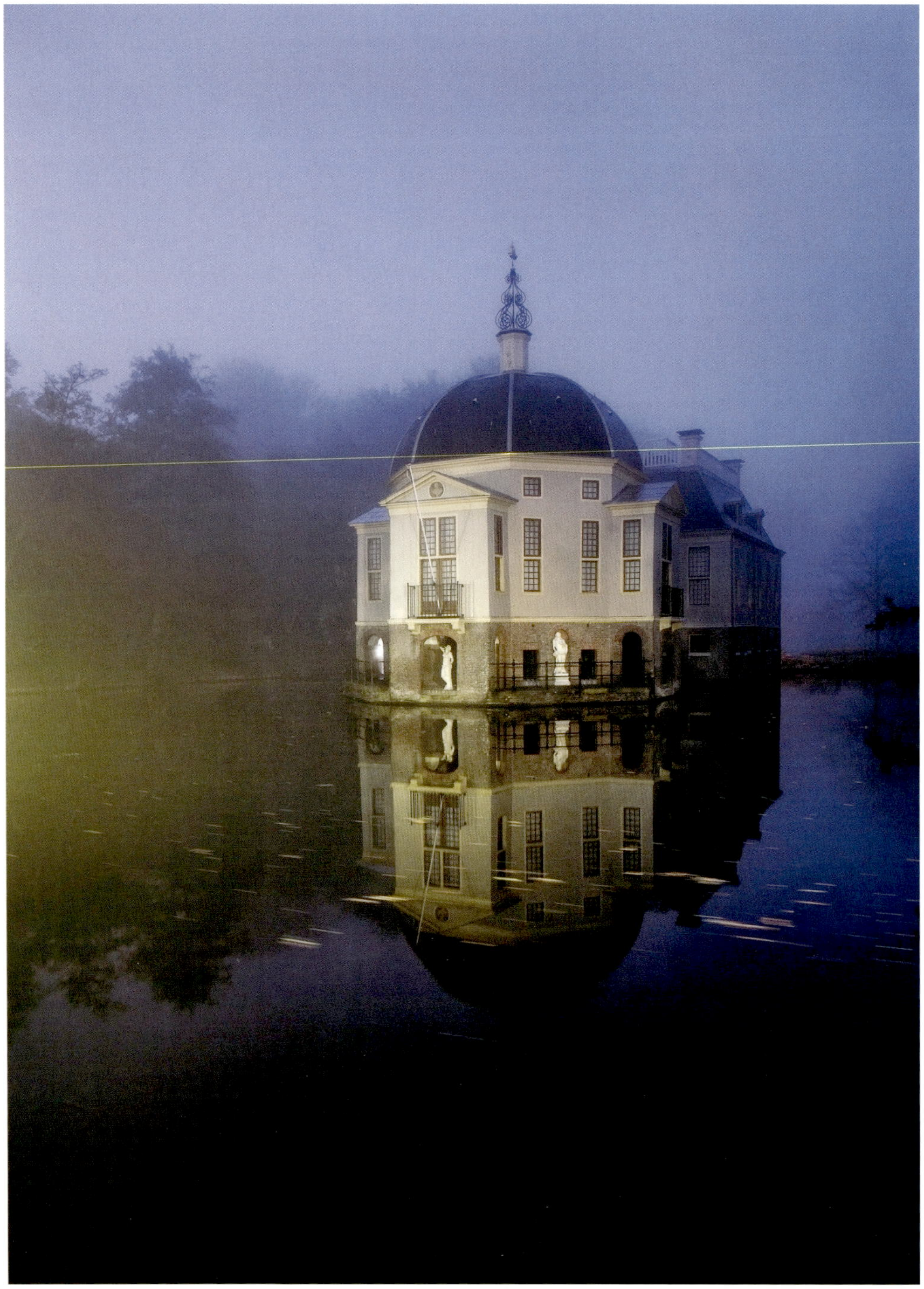

Top: Trompenburg, one of the major country estates in 's-Graveland, built for Admiral Cornelis Tromp, son of the legendary Admiral Maarten Harpertszoon Tromp.

Right: Farmhouse at 's-Graveland, depicted in the four seasons.

Following pages: The Clipper Race at Enkhuizen: a sailing competition for vessels of the Brown Fleet, traditional cargo ships that formerly had brown sails.

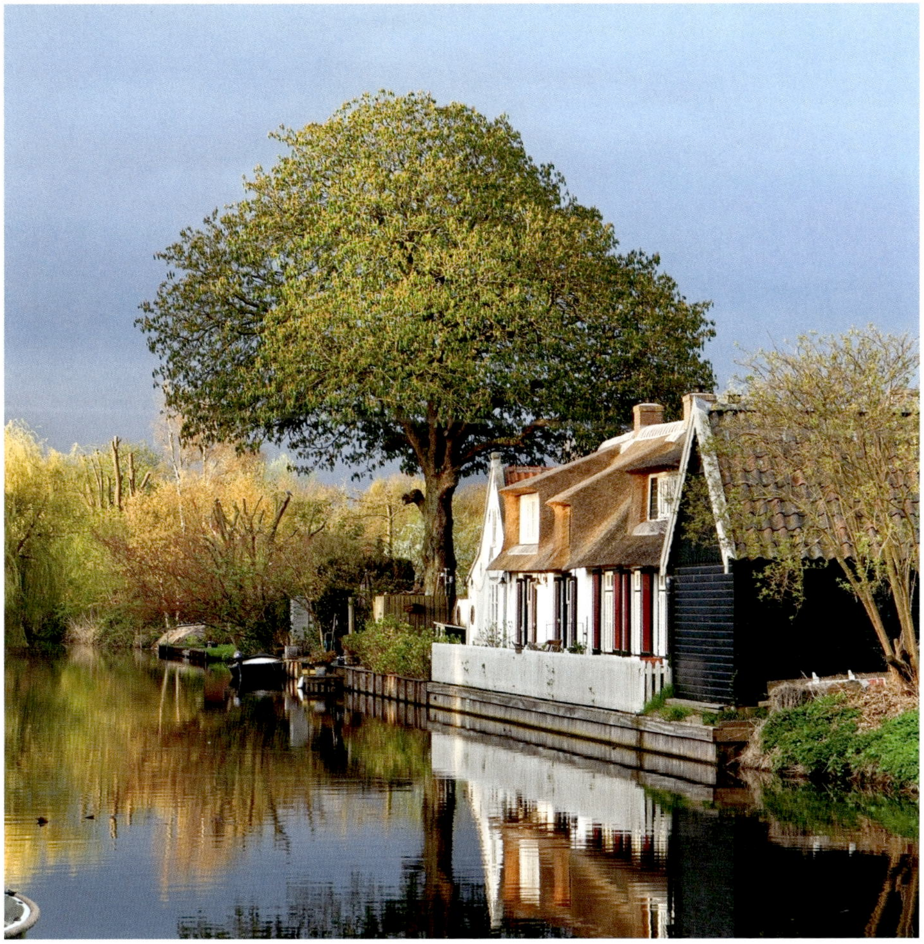
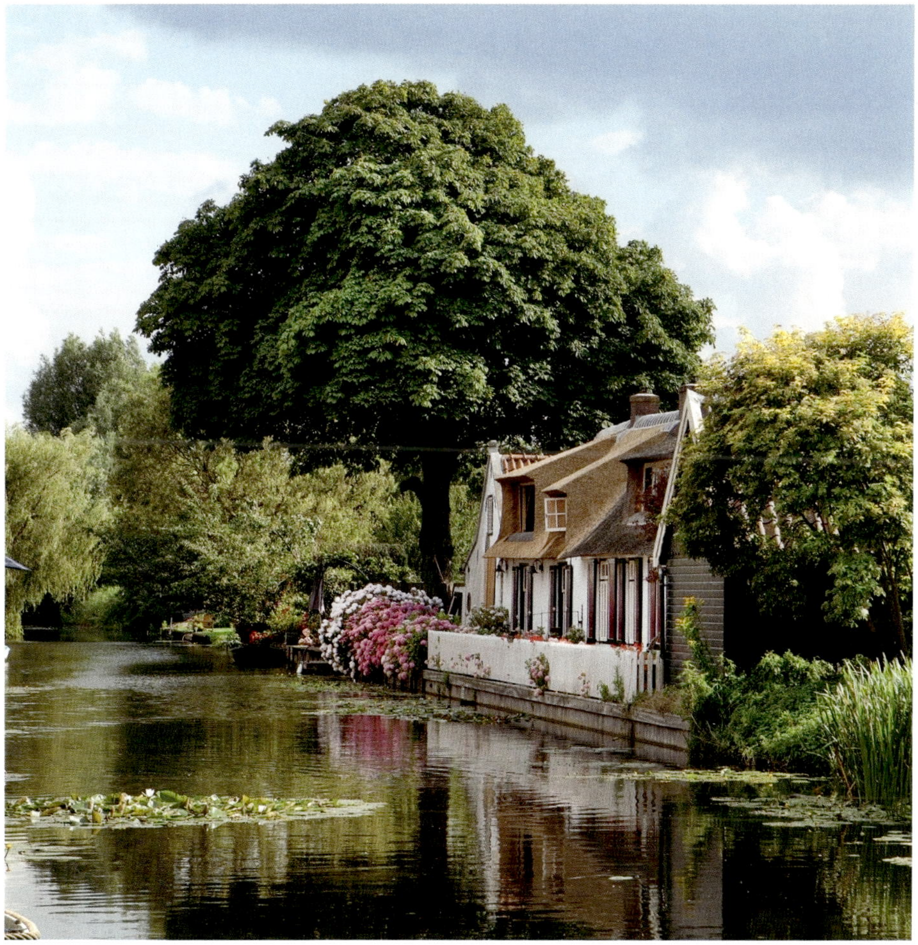
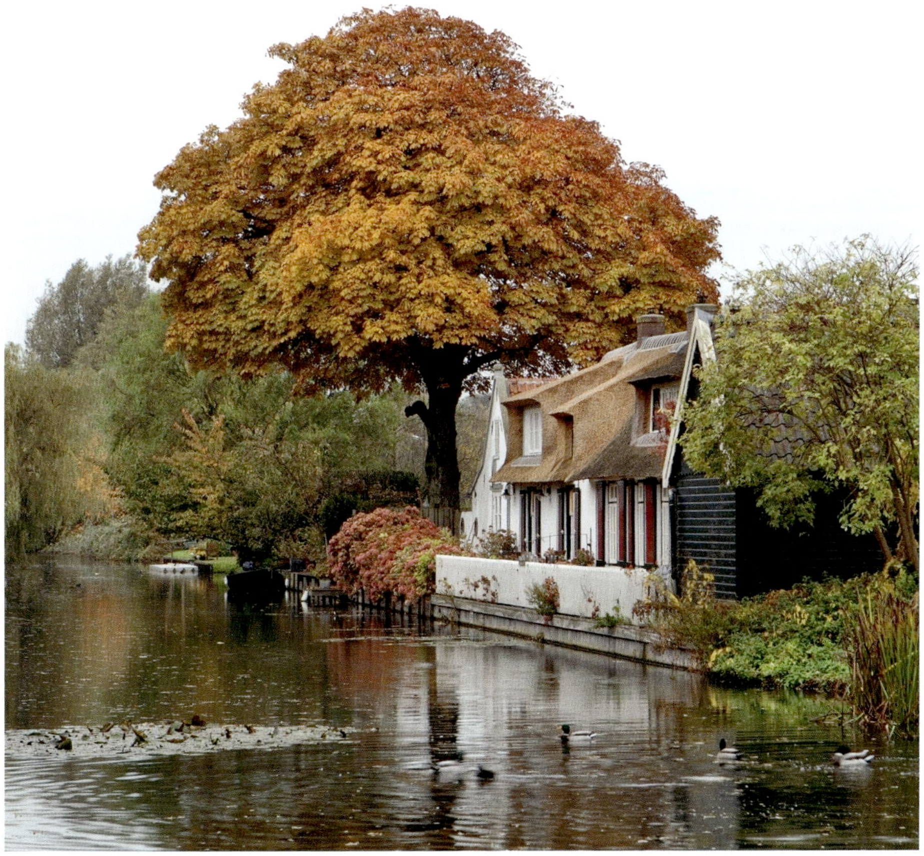
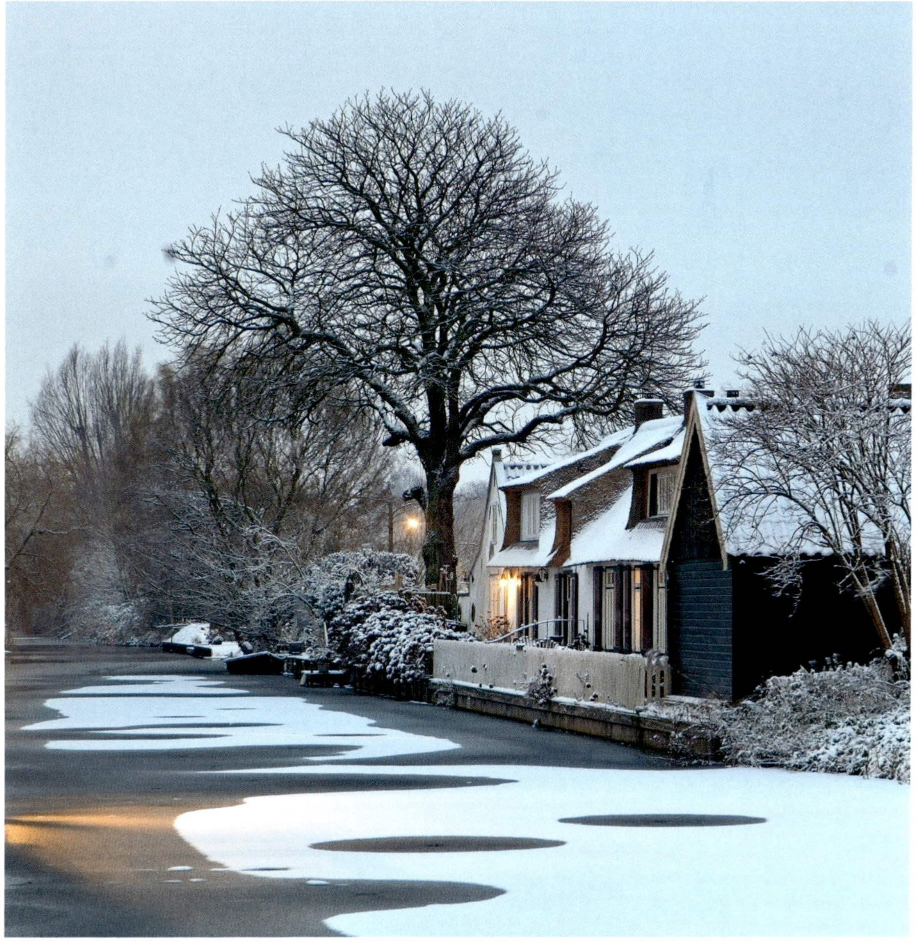

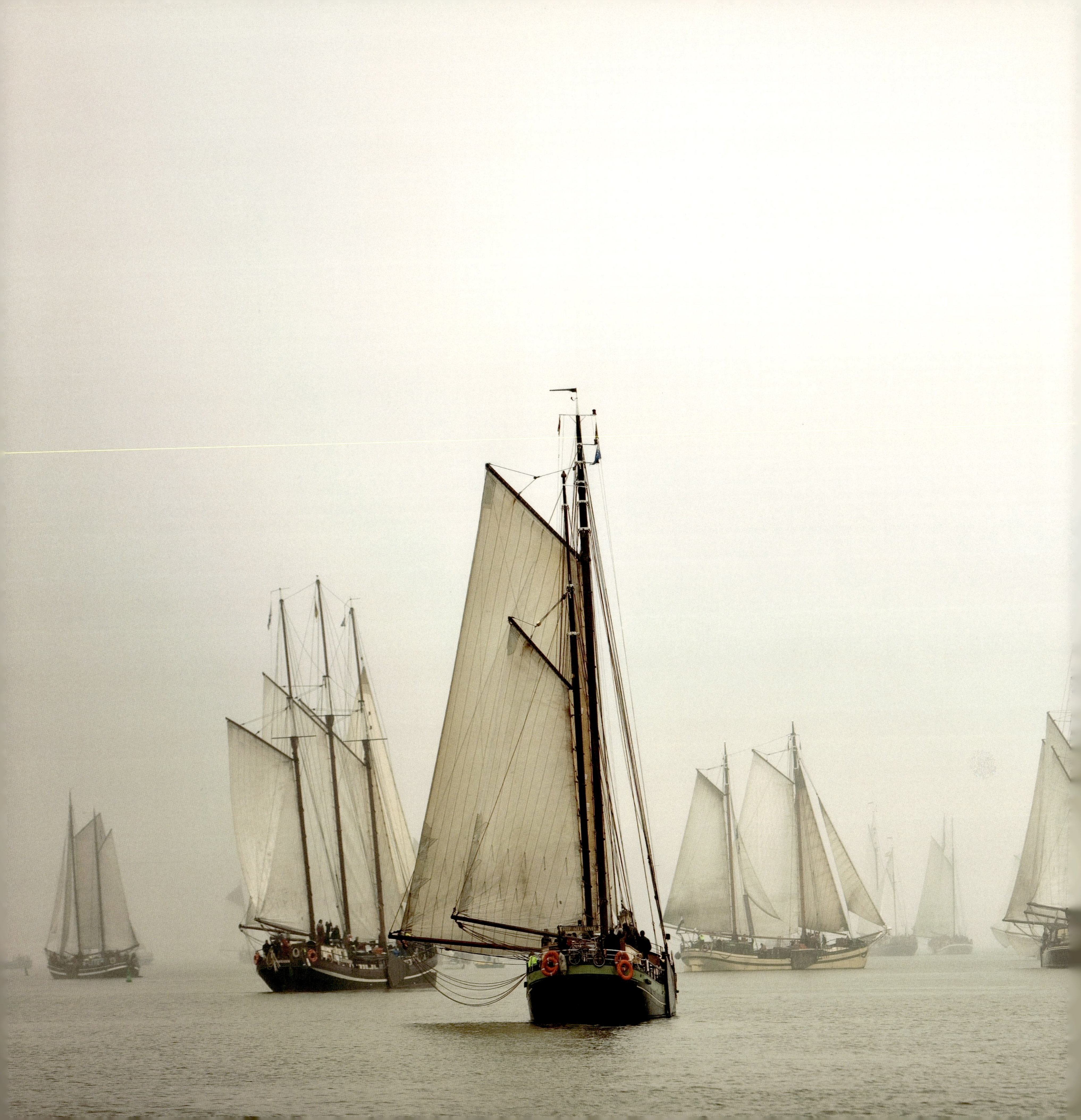

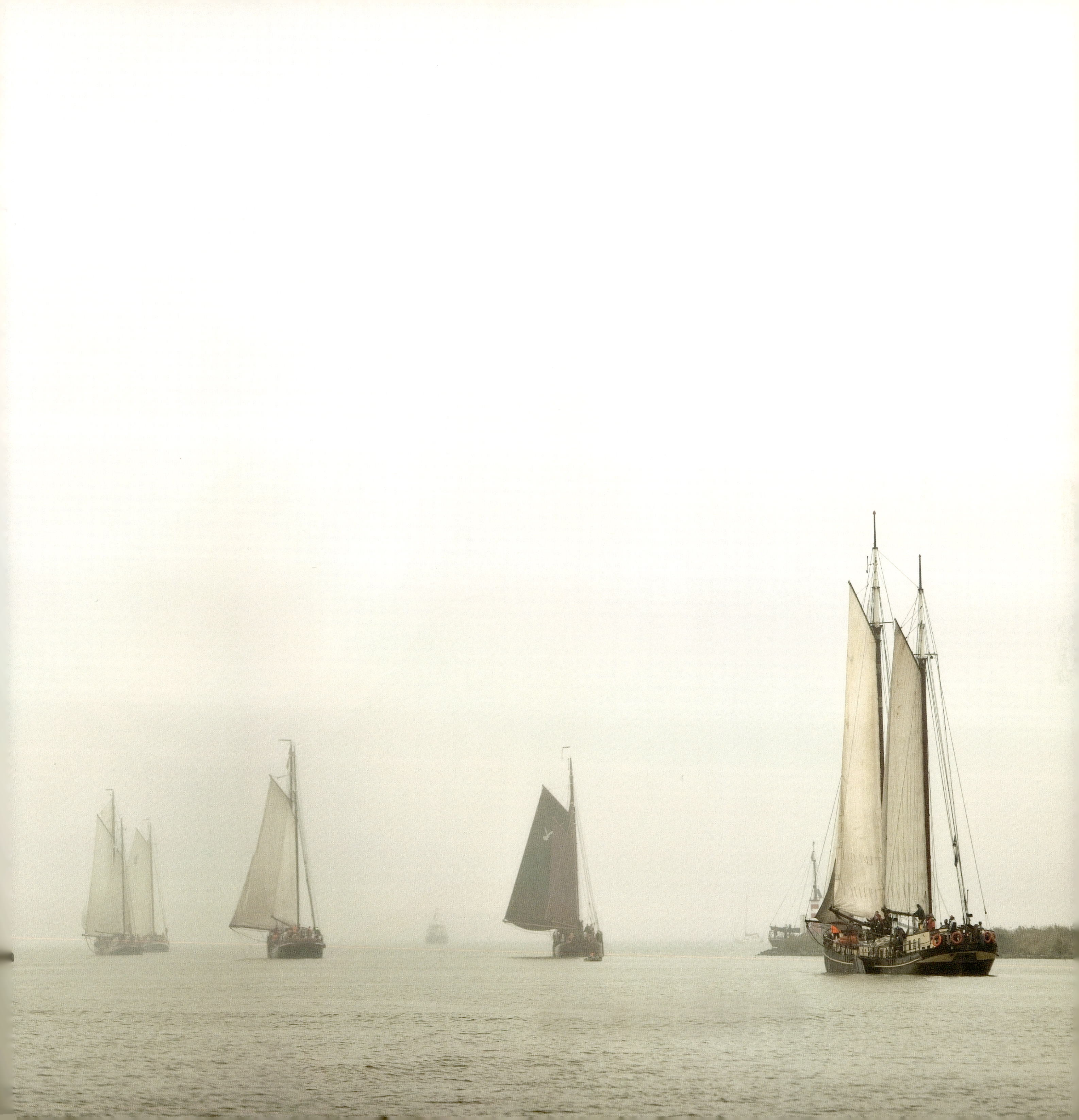

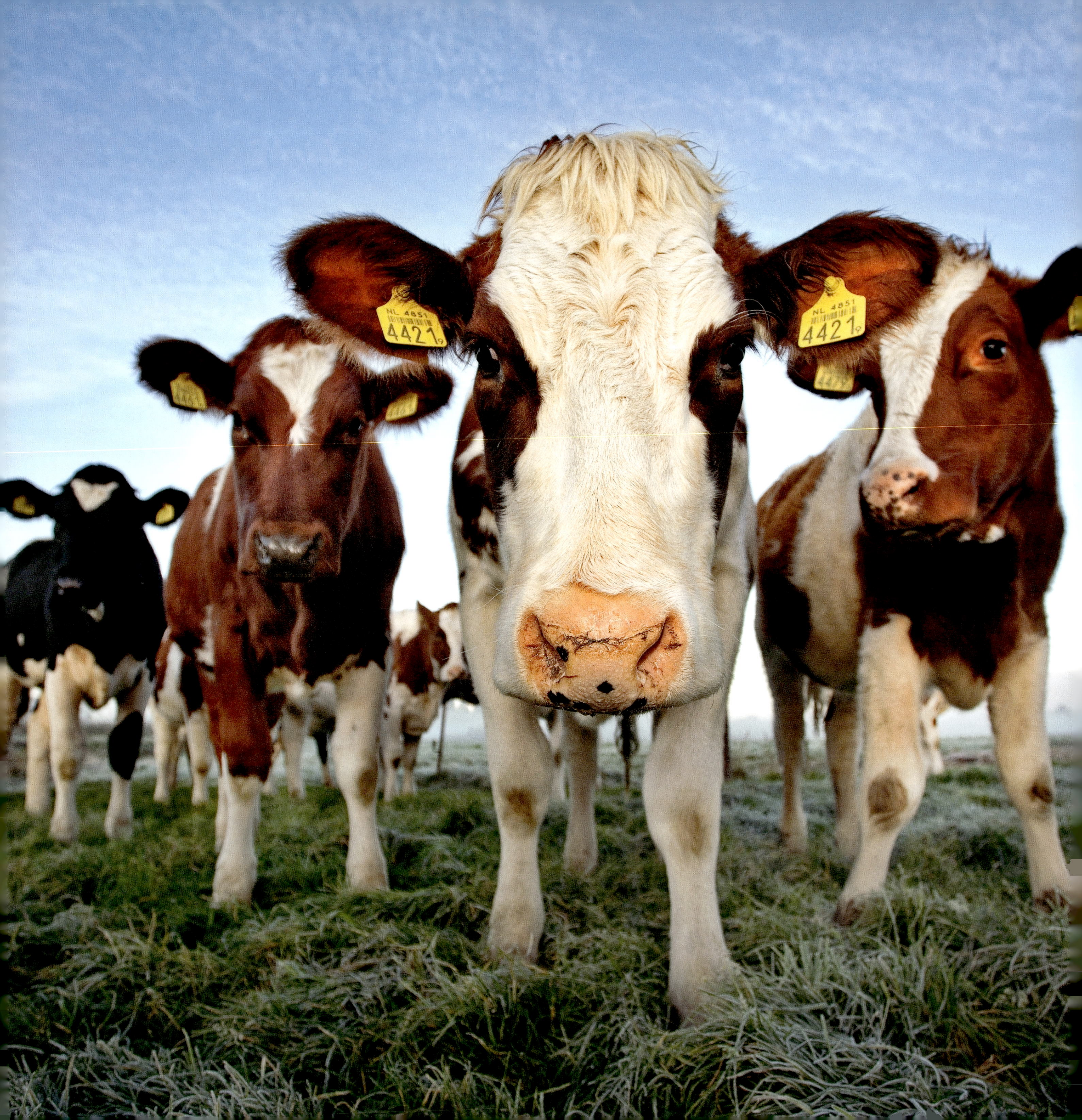
NL 4851
4421
NL 4851
4421

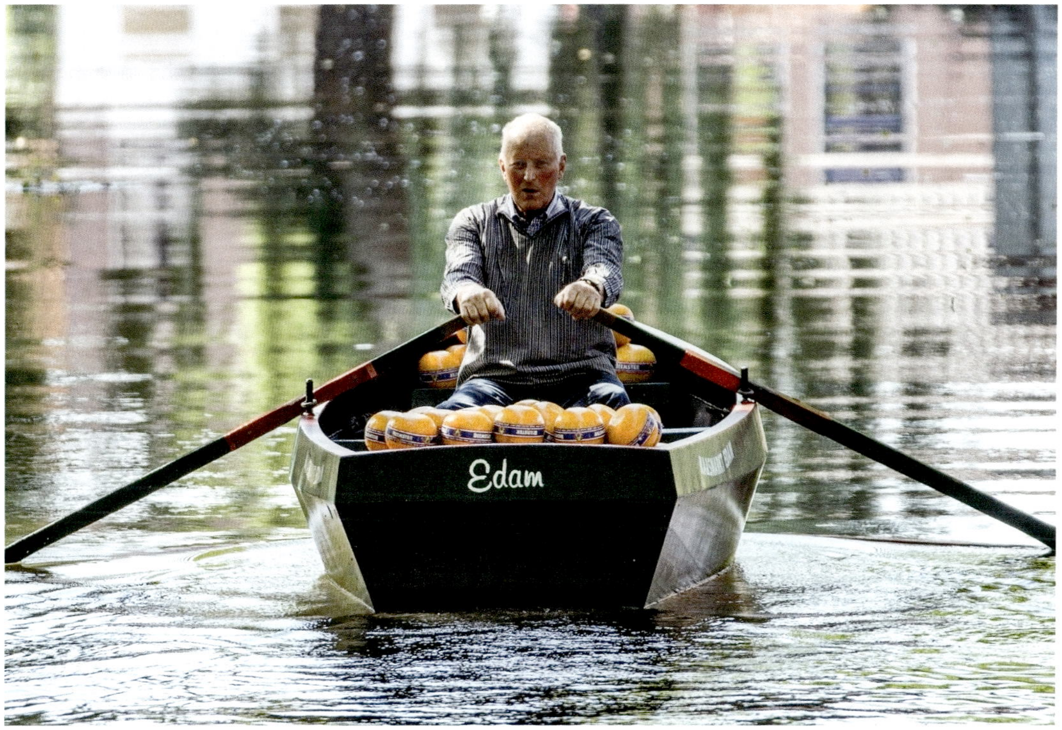

Typical features of the province of Noord-Holland are often taken to be universally true of the Netherlands – and especially form those aspects for which we are known abroad. These are such icons as windmills, cows, cheese, tulips, historic towns, sailing ships and of course the polders, one of which – the Beemster Polder – is now on the UNESCO World Heritage List.

Left: Cows in a polder at Nederhorst den Berg.

Top: Transporting cheese to the dedicated cheese market at Edam.

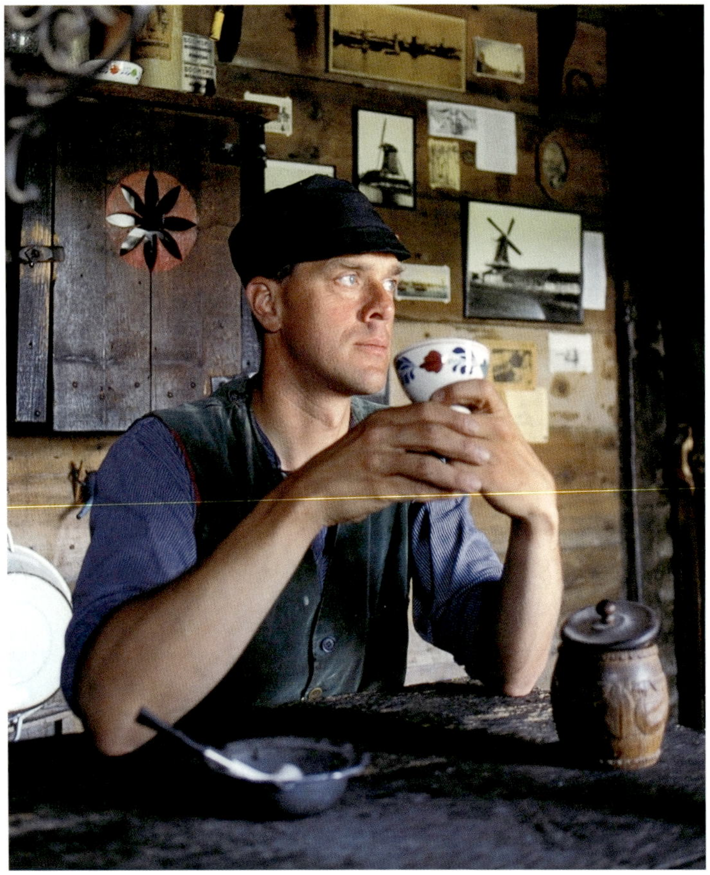

There are two types of traditional windmills: those that pump water, and mills for industrial use. There are many fine examples of both types to be found all over the country.

Top: Miller taking a break in his mill at Zaanse Schans.

Right: Three windmills at Schermerhorn. There used to be six of them in this part of the Schermerpolder: two bottom mills, two middle mills and two upper mills. They pumped the polder water out of the inner collection pool – which it had already taken fourteen polder mills to move up that far – into the Schermerringvaart waterway in three steps.

Following pages: The Zaanse Schans open-air attraction, with historic industrial mills and the unique wooden architecture of the Zaan district. The Zaan district is the oldest industrial area in Western Europe. The area attracts around 1.5 million tourists every year. Right: a saw mill; left: an oil mill; centrally: De Kat, the only paint windmill still working anywhere in the world.

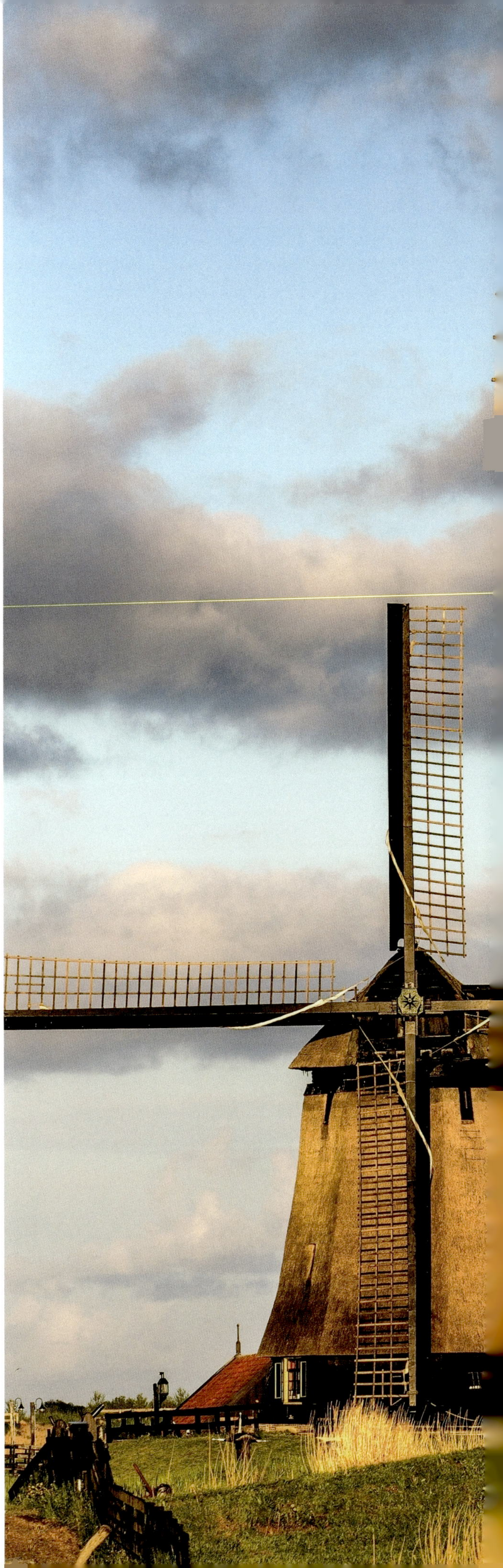

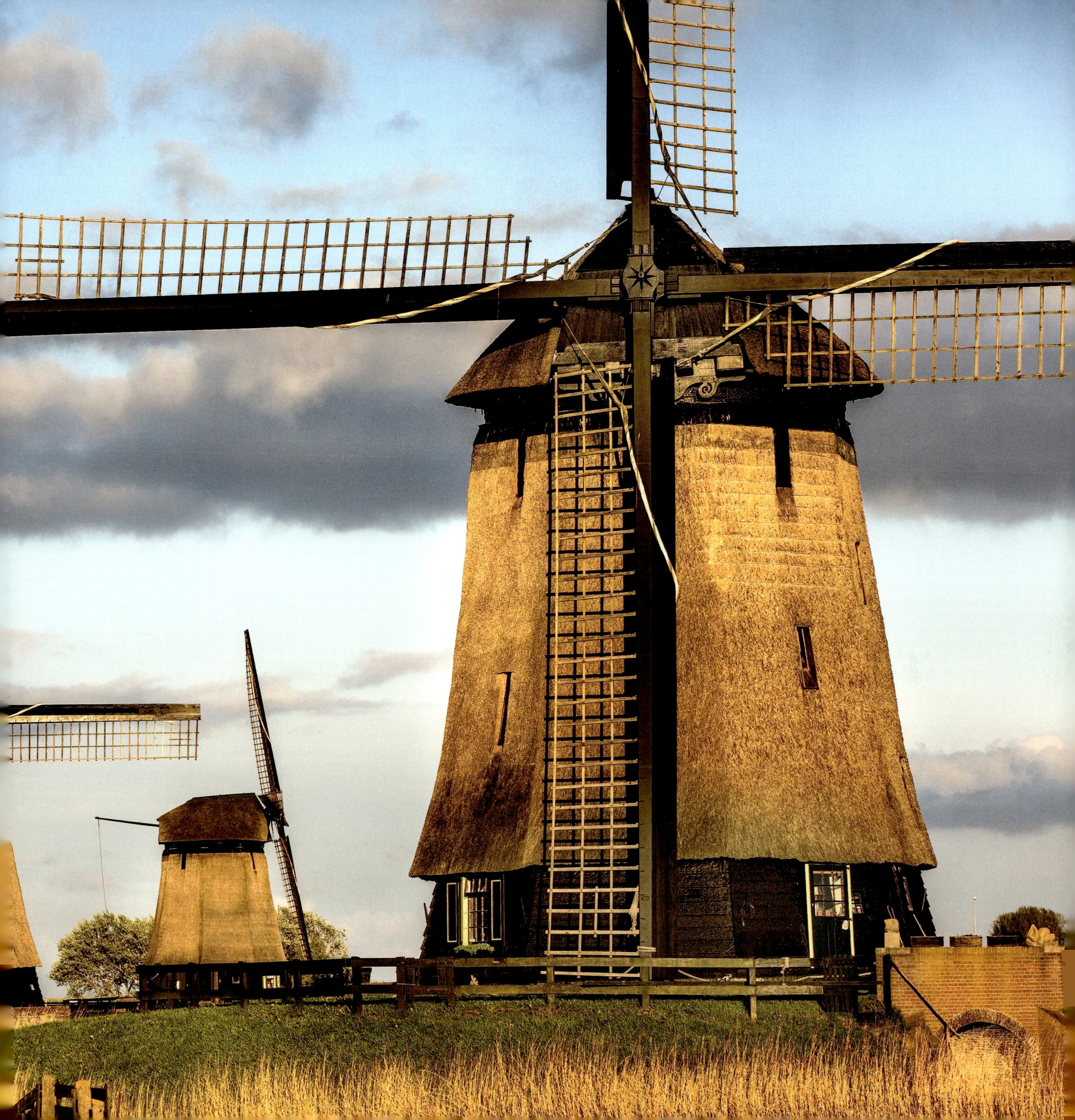

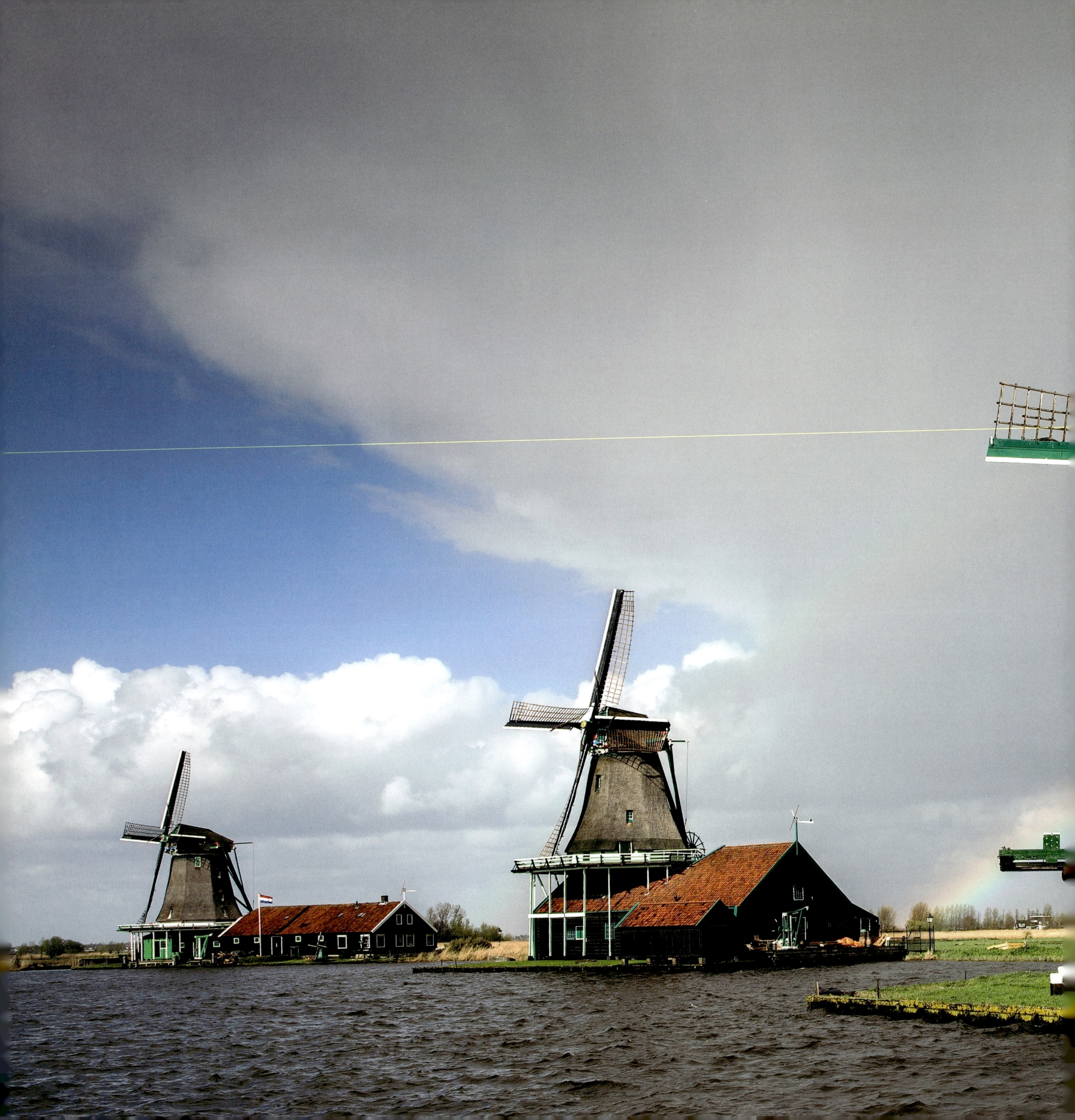

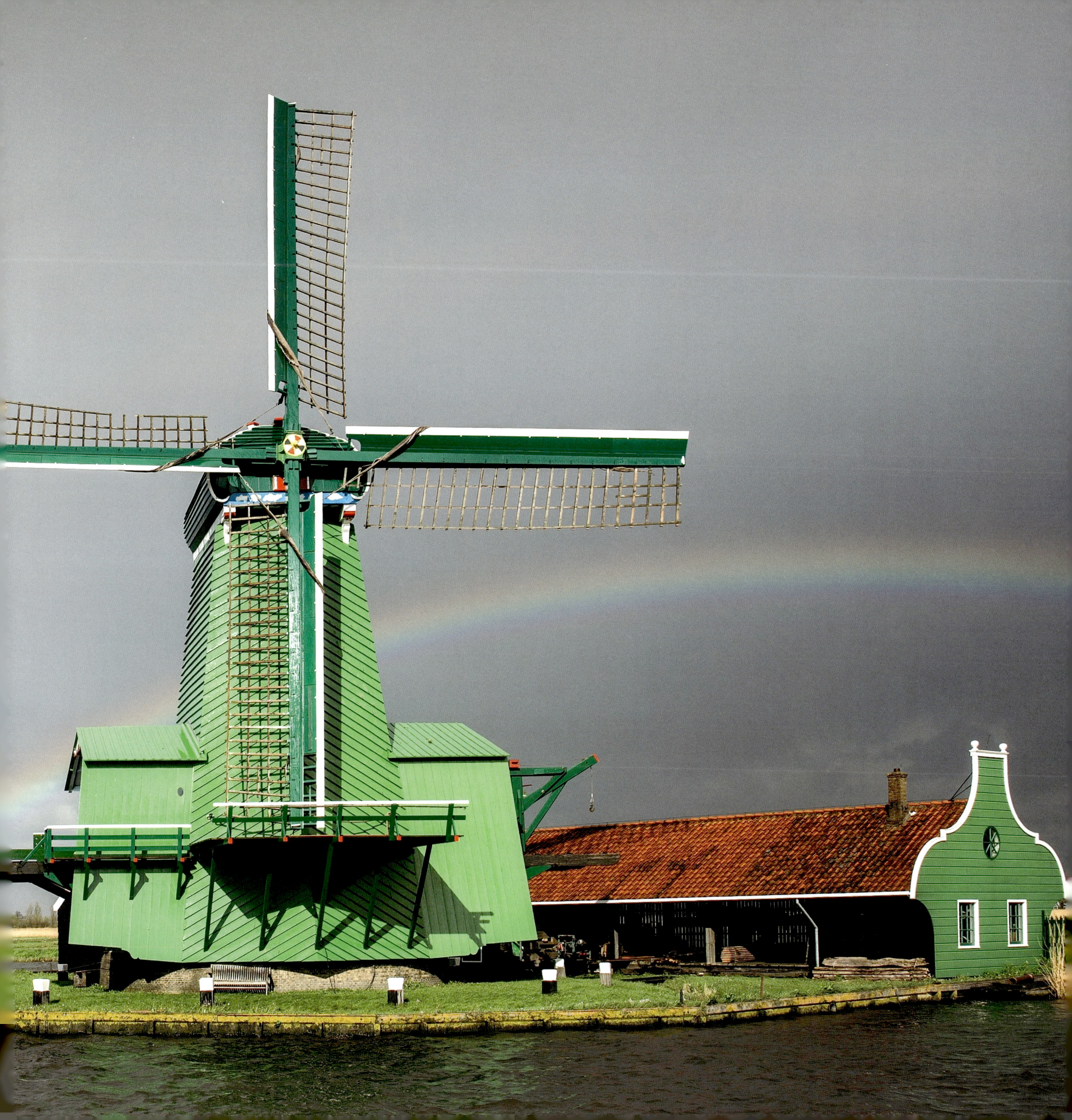

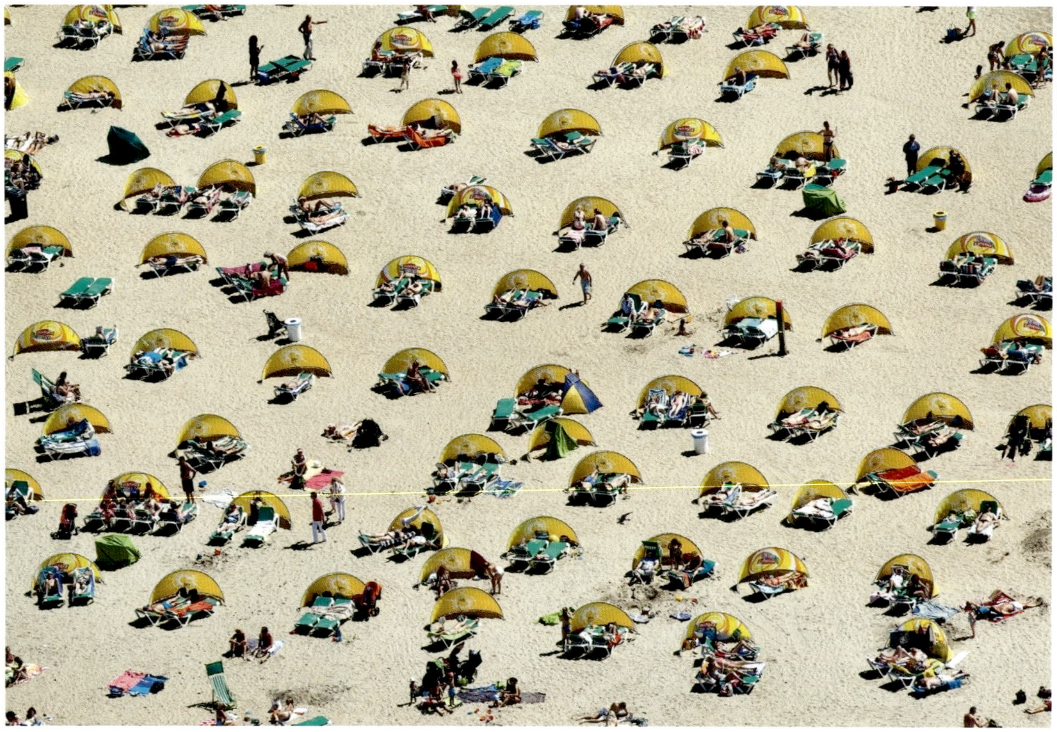

From the North Sea beaches and the Wadden Sea to the pools and lakes, canals, rivers and streams, at every turn we come across the Dutch enjoying recreation. If not in bikinis or swimming trunks, they will be found on their boats, in their caravans and – if it has frozen properly for a couple of days – on their skates.

Above and right: Zandvoort beach on a hot summer's day. Not just popular with many Dutch bathers but also beloved by our German neighbours.

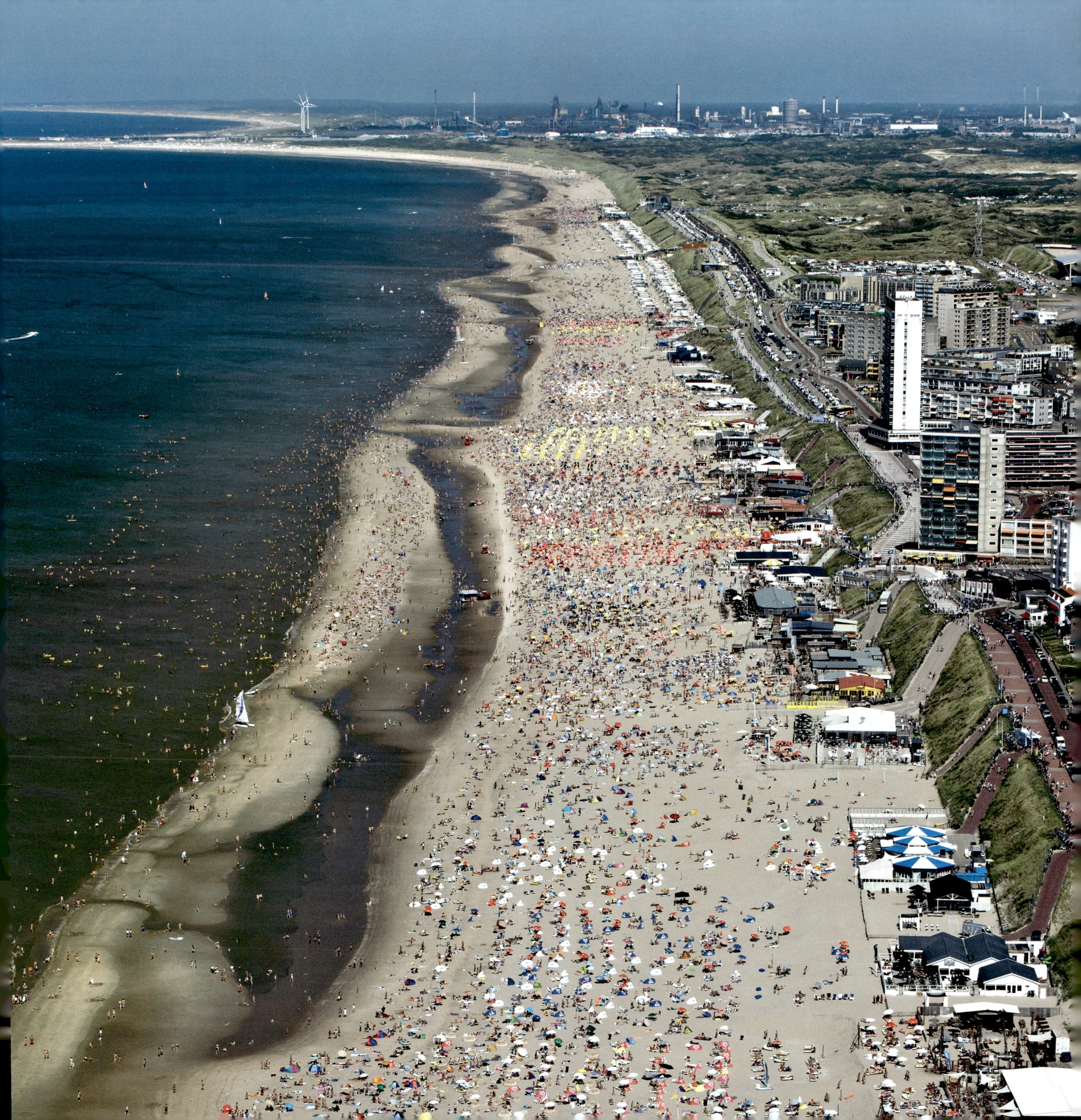

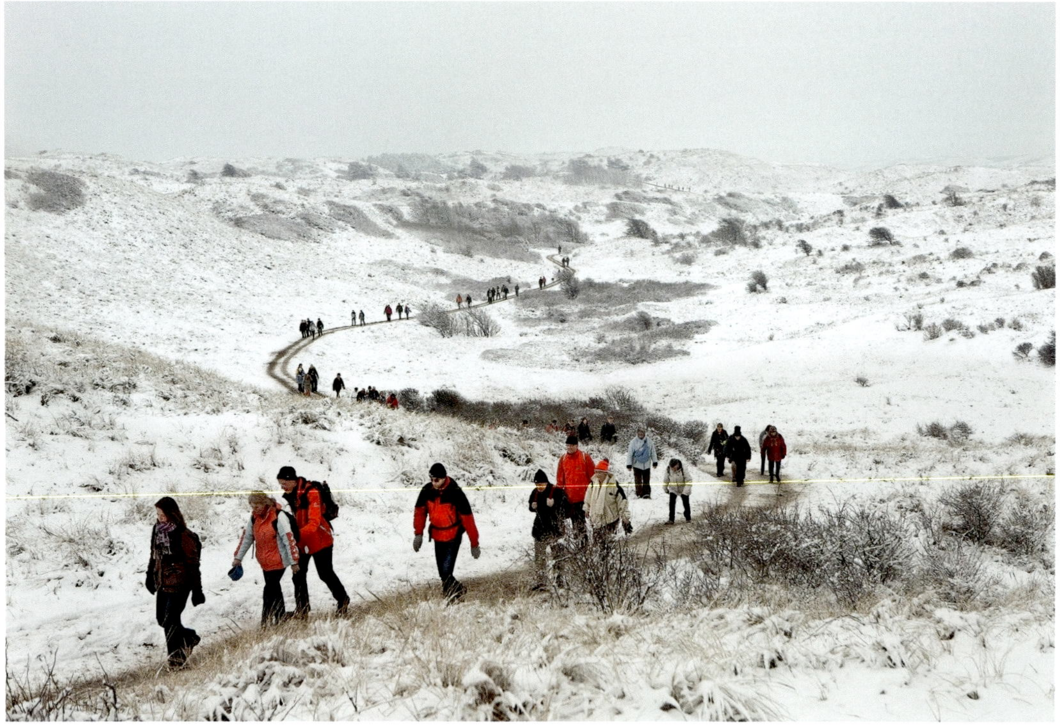

Top: The Egmond Hiking Marathon through the dunes of Egmond aan Zee.

Right: Ice sailing on the Gouwzee near Monnickendam.

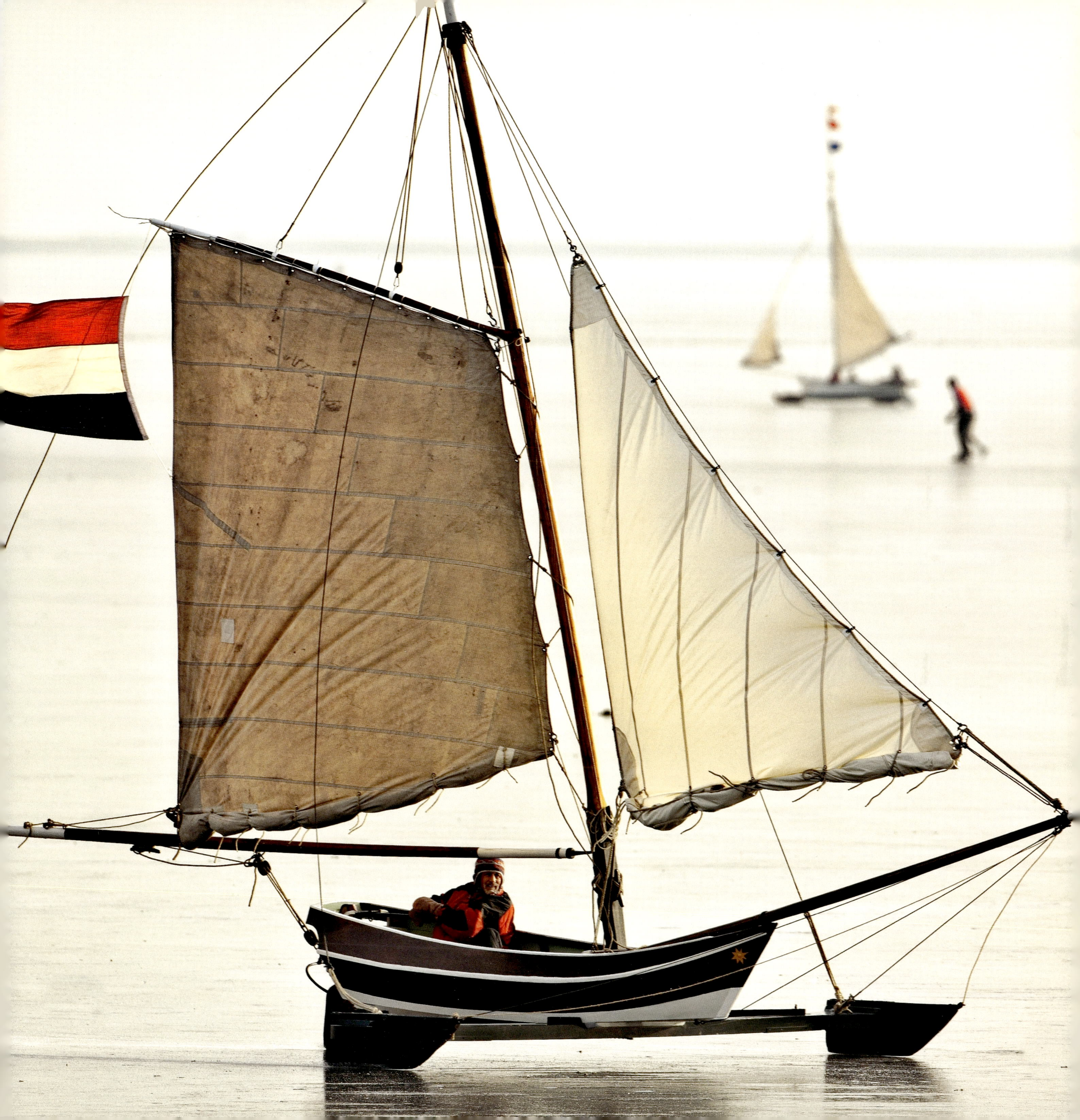

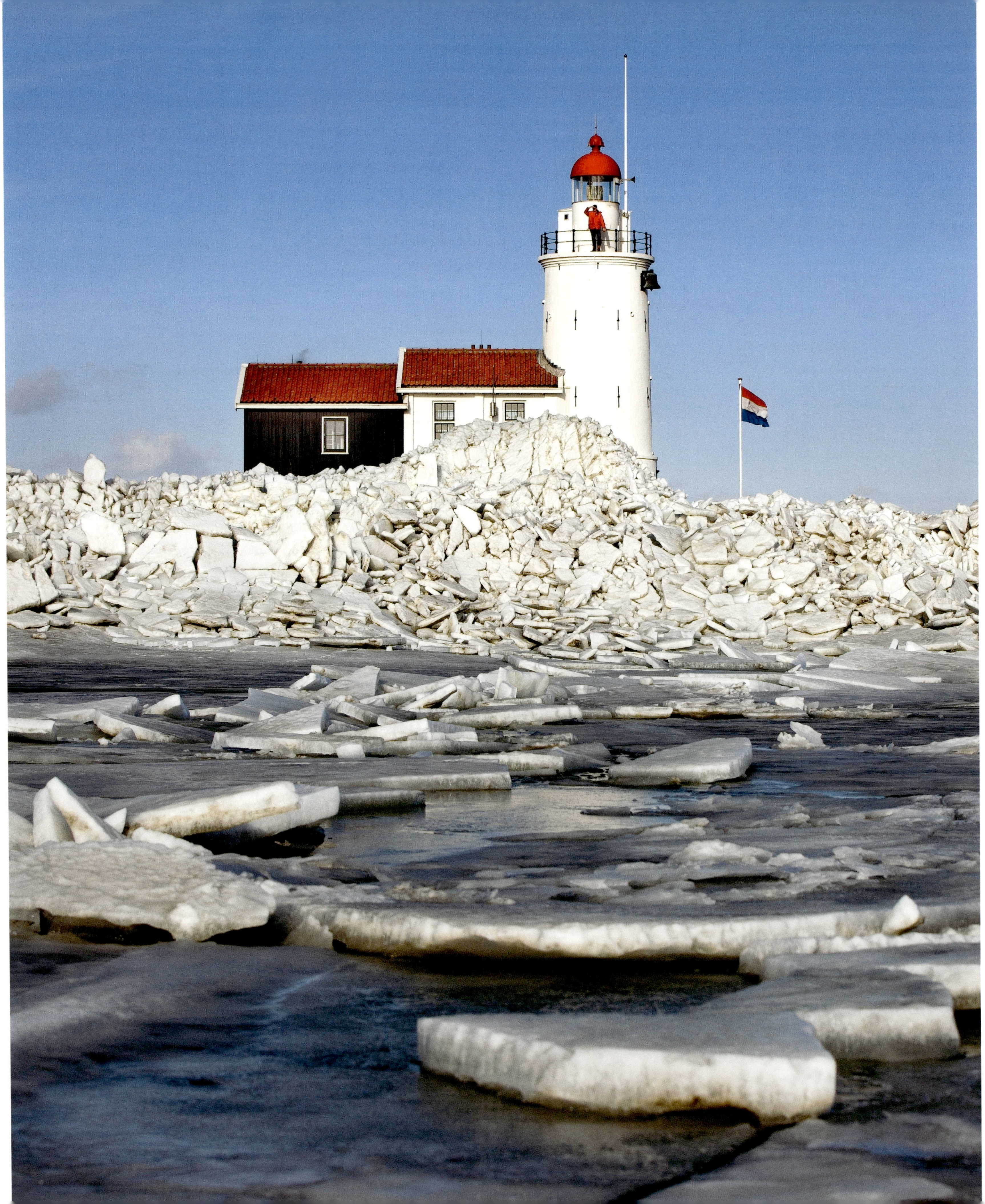

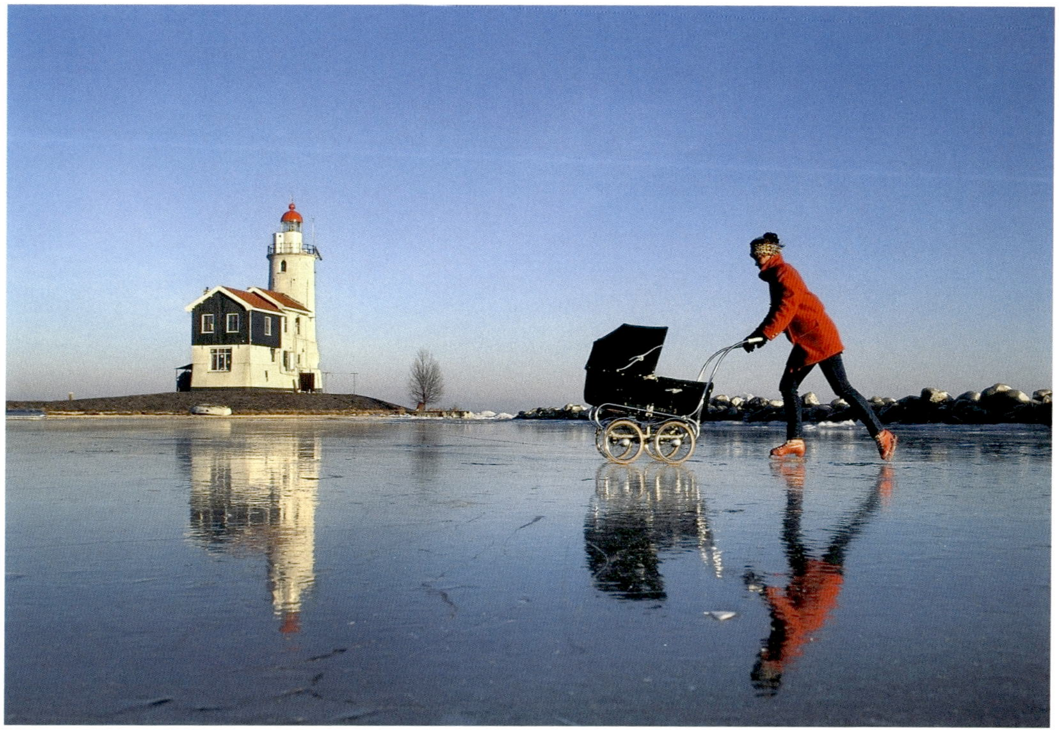

Left: Het Paard lighthouse on the Marken peninsula. From his tower, the lighthouse keeper watches the drifting ice that menaces the lighthouse.

Top: A mother skating past the lighthouse with her baby buggy on a sunny day.

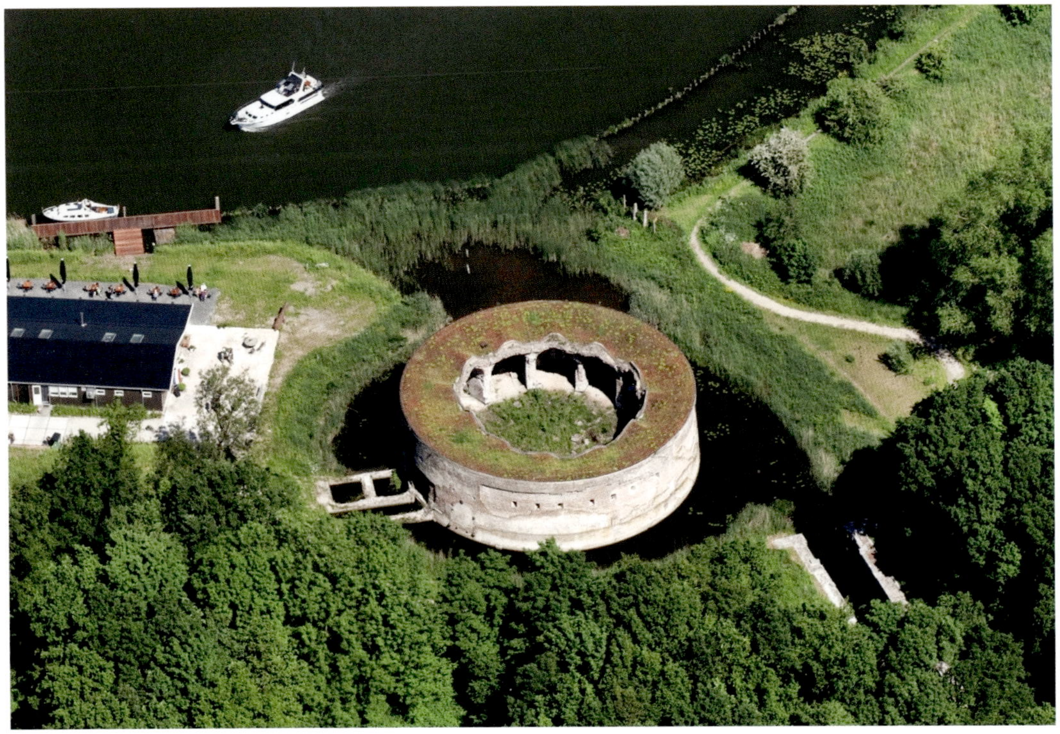

A World Heritage Site

The UNESCO World Heritage List includes ten monuments from the Kingdom of the Netherlands: the former island of Schokland, the Stelling van Amsterdam defensive line, the windmills of Kinder- dijk-Elshout, the Woudagemaal water pumping station in Frisia, the Beemster Polder in Noord-Holland, the Amsterdam canals, the Rietveld Schröder House in Utrecht, the Van Nelle factory in Rotterdam, the historic port of Willemstad on the Caribbean island of Curaçao and the Wadden Sea.

Stelling van Amsterdam defensive line

To keep the capital city out of range of enemy guns, a 135 km-long defensive line was built around Amsterdam between 1881 and 1914, fifteen to twenty miles from the city. Over time, and due to new methods of warfare, the defensive line has long lost its original purpose. However, the Stelling van Amsterdam provides a good picture of the period in which it was a serviceable structure. The Stelling van Amsterdam: its forts are well visible; it is a feat of logistical ingenuity. If it had been called upon to save Amsterdam from invasion, it would undoubtedly have worked well. In 1904, the Stelling van Amsterdam was calculated to be capable of protecting nearly 700,000 local residents and 200,000 soldiers through six months of siege.

Top: Fort Uitermeer on the River Vecht at Weesp.

Right: Fort on the Jisperweg along the North Holland Canal, which also serves as a ring waterway for the Beemster Polder.

Following pages: Politics and art fraternise at the Hofvijver (Court Pond) in The Hague. The small tower in the middle of the Hofvijver is the official workplace of the Prime Minister. To the left of the tower is the Mauritshuis, a national museum with a superb collection of masterpieces, especially from the Golden Age.

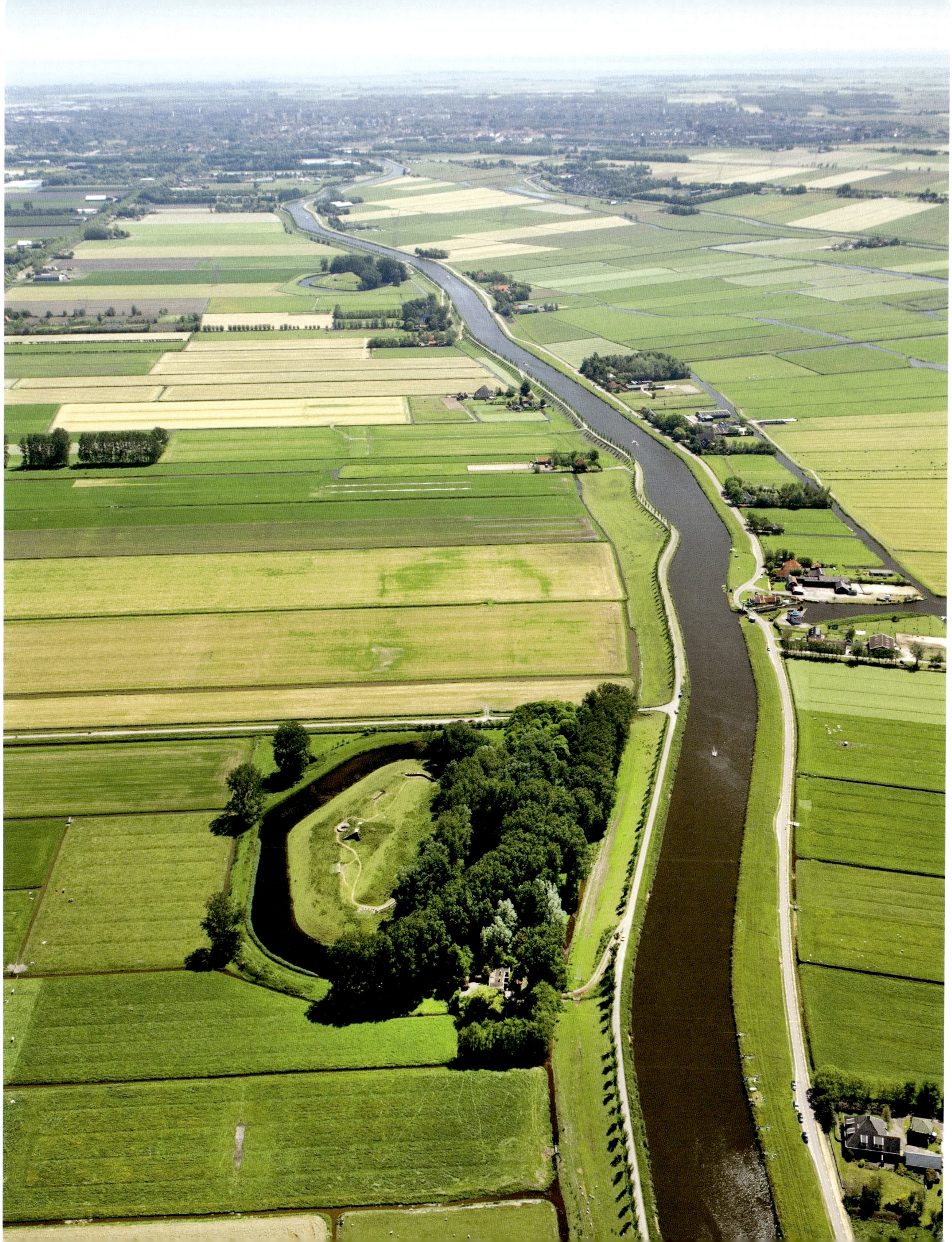

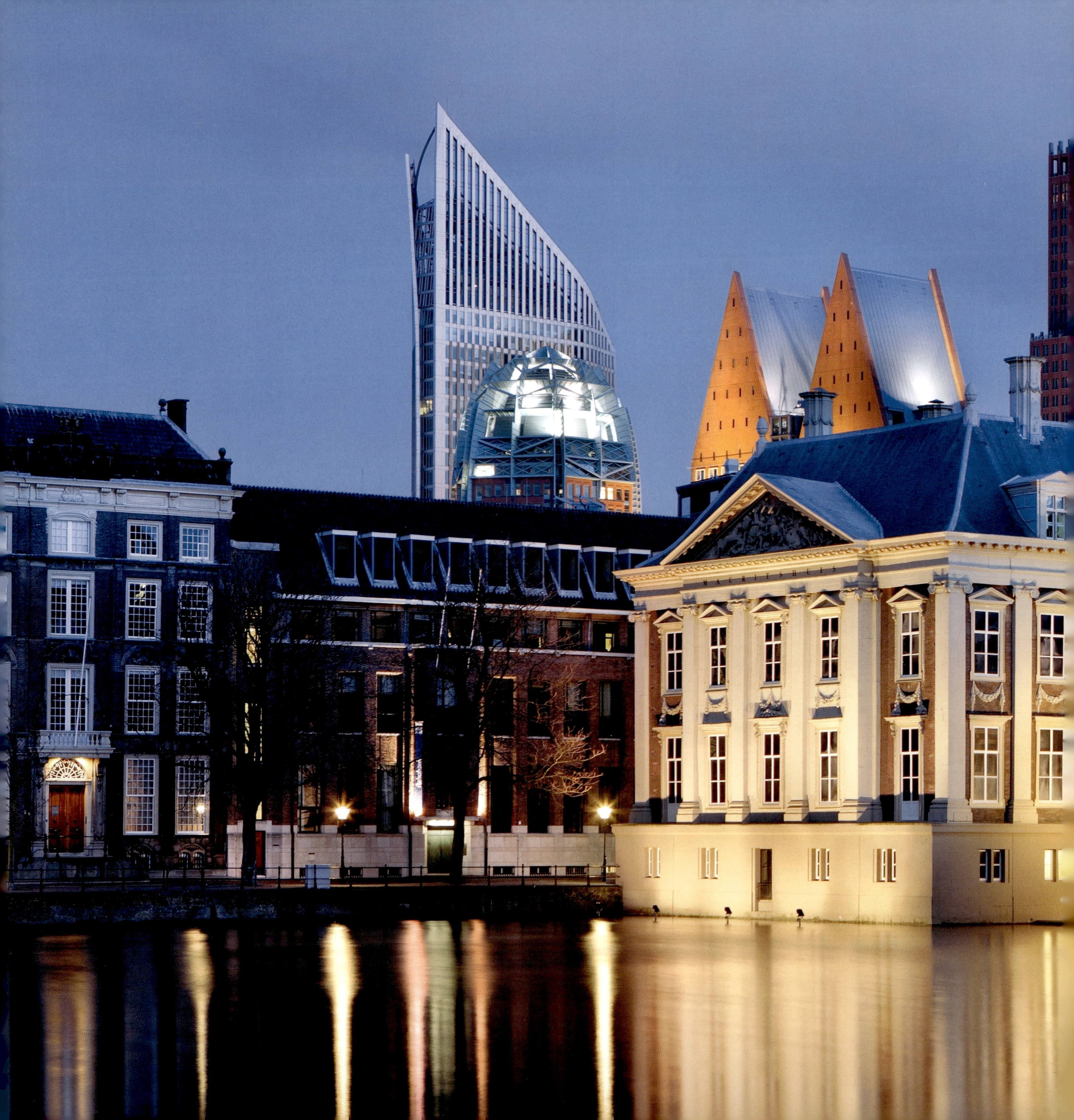
MAURITSHUIS

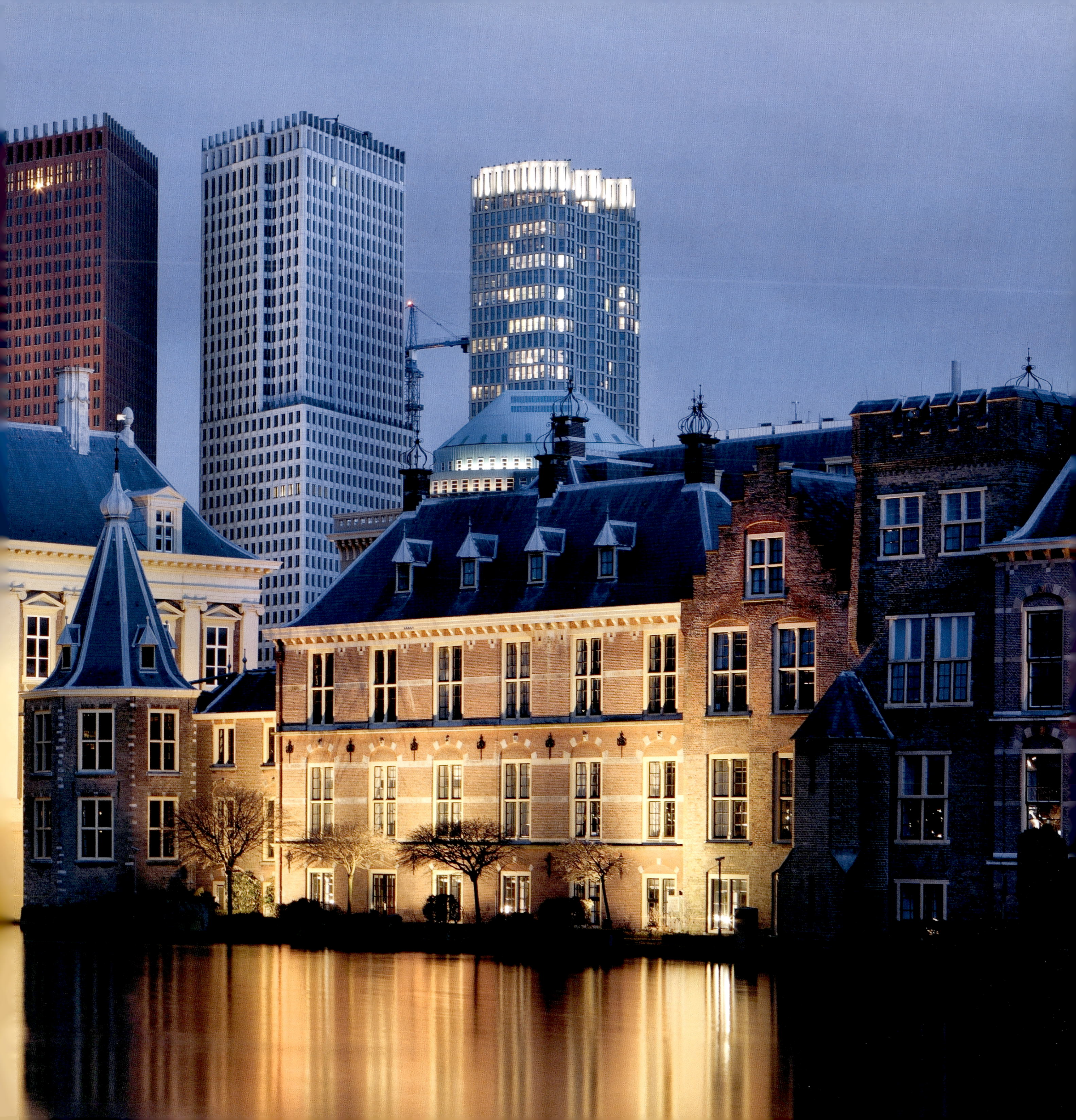

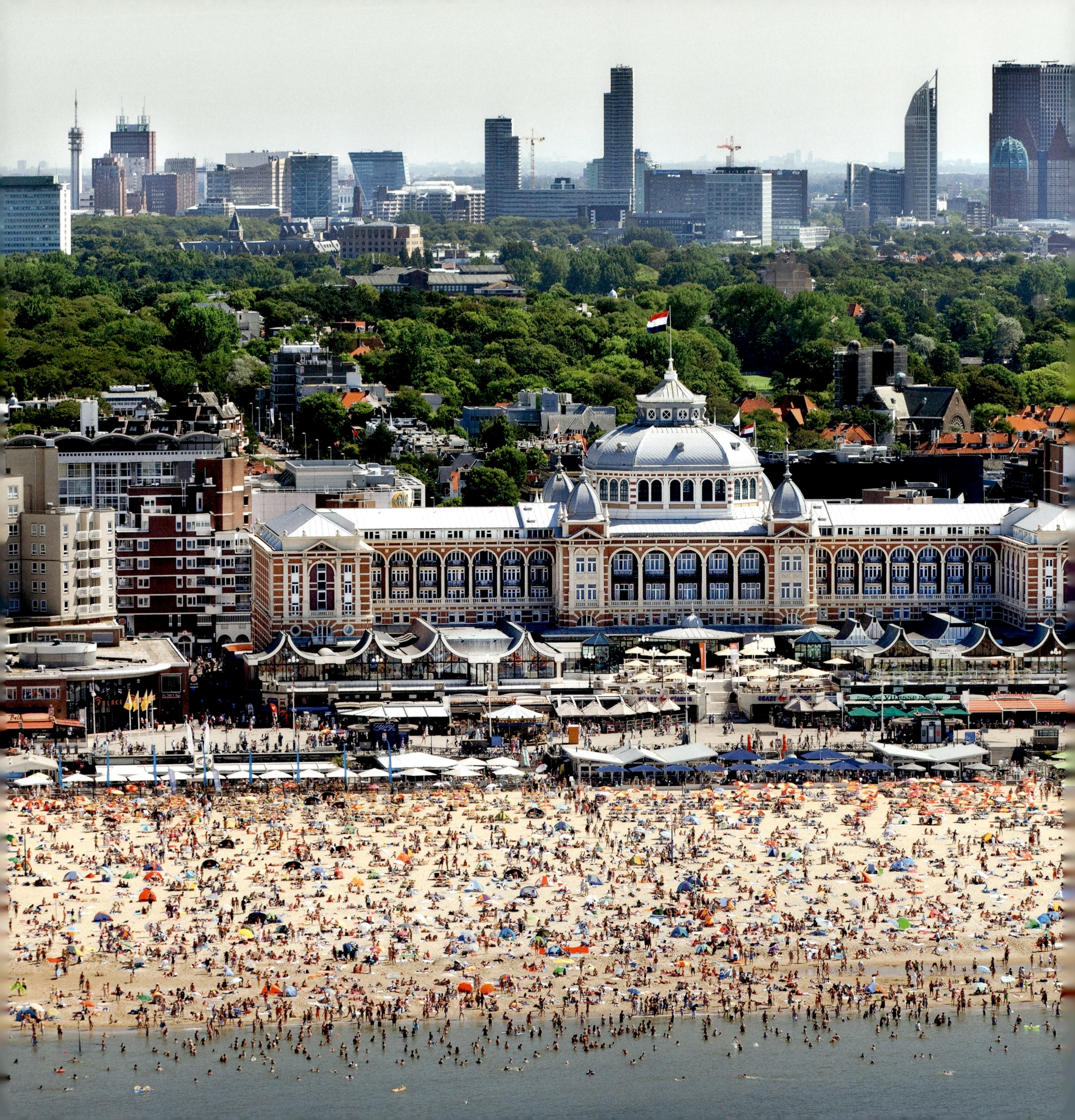

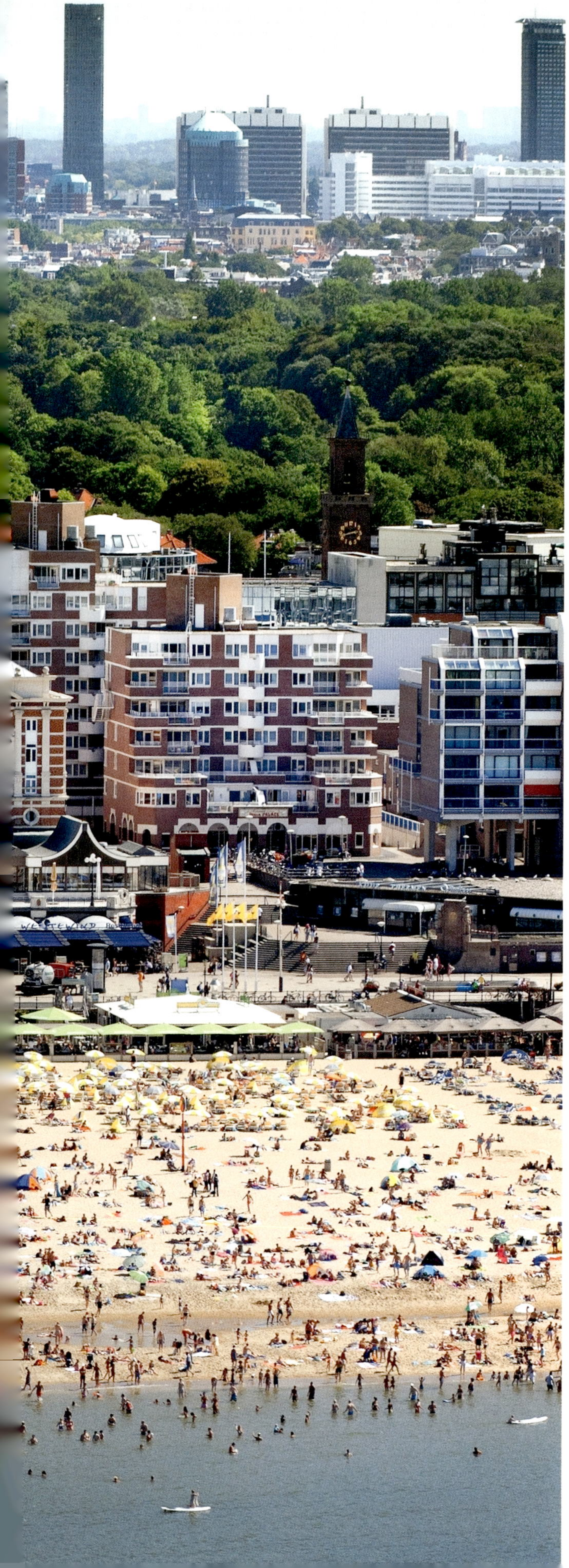

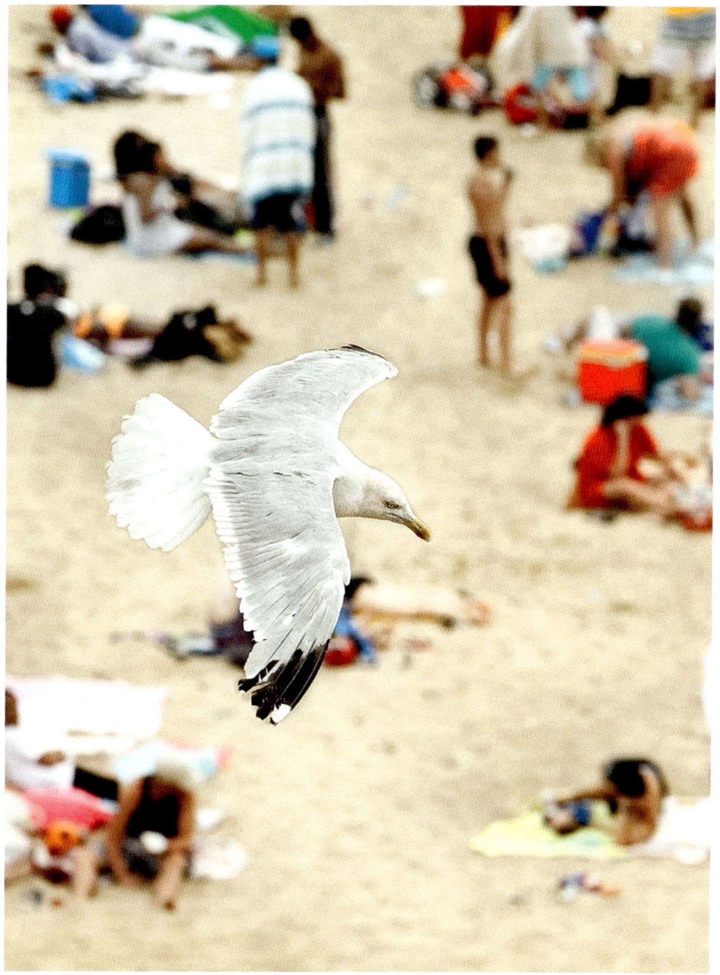

Left: Scheveningen beach with the Grand Hotel Amrâth Kurhaus. In the background, the skyline of The Hague.

Top: A seagull flies over the bathers.

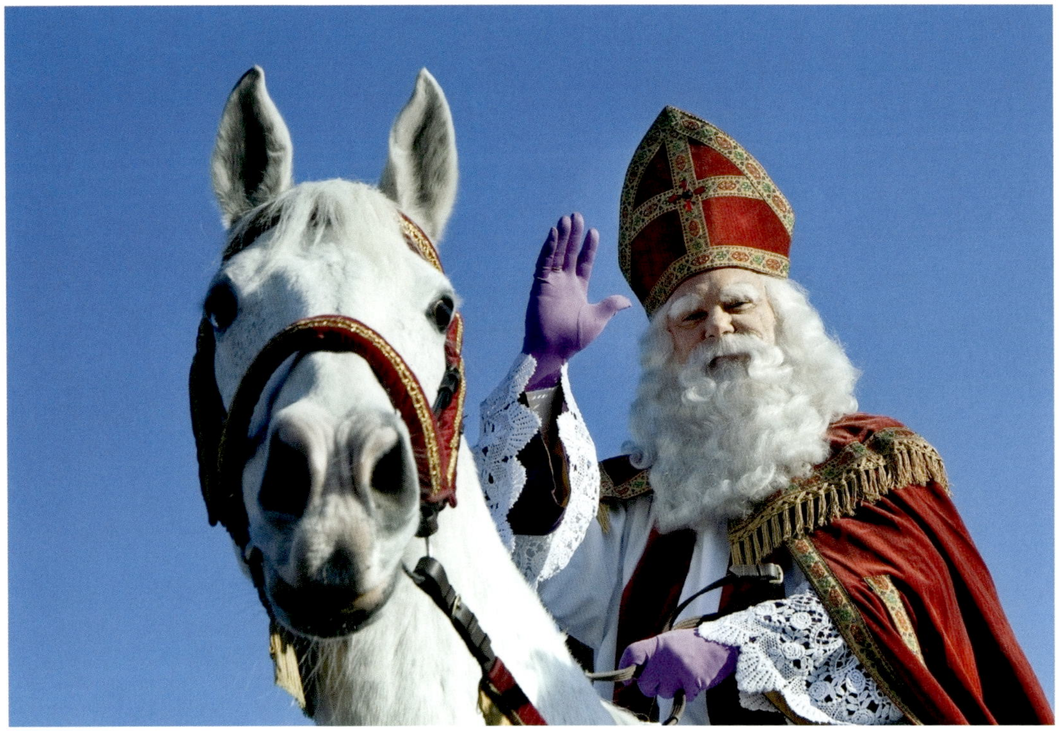

Top: Sinterklaas on his white horse, Amerigo. Sinterklaas is a children's festival held on 5 and 6 December in the Netherlands, Belgium and a few current and former Dutch colonies.

Right: On 1 January each year, to see in the new year, thousands of Dutch take part in the UNOX New Year's Dive in the cold waters of the North Sea at Scheveningen.

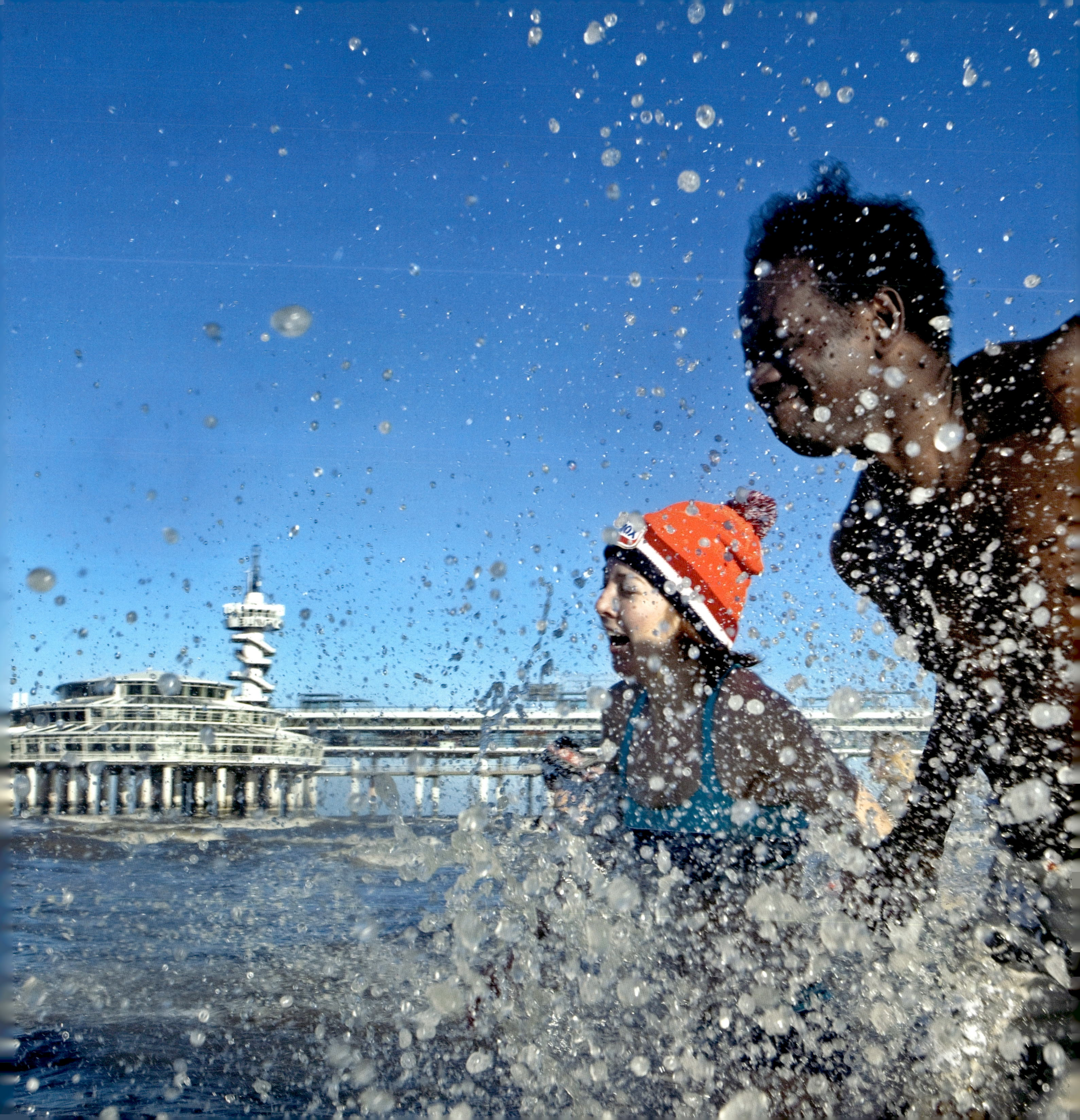

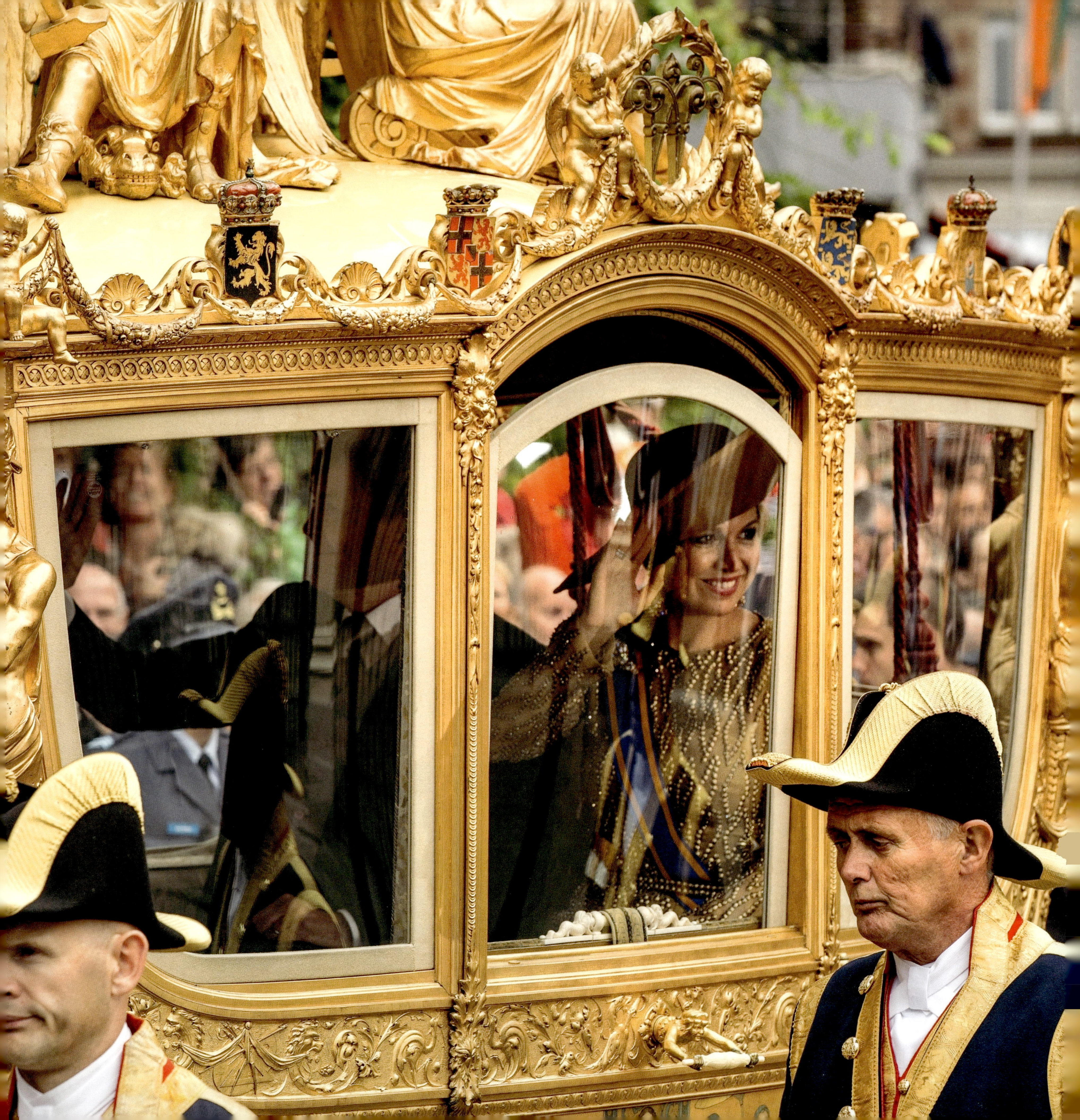

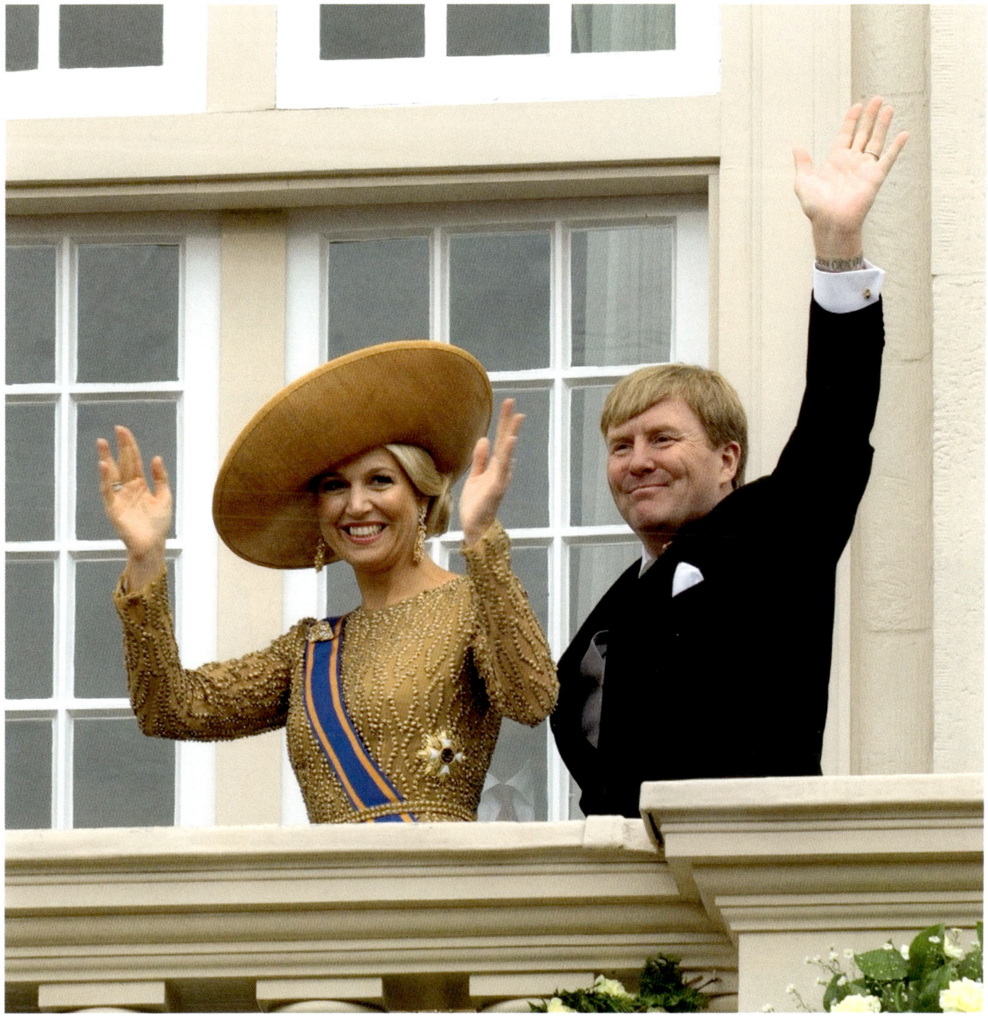

Traditionally, the monarch opens the annual parliamentary calendar on the third Tuesday of September (Prinsjesdag) each year, when the government's plans are announced. In the picture on the left, King Willem-Alexander and Queen Máxima ride through The Hague in the Golden Carriage from the Ridderzaal to Noordeinde Palace, where they wave to the adulating crowds from the balcony (top).

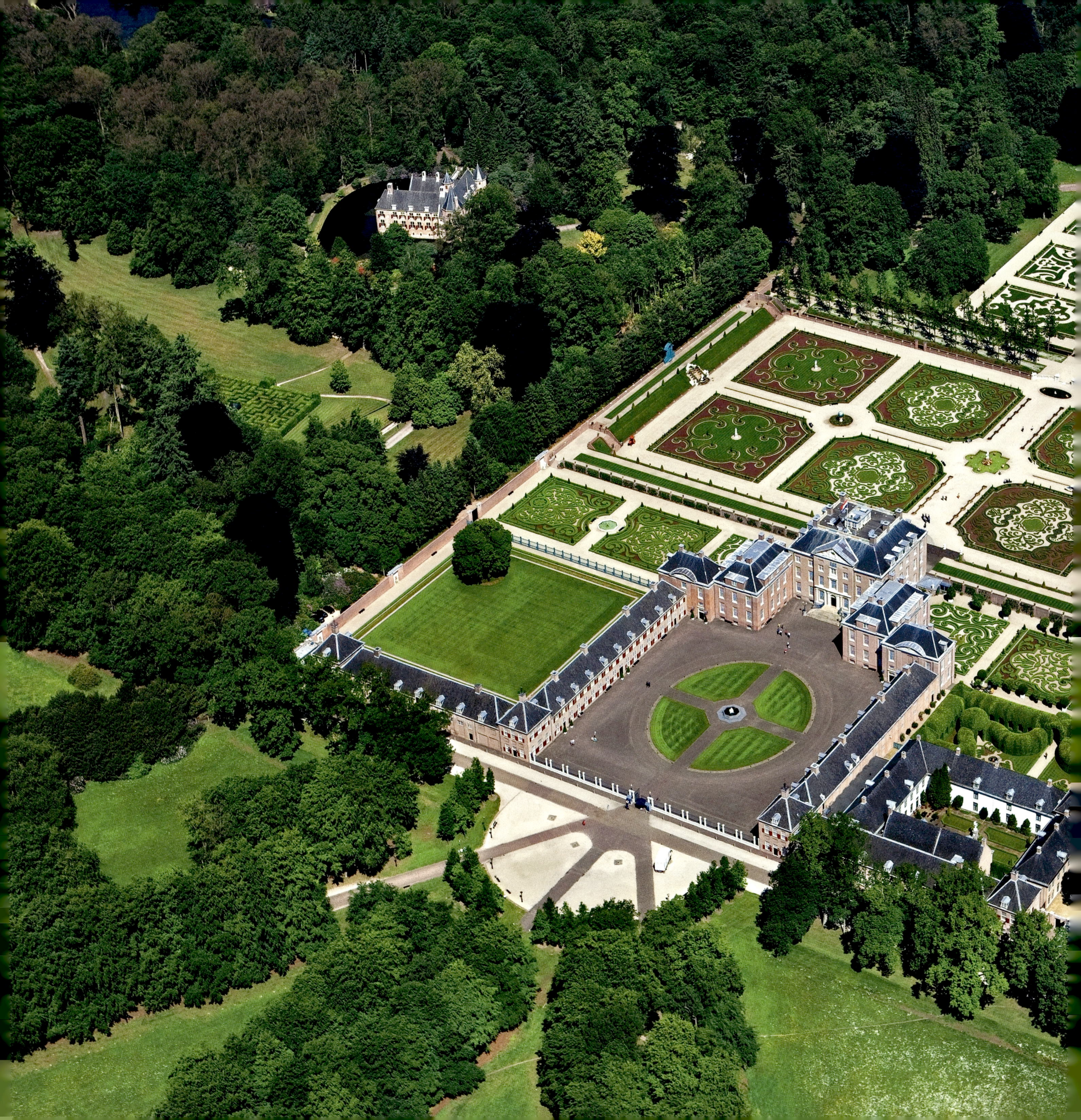

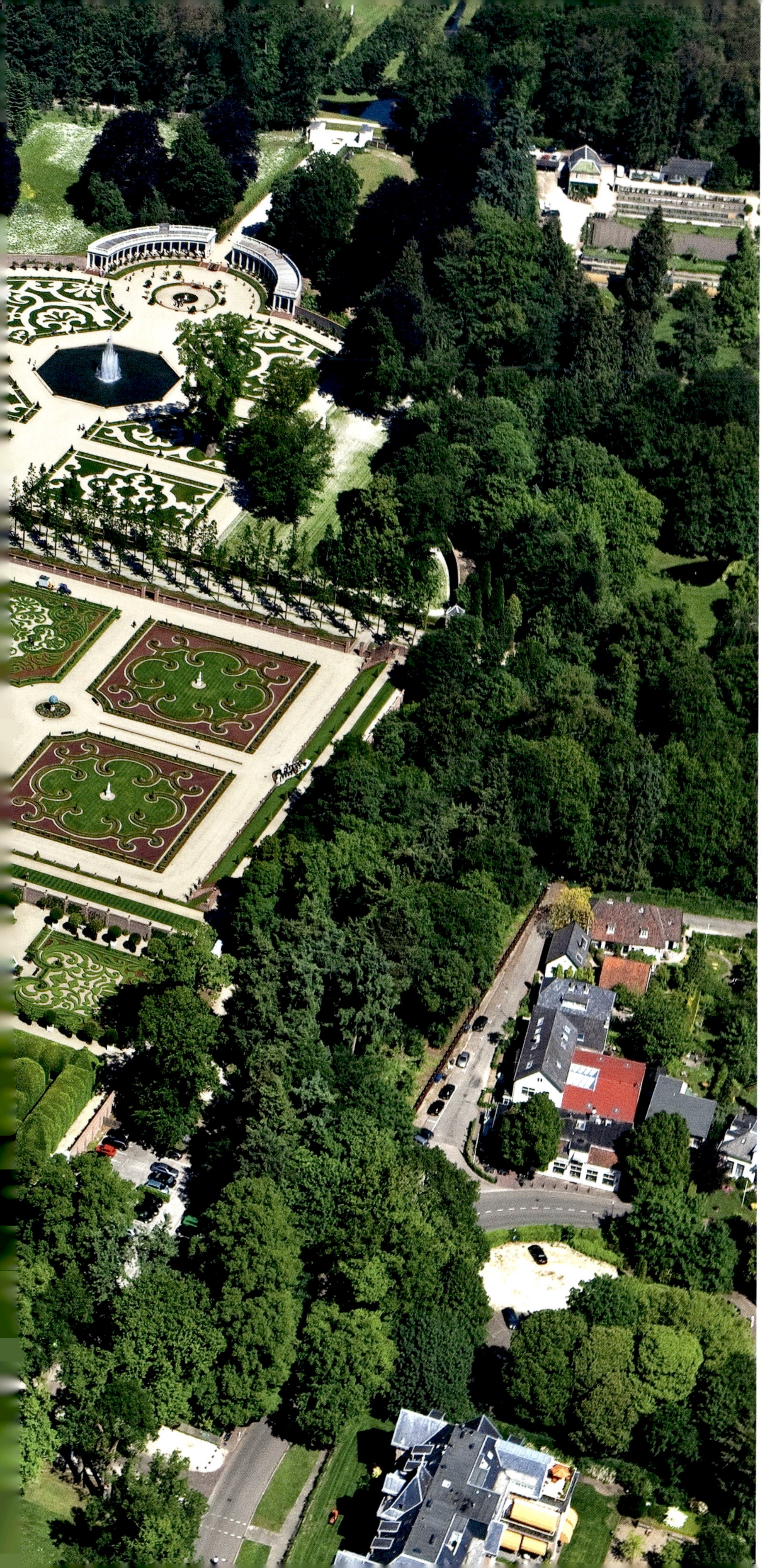

67

Left: Apeldoorn is home to the 300-year-old palace of Het Loo. Since 1984, after a thorough restoration, this former royal palace has been open to the public and has since become a National Museum. The guest rooms provide a picture of three centuries of residence by the Orange royal family: the gardens, with their fountains and flower beds, give an idea of how the surrounding park must have looked when it was still there. The Palace is located at the edge of one of the most scenic areas of natural beauty in the Netherlands: the High Veluwe.

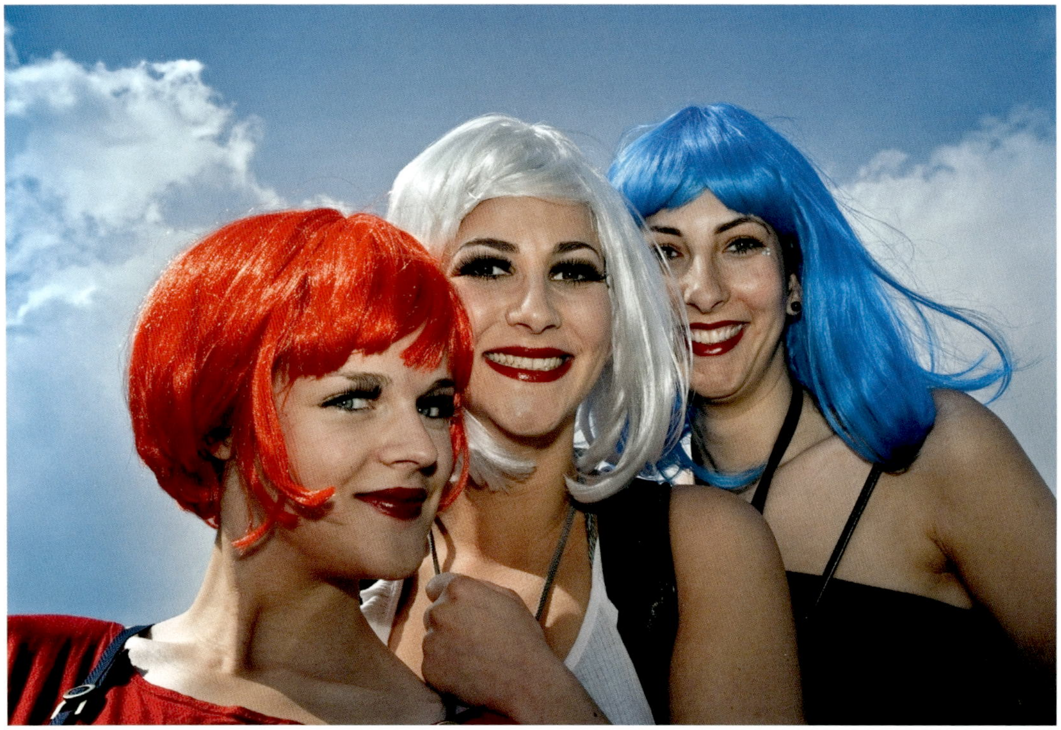

King's Day

The birthday of the king on 27 April is a joyful festival nationwide. Attending King's Day in Amsterdam is a popular way of spending the national holiday. Hundreds of thousands of visitors, including many from abroad, spend the day visiting the capital.

Top: Women wearing wigs in the national colours of red, white and blue.

Right: King's Day is celebrated enthusiastically along the Amsterdam canals.

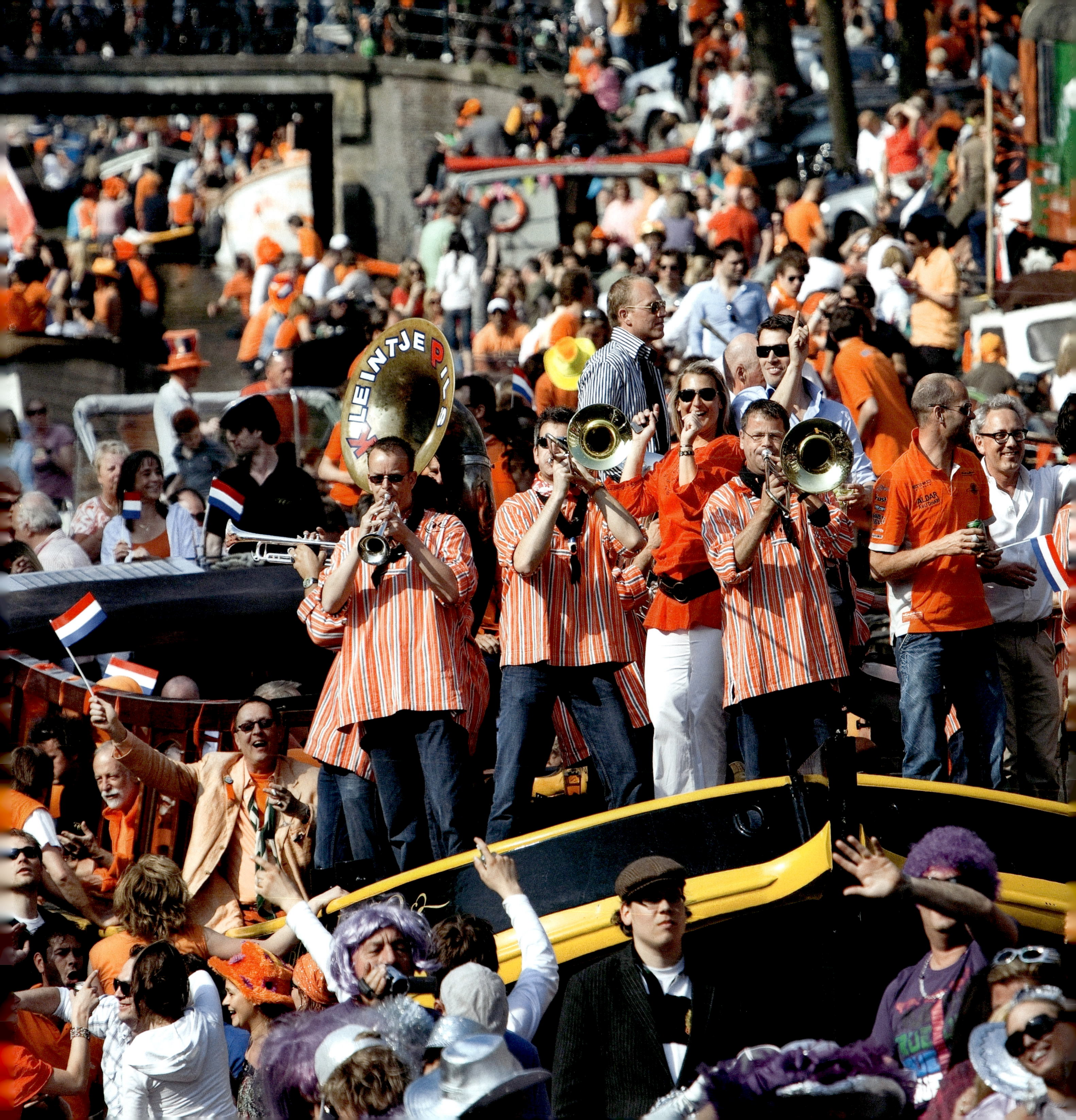
KLEINTJE PILS

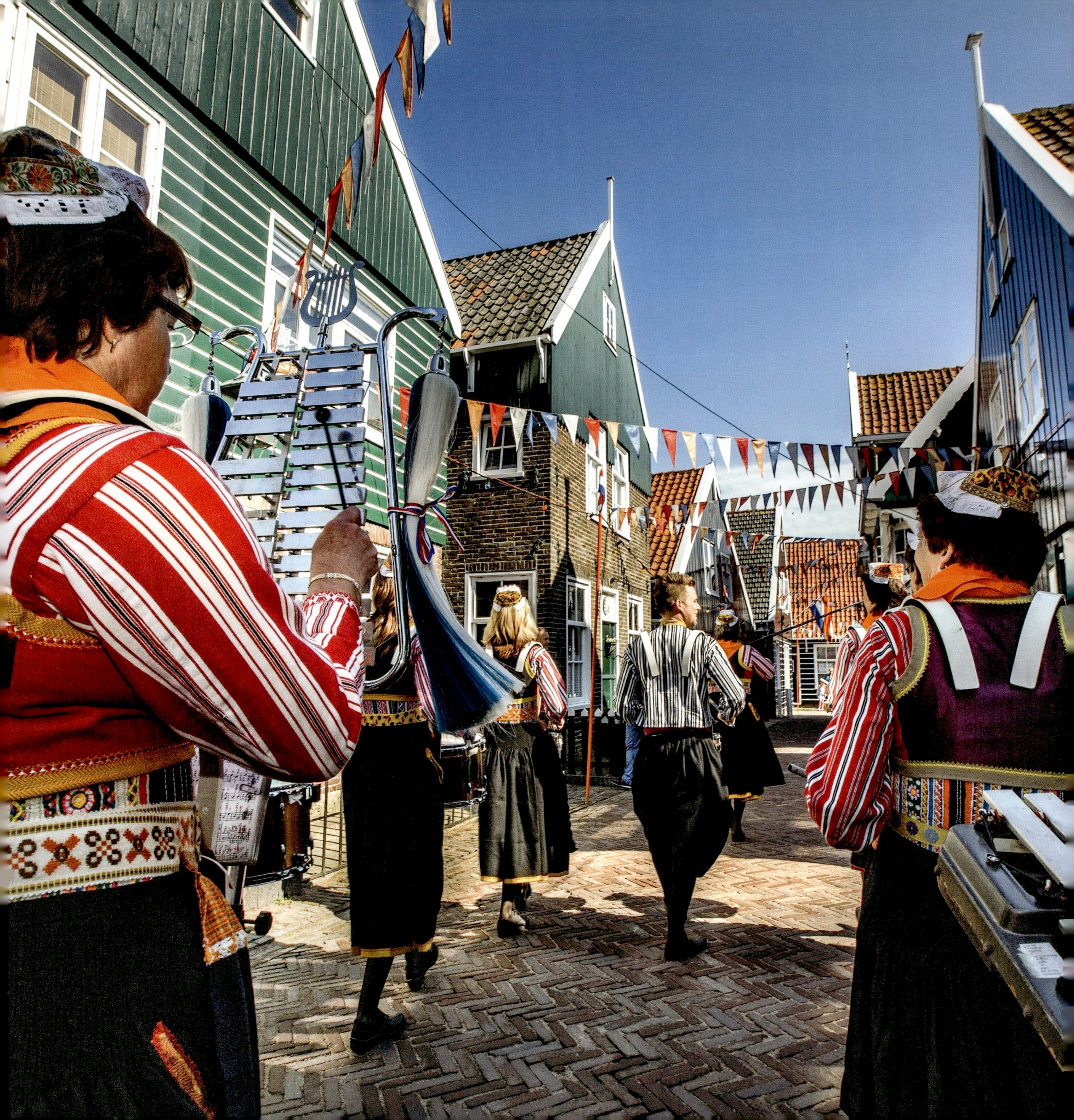

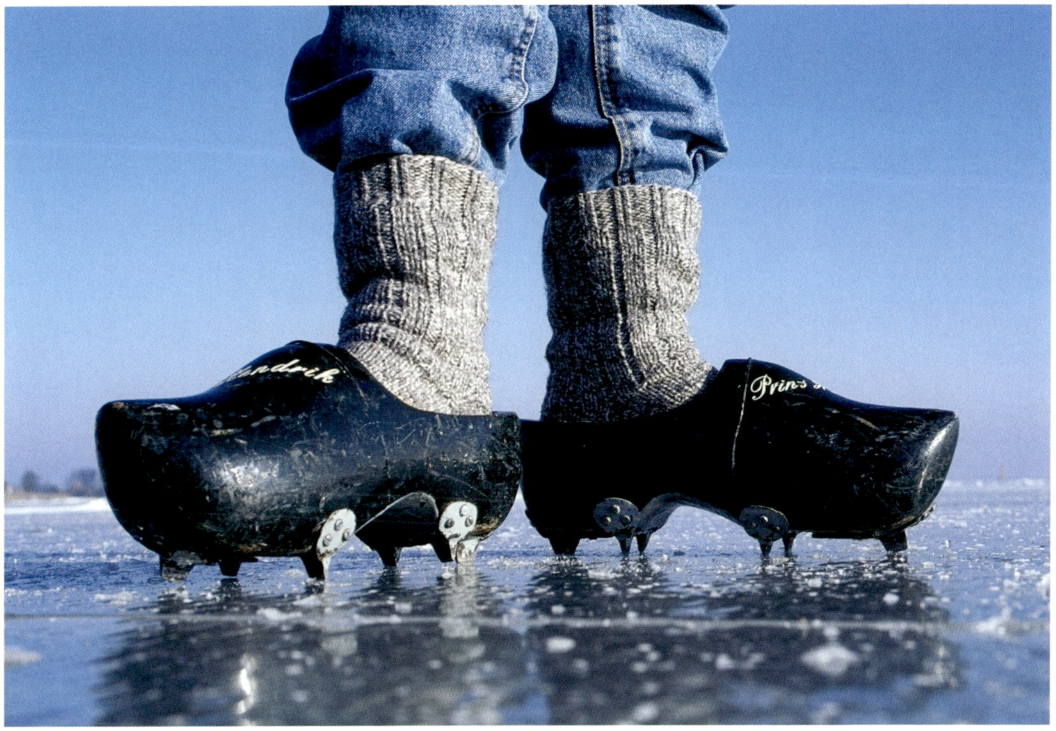

Left: Traditional national dress has almost entirely disappeared from the Dutch streets. But not on the peninsula of Marken, where many people still wear it for King's Day. In the picture: Fanfare Juliana Band marching through the village of Marken.

Top: Of course, the clog is another traditional symbol of the Netherlands. In order not to slip on the ice, there are even clogs with spiked soles.

Right: Spring near Noordwijk. Cliché or not, the vast fields of tulips and the windmills never fail to make a big impression.

Following pages: Egmond aan den Hoef. A bulb grower checks tulips for diseased specimens.

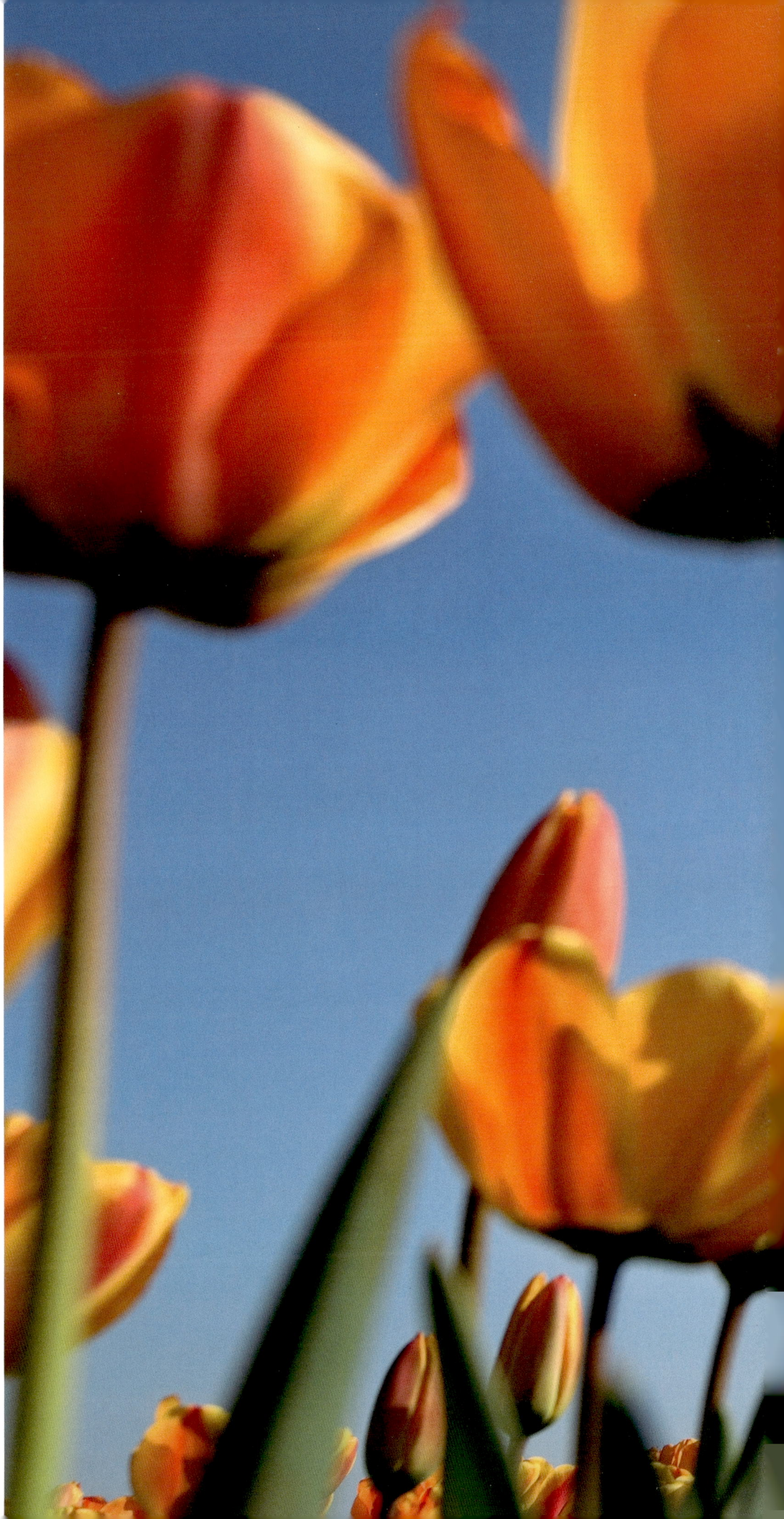

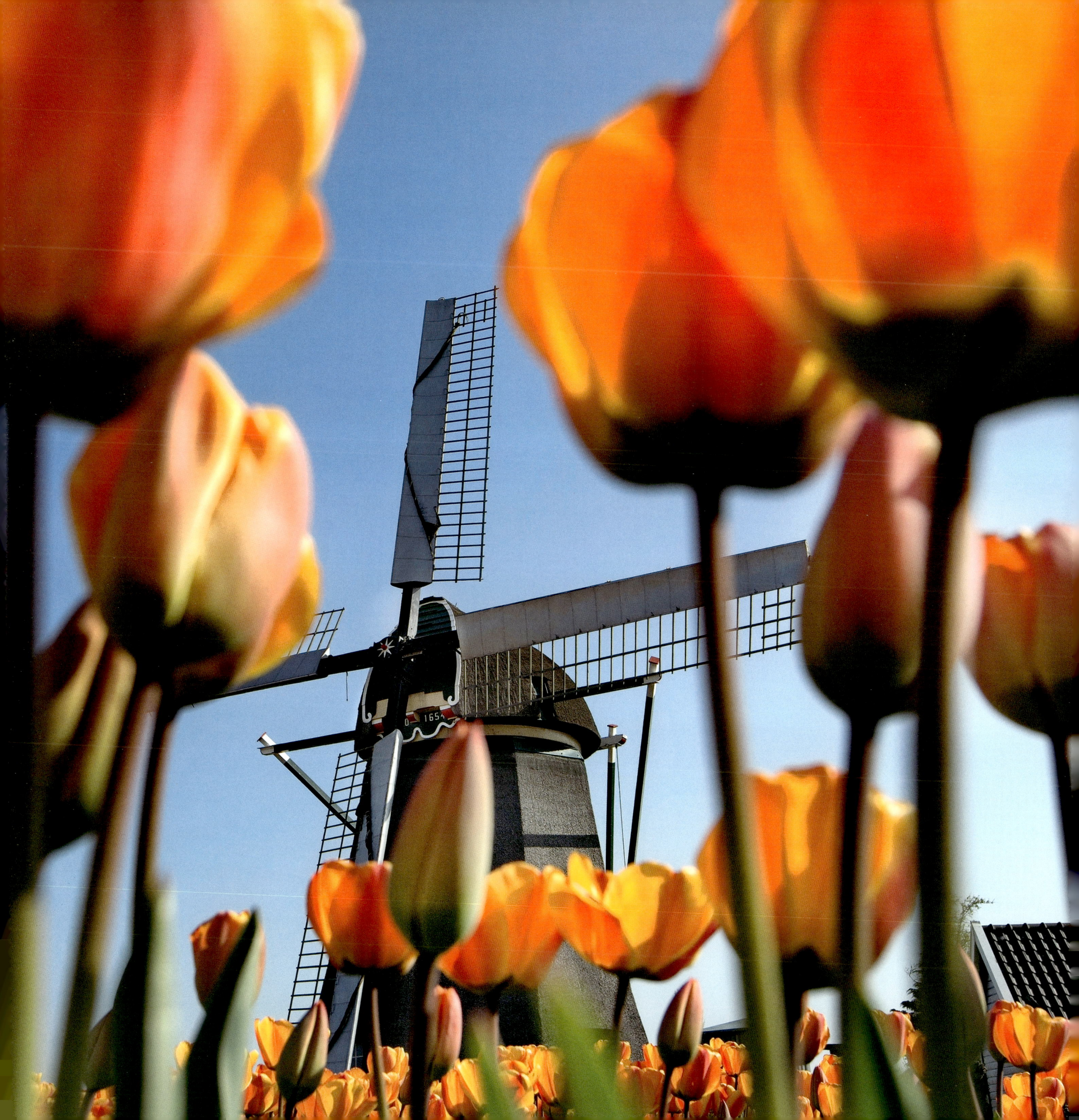

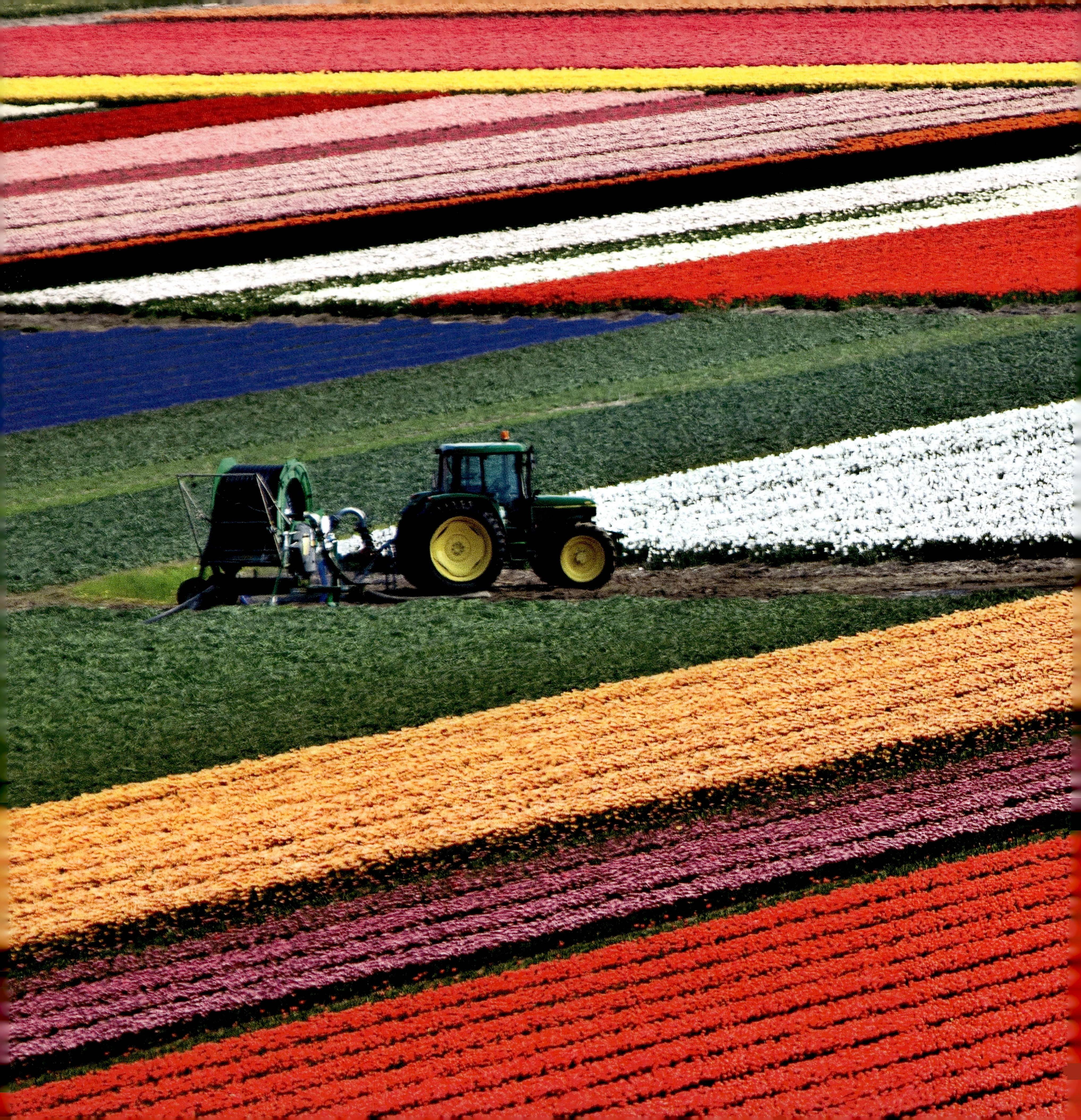

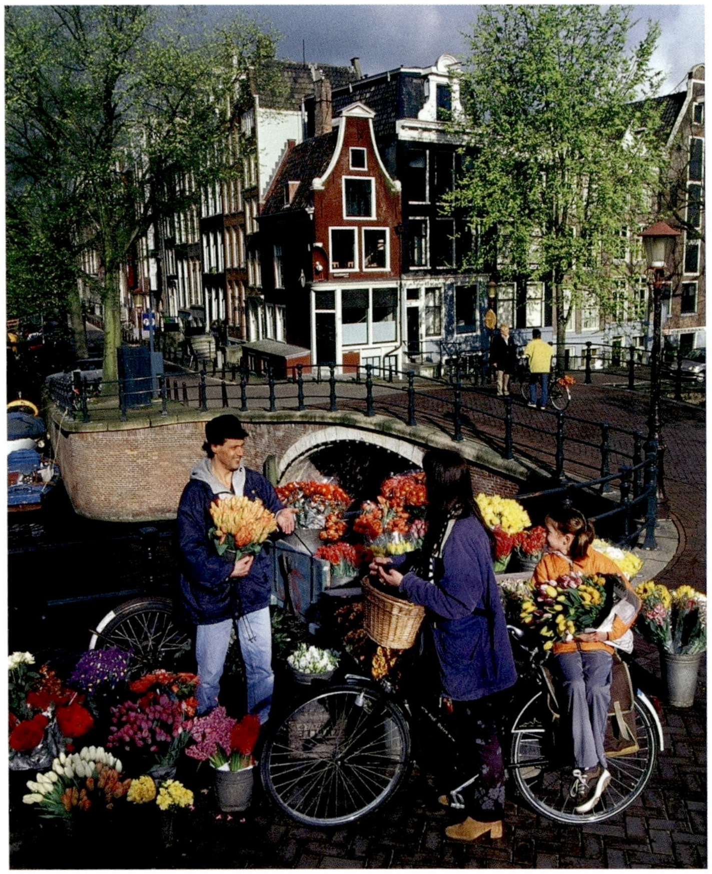

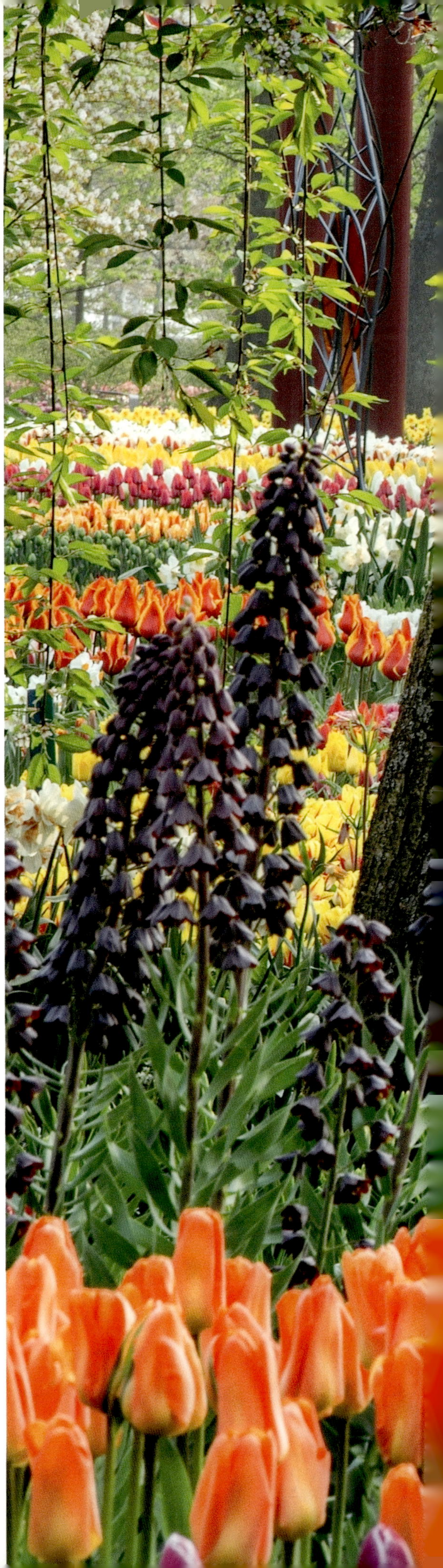

Top: Flower stall on the canals in Amsterdam.

Right: Each spring, Keukenhof, the premier flower garden of the Netherlands, attracts about one million visitors.

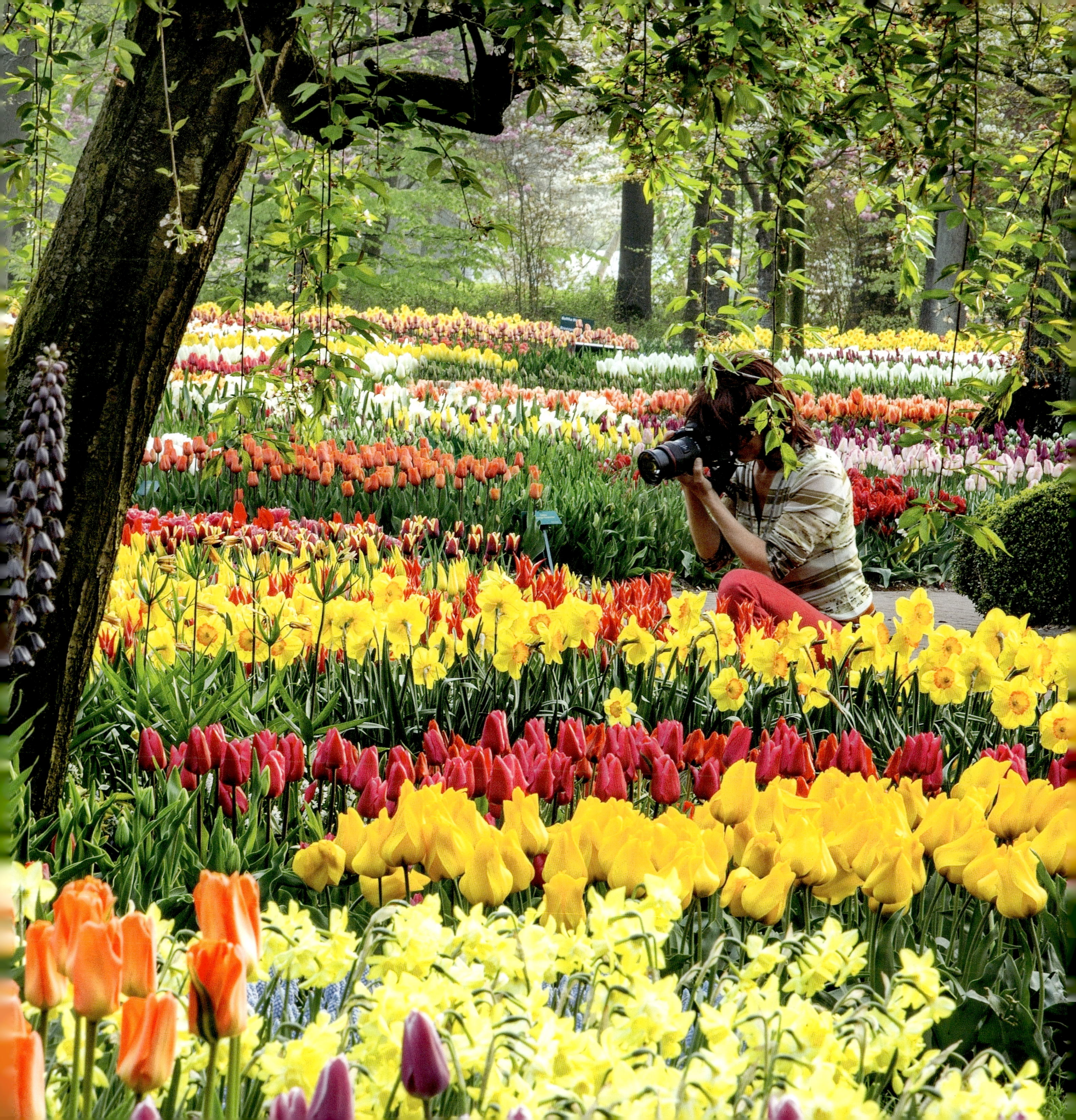

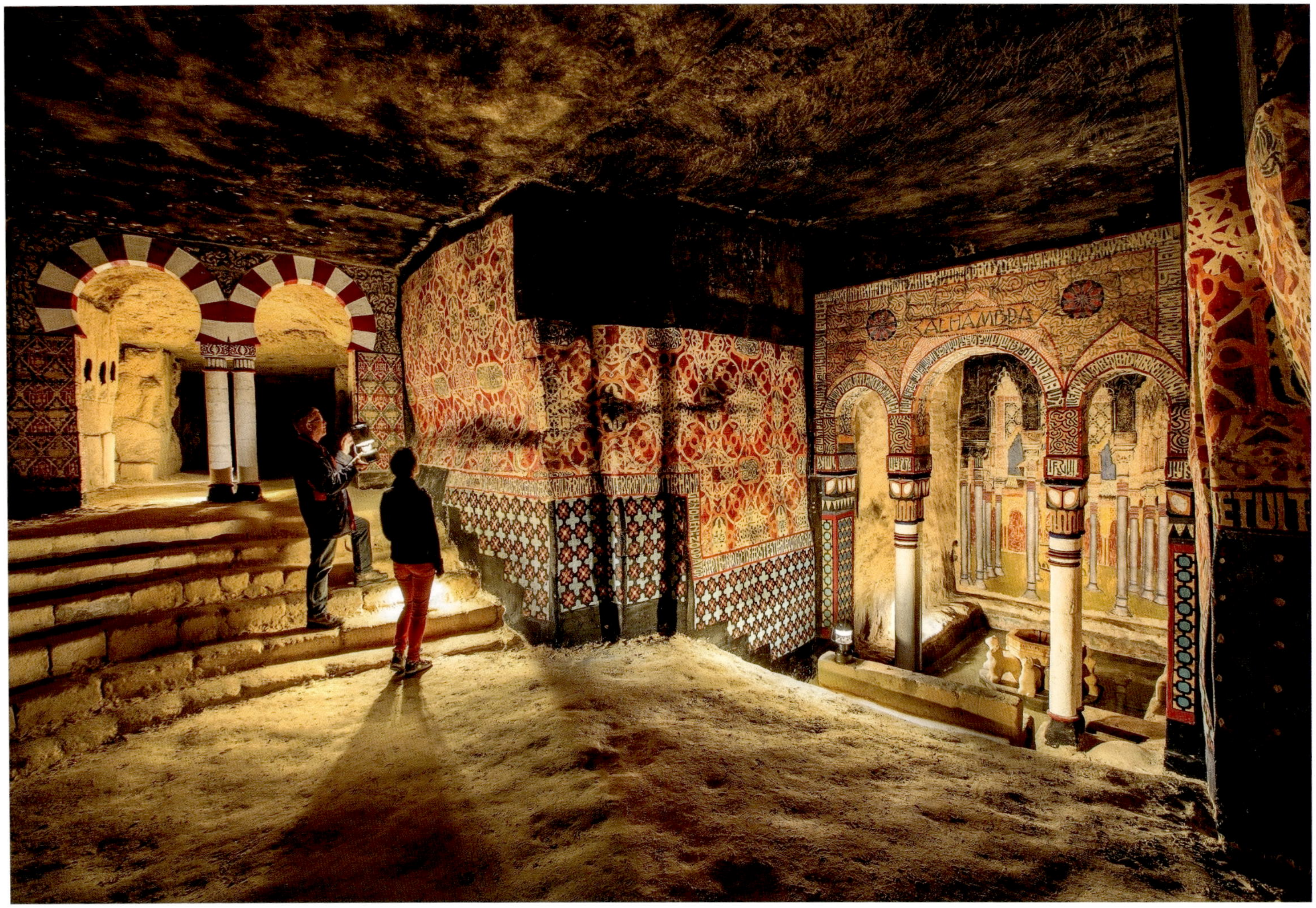

Top: The hundreds of kilometres long cave system of Sint Pietersberg in Maastricht. The cave system arose from the quarrying of marl stones. In the picture, a guide leads visitors around the works of art in the caves of Jezuïetenberg. Between 1860 and 1960, Jesuit scholars and theologians spent their free Wednesday afternoons at the quarry relaxing from their studies. They made many works of art there, including this replica of the Alhambra in Spain.

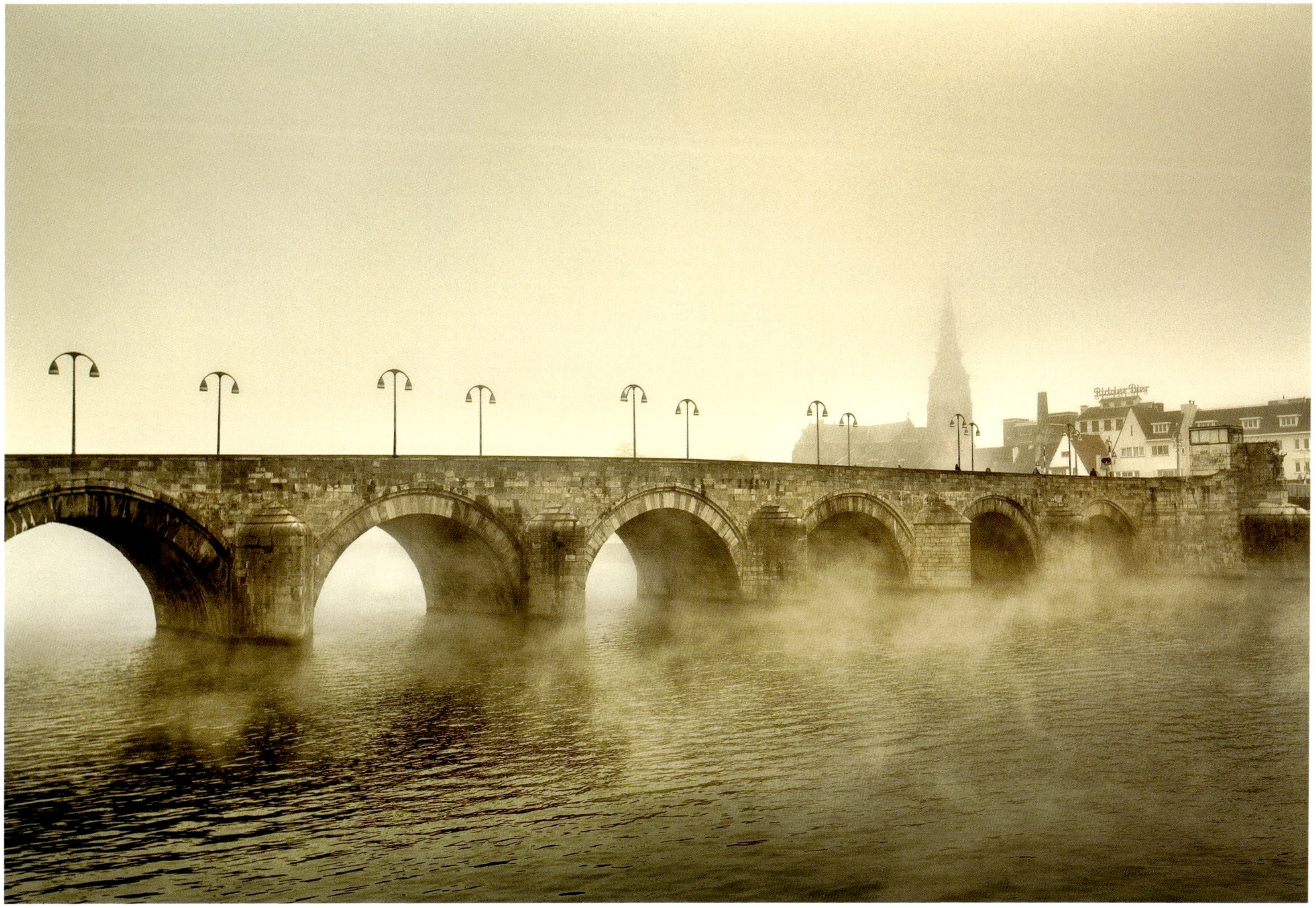

79

Top: St Servaas Bridge over the River Maas in Maastricht, partially shrouded in morning fog.

Following pages: The pictures on the previous pages were stereotypically Dutch. A very different region is hilly South Limburg, where even Dutch holiday-makers often imagine themselves to be abroad. In the picture: half-timbered houses in the rolling hills near Epen, South Limburg.

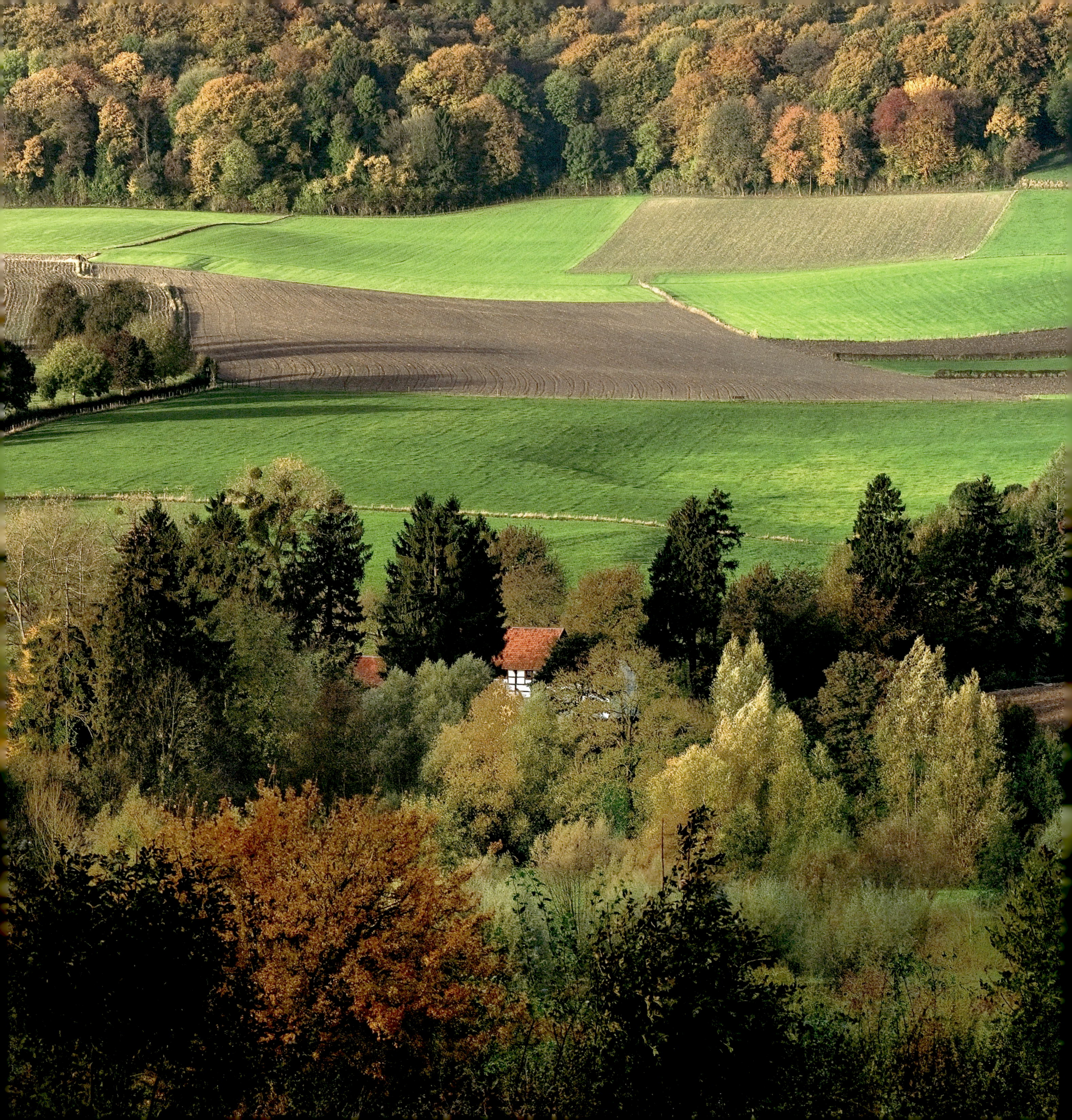

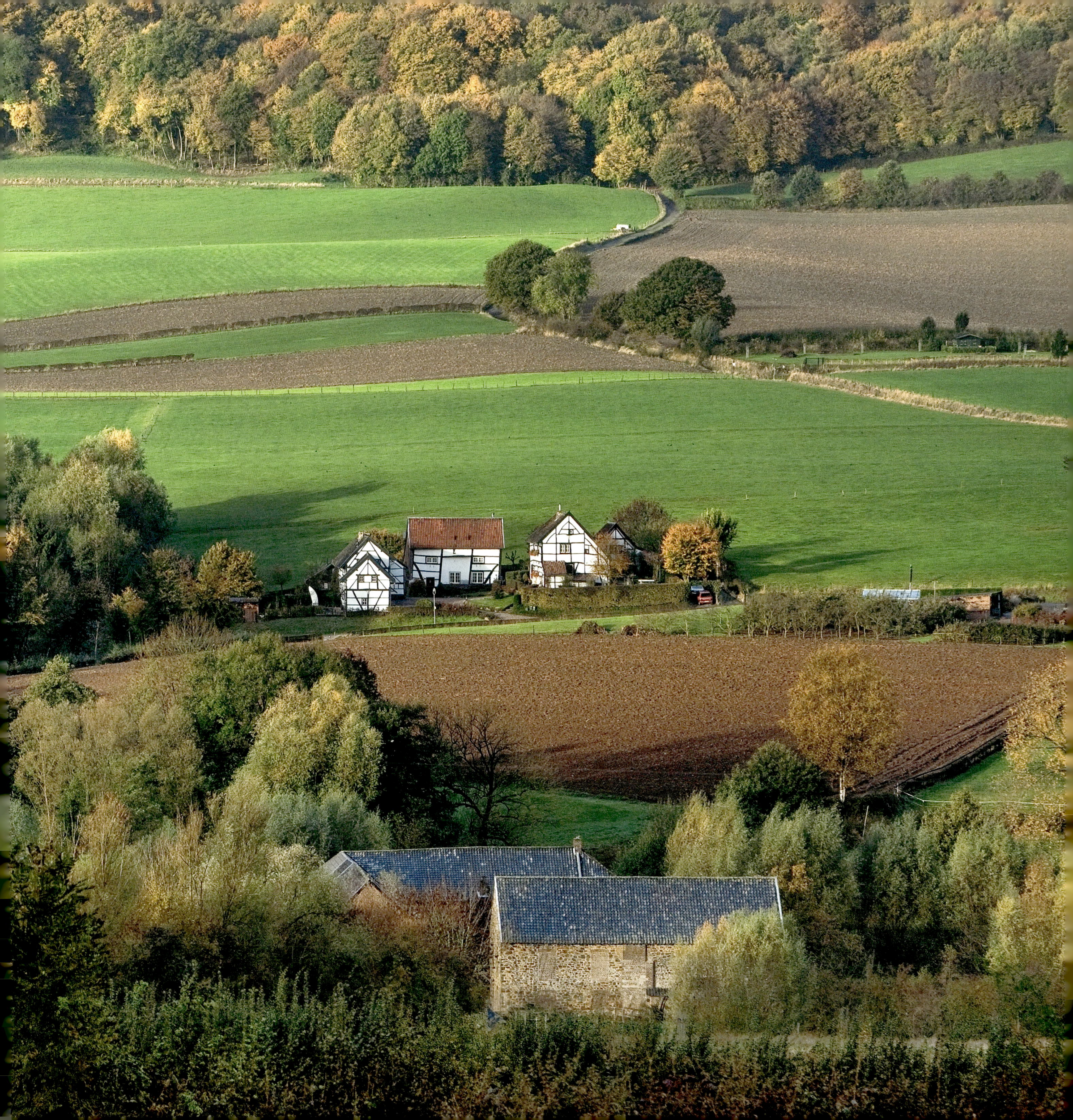

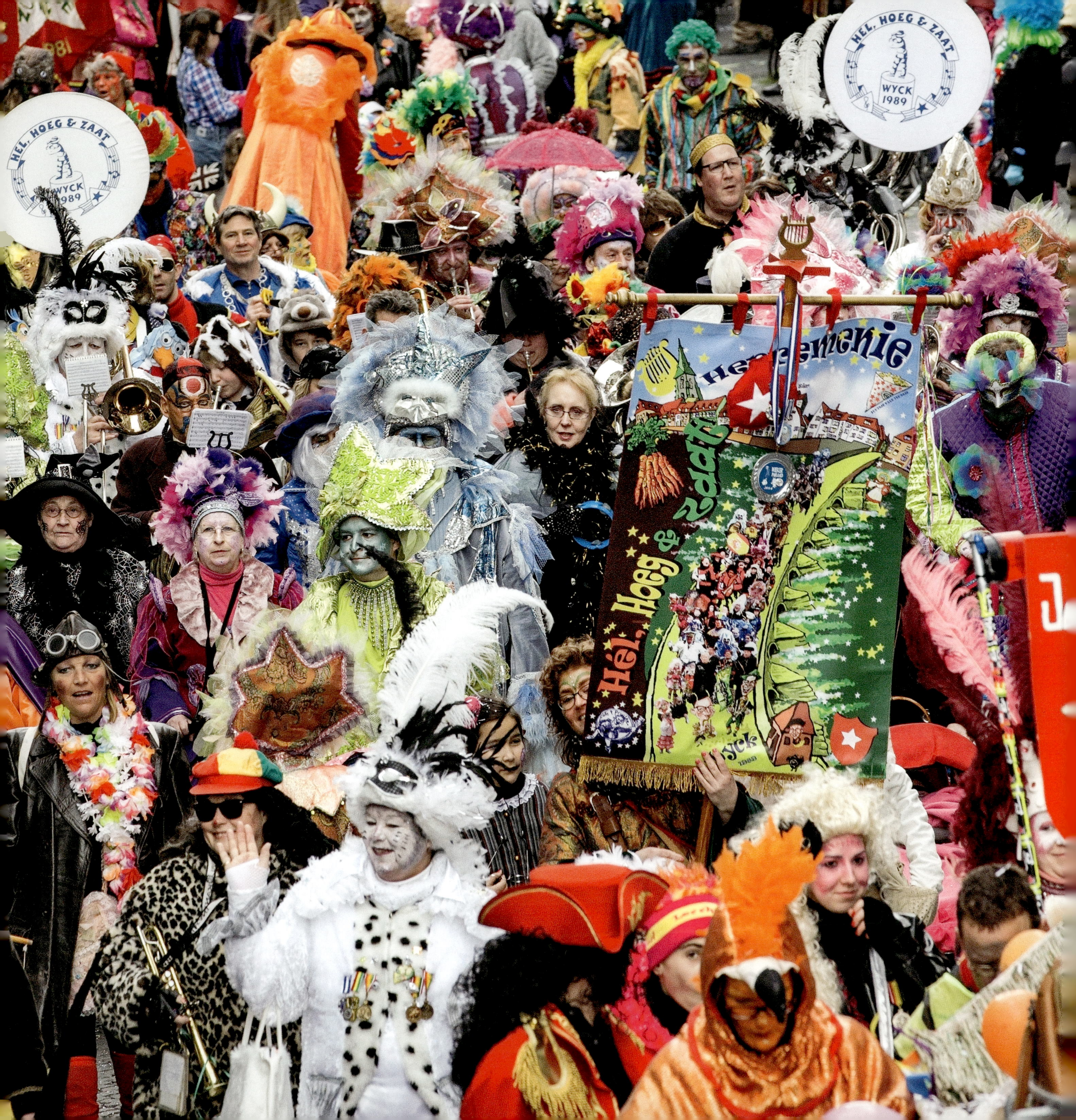
HEL, HOEG & ZAAT
WYCK
1989
HEL, HOEG & ZAAT
WYCK
1989
Hel, Hoeg & Zaat

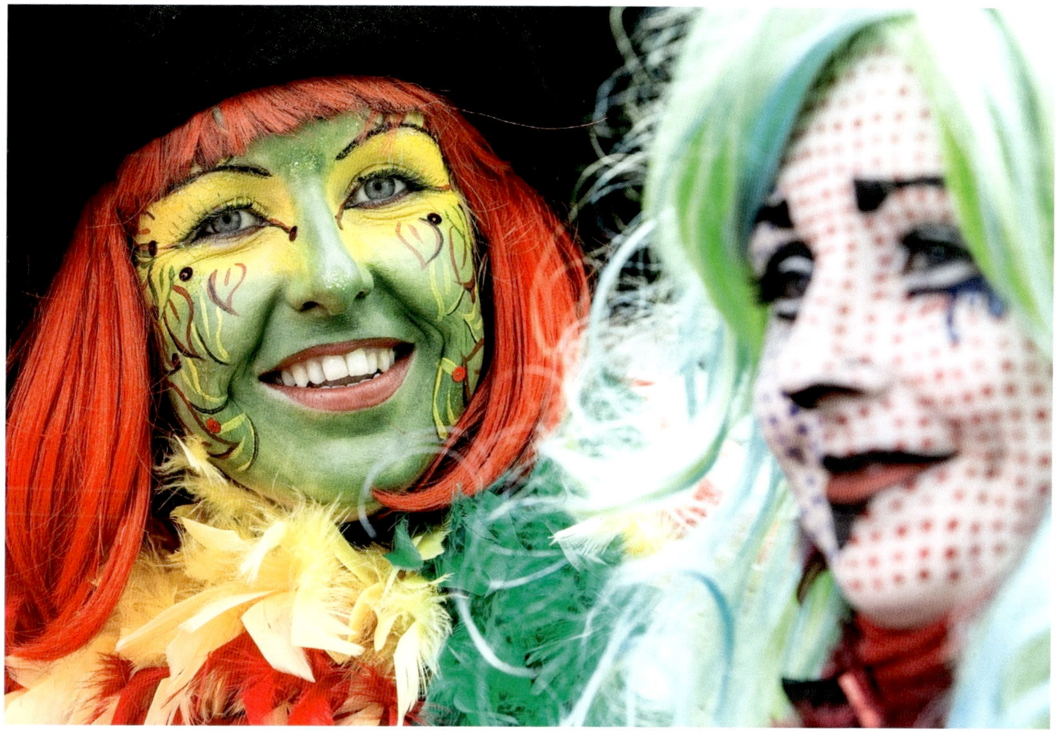

Carnival time
For three days each February or March, Carnival, originally a Roman Catholic feast, holds the southern Netherlands enthralled. In Maastricht, the numerous elaborately costumed groups and 'hermeniekes' (harmony bands) form the backbone of Carnival (left and top).

Following pages: American military cemetery from World War II in Margraten.

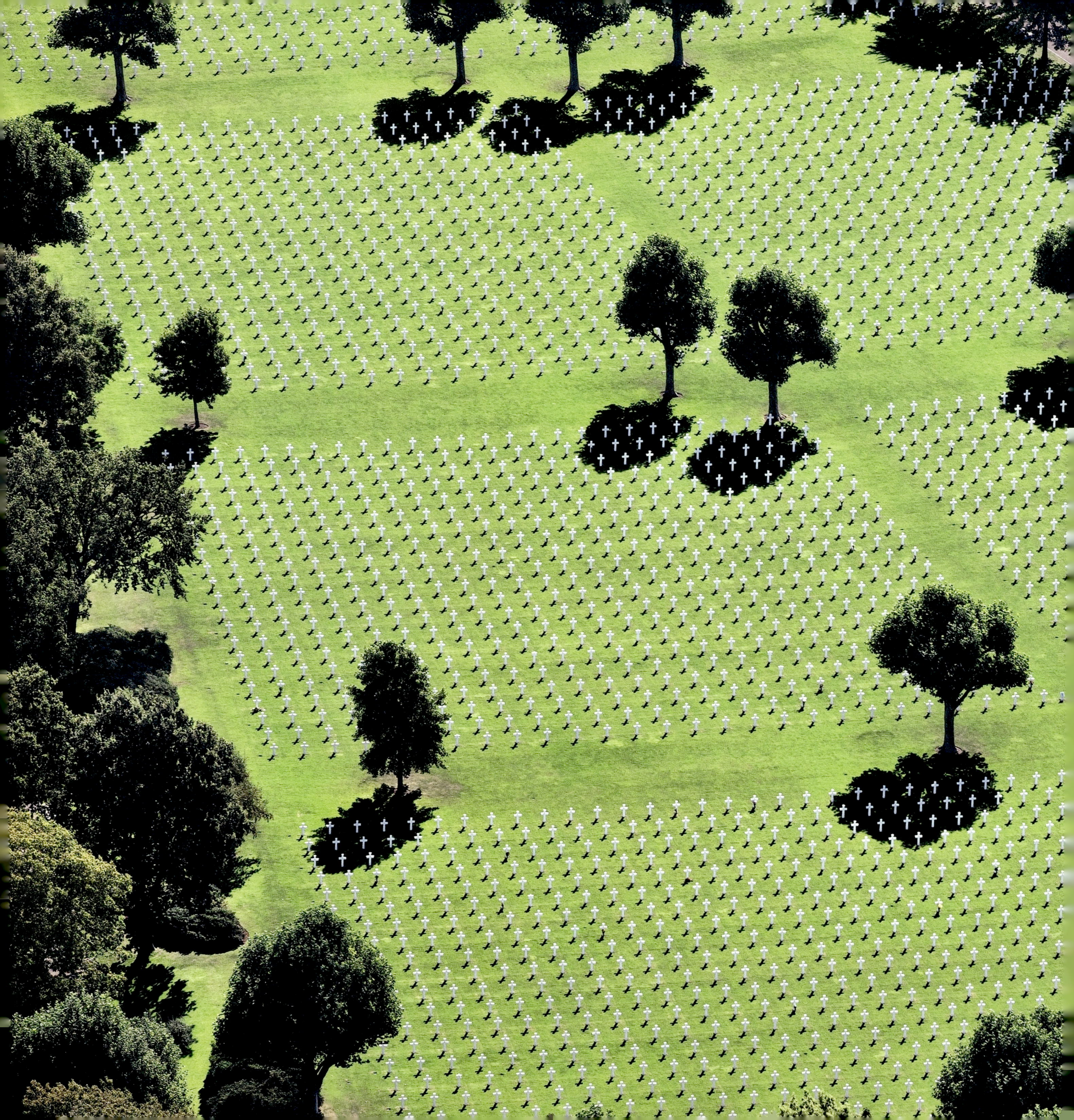

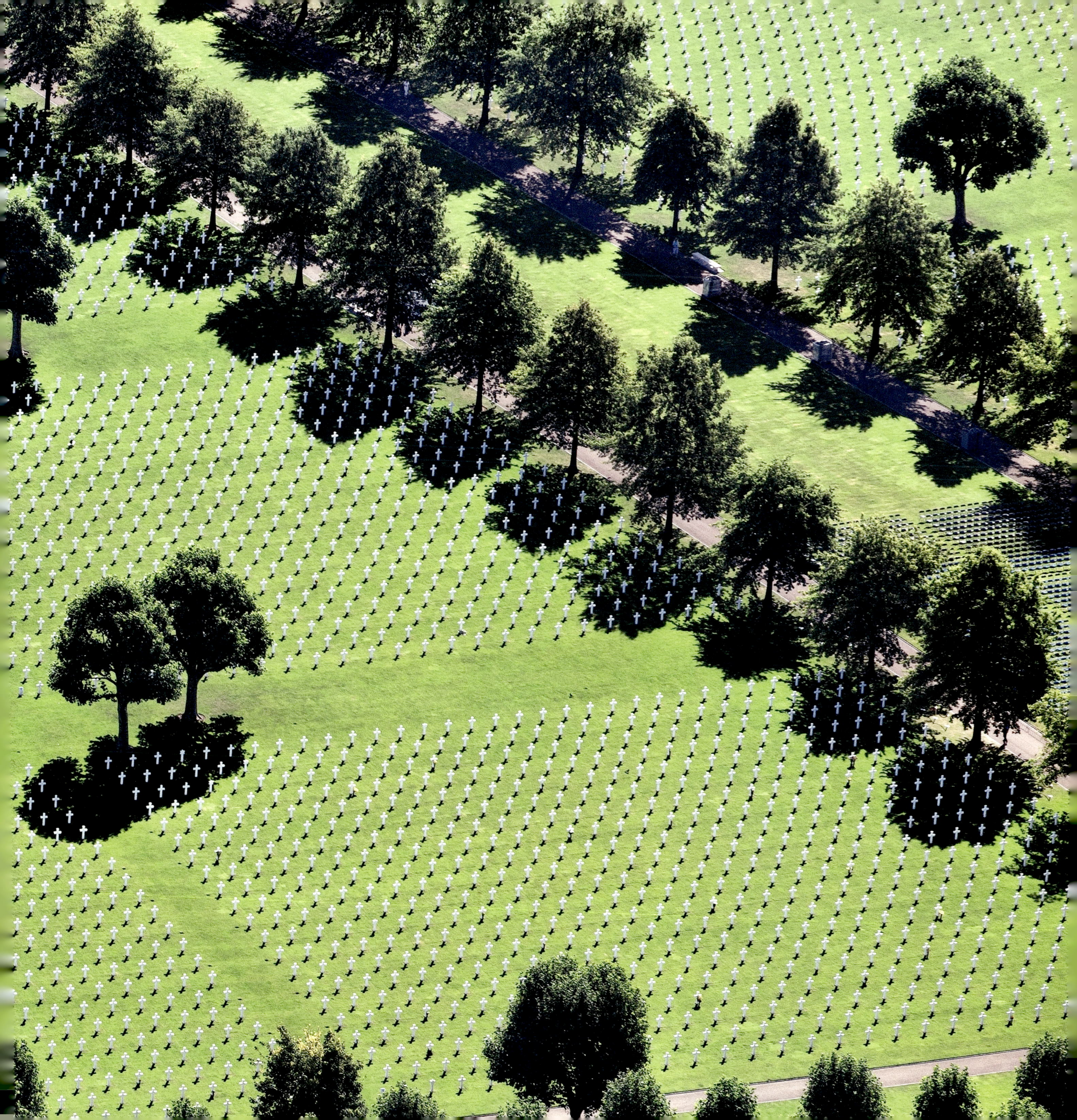

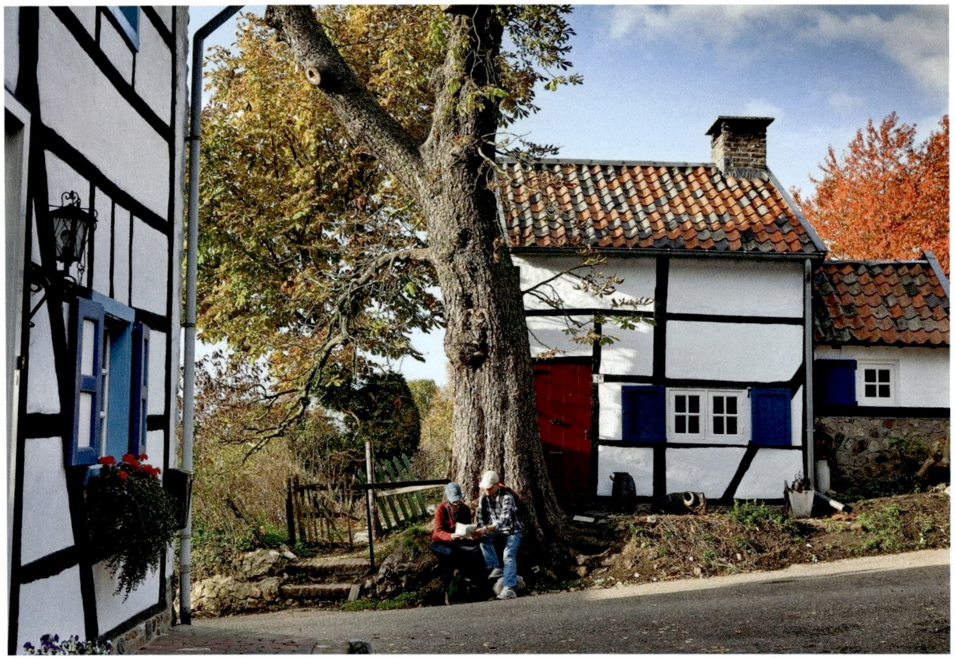

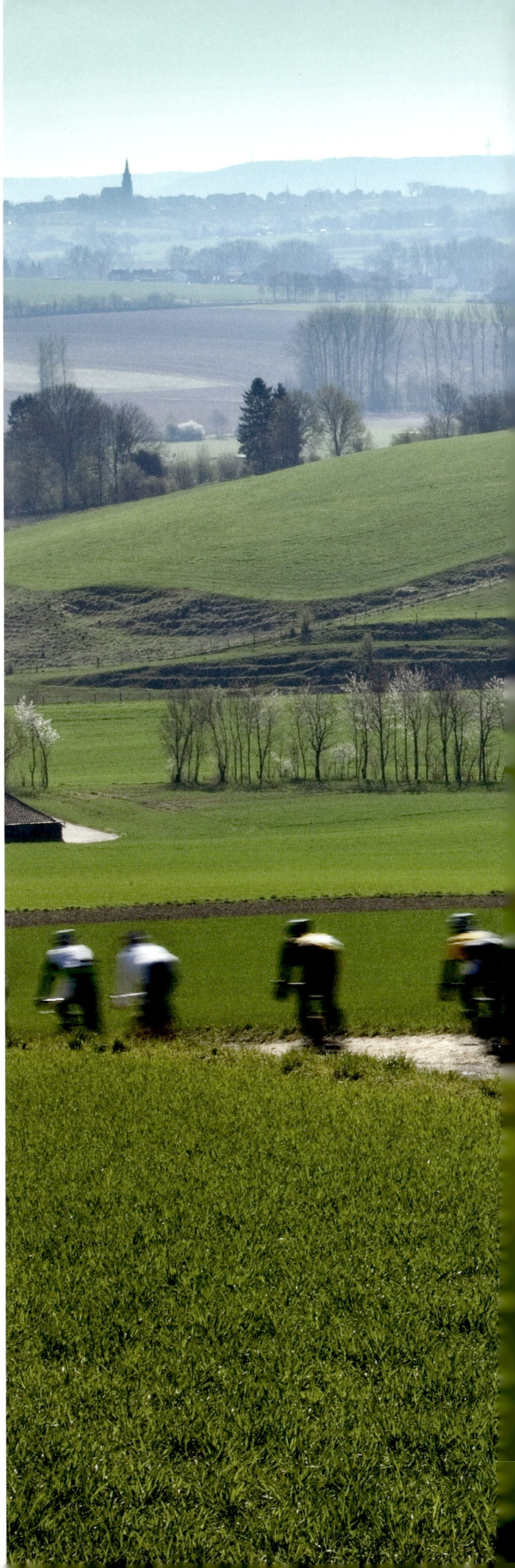

Top: Half-timbered houses in the municipality of Vijlen.

Right: Many Dutch cyclists head for the Limburg hills for recreation.

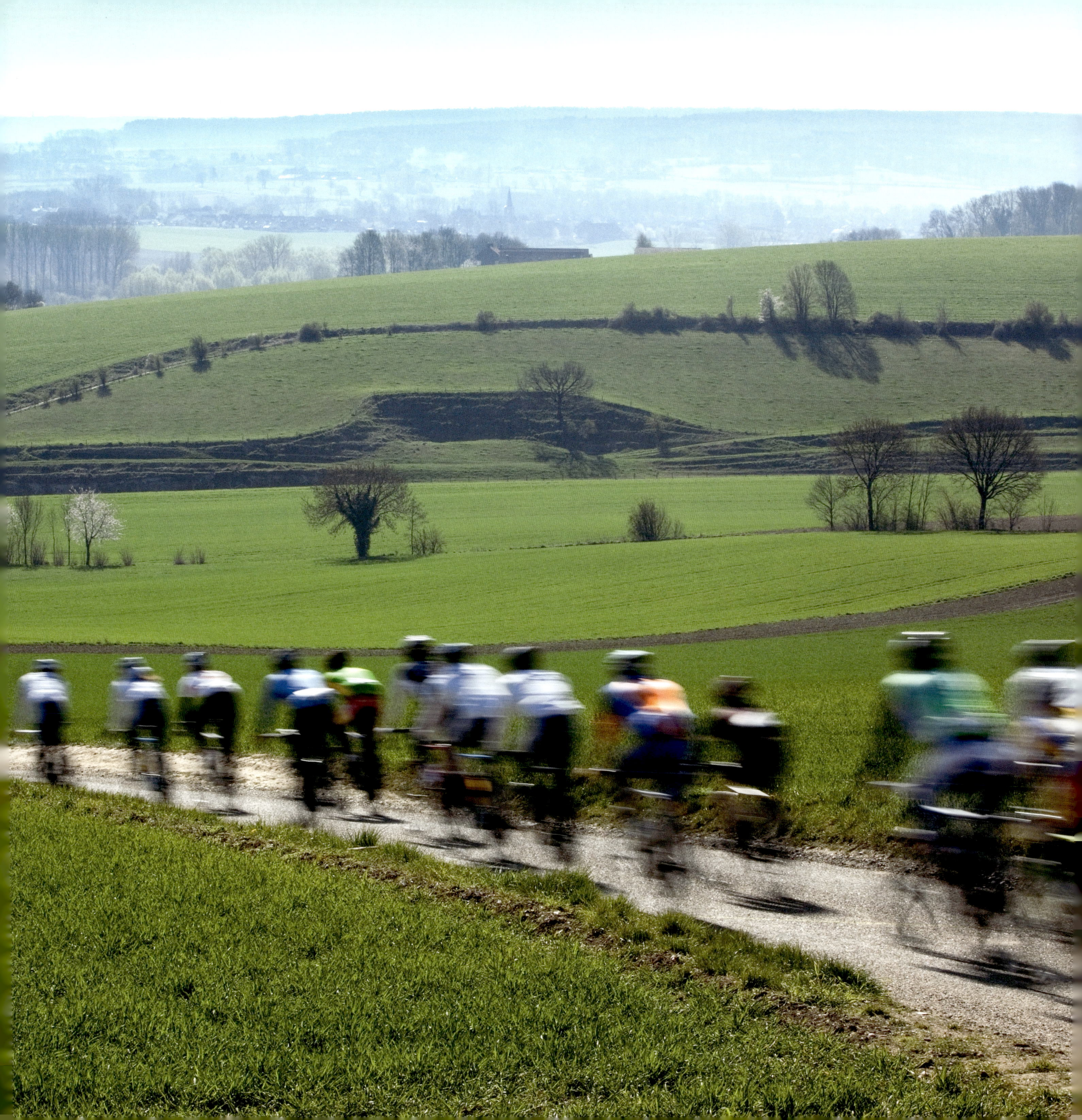

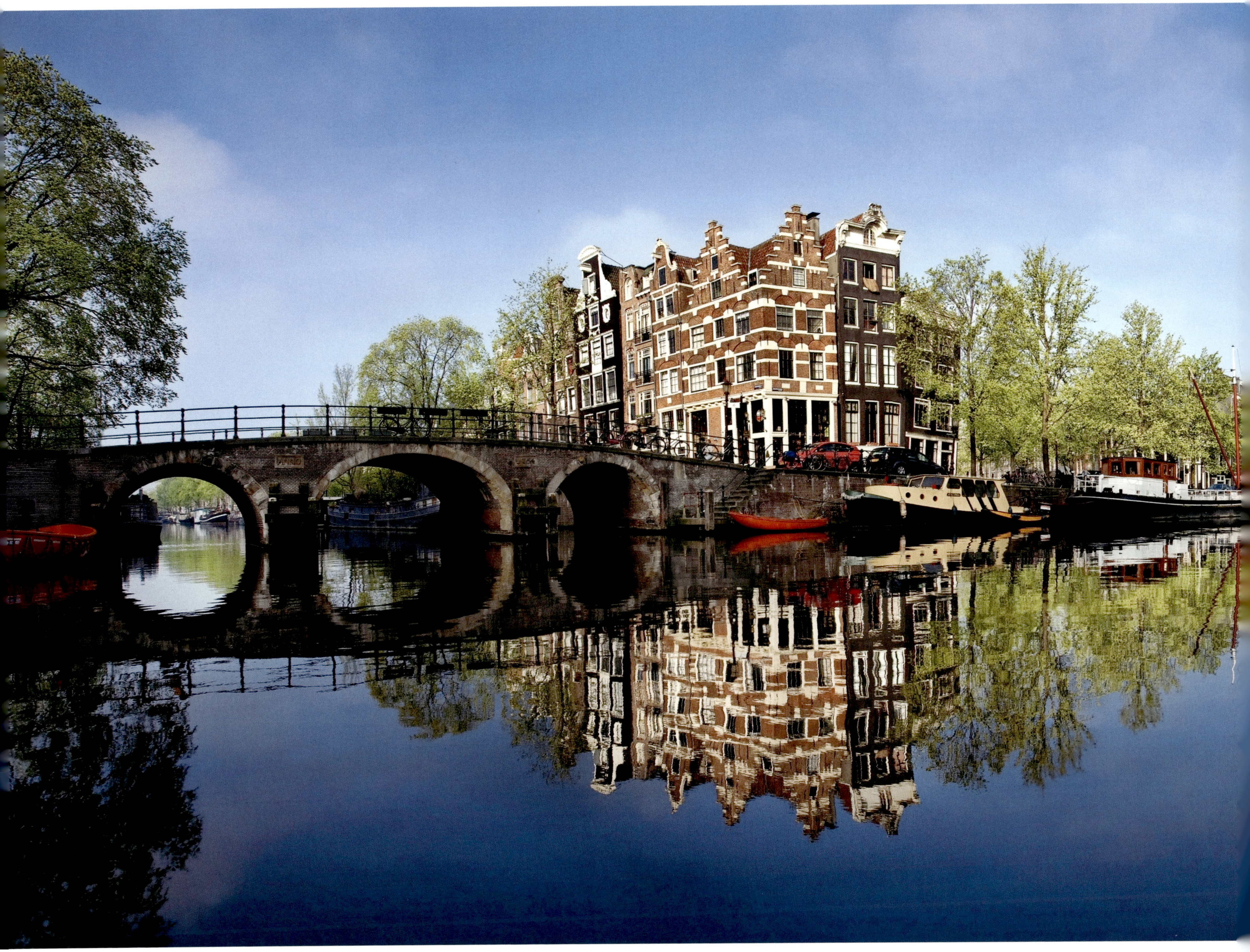

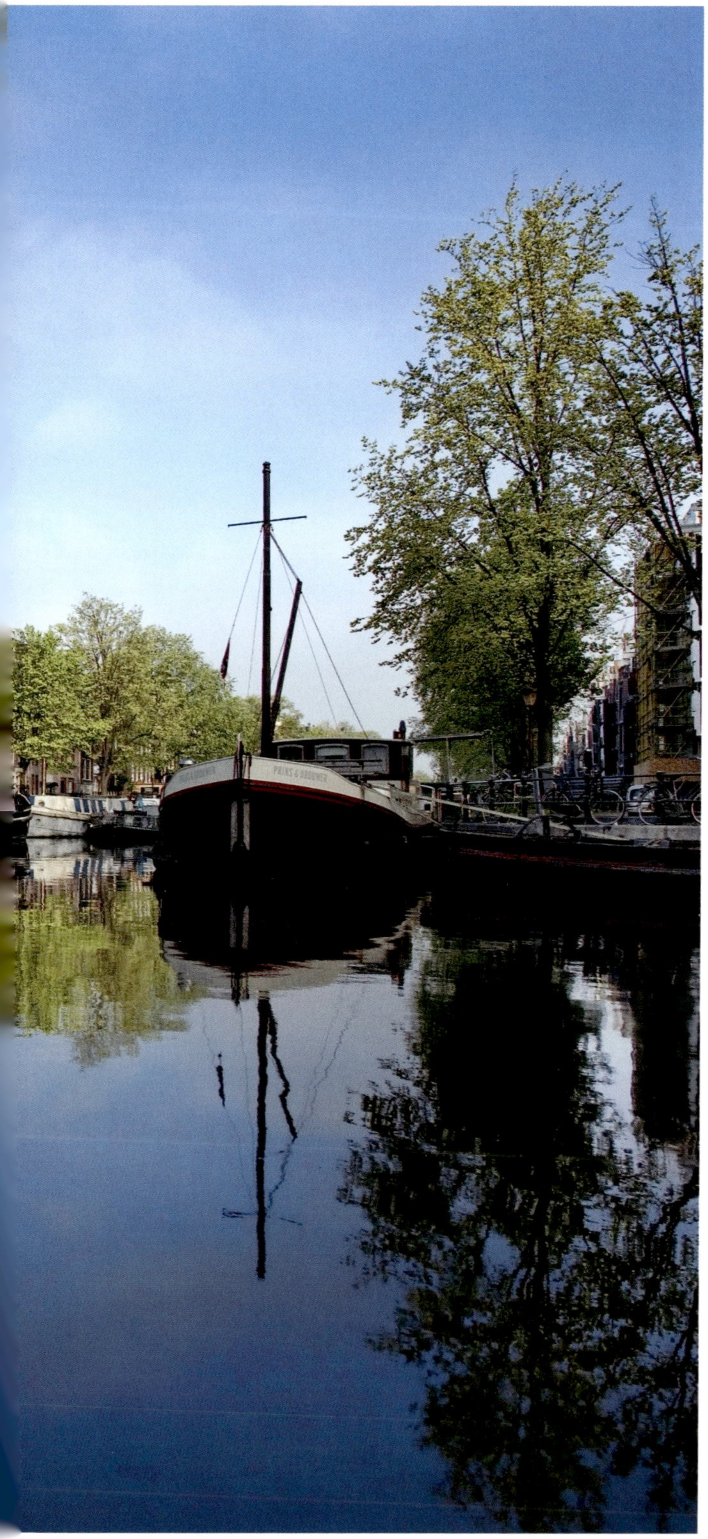

Architecture
Dutch architecture is not only praised within the country but also abroad. There are many beautiful buildings to be found, buildings which tell us a lot about the period in which they were built. For example, the Amsterdam canals (left) are admired worldwide and have thus been a UNESCO World Heritage Site since 2010.

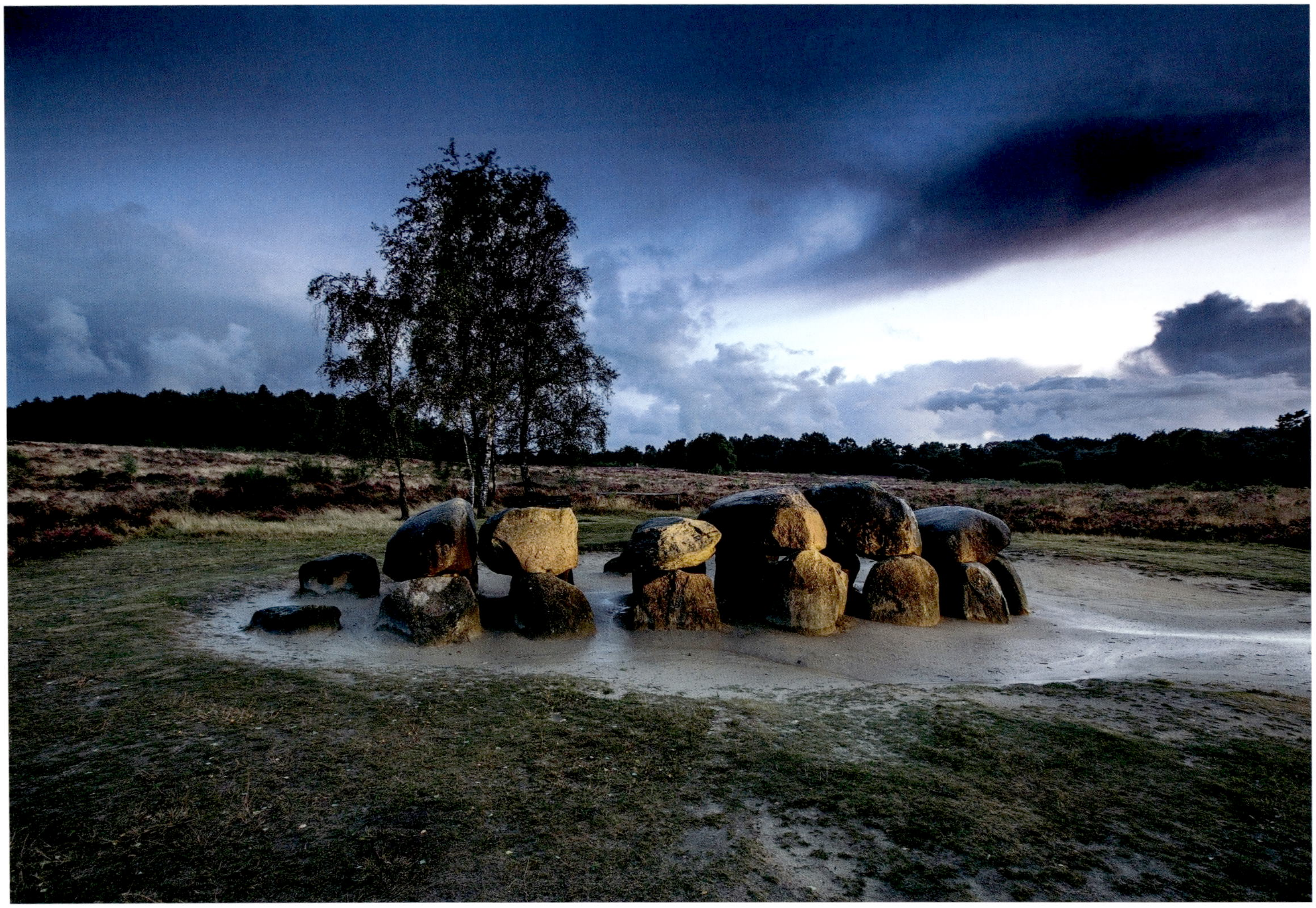

Top: The oldest buildings are the megaliths ('hunnebedden'), some of which are over 4000 years old. While they are not high architecture, they are skilful pieces of construction work. In the picture, an example at Havelte in the province of Drenthe.

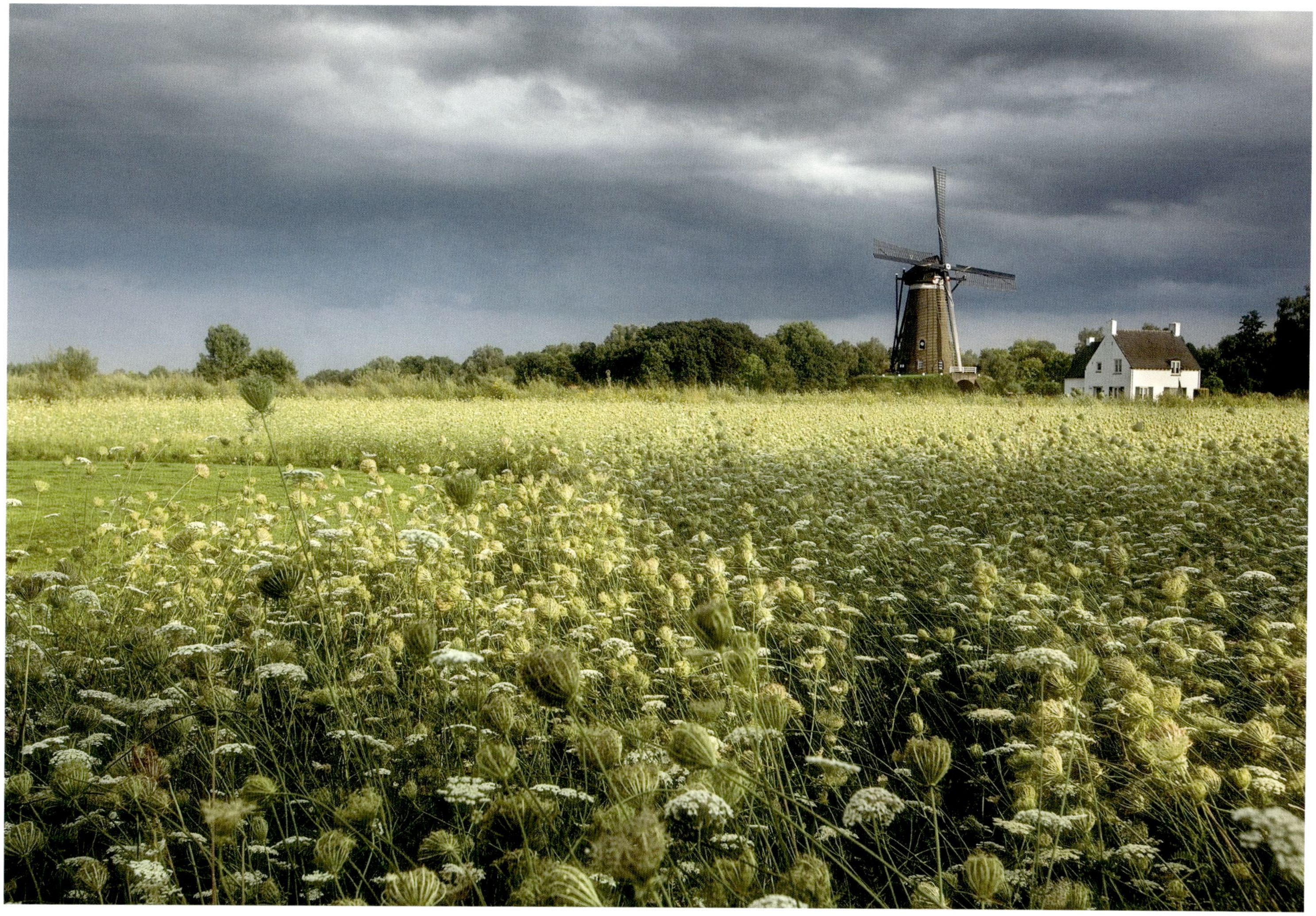

Top: Grain and oil mills are plenteous in the Netherlands; they rise majestically above the landscape to capture as much wind as possible. In the picture, *De Roosdonck* mill in Nuenen, completed in 1884. Vincent van Gogh lived and worked in Nuenen from December 1883 to November 1885. In hindsight, his stay there was one of the most important periods in his life. Van Gogh drew the mill seven times, but did not want to paint it because he did not like new buildings.

Church Styles

The first Dutch churches were built in the Romanesque style, usually in the form of a Roman cross. Little remains of the original building style, as the churches were largely rebuilt in the following centuries. The Gothic style, which originated in thirteenth-century France, was the first innovation to arrive. The distinctive pointed arch, which bore the pressure of the walls, and the buttresses, huge pillars that spread the weight of the vaulting around the church, allowed a lighter building style. From that moment on, the churches came to have larger windows, often with beautiful stained-glass religious scenes. After three centuries, Gothic architecture fell out of favour and made way for the Renaissance style, the first form of which was ornamenting the still-Gothic churches with Renaissance elements. In the wake of the Reformation, in the seventeenth century, Dutch Classicism arrived on the scene, with architect and artist Jacob van Kampen as its master builder. He designed the Dam Palace (1648-1665), the Mauritshuis and Noordeinde Palace.

Right: Aerial view of Doesburg, where the Old IJssel river flows into the River IJssel.

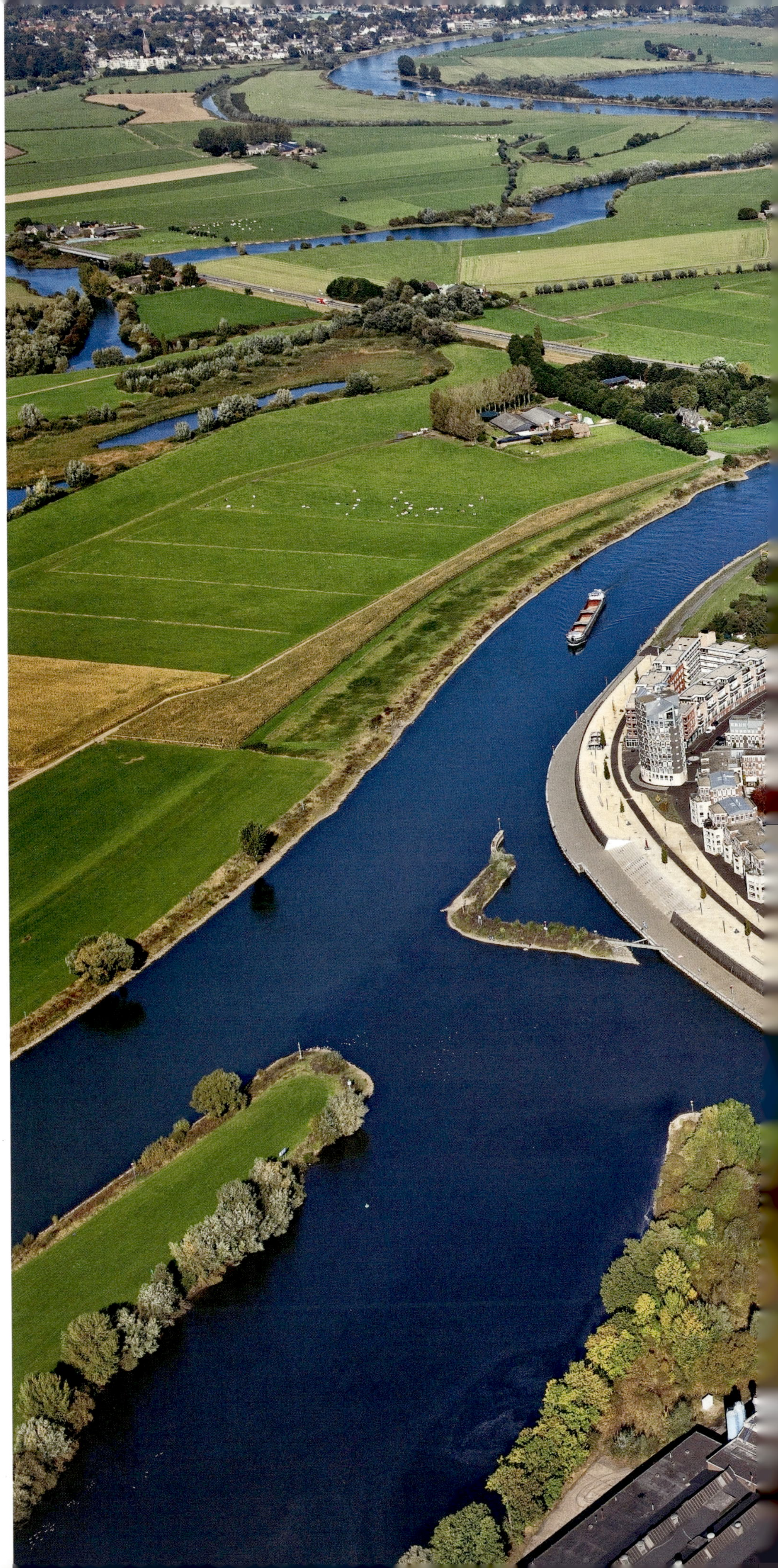

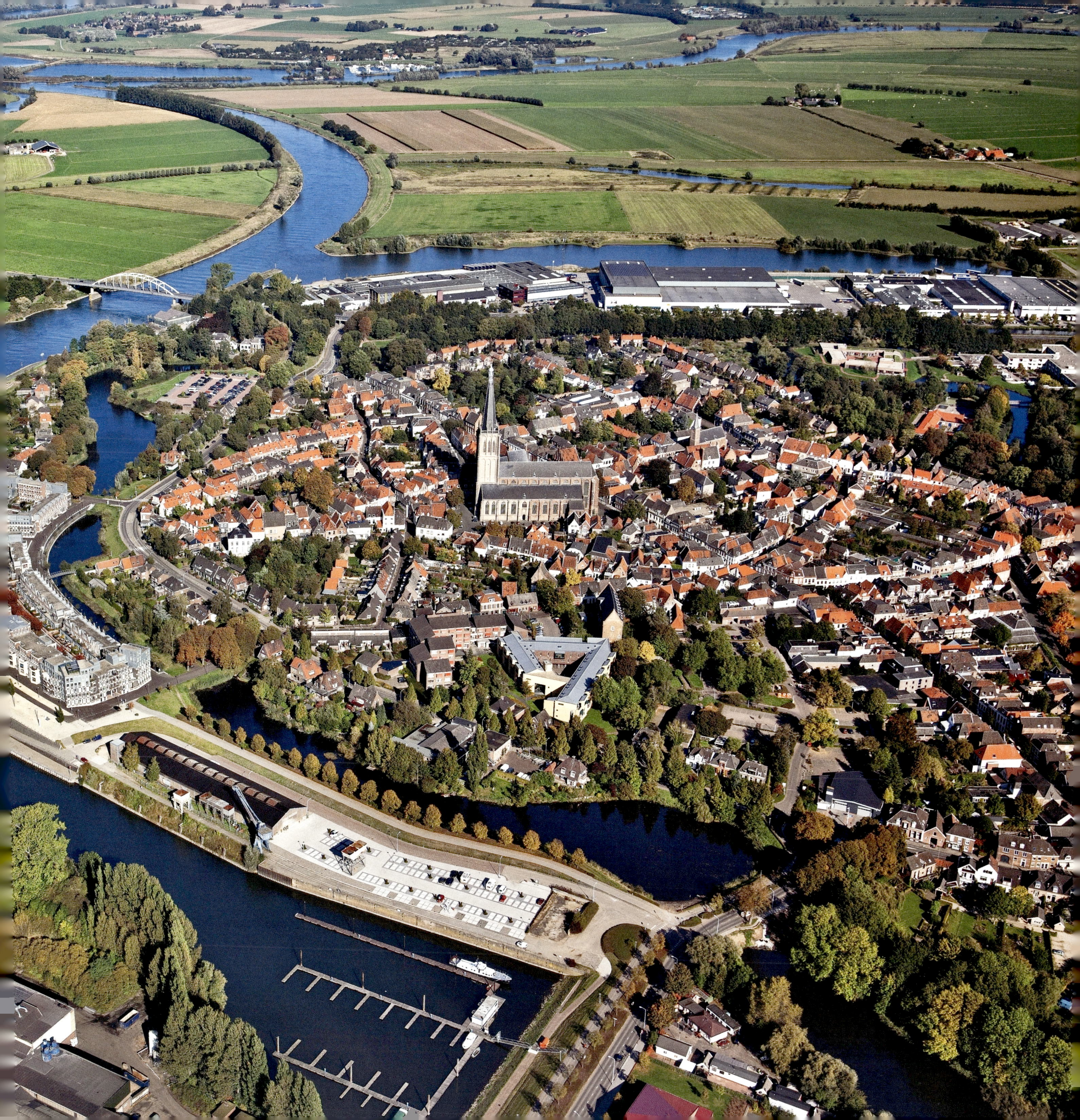

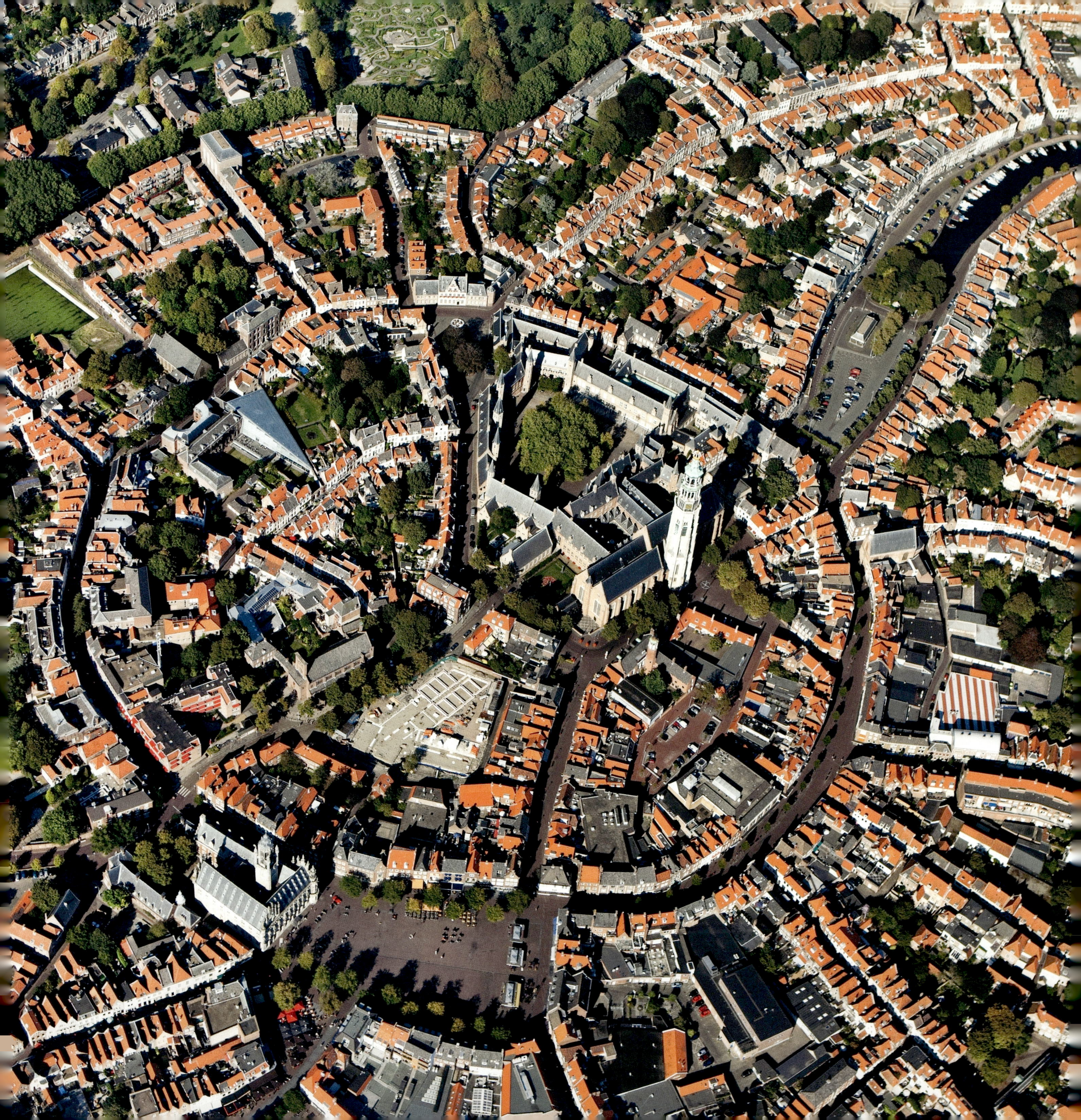

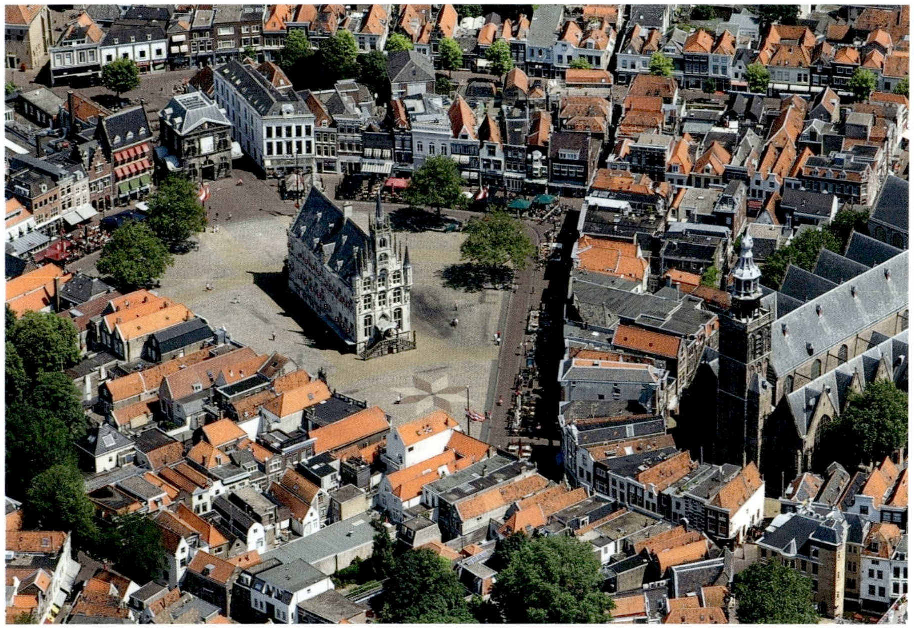

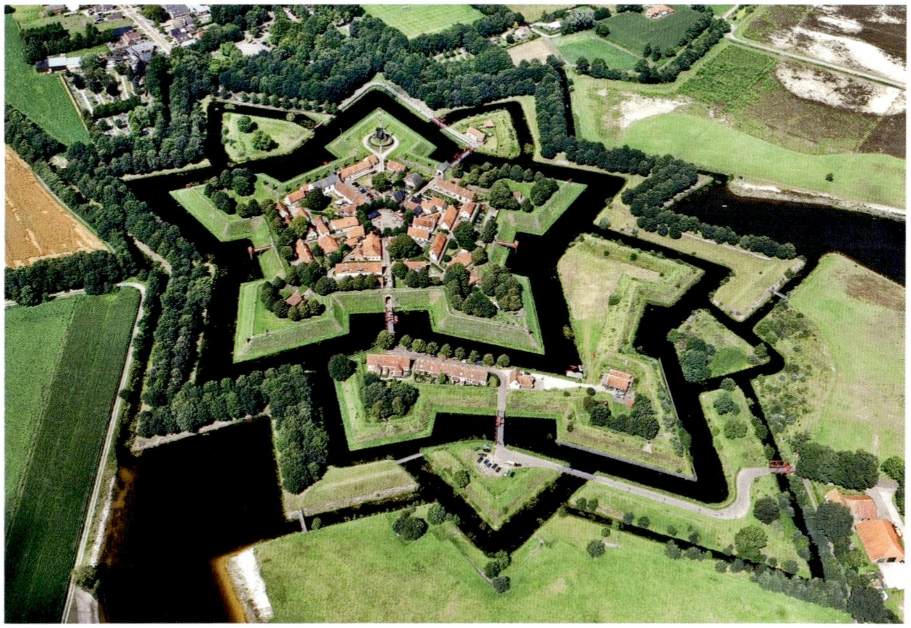

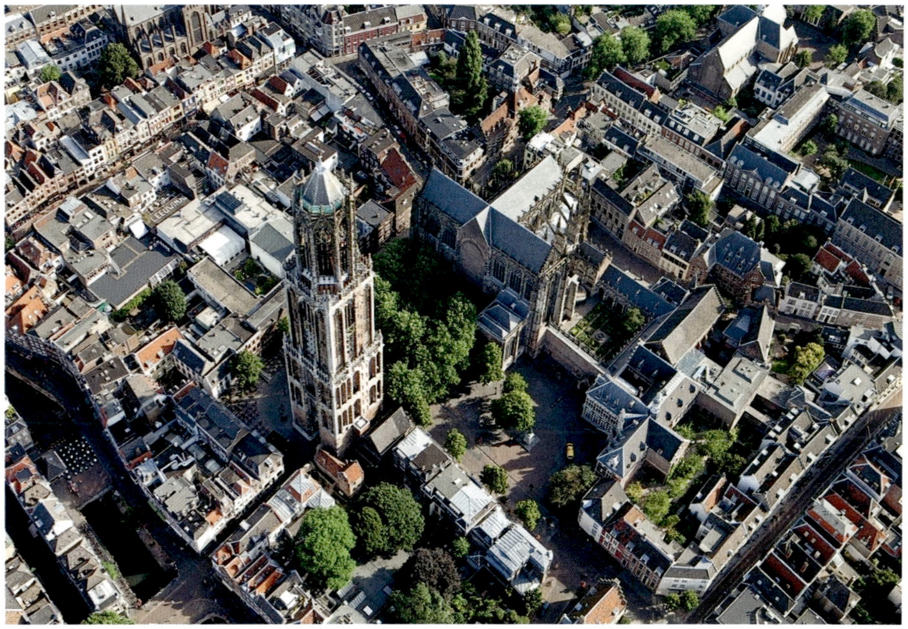

Left: The seventeenth-century centre of Middelburg, the main city for the Dutch East Indies Company (VOC) after Amsterdam.

Top right: The centre of Gouda with the former City Hall from 1459, an example of Gothic architecture.

Centre: Bourtange fortified village in the province of Groningen.

Below right: Utrecht Cathedral is a striking Gothic church. Its 112.32 metre-high Domtoren is the highest church tower in the Netherlands.

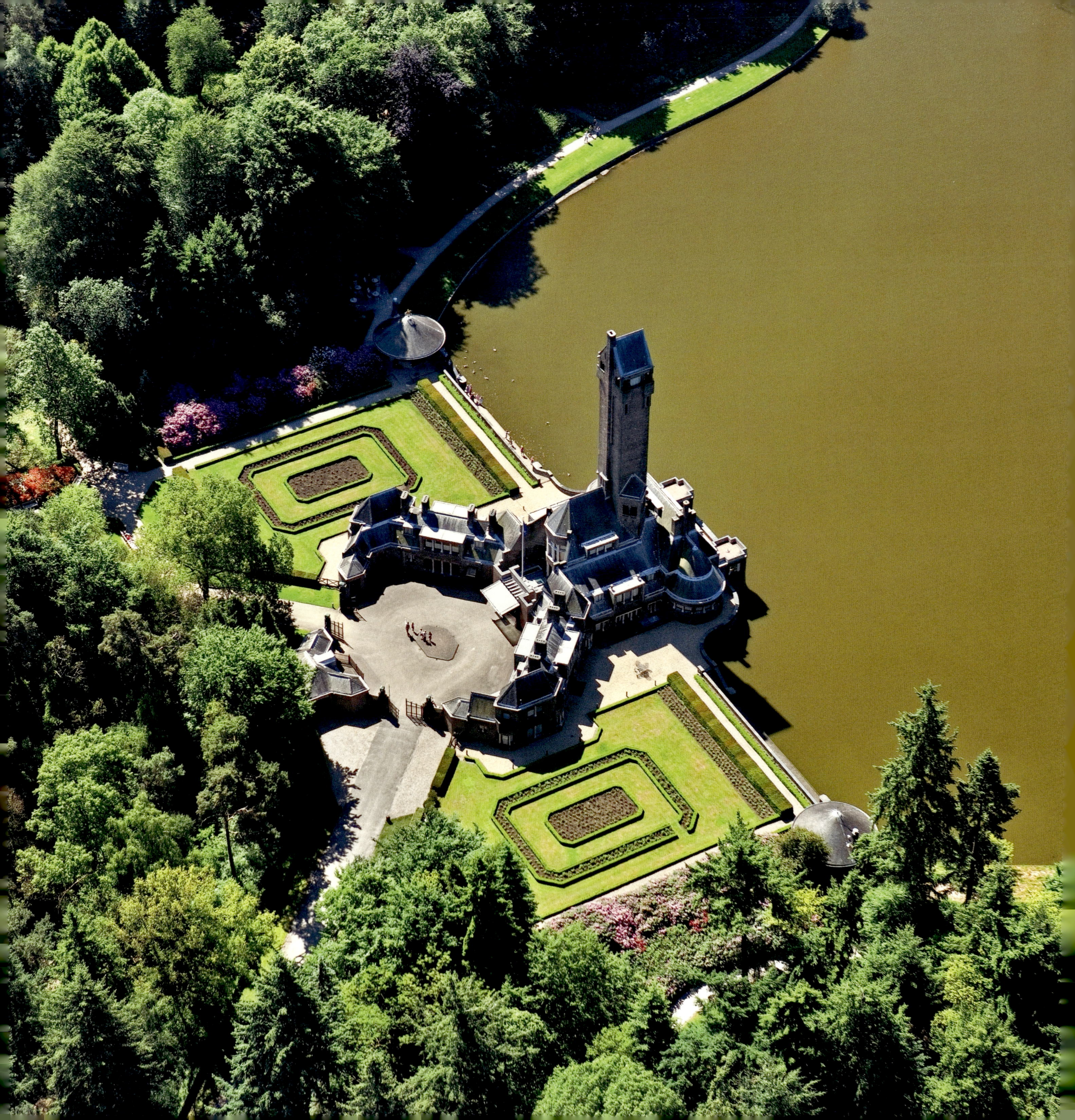

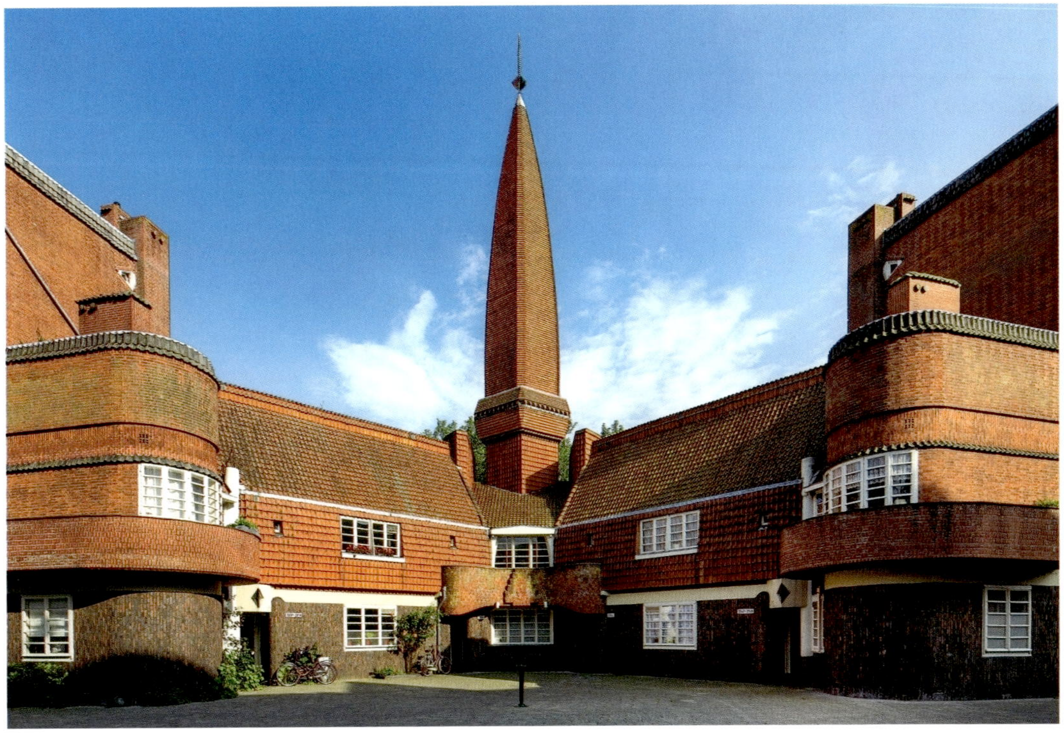

From neo to modern

In the eighteenth century, Dutch architecture was strongly influenced by French style. After this came a period of styles denoted as neo, which echoed earlier Gothic, Renaissance and Baroque themes. The most famous architect of that period was Pierre Cuypers, he designed the Rijksmuseum and Amsterdam Central Station. With Berlage, modern architecture made its entrance – unmistakably Dutch in terms of its signature and often erroneously compared with the Amsterdam School.

Amsterdam School

Generous use of brick, flowing undulations in the walls, ladder windows, steep roofs and the sometimes symbolically-presented supporting structures are typical of the Amsterdam School. This style has undoubtedly had much influence on Dutch architecture.

Left: In the Hoge Veluwe national park, the Kröller-Müller family had the imposing hunting lodge of Sint Hubertus built to a design by architect H.P. Berlage. The building has a floor plan in the shape of a deer antler.

Top: Residential blocks in the Amsterdam Spaarndammerbuurt by architect Michel de Klerk. This project has been called the zenith of Amsterdam School architecture. For working-class residences, the detailing is considered exceptionally rich.

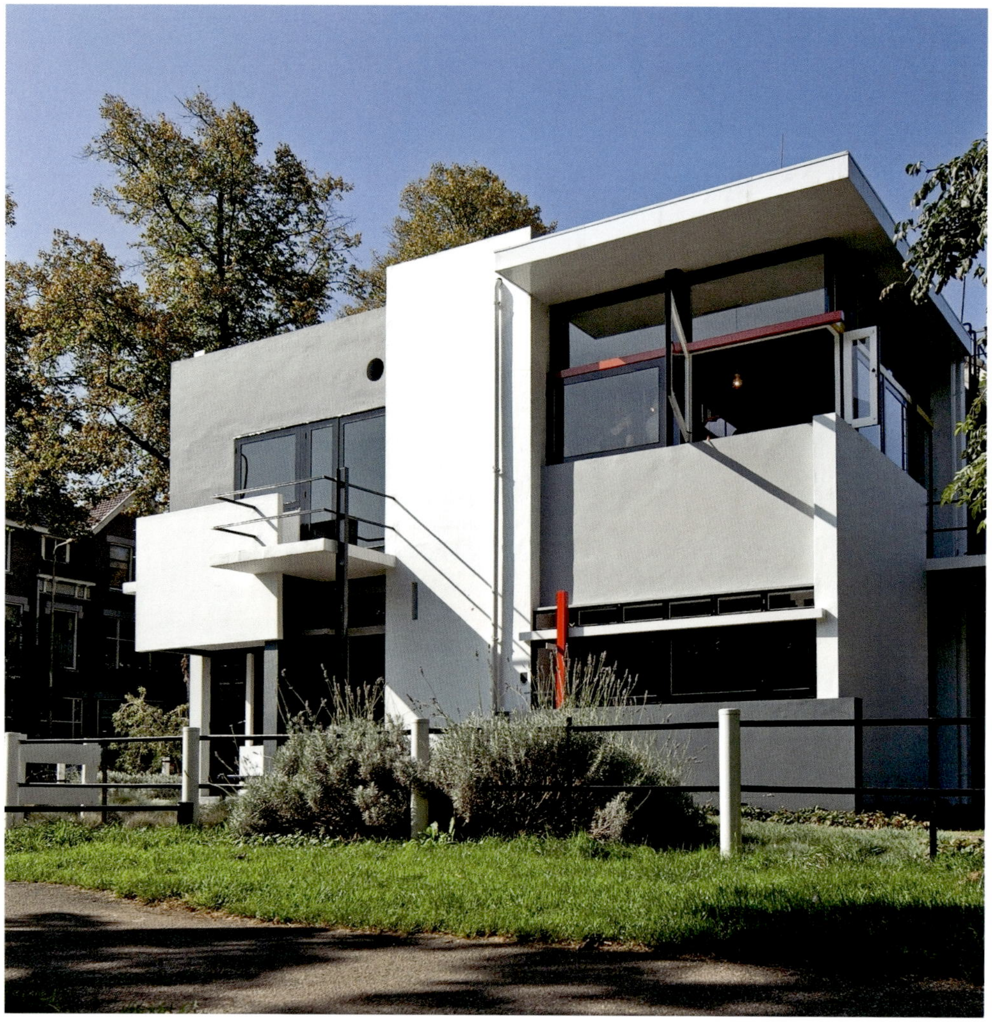

De Stijl

The Dutch art movement De Stijl was founded in 1917 by Theo van Doesburg. This movement – renowned members included Piet Mondrian and Gerrit Rietveld – sought a revolution in art by bidding a firm farewell to traditions and dogmas. This resulted in an abstract design as simple as possible, that only allowed the use of primary colors in combination with grey, white and black.

Top: The Rietveld Schröder House (1924) in Utrecht is built entirely in accordance with the principles of De Stijl and is on the UNESCO World Heritage List.

Right: Willem Dudok accomplished more than seventy buildings in Hilversum. The town hall (1931) is the most notable design of his oeuvre. Dudok did not belong to any one particular school, but is generally regarded as one of the most famous exponents of modern Dutch architecture.

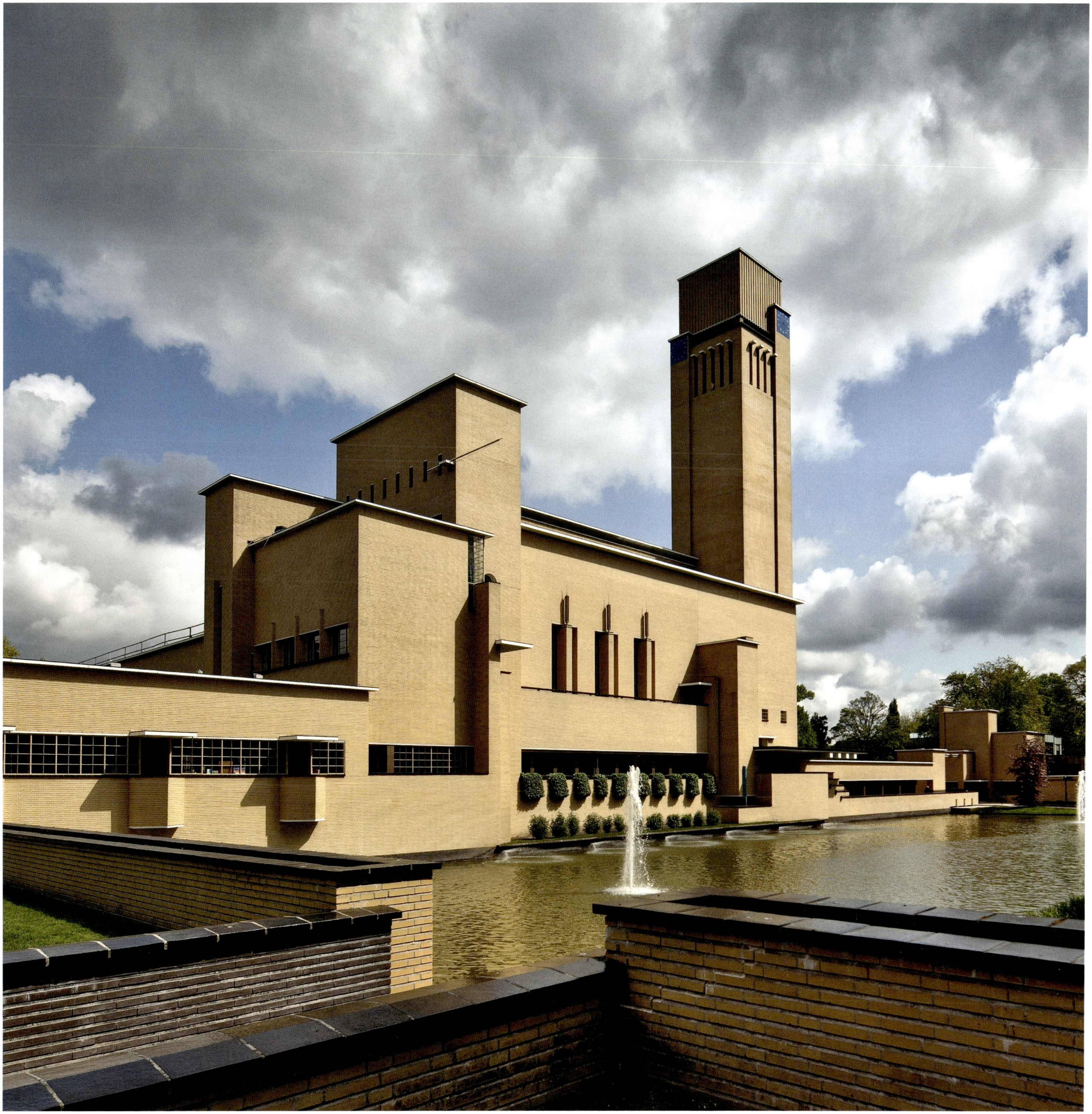

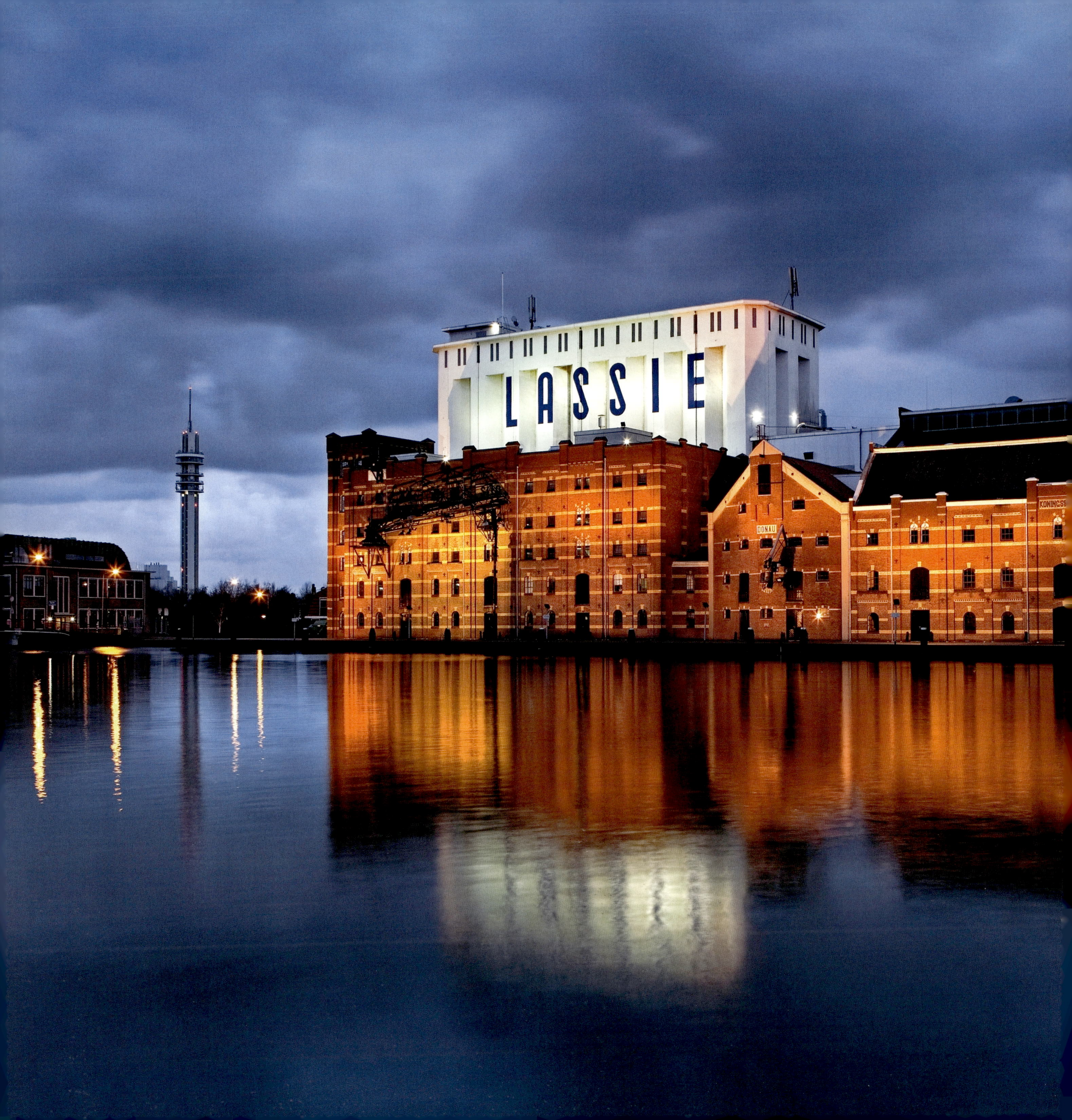
LASSIE
DONAU

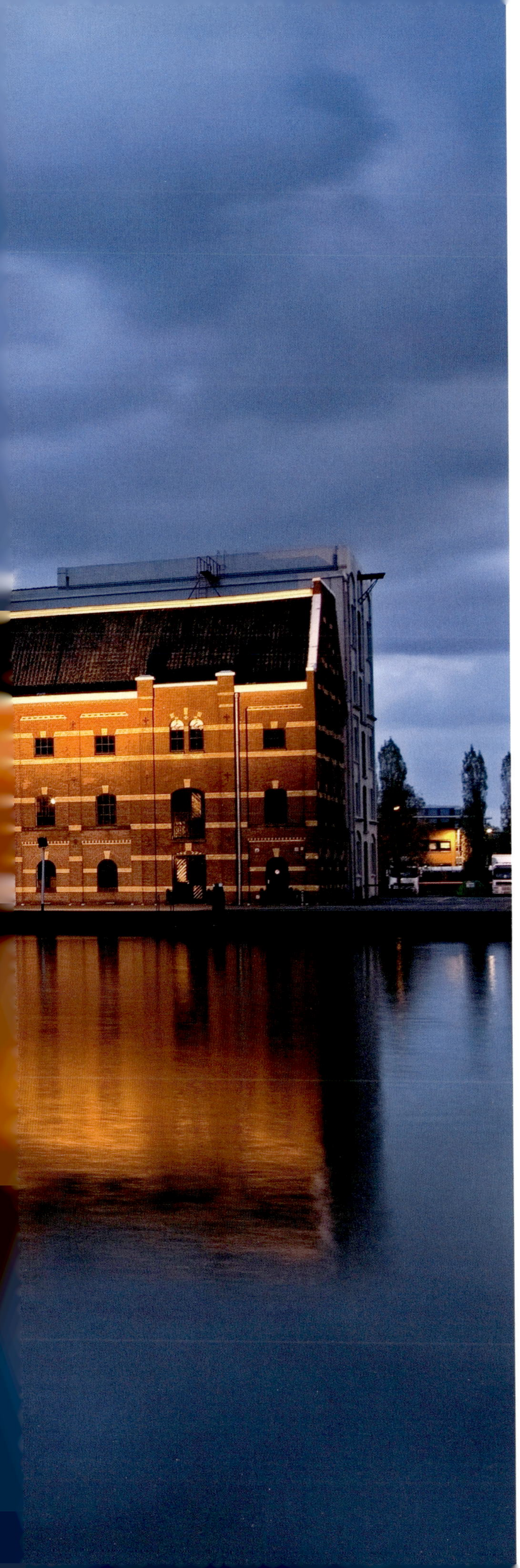

Left: Industrial architecture along the River Zaan: the warehouse complex of Lassie in Wormer, restored and still in use for the processing of rice. The white silo is a remarkable example of concrete building from the 1920s.

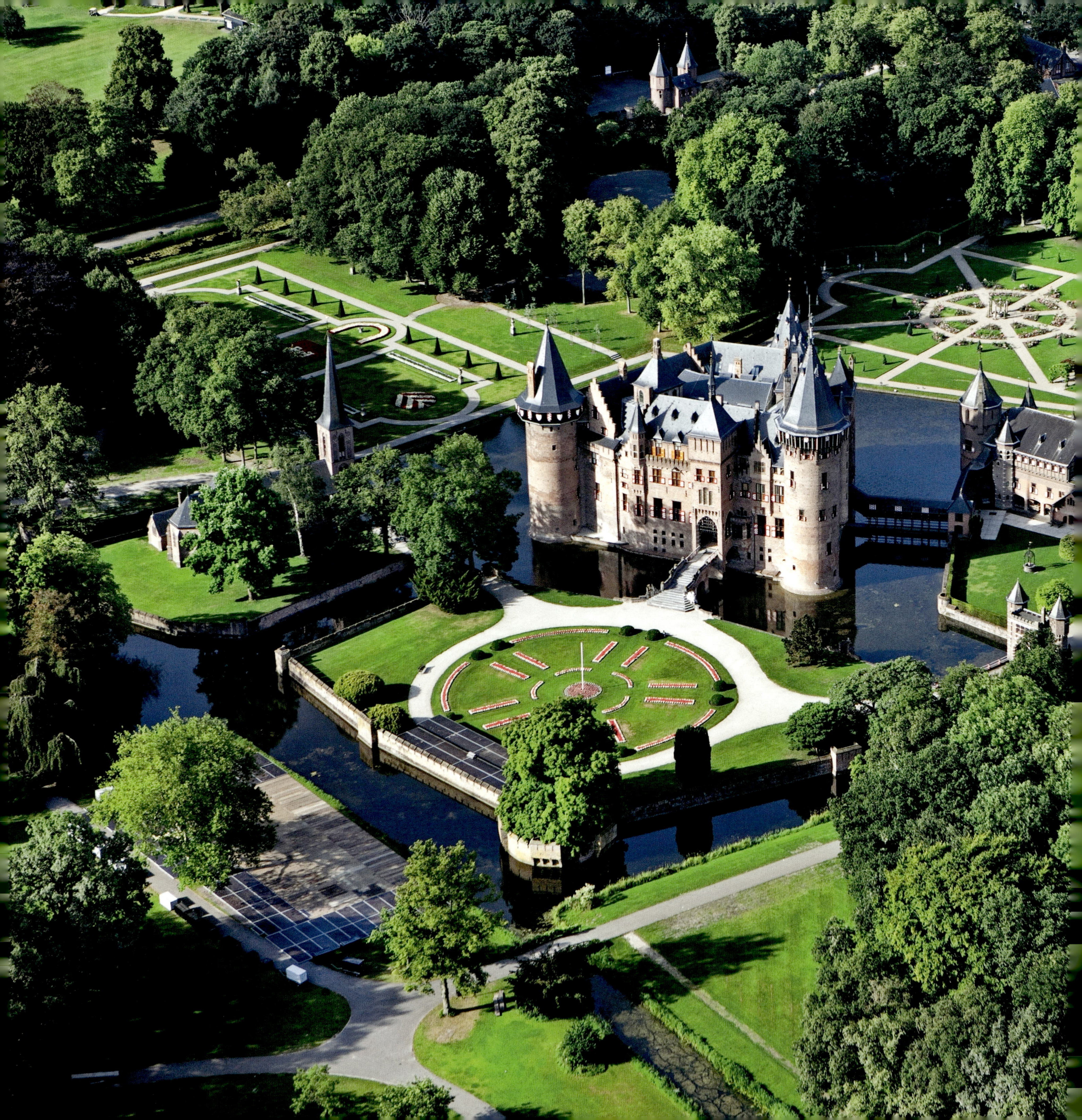

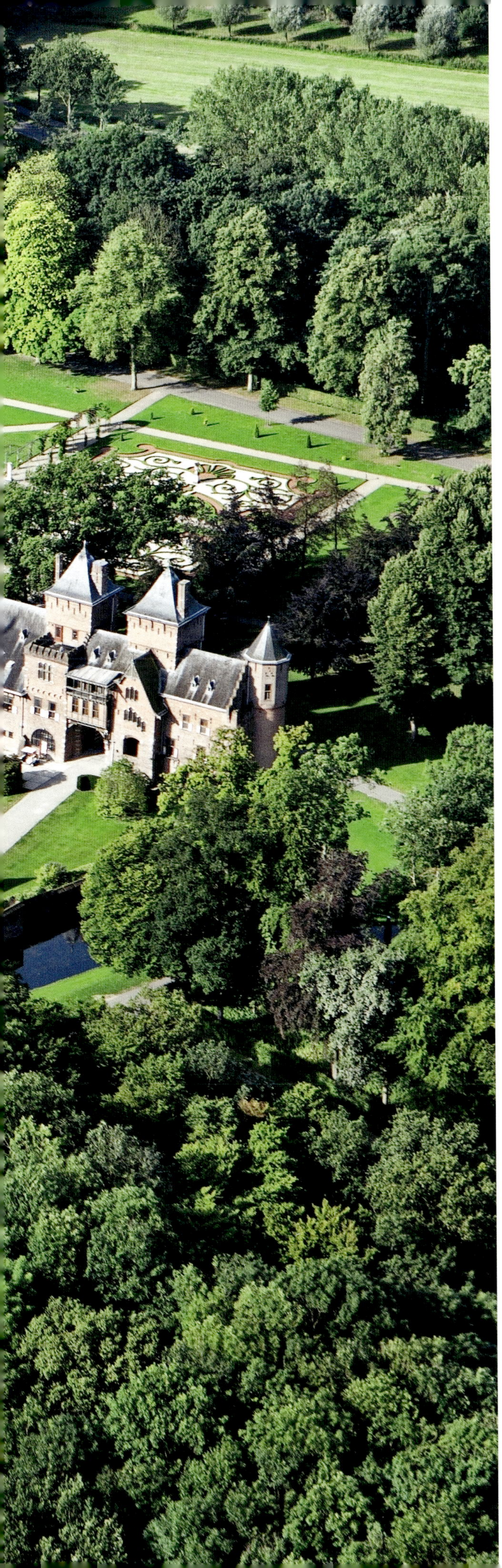

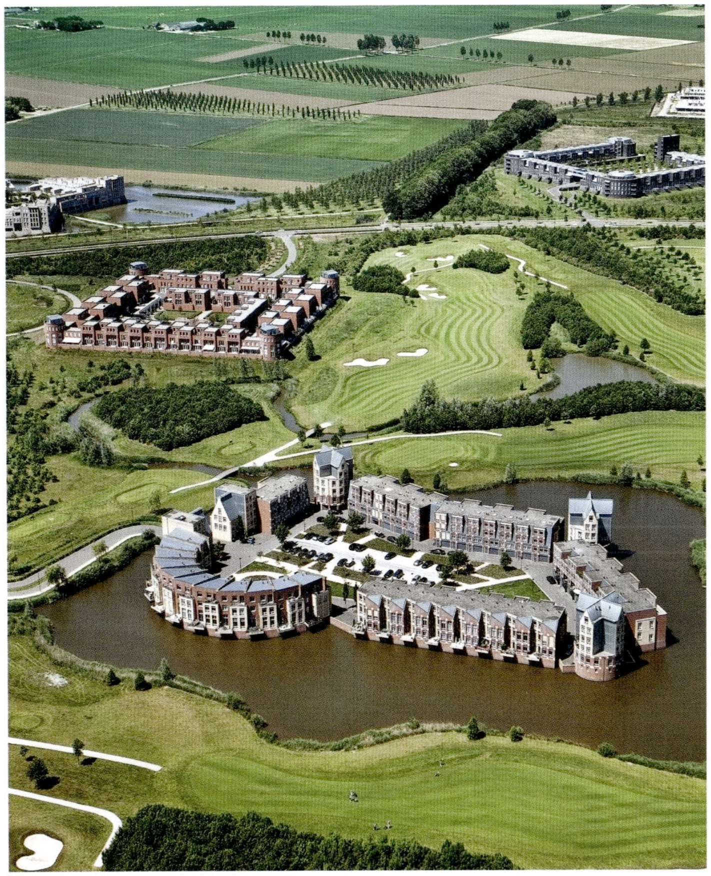

Left: Kasteel De Haar, at Haarzuilens, is the largest castle in the Netherlands. Dating from 1892, it is rebuilt on the ruins of the old castle in Gothic Revival style.

Top: A series of modern 'residential castles' at Engelen, each with their own architectural design.

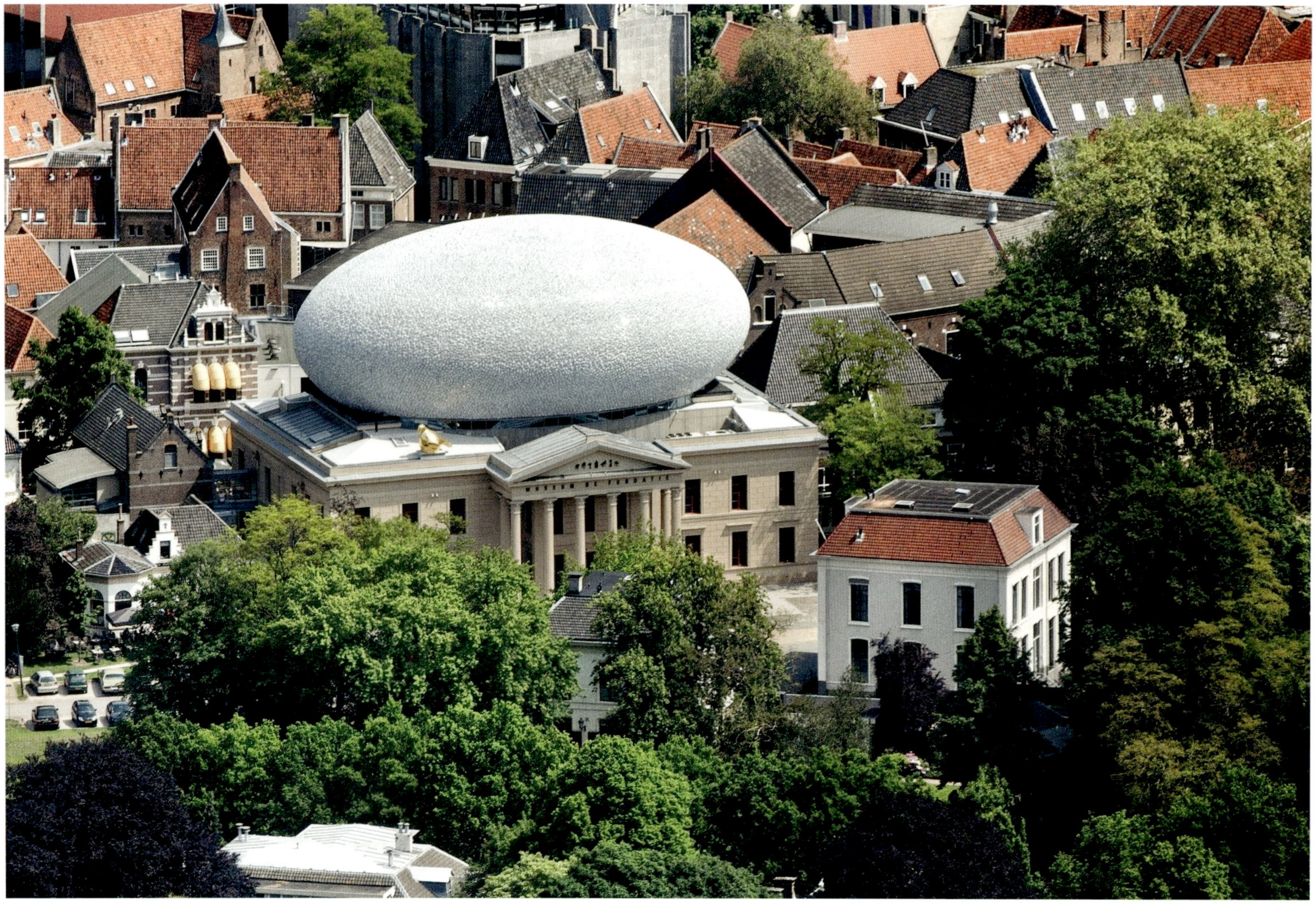

Top: Museum De Fundatie is a museum for visual arts in Zwolle. In 2012-2013, the museum expanded with a new exhibition space on the roof of the existing building. The design is by Bierman Henket Architects.

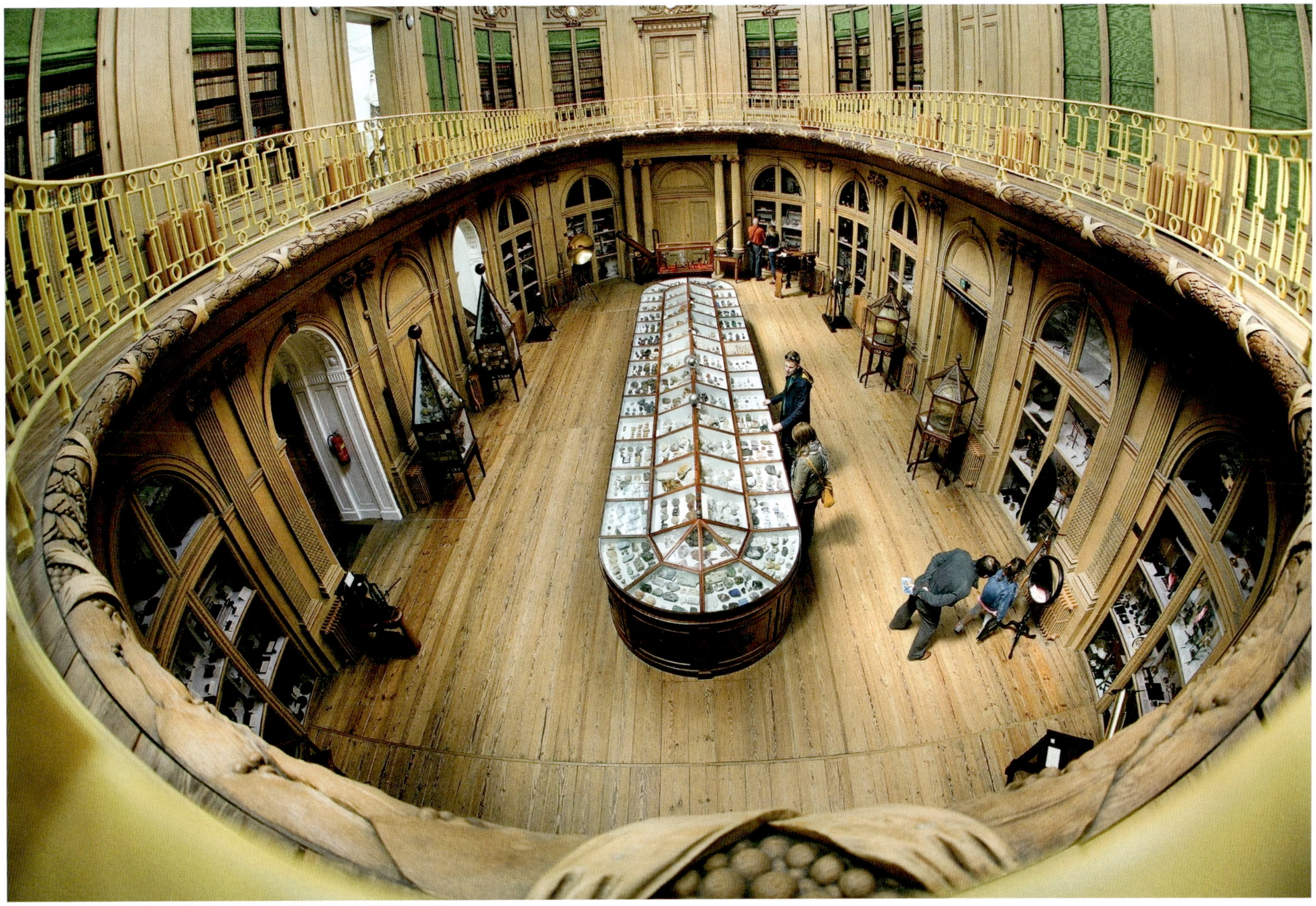

Top: The Oval Room in the Teylers Museum in Haarlem. The Teylers Museum, founded in 1778, was the first museum in the Netherlands that was open to the public.

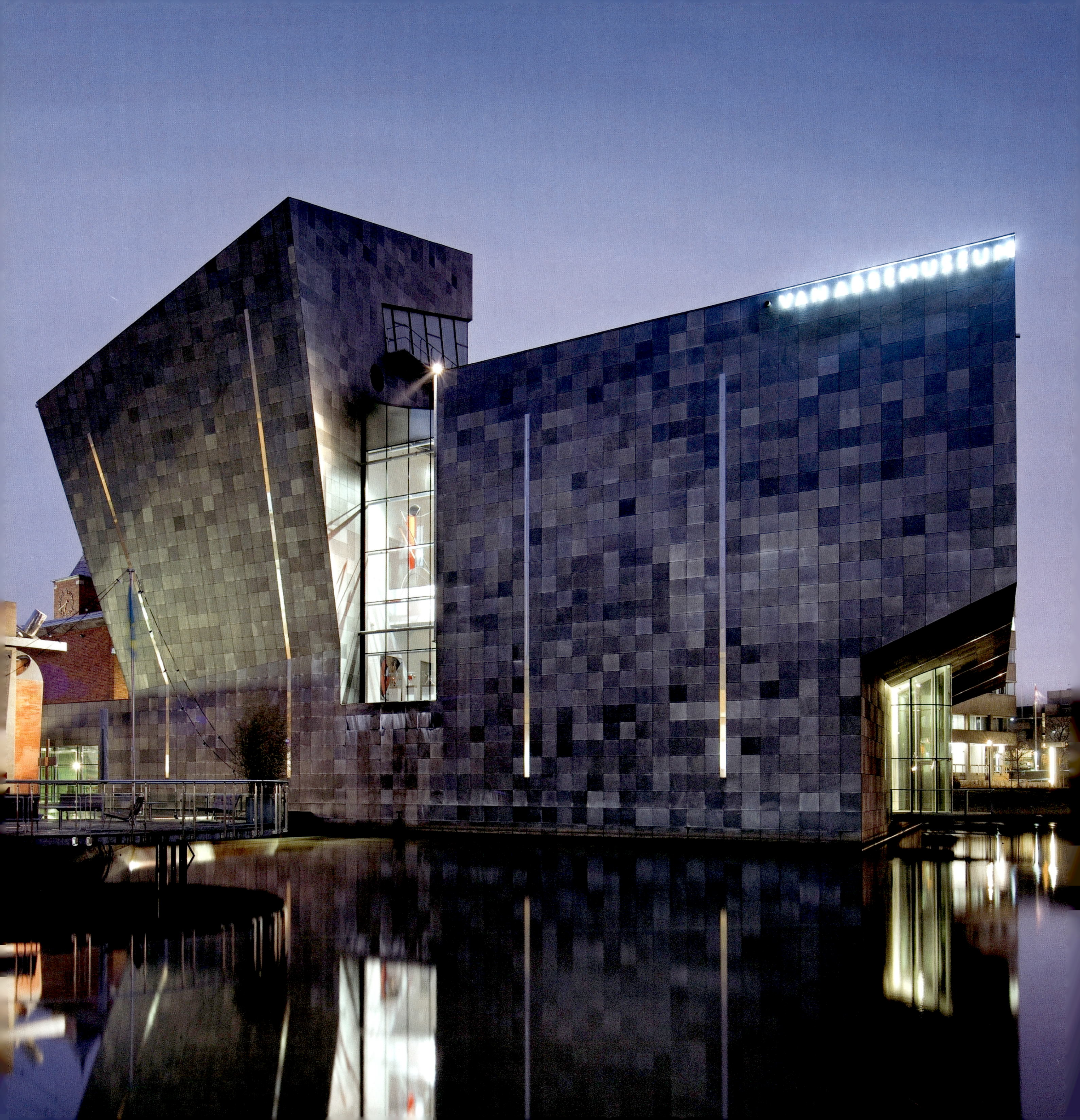
VAN ABBEMUSEUM

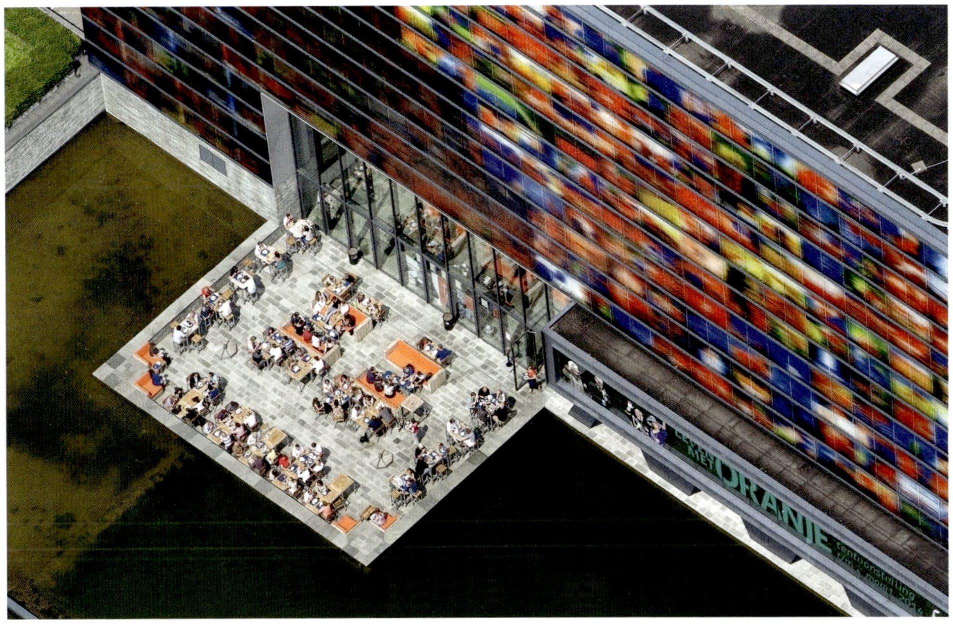

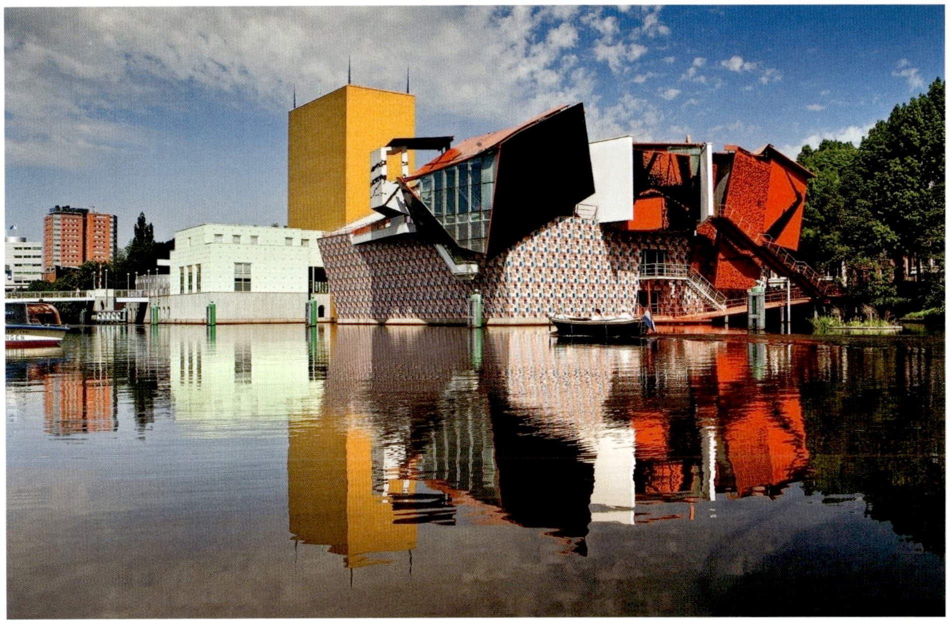

Left: The Van Abbe Museum in Eindhoven (by Abel Cahen). Many modern museums have a special character and are often designed by leading foreign architects.

Top: The Groninger Museum (by Alessandro Mendini), and an aerial photograph of the Netherlands Institute of Sound and Vision in Hilversum (by Neutelings Riedijk).

On page 27: Amsterdam museums EYE Filmmuseum (by Delugan Meissl) and the Science Center NEMO (by Renzo Piano).

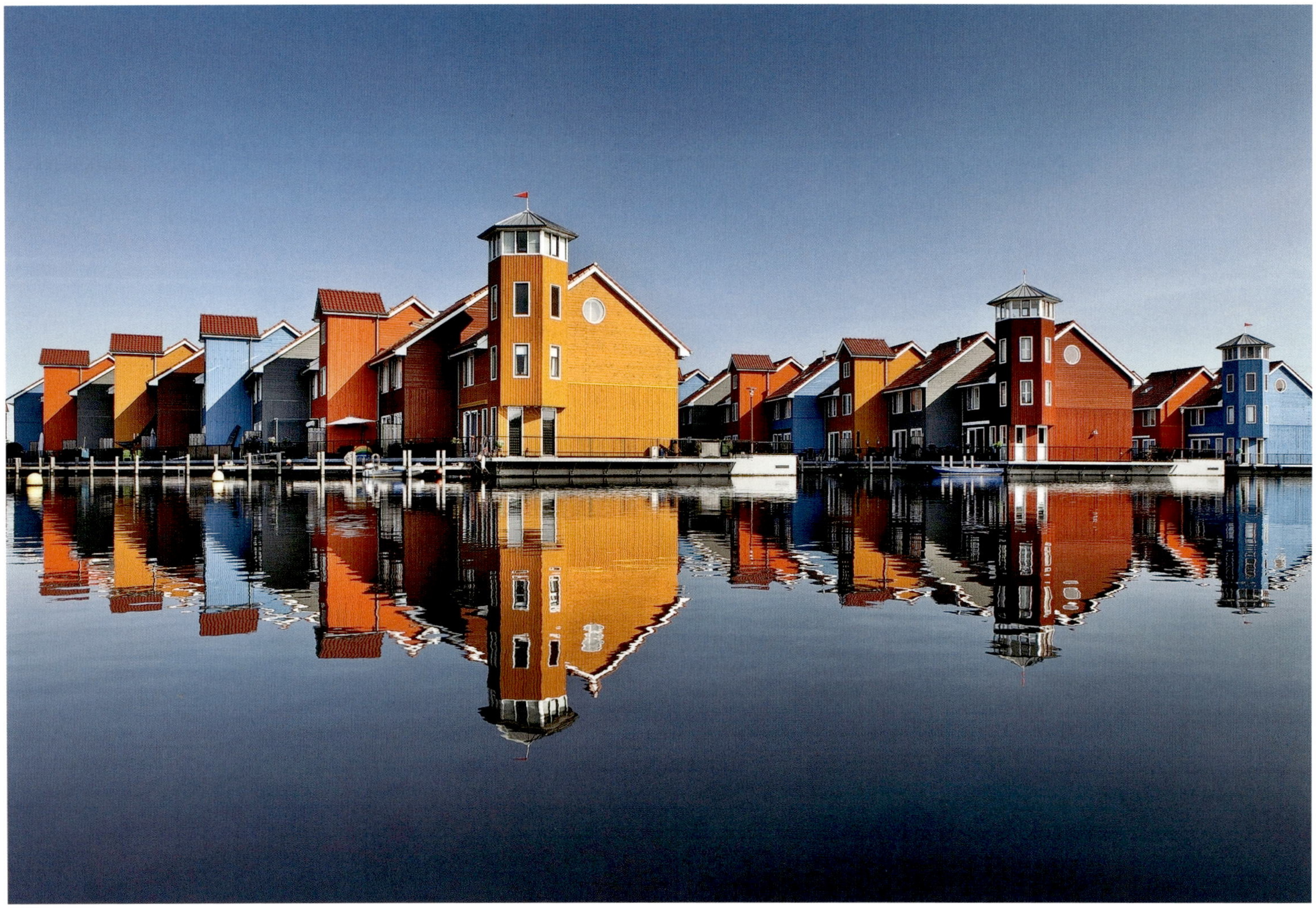

Top: Holiday homes at Reitdiep city marina in Groningen.

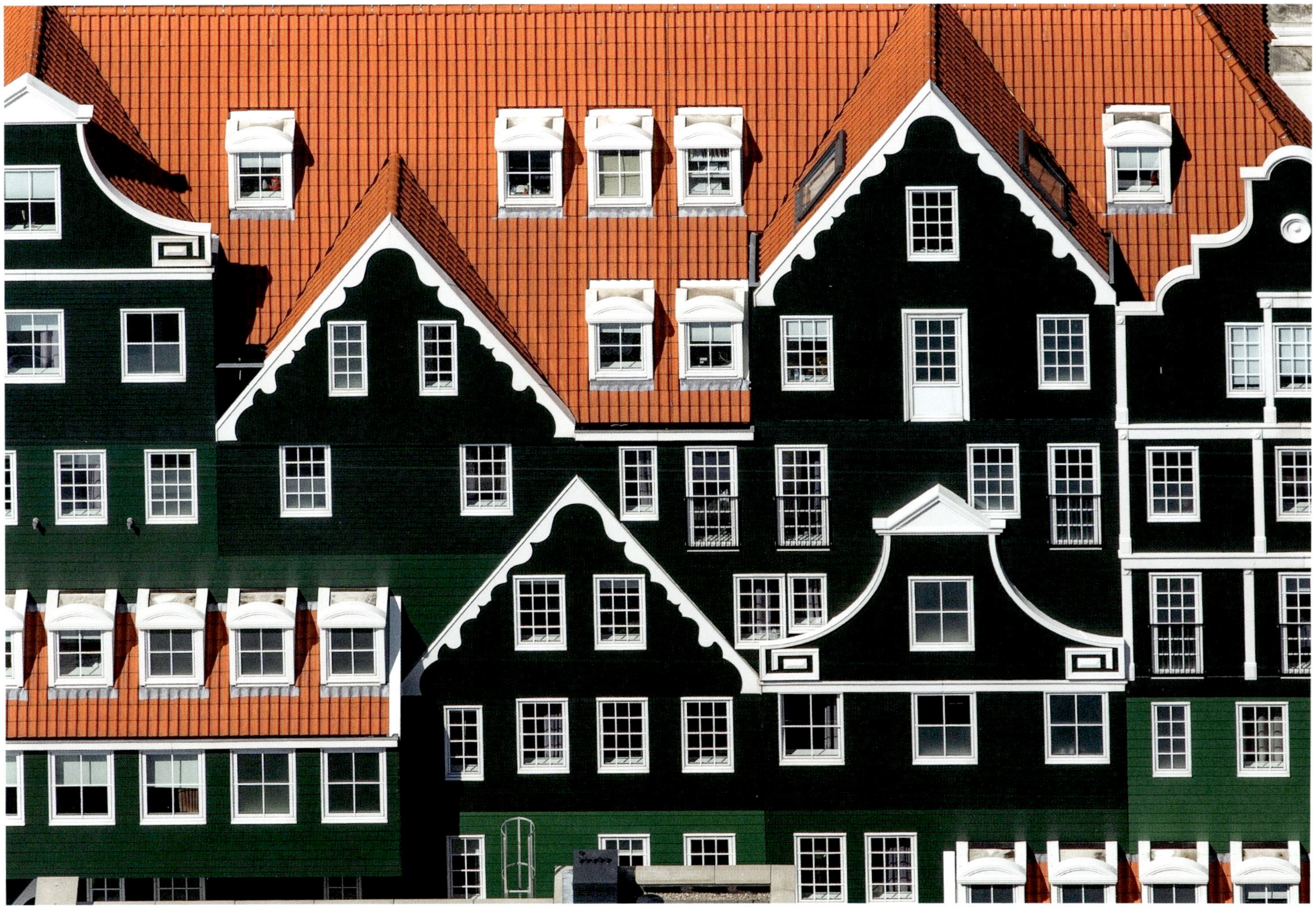

Top: Detail of the Inntel hotel in Zaanstad – designed by Sjoerd Soeters – in the style of traditional Zaan houses.

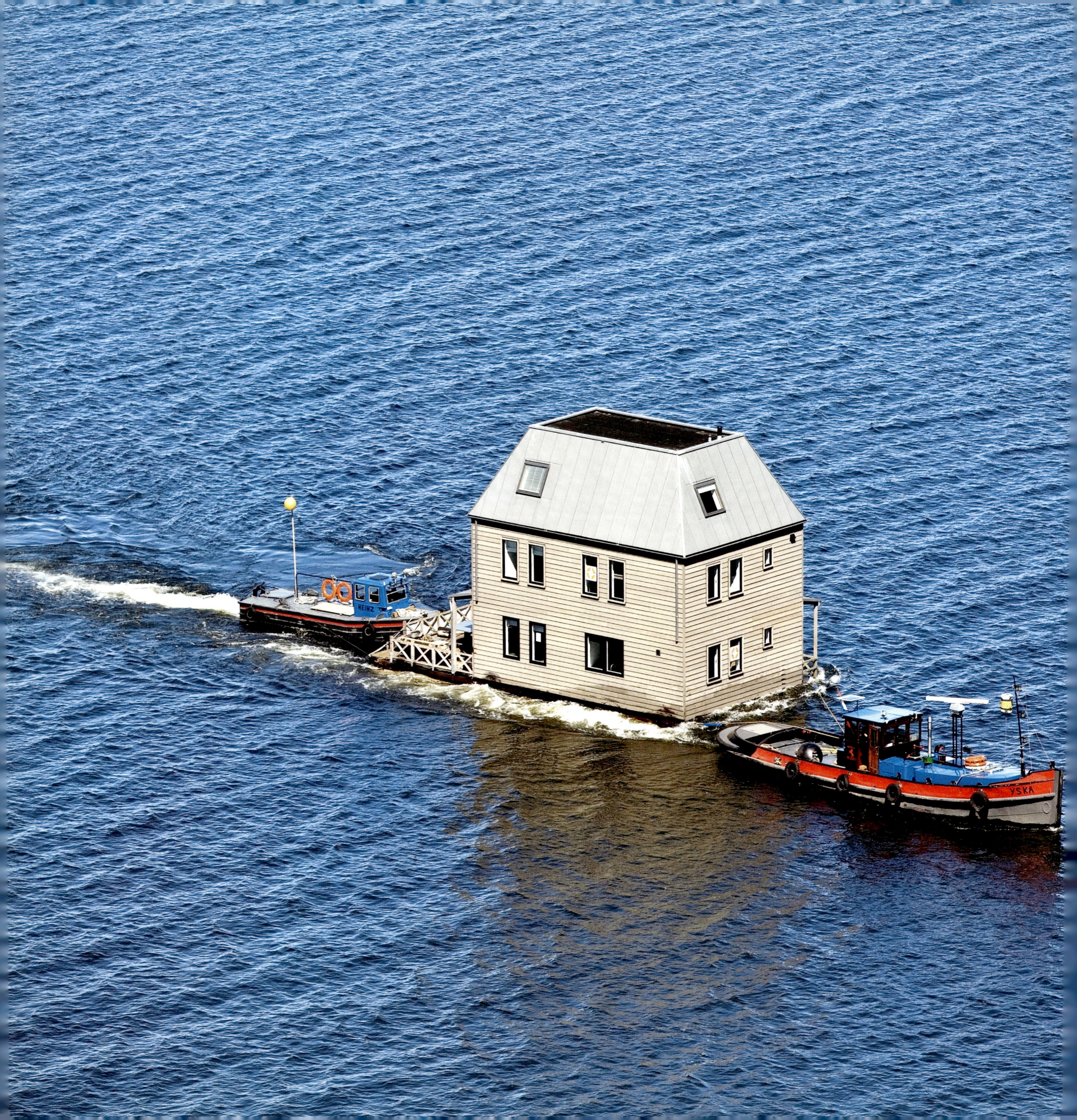
HEINZ
YSKA

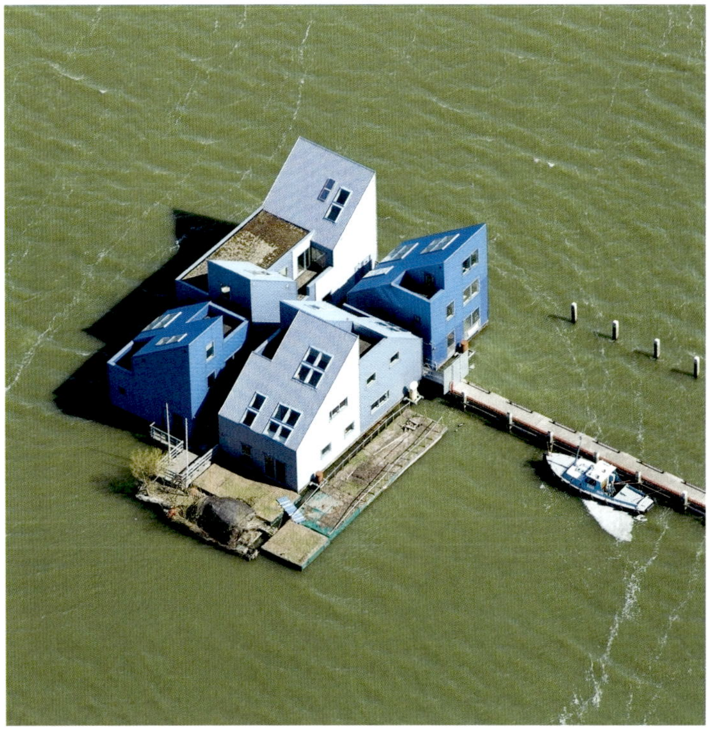

Left: Transport of a water villa across the IJsselmeer from Amsterdam to Almere.

Top: Floating villa in the IJsselmeer at Almere, an example of flexible living and working.

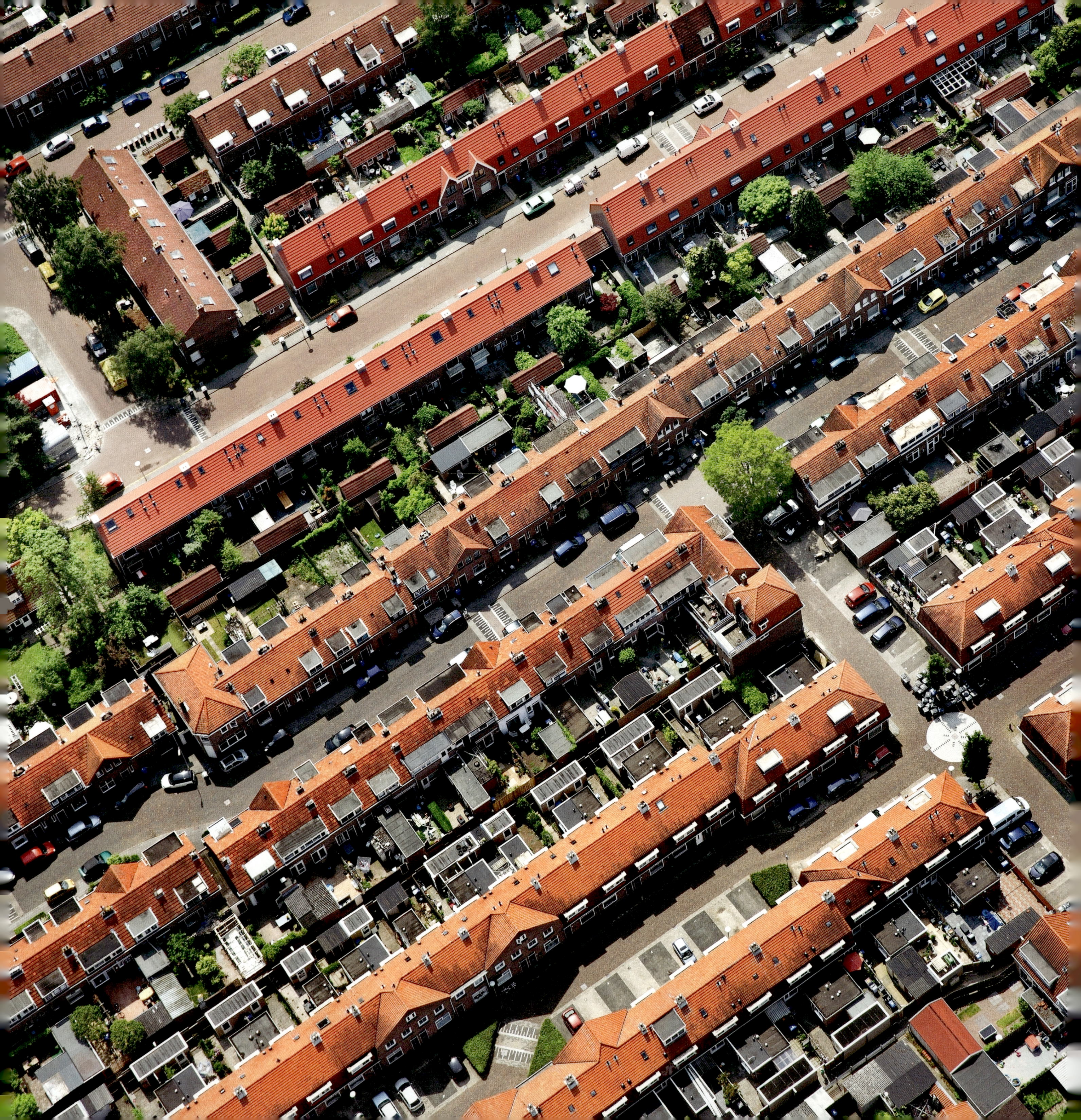

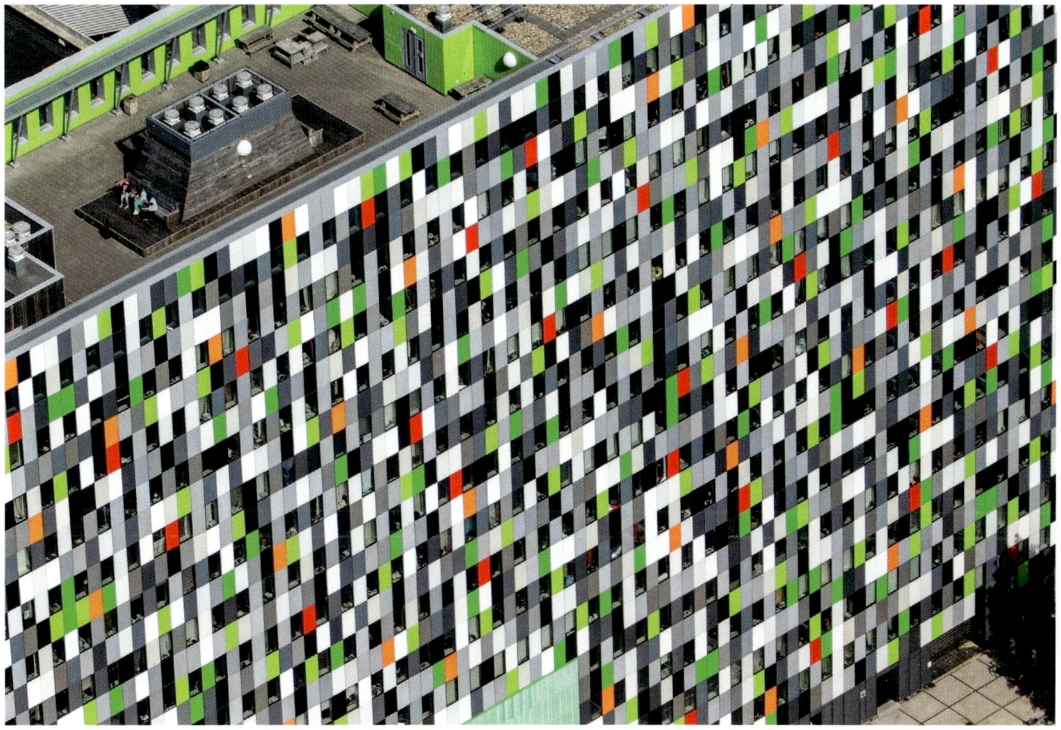

Left: The terraced house is the most common type of property in the Netherlands. In the picture, an example from Zwolle.

Top: The colourful hall of residence Casa Confetti in Utrecht, built in 2008, has 377 student flats. It was designed by Marlies Rohmer Architects.

Following pages: Skyline of Kop van Zuid in Rotterdam, with the Erasmus Bridge (by Ben van Berkel) on the left and De Rotterdam (by Rem Koolhaas) on the right, the largest building in the Netherlands.

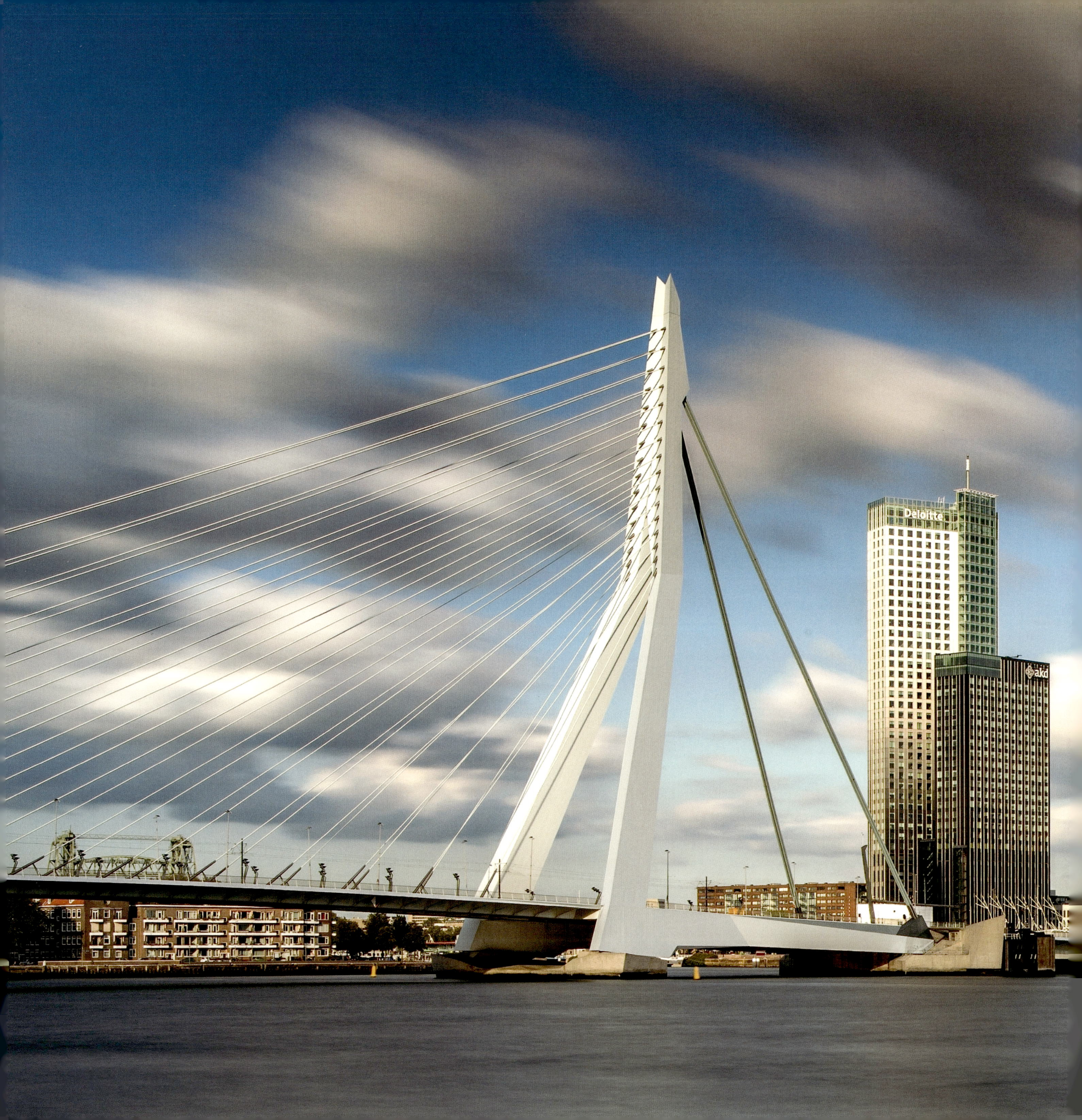
Deloitte

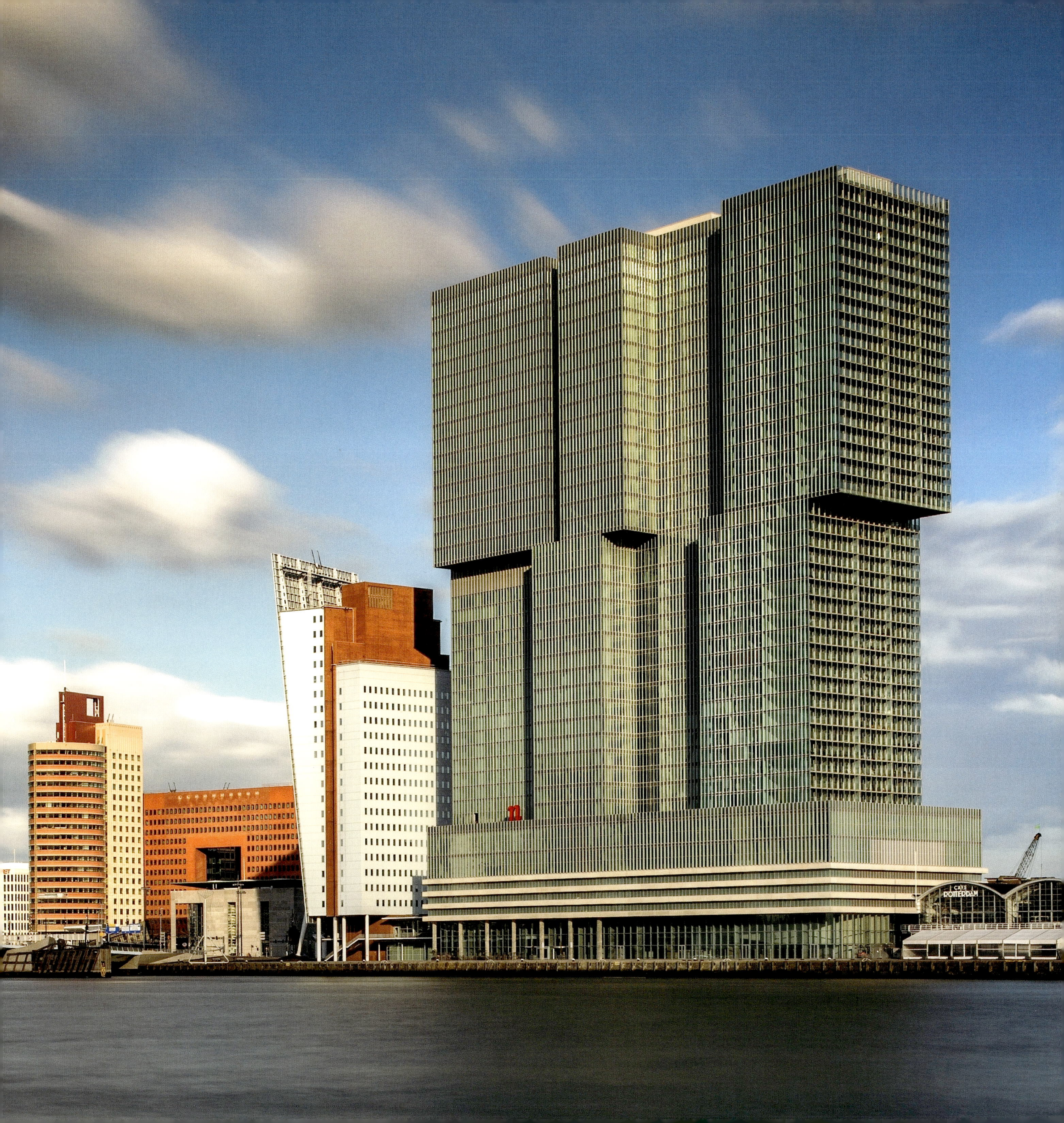
ROTTERDAM

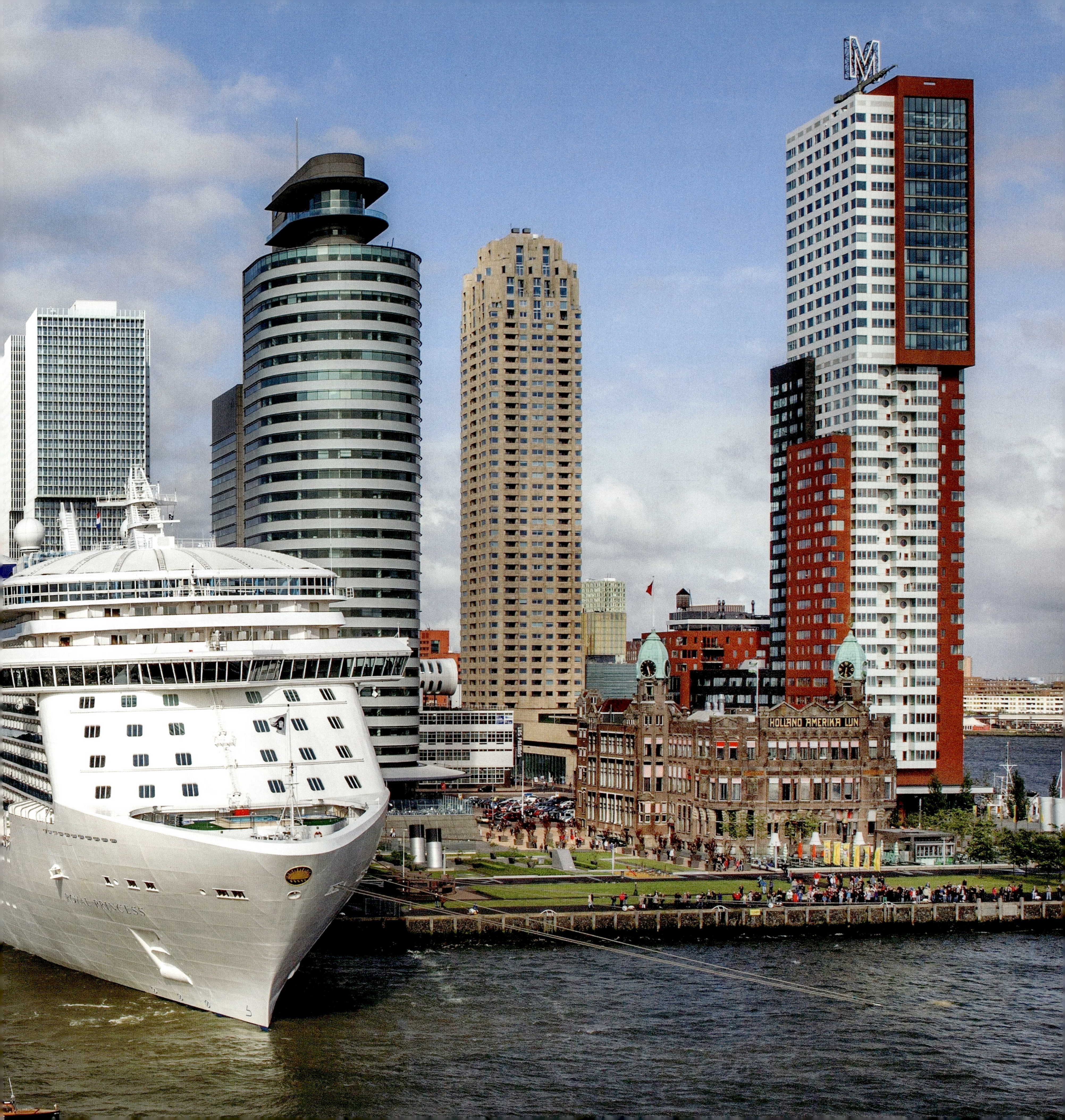
HOLLAND AMERIKA LIJN

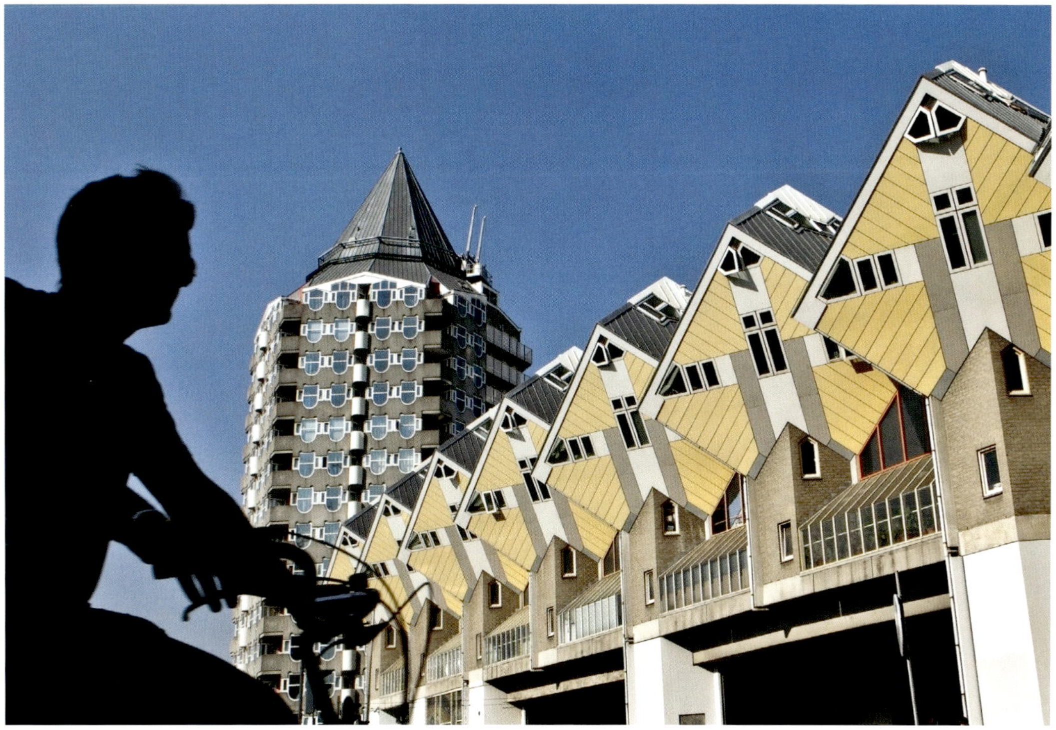

Capital of Architecture
Rotterdam is seen as the architectural capital of the Netherlands, at least as far as modern architecture is concerned. The city was almost completely destroyed during World War II, which meant there was an opportunity for new housing and utility projects.

Left: The relatively young Rotterdam district of Kop van Zuid is a good example of how modern and historic architecture can go hand in hand. In the shadow of the gigantic towers is the historic Hotel New York from 1901 – formerly the headquarters of the Holland America Line. The imposing Ocean Princess moored at the cruise terminal.

Top: In the postwar period, Rotterdam offered plenty of space for experimental construction, such as the famous cube homes by Piet Blom.

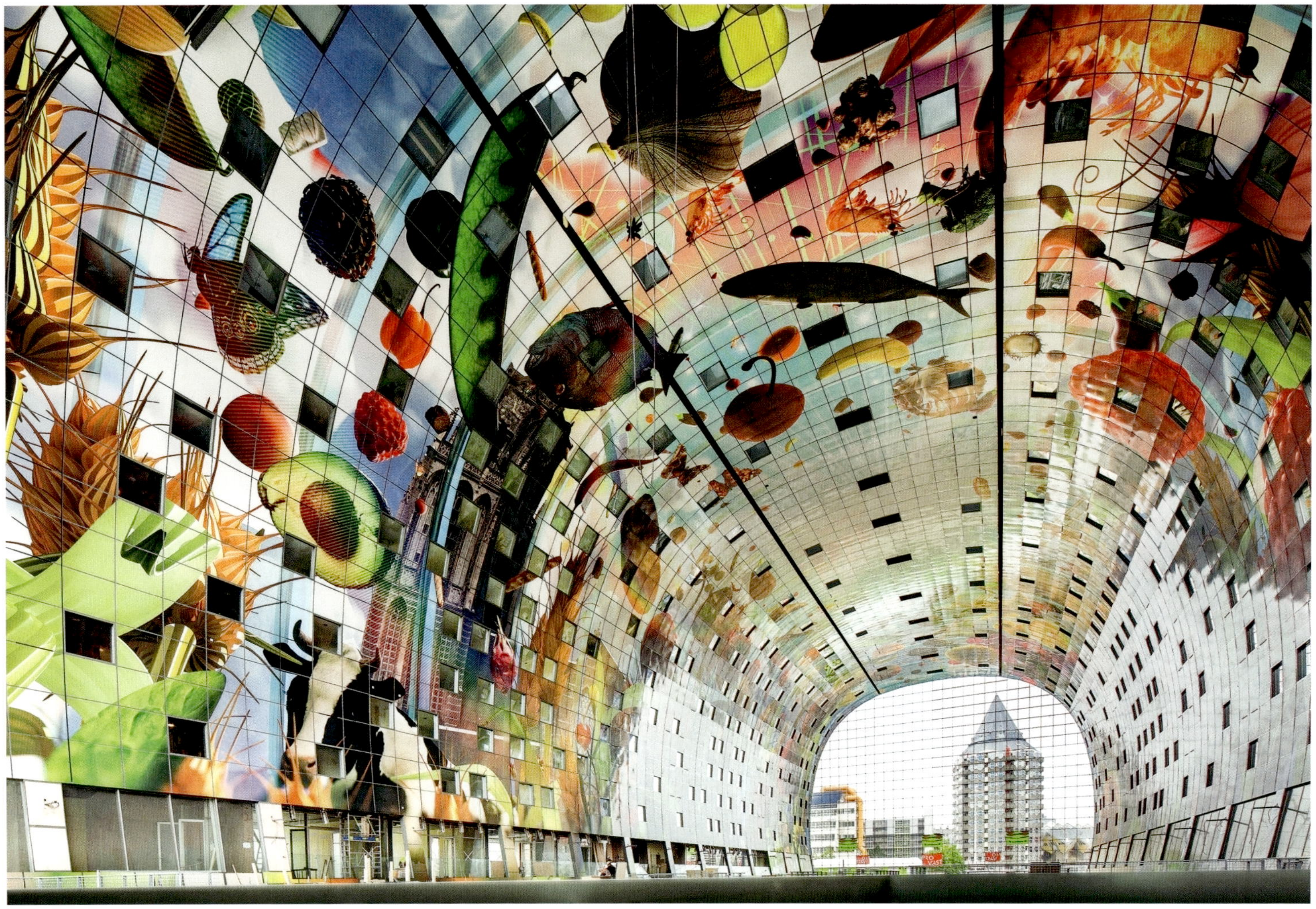

Top: The Market Hall, an indoor market topped by ten floors of over 200 apartments. The striking, horseshoe-shaped building was designed by architect Winy Maas. The interior artwork of the building is by Arno Coenen.

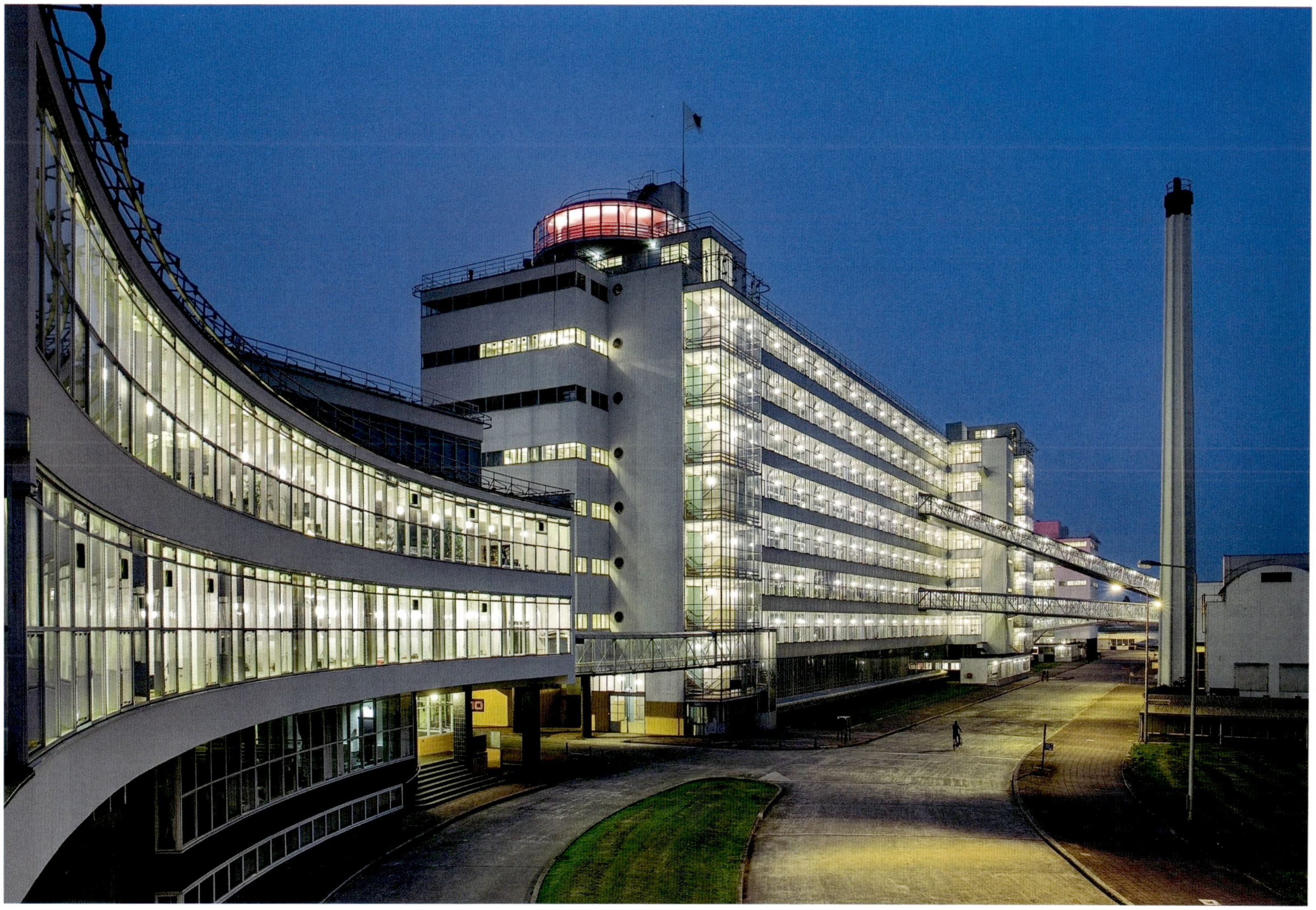

Top: Van Nelle, a former coffee, tea and tobacco factory in Rotterdam – the most important industrial monument in the Netherlands. It is a classic example of Het Nieuwe Bouwen style – the design is by Leendert van der Vlugt – and was built between 1927 and 1930. Since 2014, the building has been on the UNESCO World Heritage List.

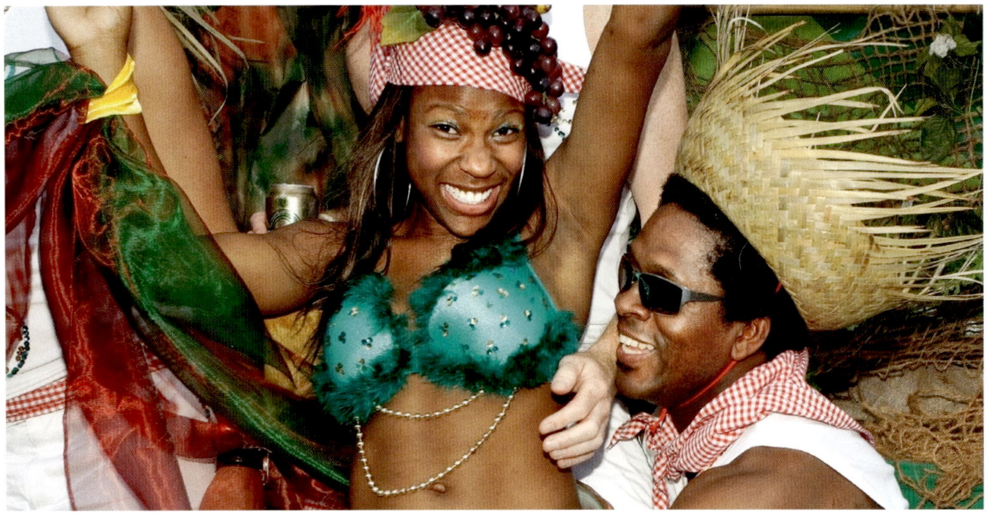

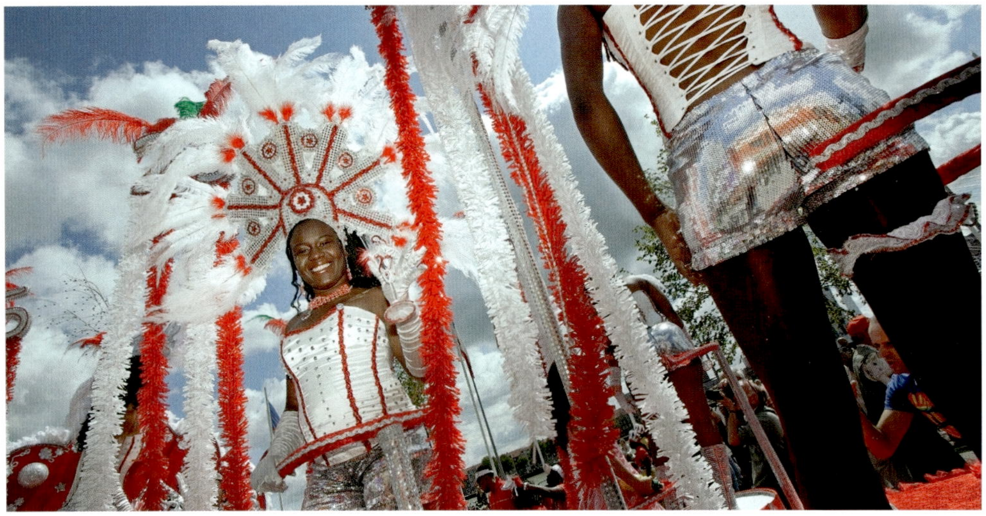

Antillean Carnival

The counterpart of the traditional Dutch carnival is Summer Carnival (from the Antilles), celebrated in Rotterdam around the last Saturday in July. More than 900,000 people attend. The Summer Carnival has become a major multicultural event, bringing together the various ethnic groups (top and right).

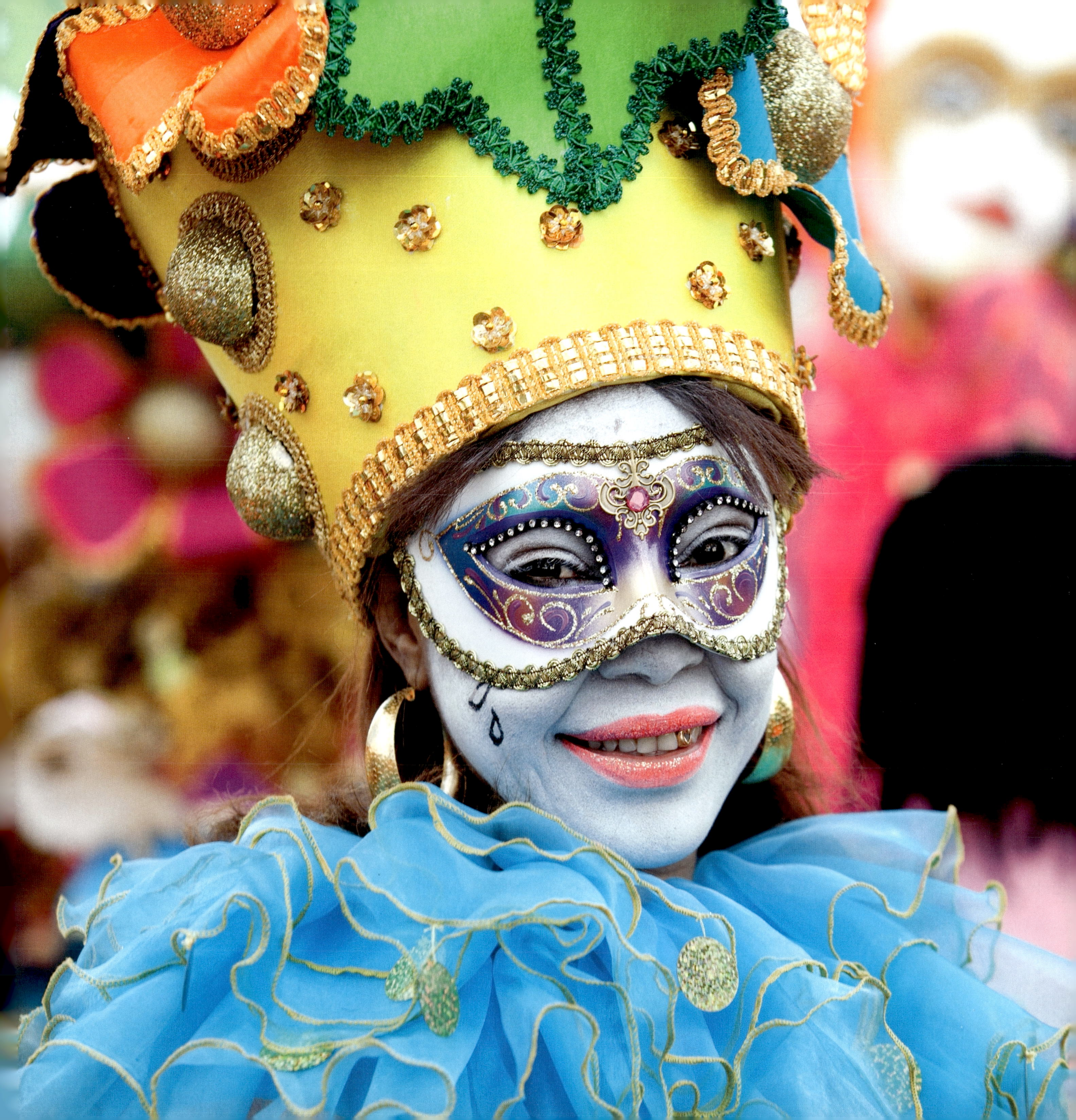

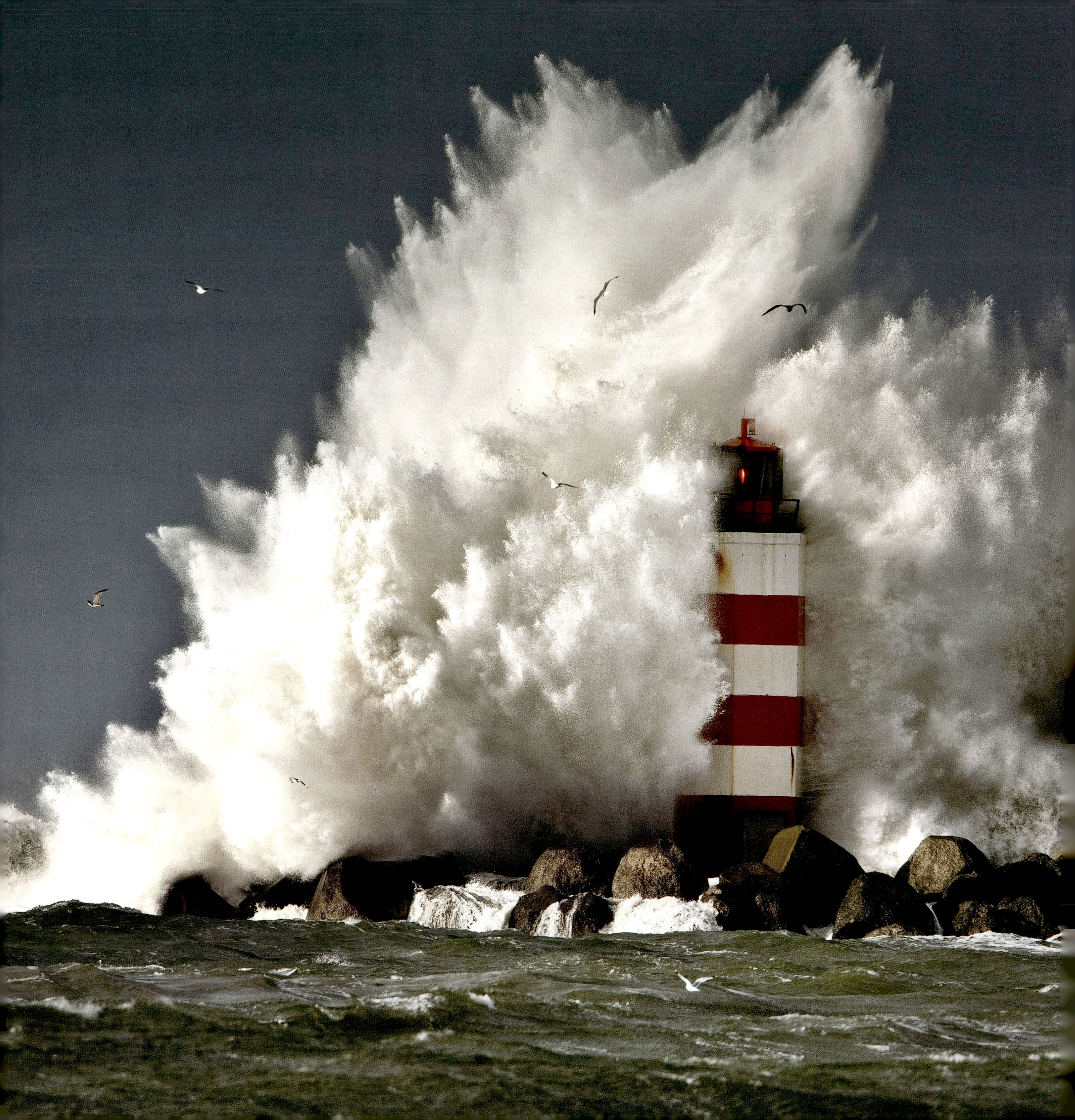

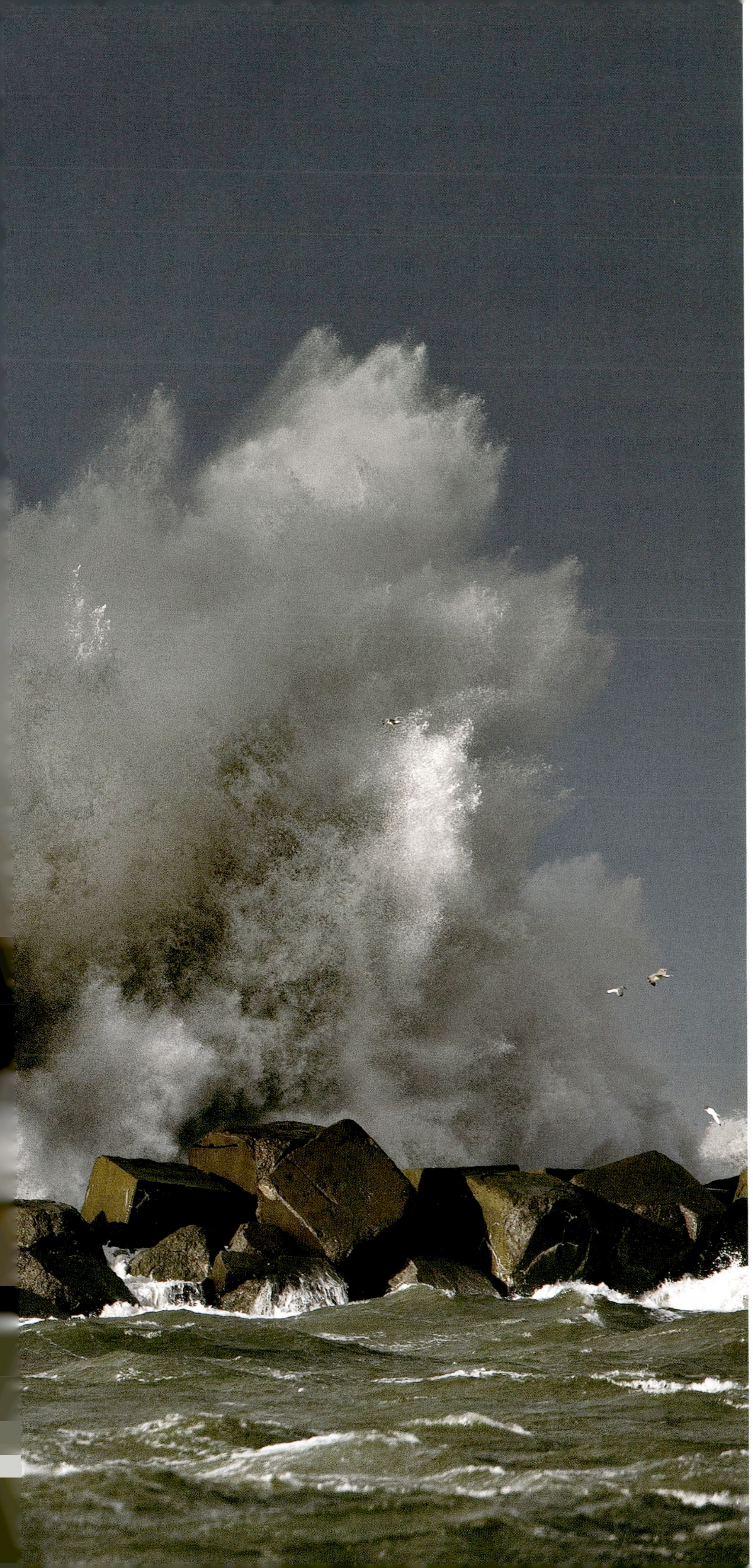

Water

The Netherlands, the Low Countries, les Pays Bas – the country's various names tell us what is characteristic of this country: its low elevation. Very low: about 20 per cent of its territory is below sea level. For foreign visitors, this sometimes sounds alarming, but the Dutch have lived with this fact for thousands of years. The battle against the water is not only visible in the landscape. The ingenuity with which the lowest and wettest part of Western Europe was made habitable has given the Netherlands worldwide fame. In the future, that ingenuity will be needed again, because the sea level is still rising and the land behind the dikes continues to sink.

Rich in water

The Netherlands is a water-rich country. Of the total area (41,160 sq. km), at least 18 percent consists of lakes, ponds, rivers, streams, open and closed estuaries, streams, canals and harbours. Over the centuries, 630,000 hectares of land were reclaimed from the water. Equally impressive are the defences built to ensure that the country remains dry. In addition to the 260 km of dunes – the country's natural sea wall – the Netherlands has 430 km of sea dikes, dams and barrages, and 2,445 km of dikes along lakes and rivers. This system is also called the 'primary water defence' and is intended to absorb the biggest blows. The dikes, dams and embankments at the local level, the 'non-primary defences', are approximately 14,000 km long. Converted, this figure means that there is one metre of water protection available for each inhabitant.

Water Top Sector

It is not surprising that 'water' is regarded as a top industrial sector by the Dutch government. The Netherlands is keen to remain a world leader in secure and clean solutions. This particular 'top sector' focuses not only on the protection of land, but also on obtaining energy from water, water reuse technologies, and on smart, safe ships.

Left: Waves crashing into the lighthouse of the North Pier at IJmuiden.

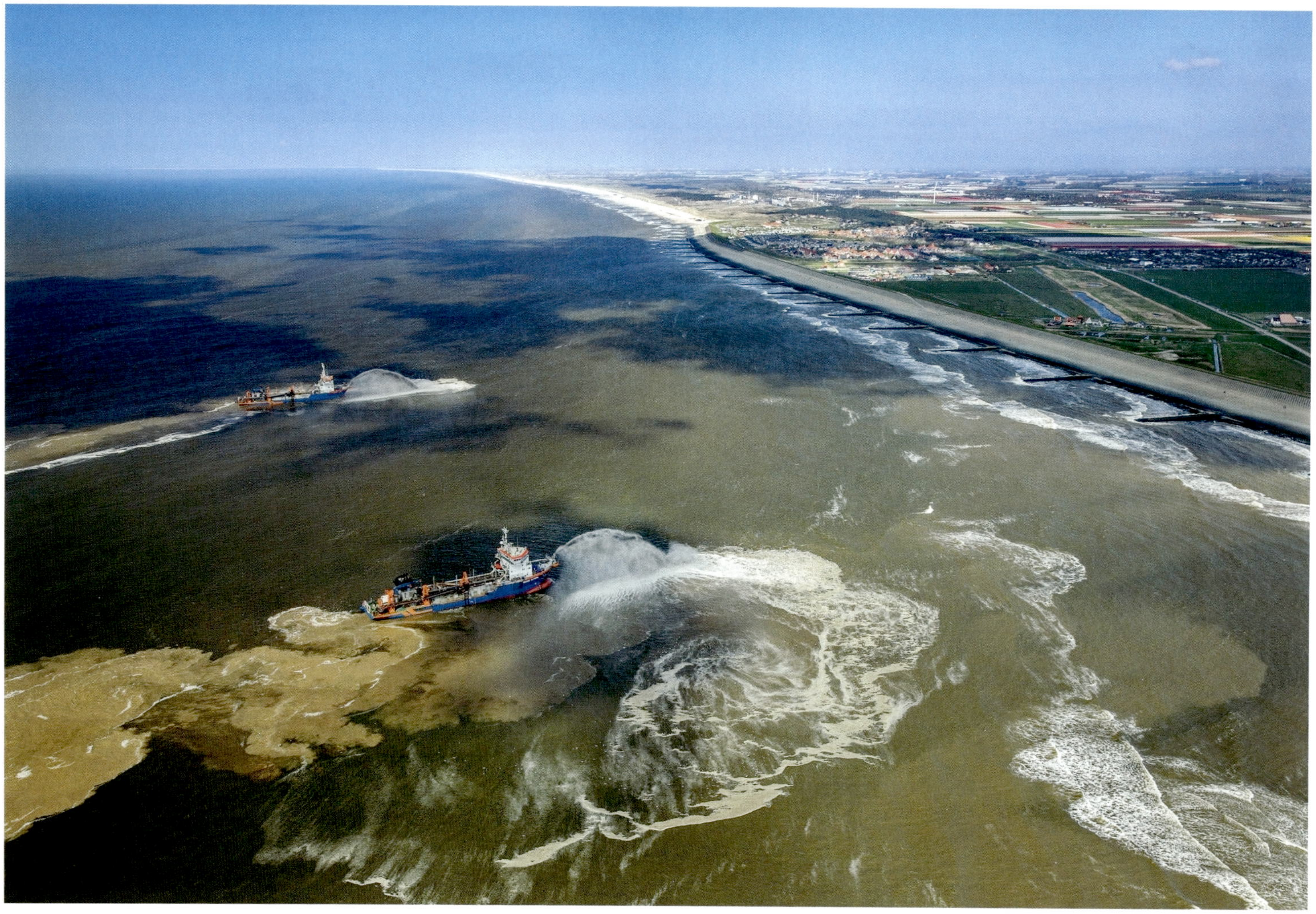

Zuiderzee becomes the IJsselmeer

After the flood of 1916, in which more than fifty people died and large parts of the Netherlands were inundated, the Dutch government finally decided to close the Zuiderzee off. This was not only for safety, but also because World War I had led to food shortages. This meant there was a great need for new farmland. Two years later, Parliament agreed on the plan, whereupon the Zuiderzee Law was adopted. Engineer Cornelis Lely carried out the plan, and ultimately, through further land reclamation, dike reinforcement and the construction of the Afsluitdijk in 1932, the Zuiderzee was no longer a sea but a lake: the IJsselmeer. What followed was the largest land reclamation project in history. Between 1936 and 1968, pumping stations in this area pumped polders dry that totalled 145,000 hectares. The Netherlands acquired a new province: Flevo- land.

Top: Dike reinforcement by spraying sand, off the coast of Hondsbossche sea wall at Petten in Noord-Holland.

Right: Aerial view of the Afsluitdijk, seen from Den Oever in Noord-Holland.

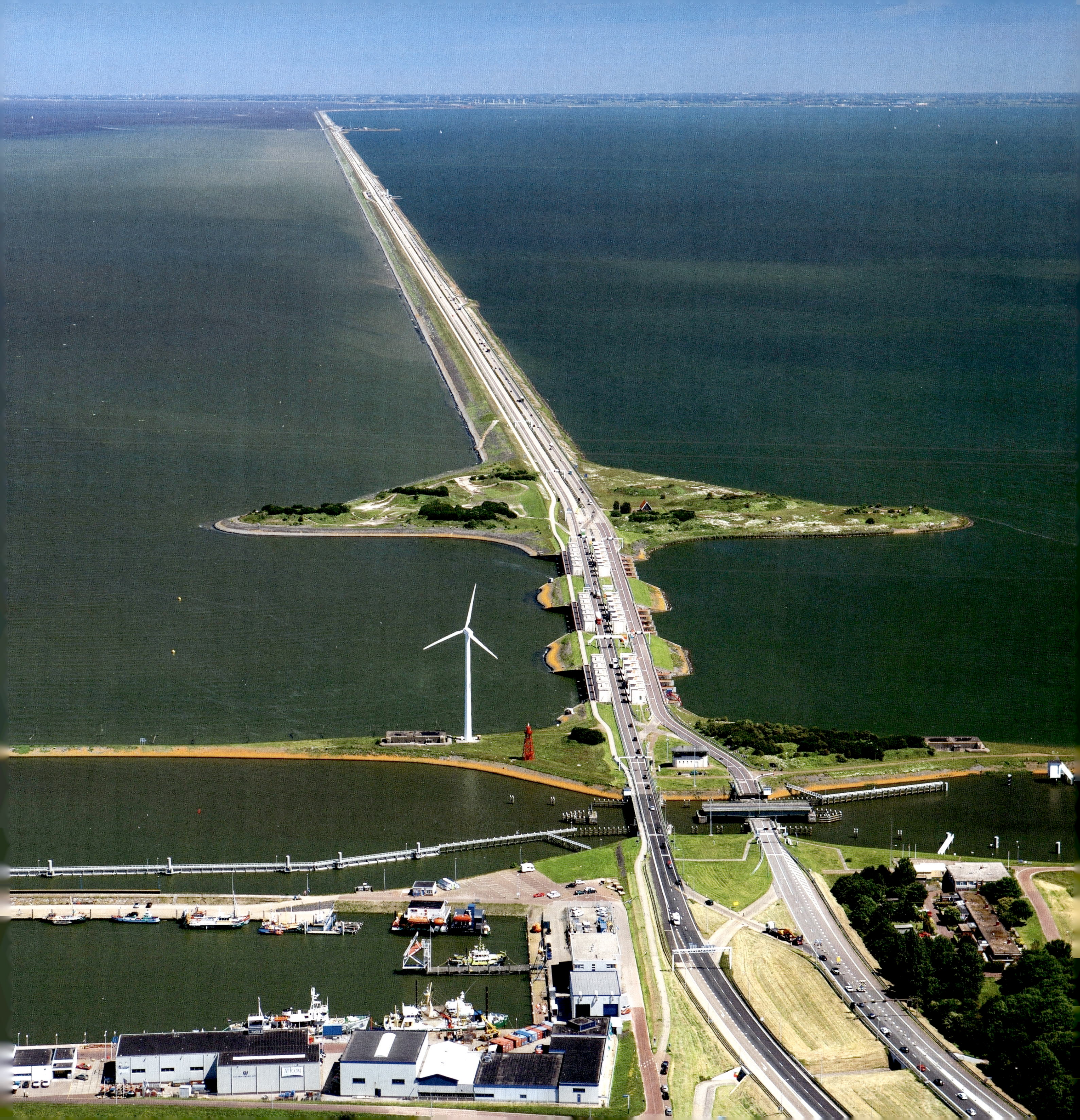

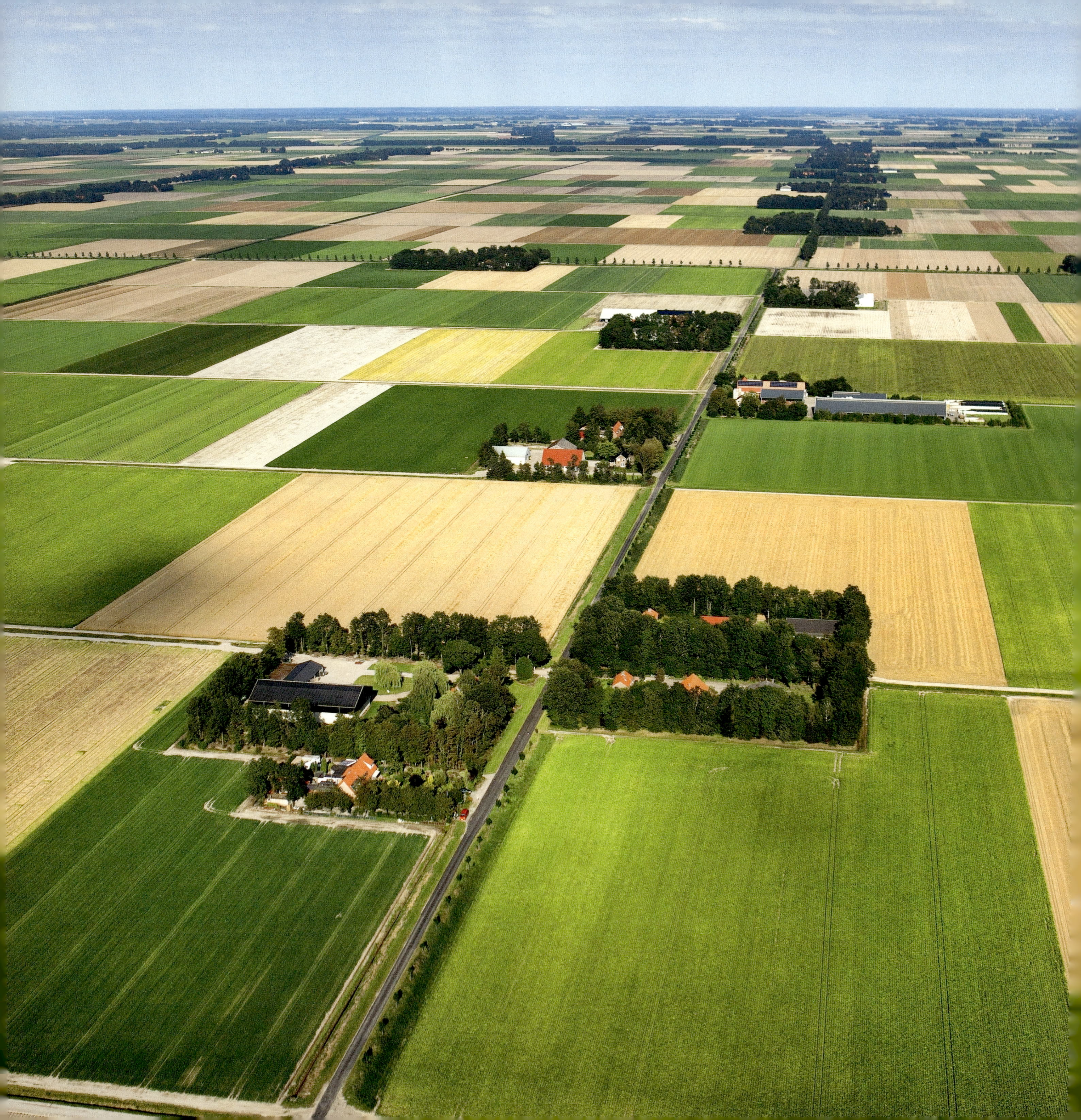

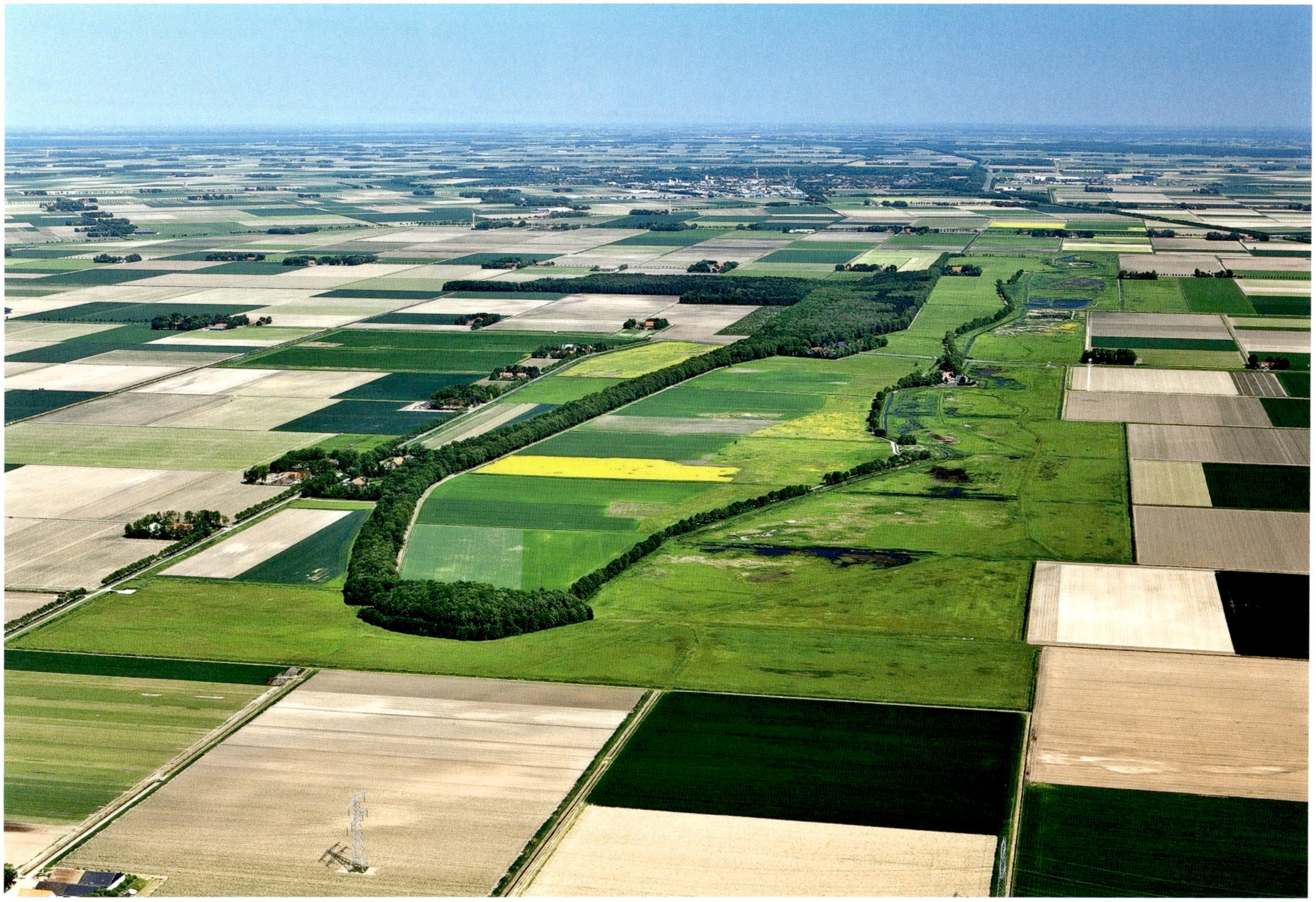

Left: The genesis of the polders in Flevoland was also of great importance for agriculture.

Top: The UNESCO World Heritage Site of Schokland, for centuries an island in the Zuiderzee, but anchored to the mainland by the reclamation of the Northeast Polder in 1942. In the picture, the outlines of the former island can still be seen.

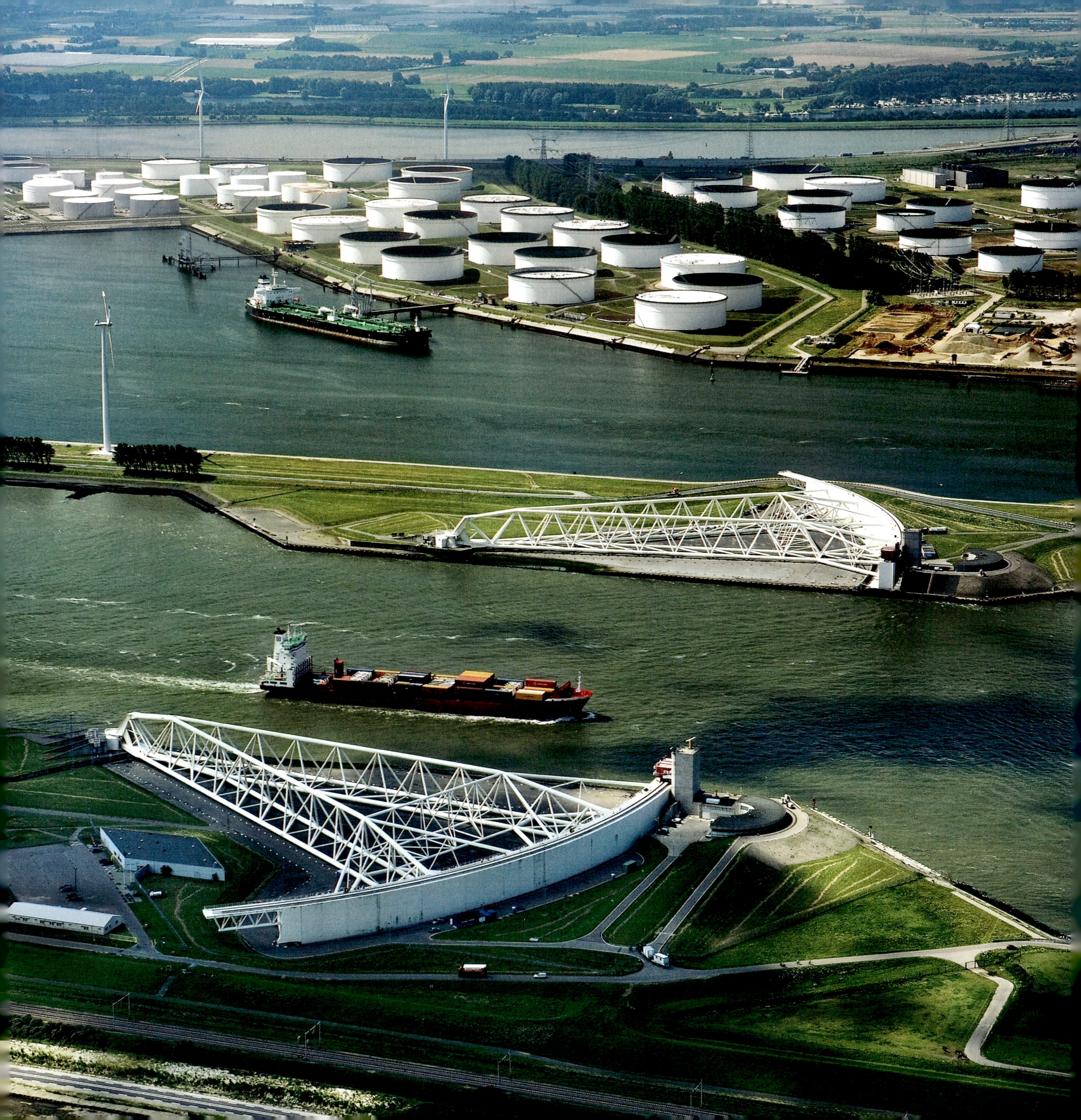

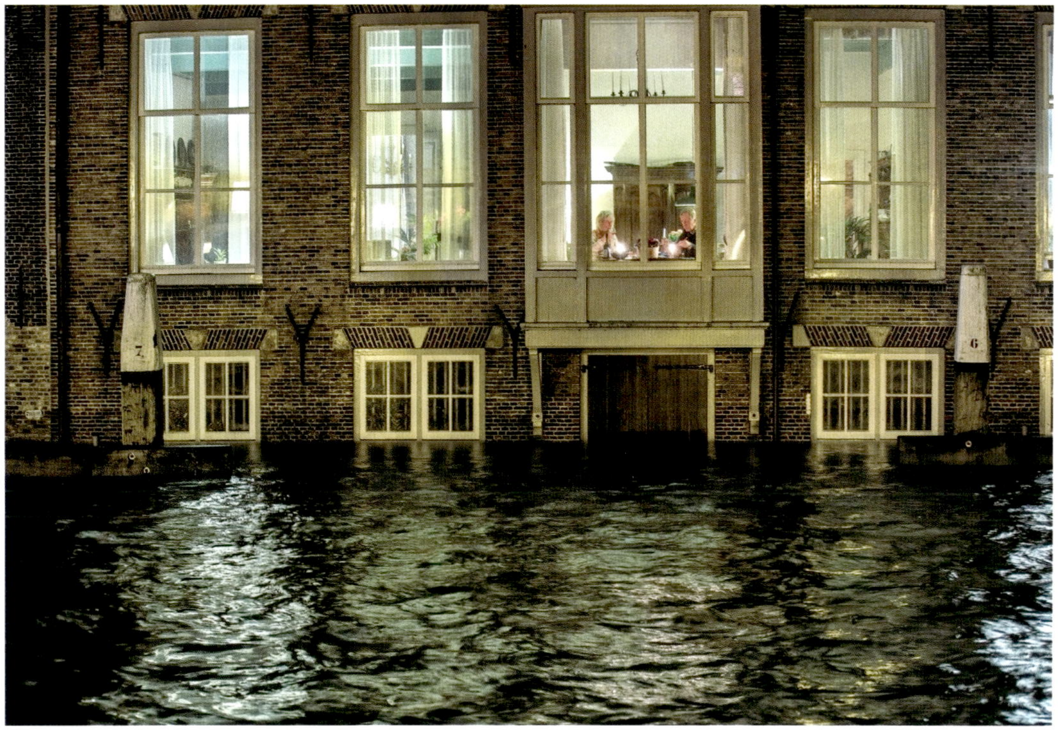

Delta Works

On the night of January 31, 1953, a northwesterly storm piled up the seawater along the coastal provinces so high that hundreds of dikes burst. 1,836 people drowned and the damage was enormous. The 1953 flood was a pretext to speed up the implementation of the already-existing Delta Plan. This plan provided for the closure of the estuaries of Zeeland and Zuid-Holland using fixed or movable water barriers. Between 1953 and 1997, billions of euros were invested in the Delta Works, a series of dikes, dams and barrages intended to protect Zeeland and Zuid-Holland against a great storm.

Left: The Maeslant Storm Surge Barrier near Hook of Holland. The two huge curved submersible gates – each 210 metres wide – are connected to land by the largest ball joints in the world. With the commissioning in 1997 of the Maeslantkering in the New Waterway, the Delta Works were complete.

Top: Even now, the historic city centre of Dordrecht can flood at extreme high tides. The couple in this house do not seem unduly bothered, though. If the water should rise further, the barrier would be closed.

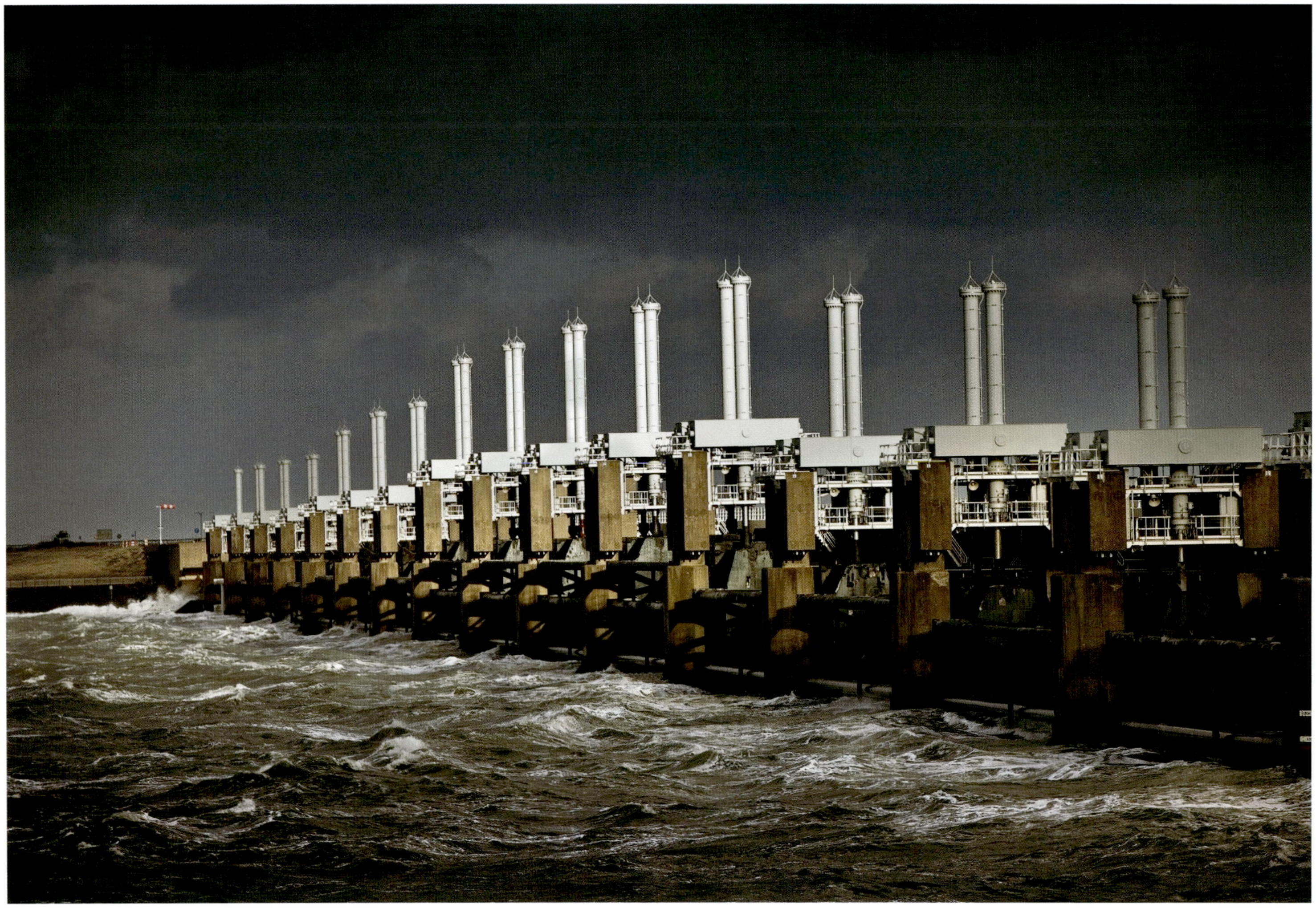

Top and right: The Oosterschelde (Eastern Scheldt) storm surge barrier, part of the Delta Works, is one of the most complex engineering works in the world, because the defensive structure can both open and close. In extreme conditions, the connectors between the huge pillars can be lowered so as to close the barrier. The system is left open in normal conditions, to allow for the preservation of the saltwater environment of the Oosterschelde, including its oyster acquaculture.

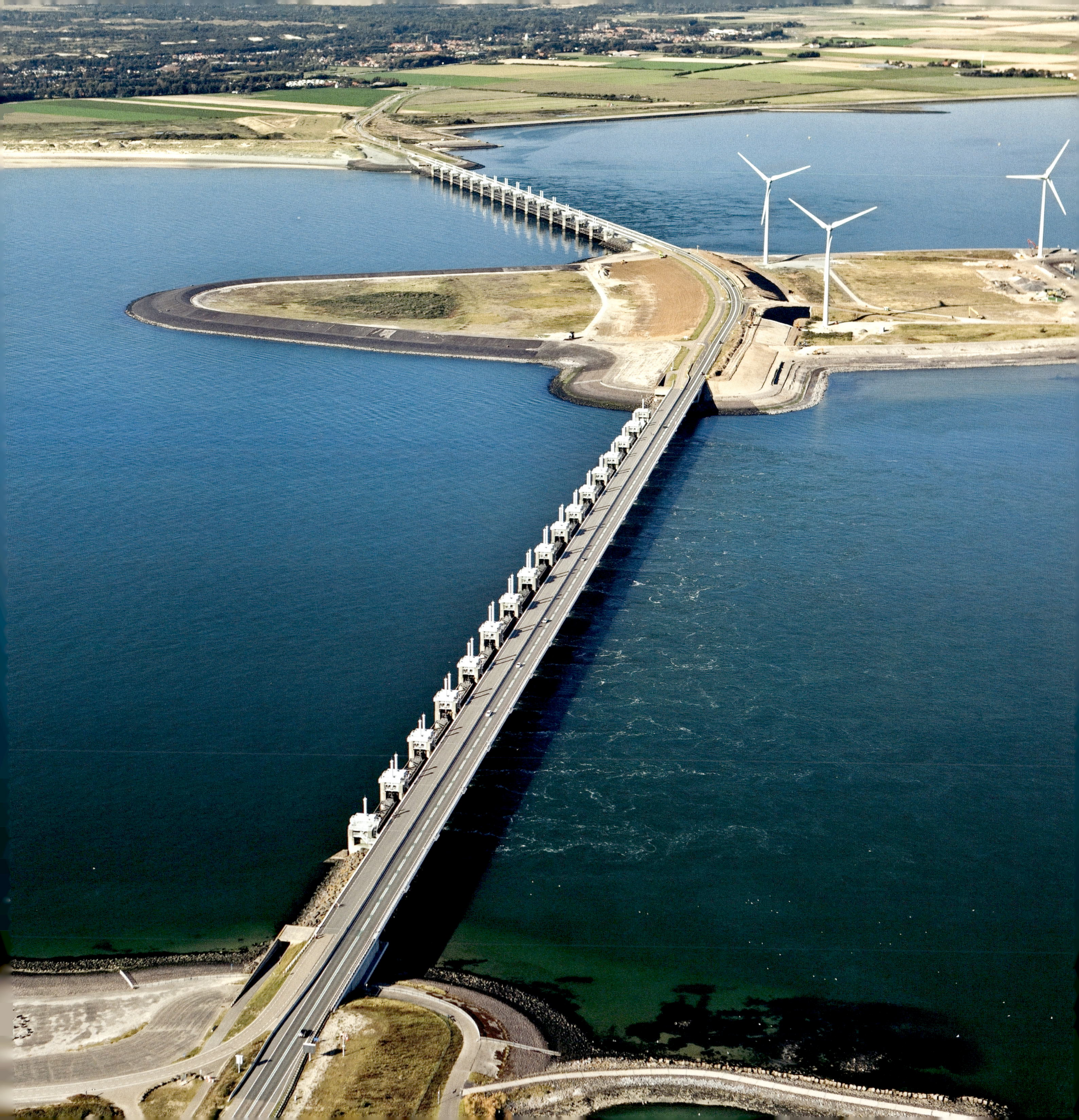

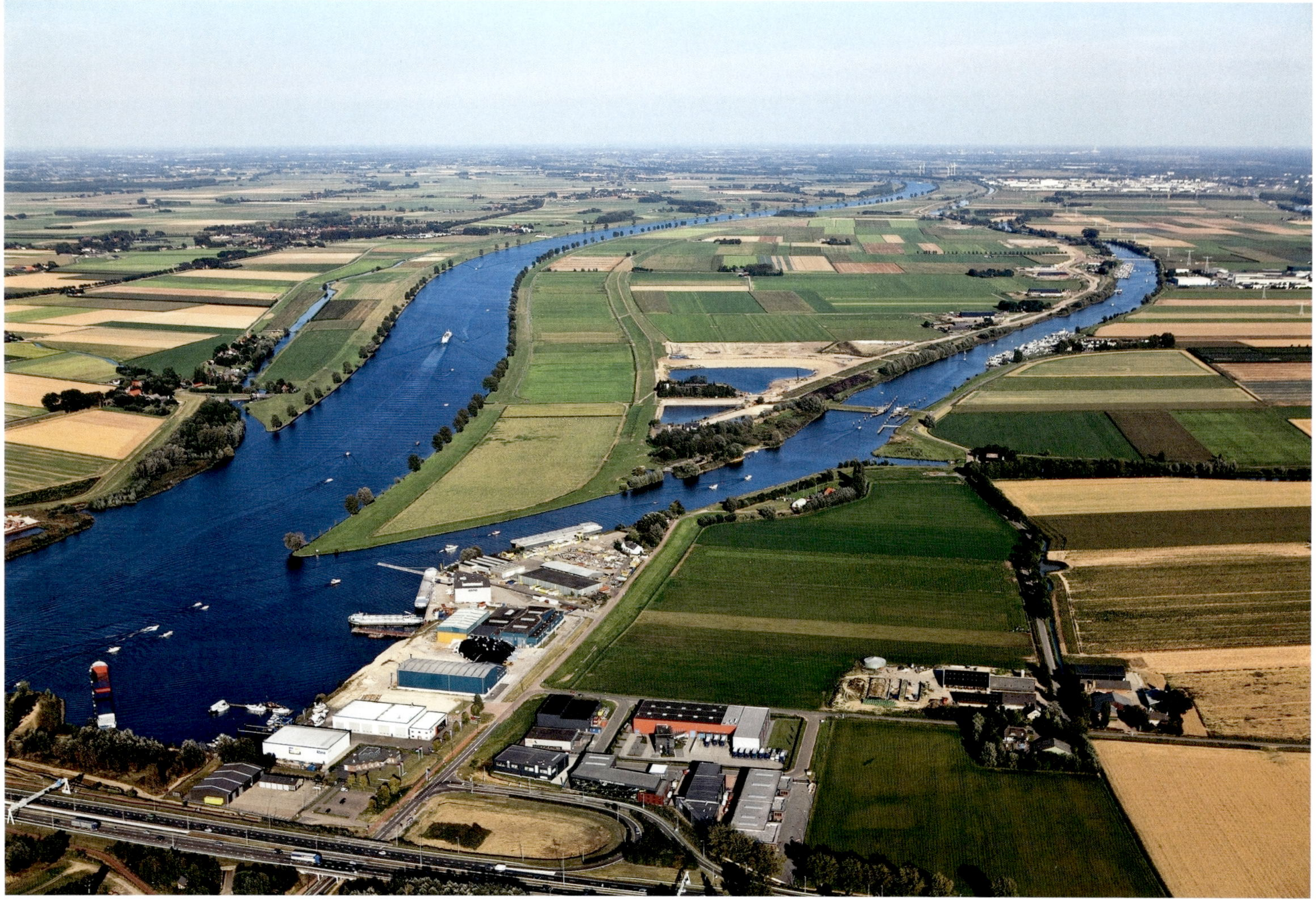

Water management

The Delta Works are an example of the more traditional battle against the water. There are now some even newer ways available to reduce flood risks. Room for the River is one such project; it focuses on reducing the risk of rivers bursting their banks. Between 1995 and 2015, more than 30 locations along the Rhine, Lek, IJssel, Waal and Lower Rhine rivers have had plans made for this project, allowing the water to flow more freely and literally to enjoy more space. Costs: 2.3 billion euros, but we do have to bear in mind that this is in the interests of the safety of 4 million people. In the Overdiepse Polder (top) project, mounds – our oldest form of protection – have once again been raised.

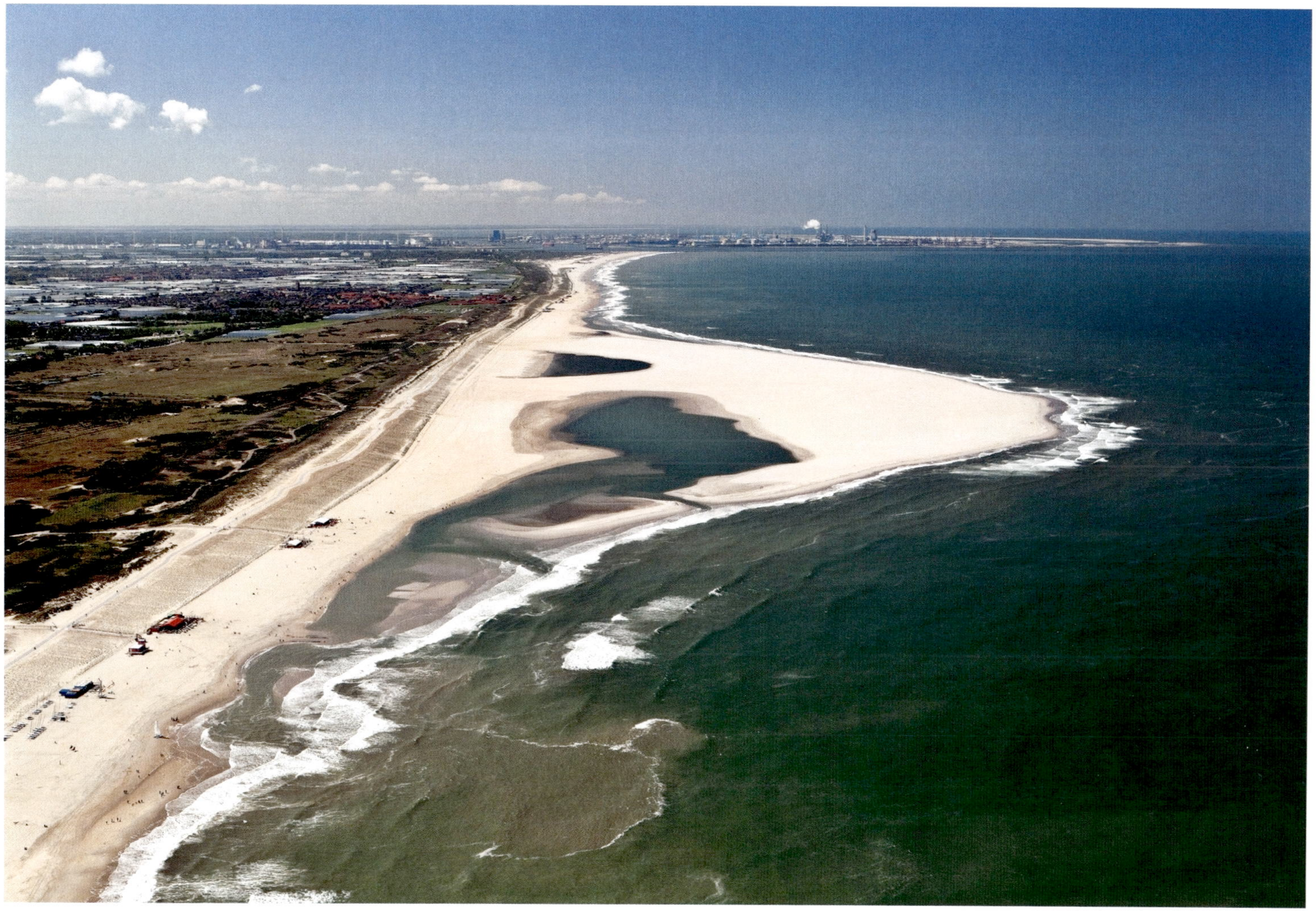

The Sand Motor

Another example of modern water management: the Sand Motor. The Sand Motor (top) is a landscaped peninsula between Ter Heijde and Kijkduin covering 128 hectares. Wind, waves and currents will spread the sand over the next twenty years along the coast between Hook of Holland and Scheveningen. This will form a new beach and dune, needed to protect the land against rising sea levels; in addition, it will provide space for nature and recreation. Government, industry and science are working together on this project; in time, the experience of Ter Heijde will profit coastal regions all over the world.

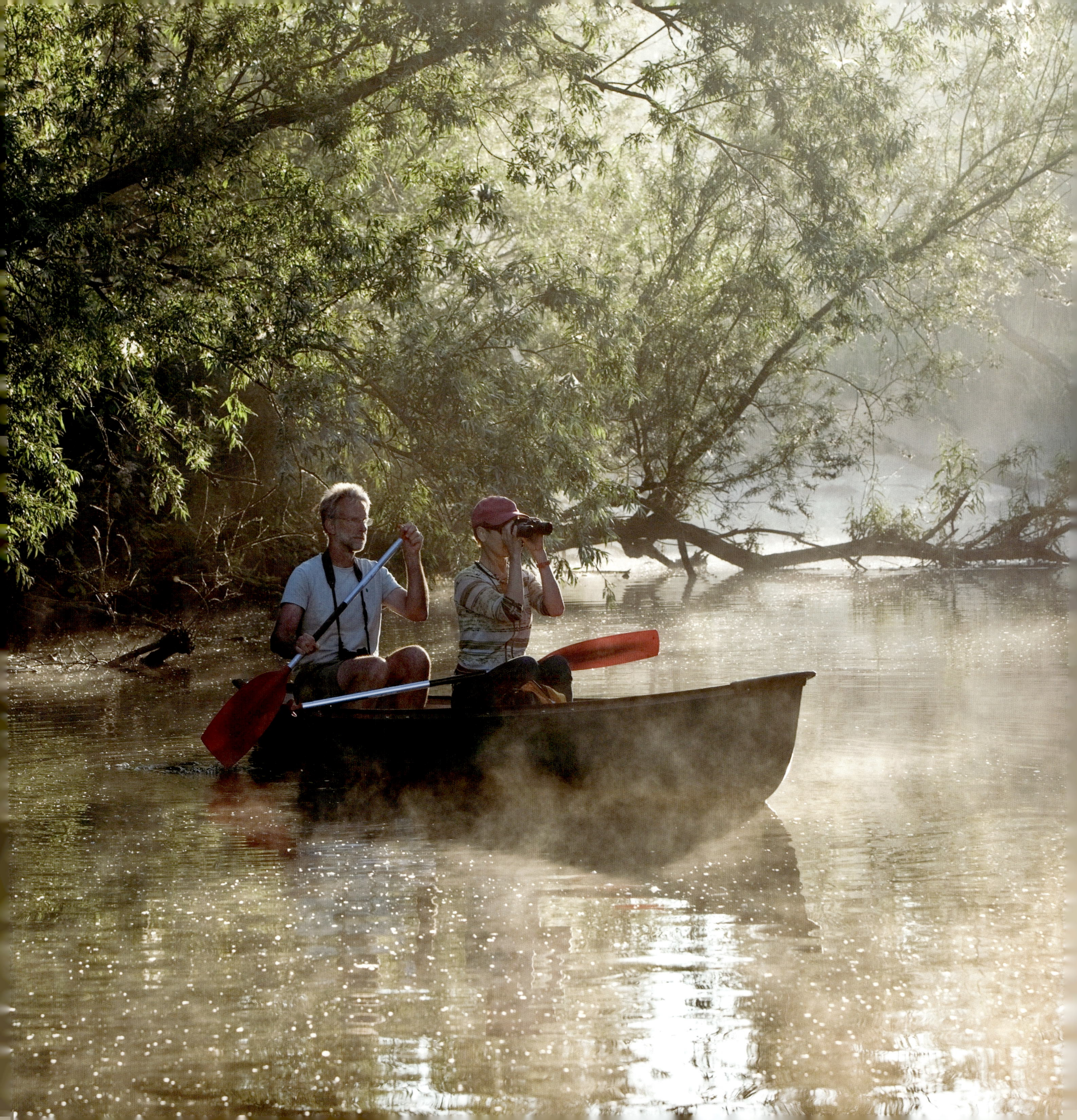

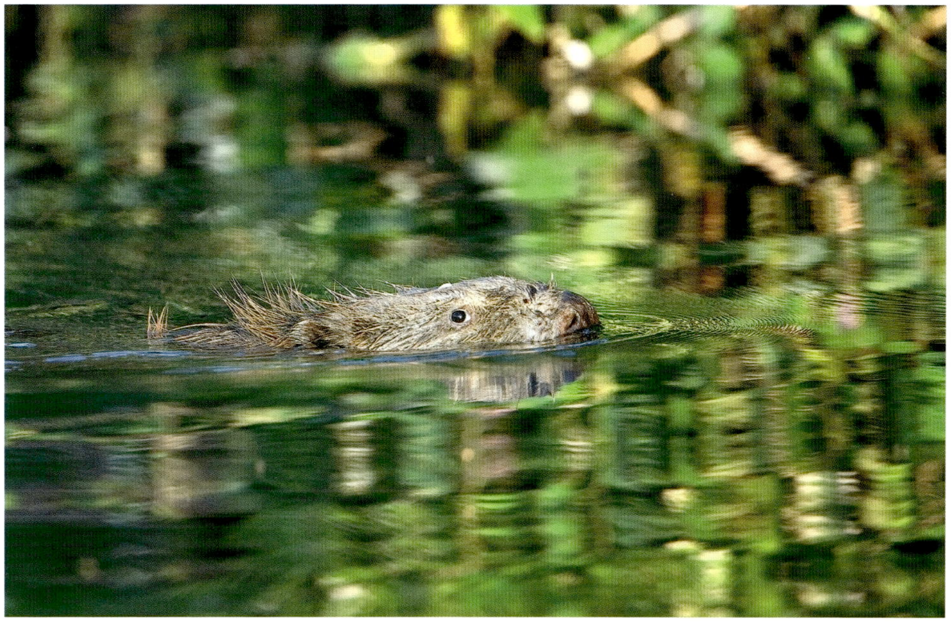

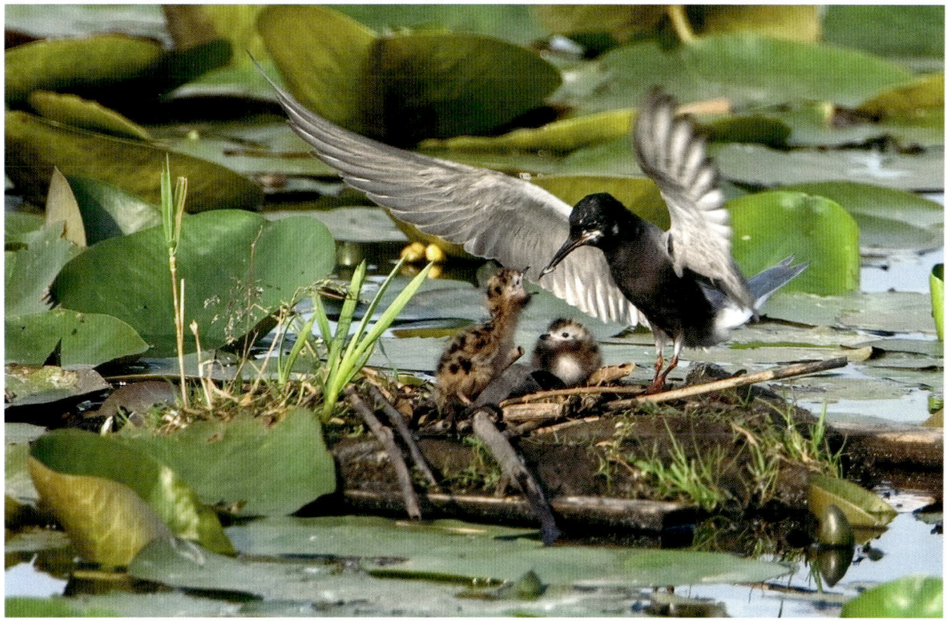

De Biesbosch

De Biesbosch is a beautiful national park with sand flats and mudflats, creeks, wild willow woods, reed beds, and many plant and animal species. The de-poldering of the surrounding land has ensured that this area has grown significantly and that it can also serve as an intended flood area as part of the Room for the River scheme.

Left: Exploring De Biesbosch in a kayak.

Top: A beaver swimming. Below: A black tern feeds its young at its nest in the Zouweboezem, a body of water in the polder of Alblasserwaard.

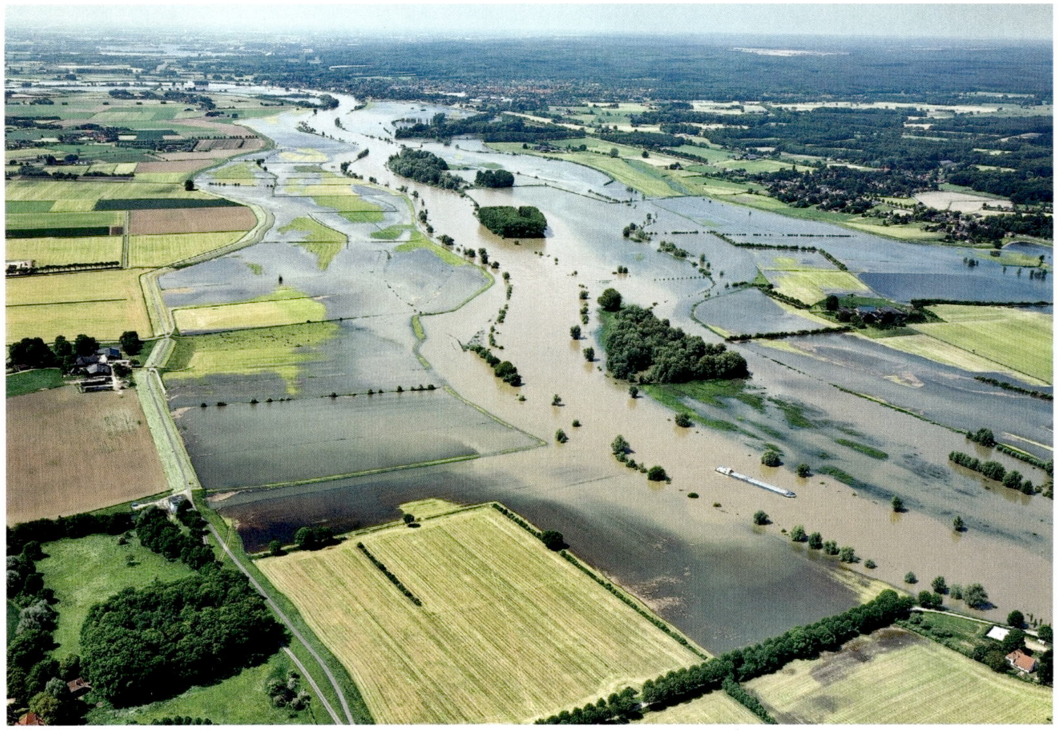

Rivers

Dutch rivers have traditionally served as transport and trade routes. At present, about half of our international transport is done by water. However, due to climate change, it has started raining more in the upper catchment areas. This means the rivers have more and more water to drain, which they do not always manage.

Top: Barge on the IJssel near Brummen at high tide.

Right: The Amerongen lock and dam complex in the Lower Rhine at high tide. When the water is high, the weirs open so that the excess water can drain away. Handy for the barges, as they then do not have to go through the lock.

Following pages: A passenger ferry crossing the Overijsselse Vecht river near Haerst.

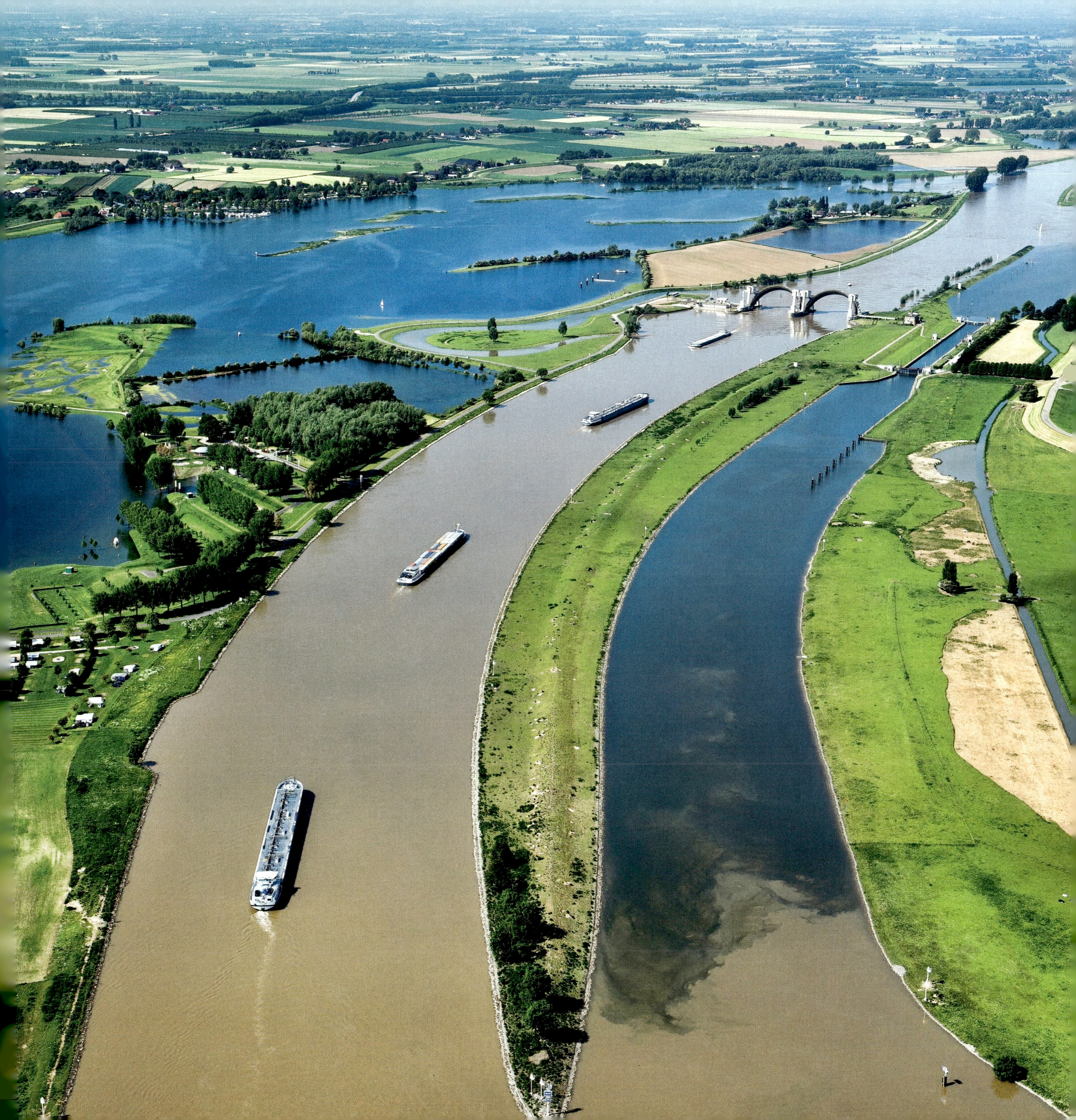

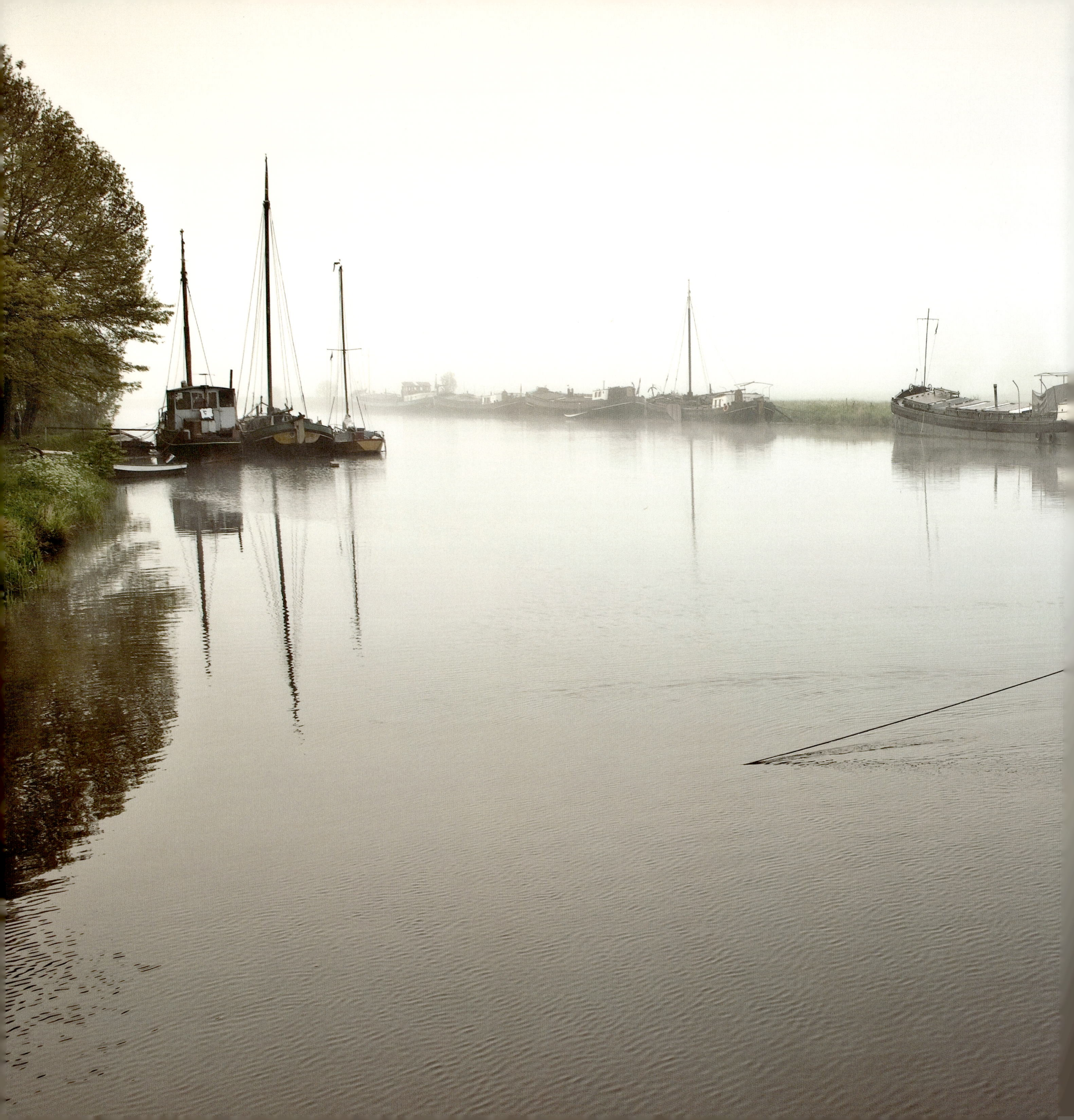

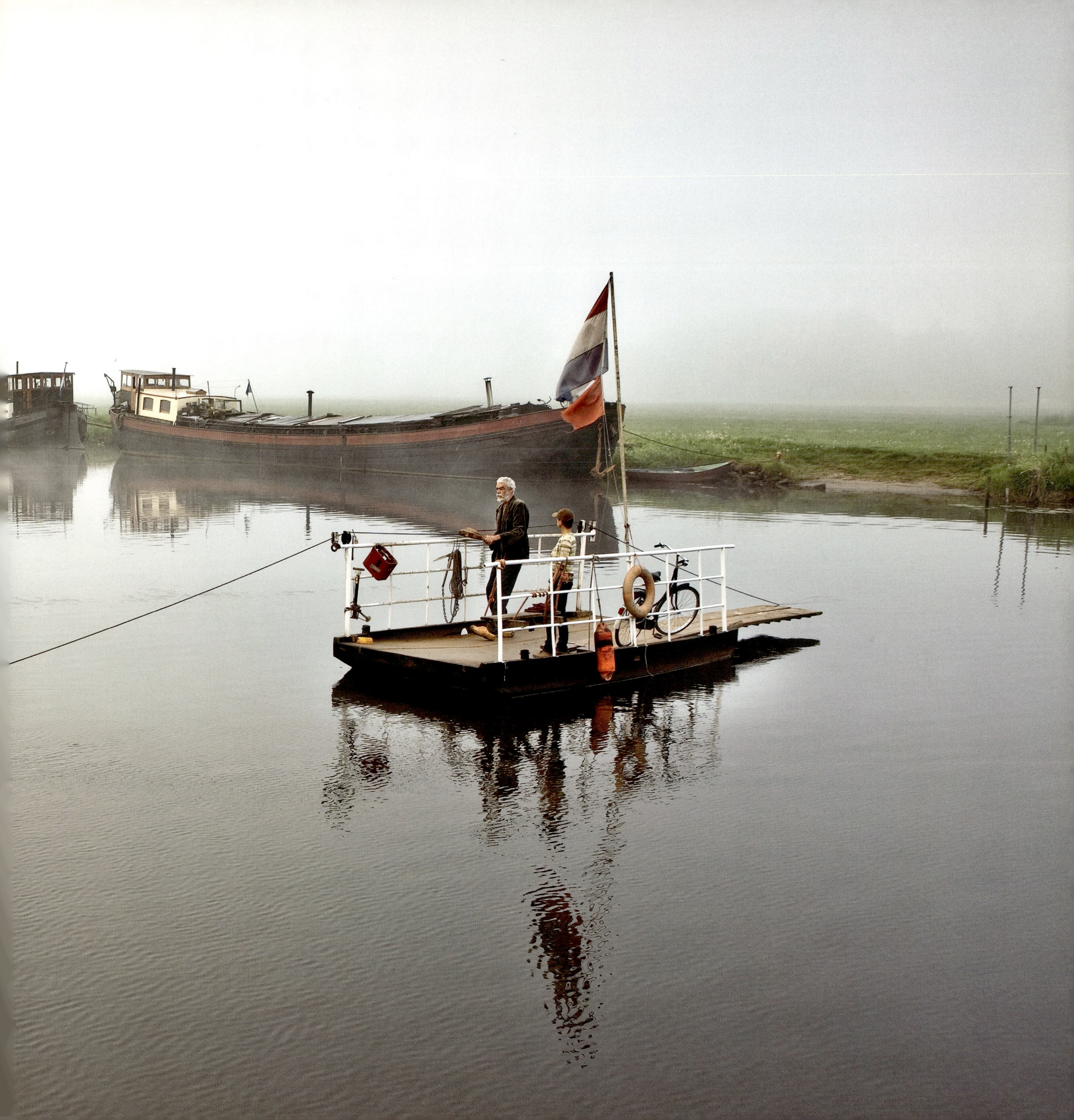

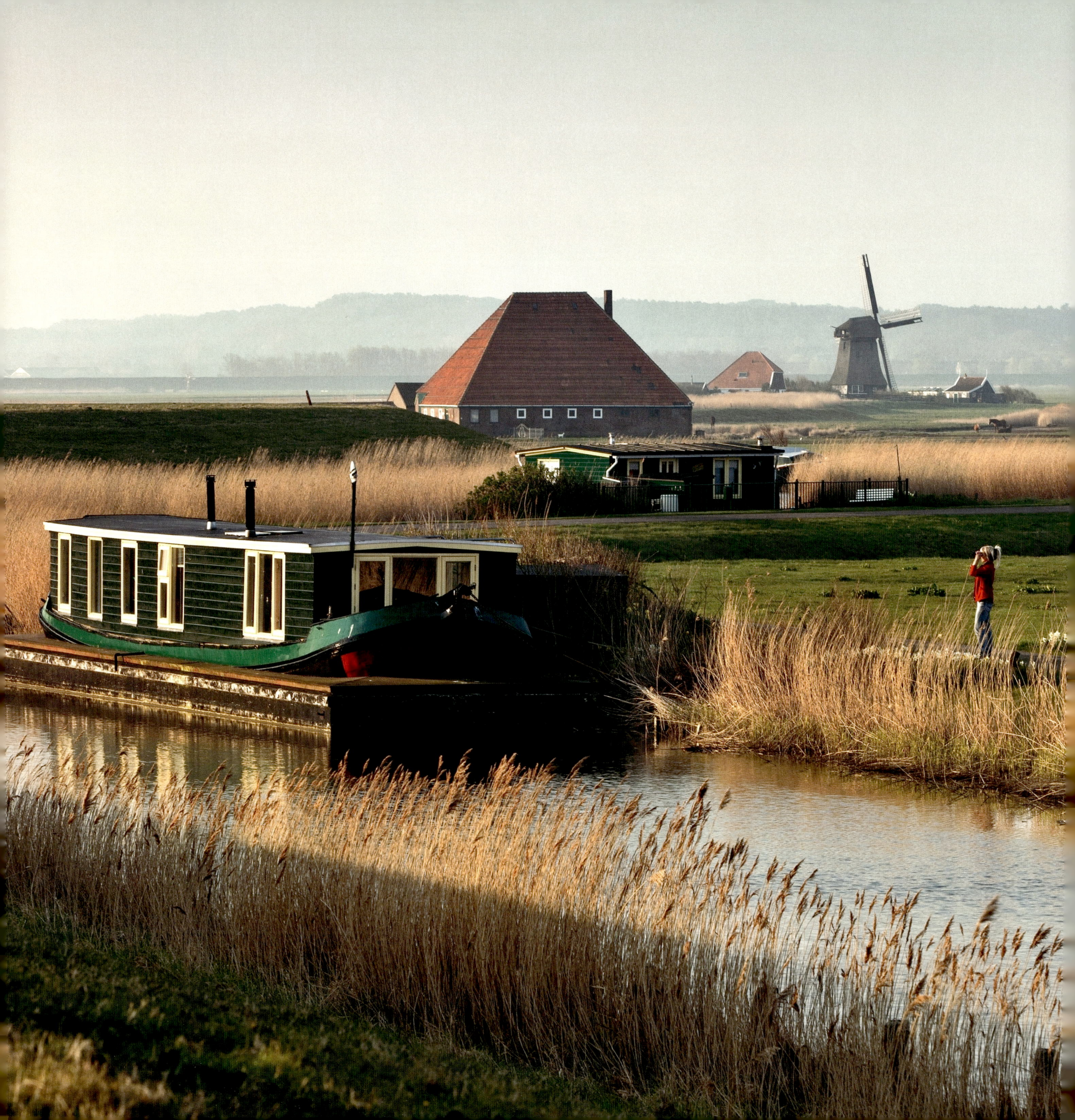

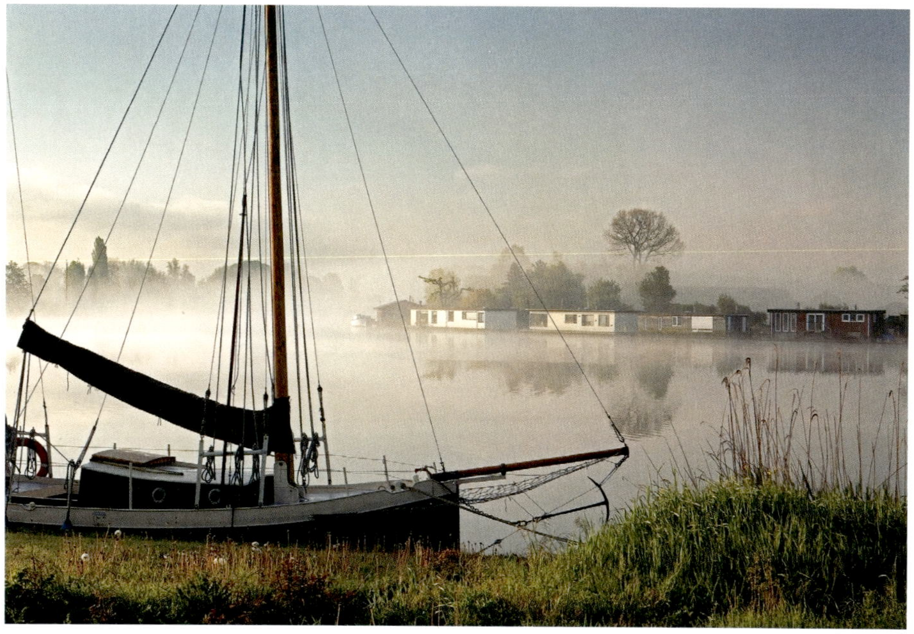

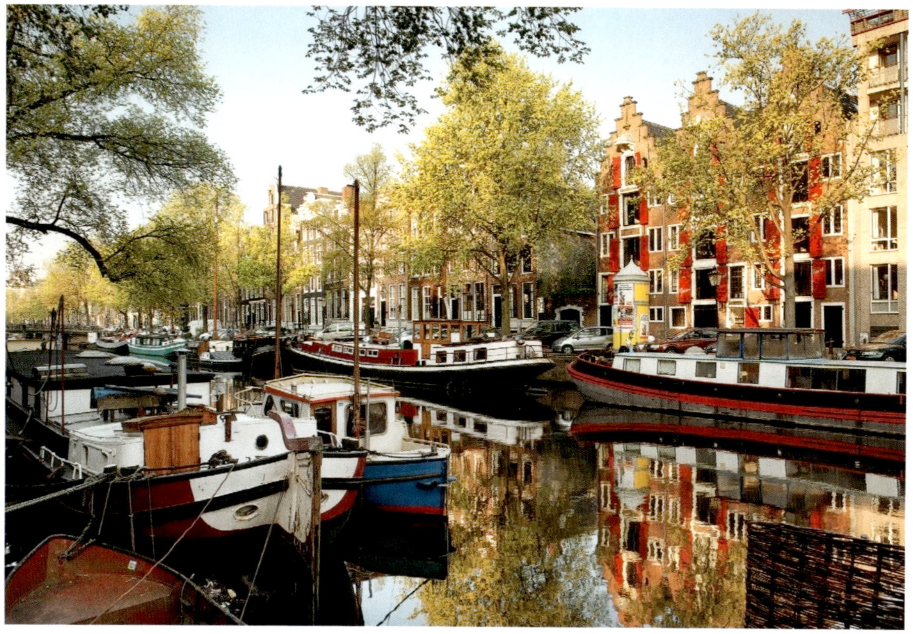

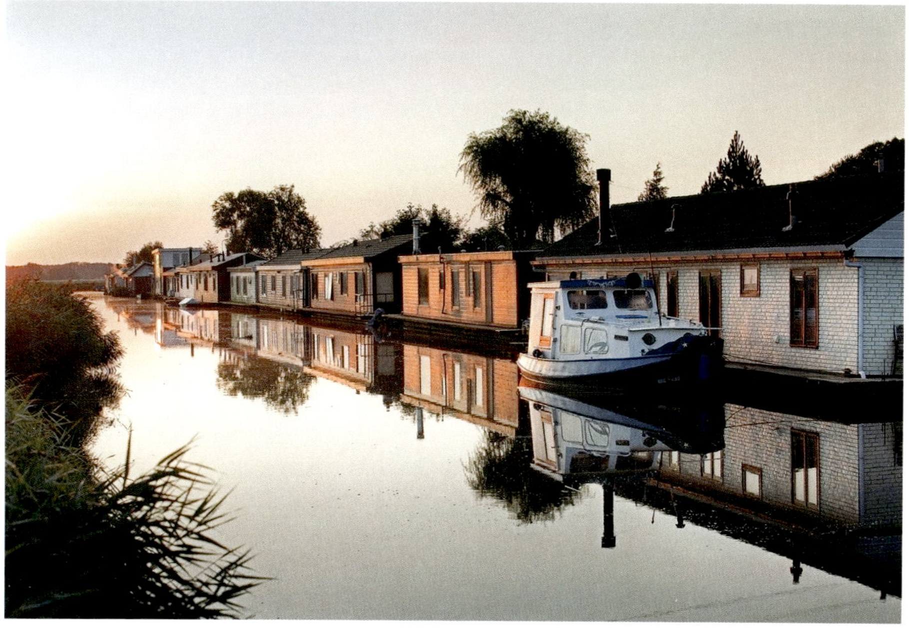

The houseboat

The Netherlands has about ten thousand official moorings for houseboats and an unknown number of other places where the authorities tolerate moorings. These are still far too few, because the houseboat is a very popular type of housing in the Netherlands.

Left: Houseboat in a channel of the Harger- en Pettemerpolder.

Top right: Beautiful moorings on the River Vecht in Weesp.

Centre: Houseboats on the Keizersgracht in Amsterdam, where a total of about 2,500 houseboats are tied up.

Below right: Living on the water, near the hamlet of Neck on the edge of the Wijdewormer Polder.

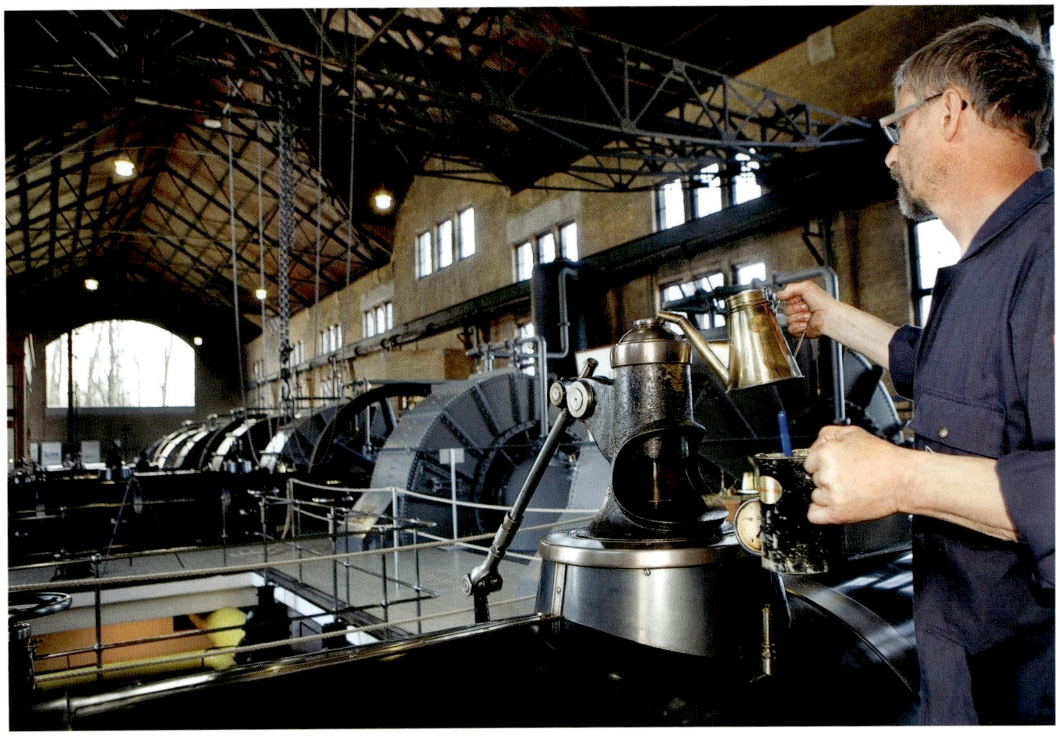

Woudagemaal

The Woudagemaal, near the Frisian town of Lemmer, is the largest steam-powered pumping station in the world that still operates. Take a look (top and right) at the exterior and interior, and you will immediately recognise the characteristics of the Amsterdam School. In the huge machine hall, four sturdy machines with huge flywheels recall earlier times. It takes a great deal of coordination to run a pumping station at full speed. A team of at least eleven people is needed to fill the boilers, to bring the stoking oil up to temperature, and to start up the eight pumps. A process that can easily take six hours. The Woudagemaal came into service in 1920 and is now a UNESCO World Heritage Site. The construction of the pumping station was necessary because the natural discharge of water through locks was no longer sufficient. Even nowadays, the Woudagemaal is used to lower the level of the Frisian waterways, but only during extreme high tides.

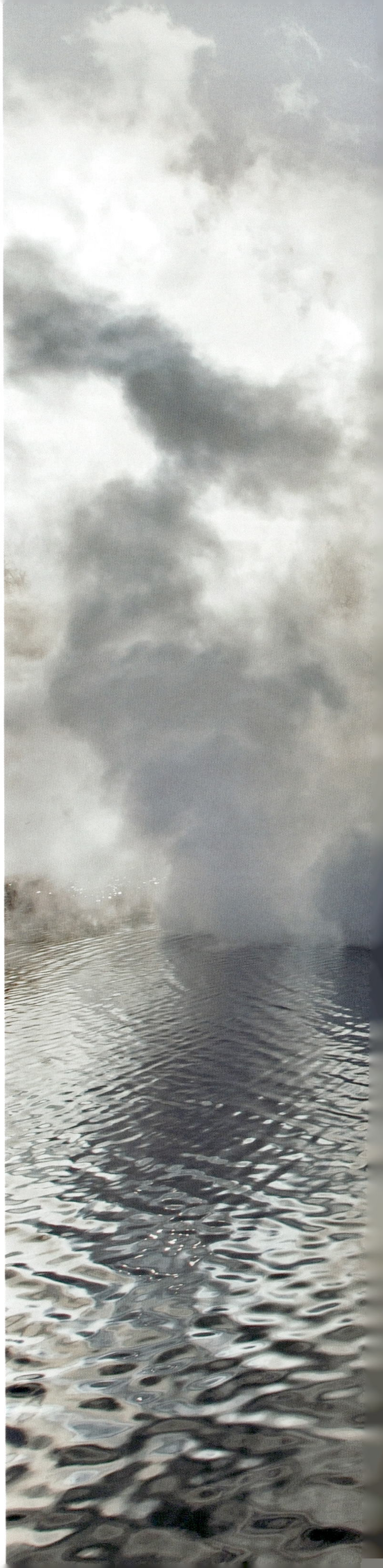

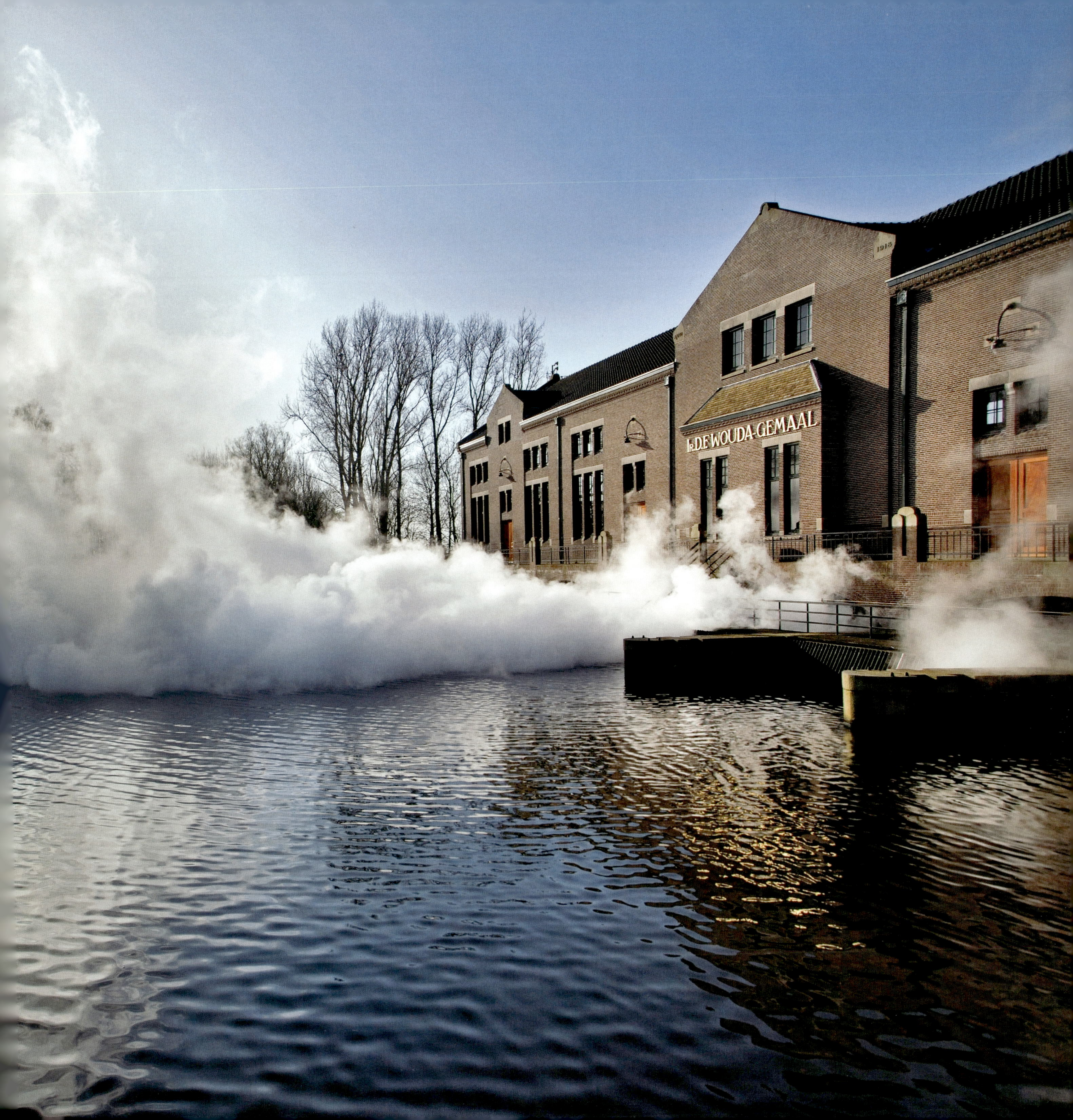
Ir.D.F.WOUDA-GEMAAL

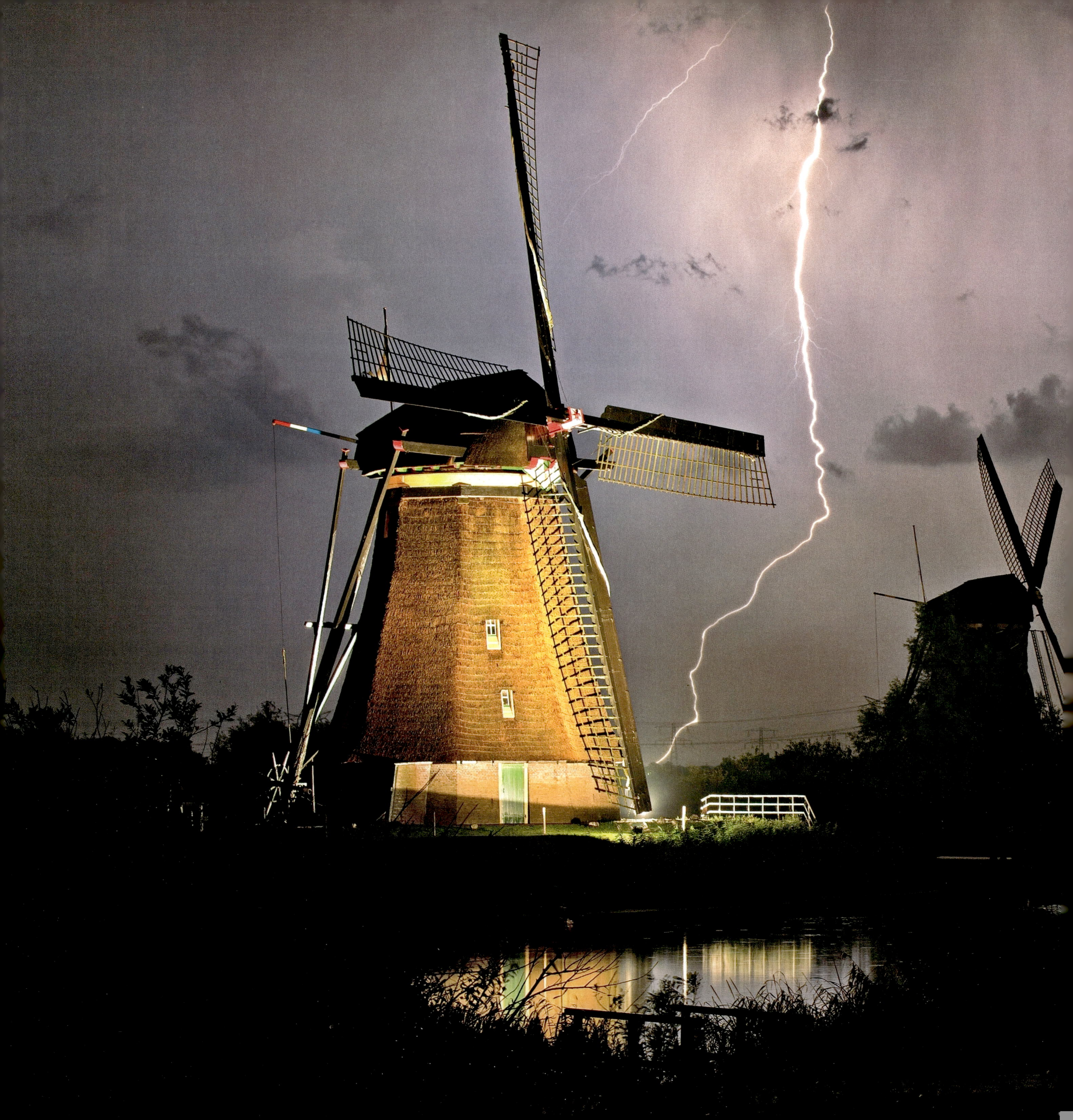

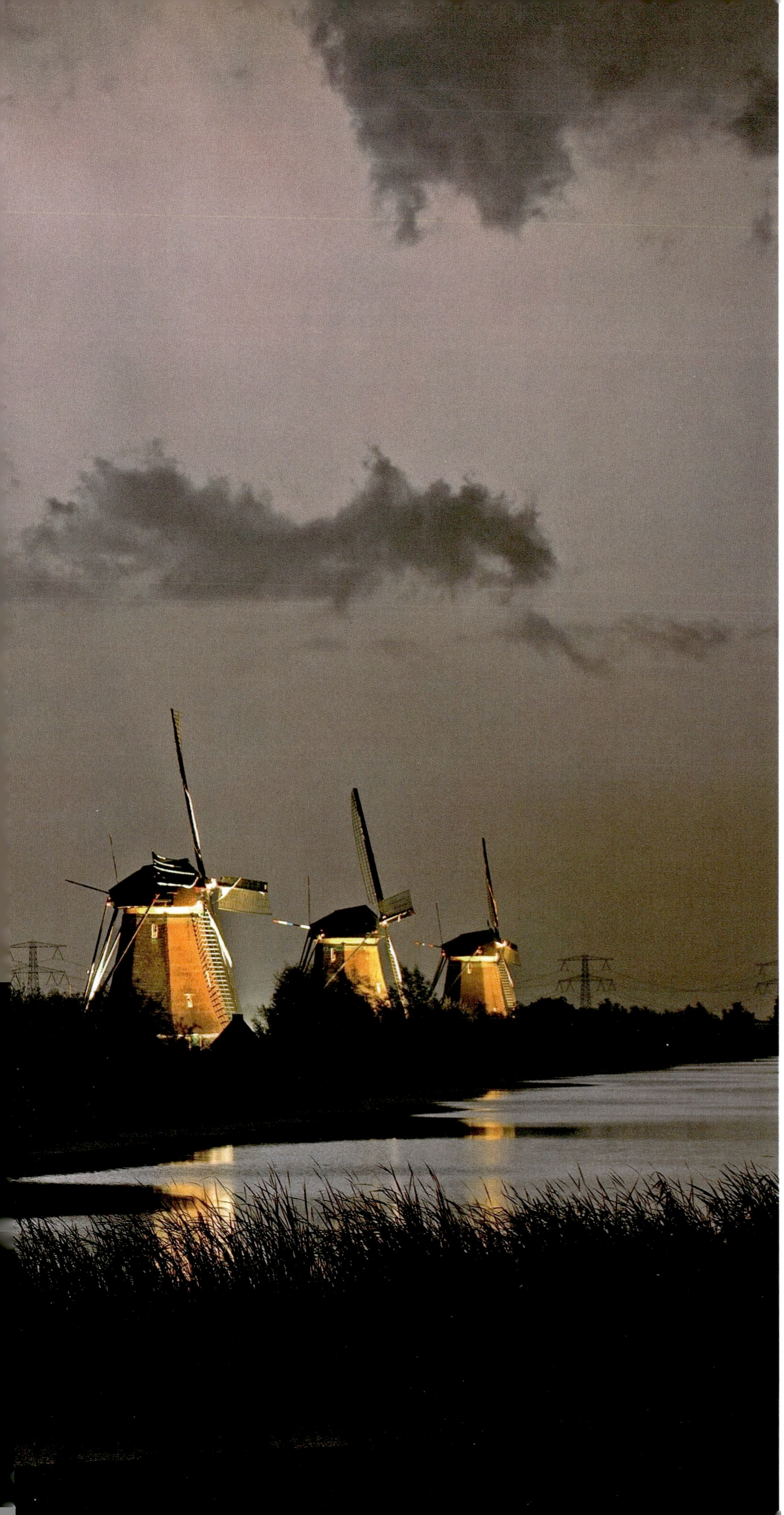

Kinderdijk
For many foreigners, the Netherlands is windmill territory par excellence. Not surprising when we think of the history of the creation of the numerous polder landscapes. We think of the mill complex in Kinderdijk-Elshout, for instance. Nowhere else are there so many mills in one place as in this stretch of the Alblasserwaard (left). The nineteen polder mills (drainage windmills), which were built between 1738 and 1740, ensured with their solid sails and powerful blades that the excess water of the Alblasserwaard was discharged into the River Lek. Although the polder mills are perfectly preserved and can still turn, they are now no longer required for drainage. As tourist highlights, the windmills of Kinderdijk, a UNESCO World Heritage Site, epitomise the struggle of the Dutch against the water.

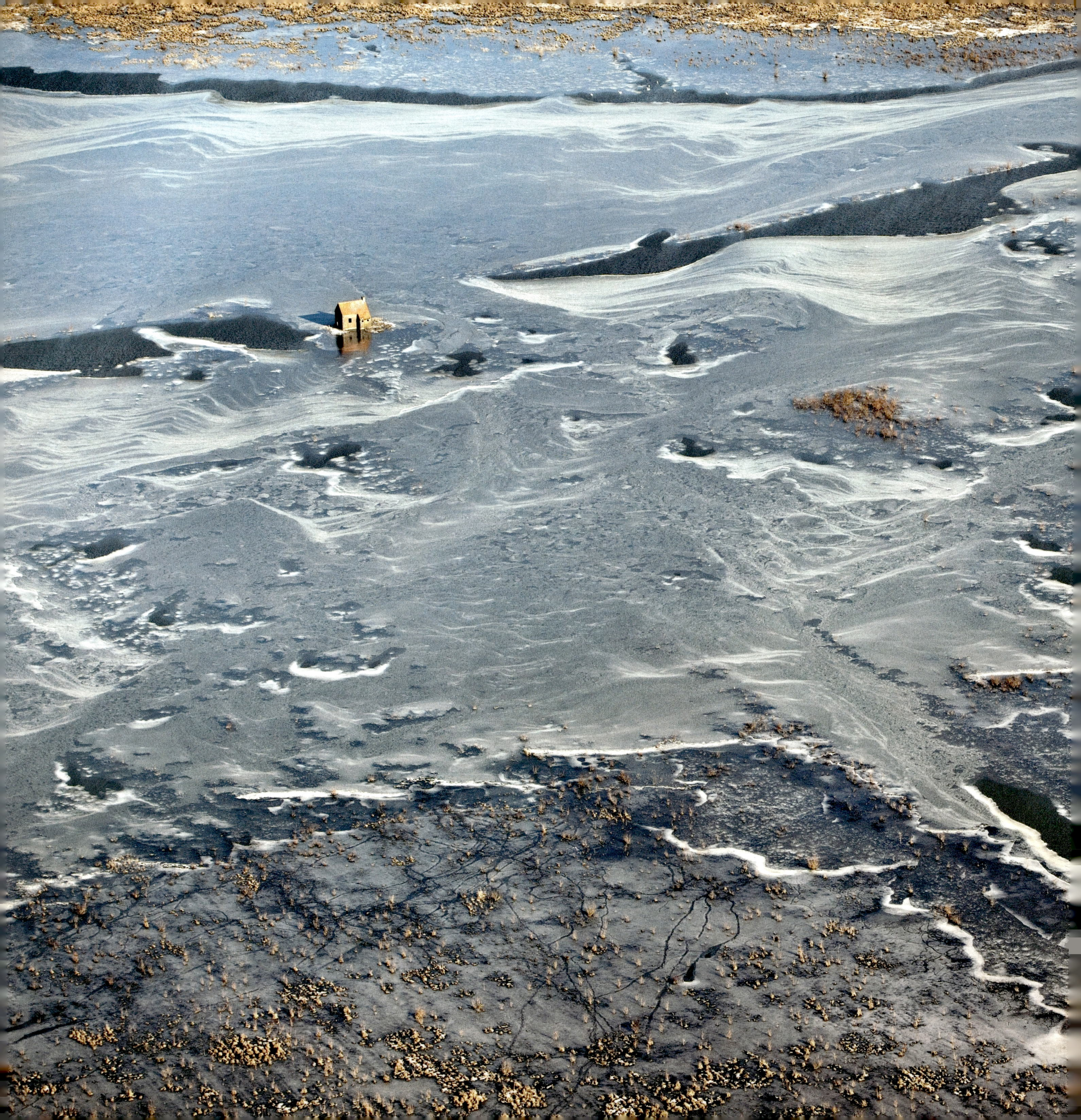

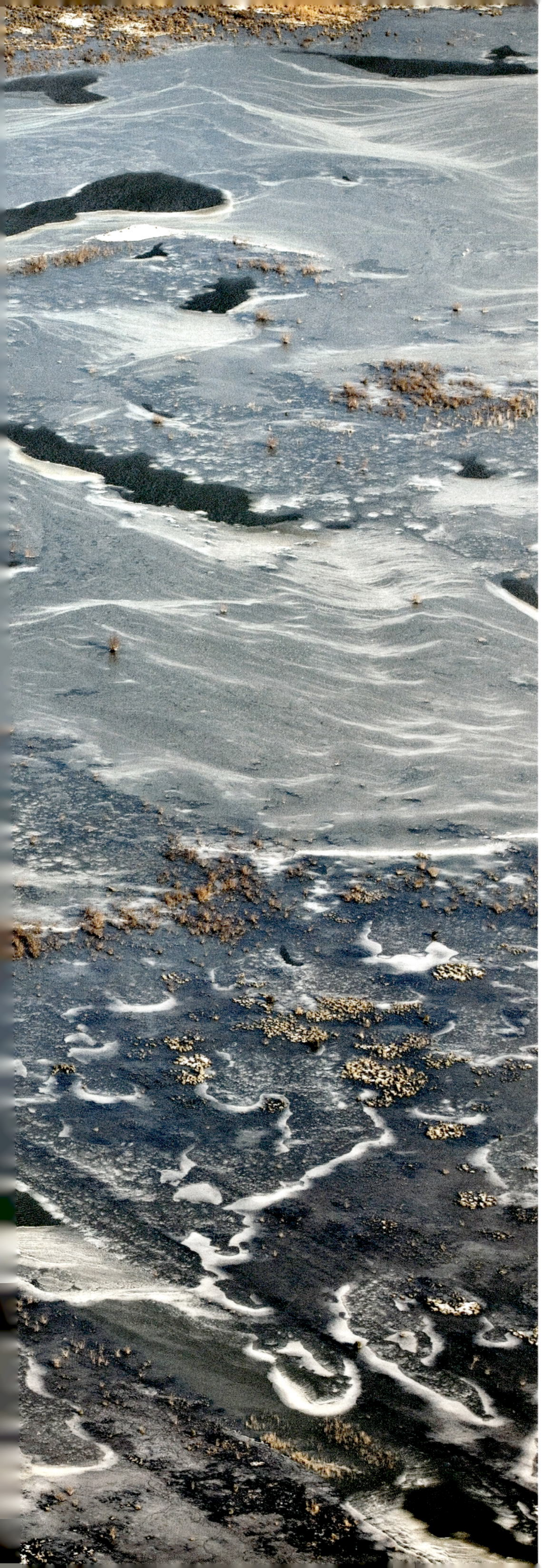

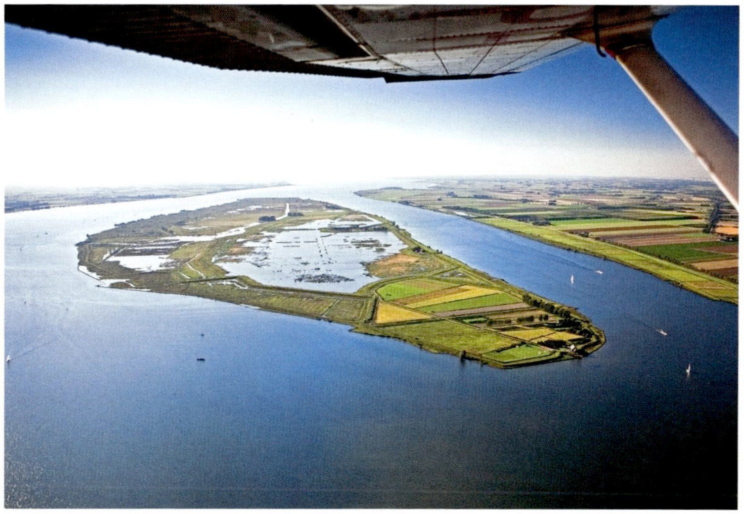

Tiengemeten

Tiengemeten is a special island in the Haringvliet estuary. In the East Indies Company (VOC) days, it was a quarantine island for ships returning from the Orient bound for Dordrecht and Rotterdam. Later it was used for agricultural purposes and, since 1997, it has been redeveloped as a nature reserve.

Left: A deserted shed, surrounded by ice.

Top: Half of the island is now occupied once again by the water.

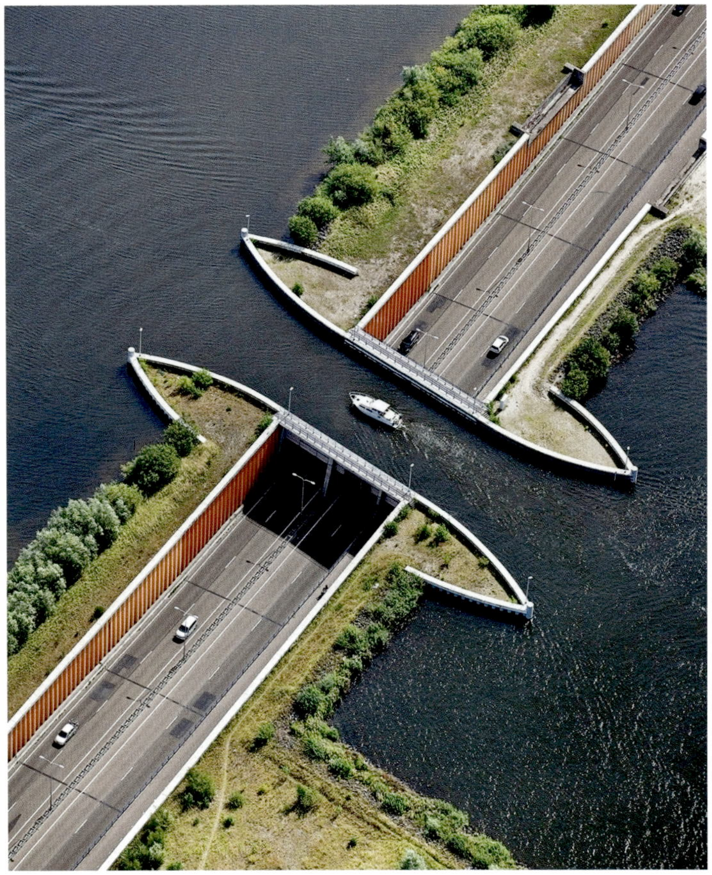

Top: A yacht sailing across an aqueduct to Harderwijk.

Right: Northern entrance of the Zeeburgertunnel that connects the Amsterdam-Noord and Amsterdam-Oost urban districts.

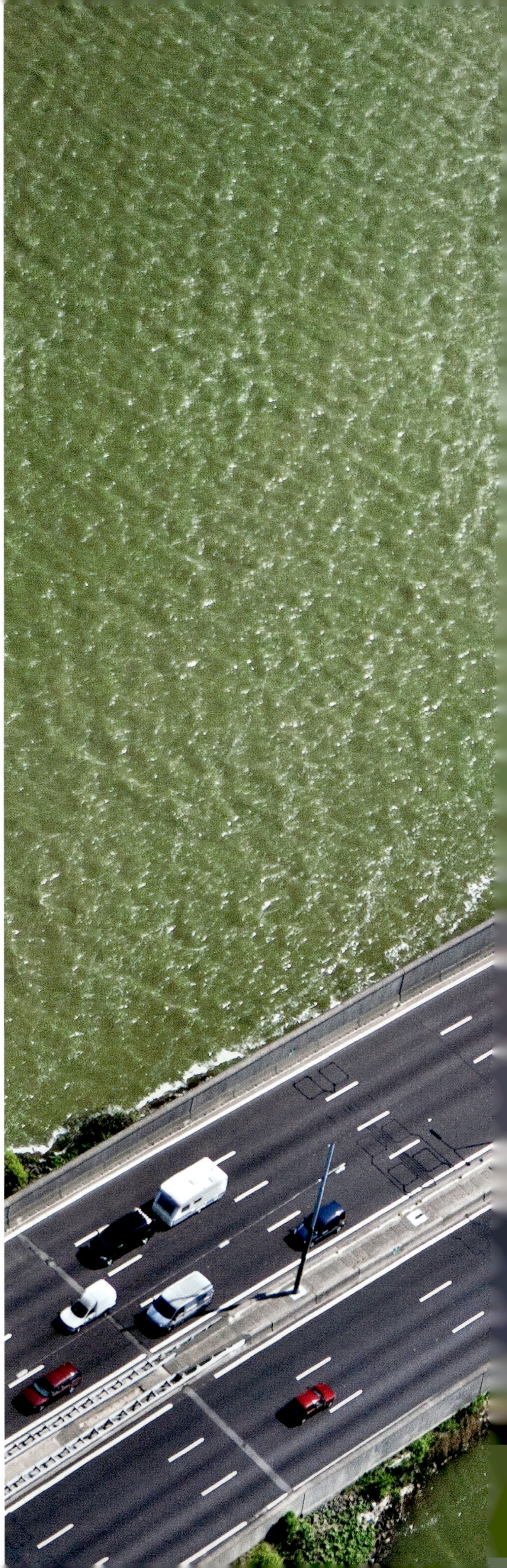

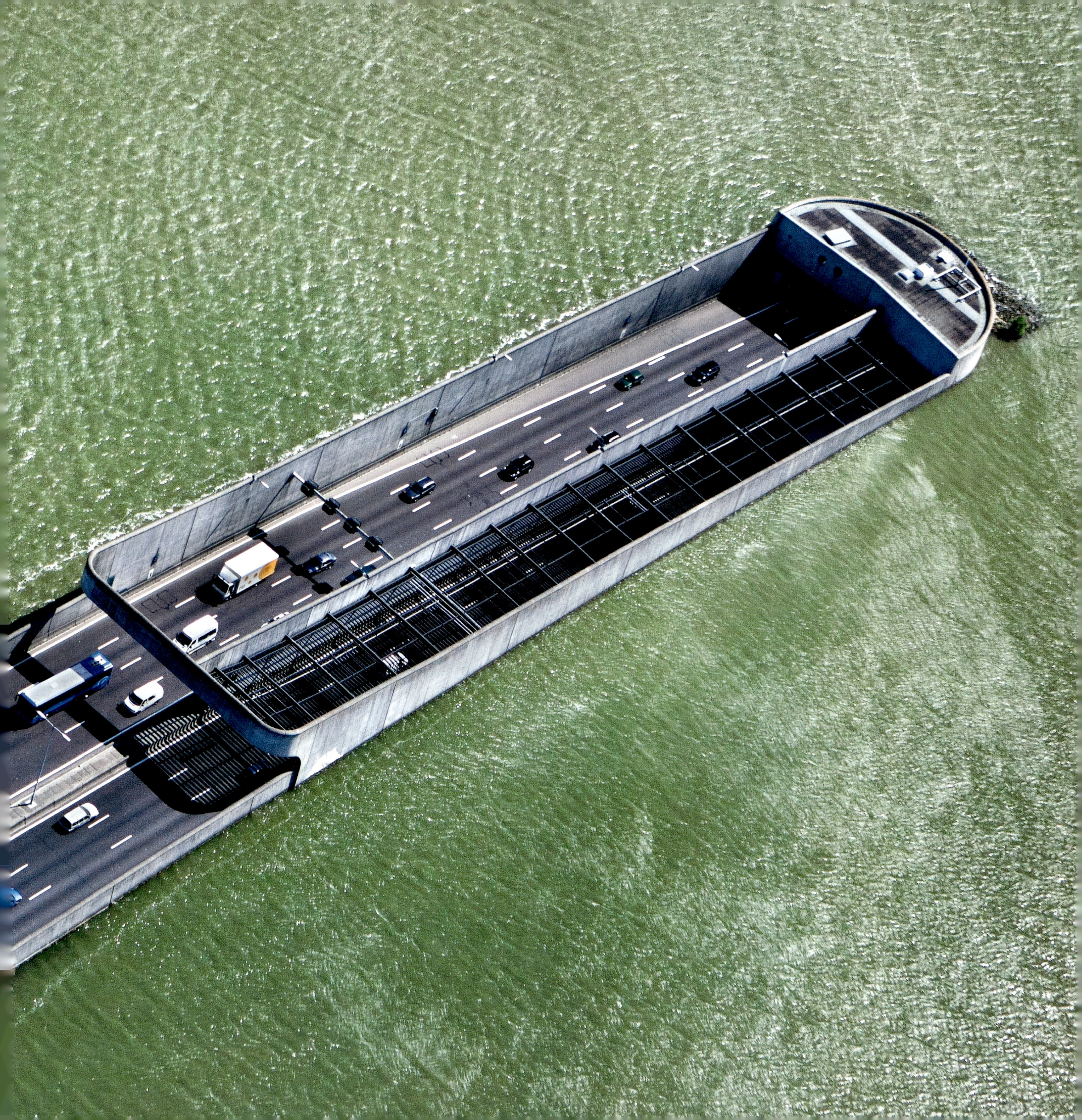

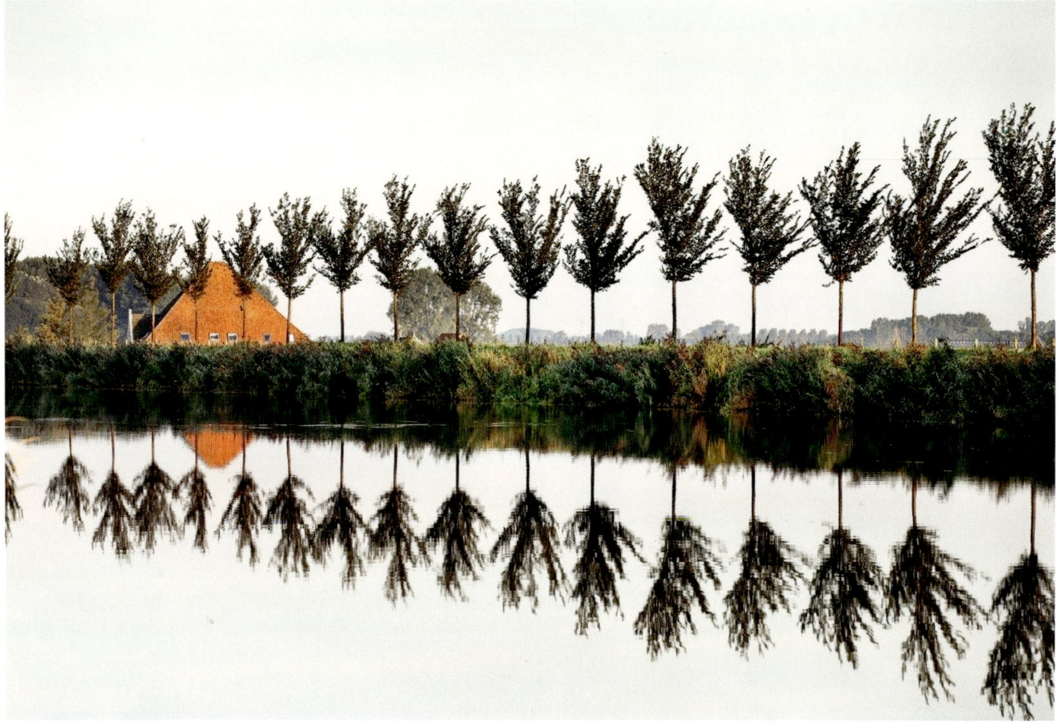

Beemster Polder

Many of the Dutch sites on the UNESCO World Heritage List have to do with combating water. This is also true of the Beemster Polder in Noord-Holland. The area was – due to the need for more agricultural land and estates – drained in 1612 by Jan Adriaan Leeghwater, whose very surname means 'Empty Water'. This was done with the aid of 43 drainage windmills (polder mills), making the Beemster the first large-scale landscaping project in the world. From this period, the area derives its distinctive plot structure, untouched over the centuries, which cuts through the landscape in pure squares. The fertile soil ensured that the Beemster was an immediate economic success. Even after the reclamation, fifty mills were needed to keep the polder dry. In the early twentieth century, these mills were replaced by pumping stations.

Top: Farm in the Beemster Polder behind the dike of the North Holland Canal.

Right: This aerial view of Middenbeemster shows the structure of the Beemster Polder well.

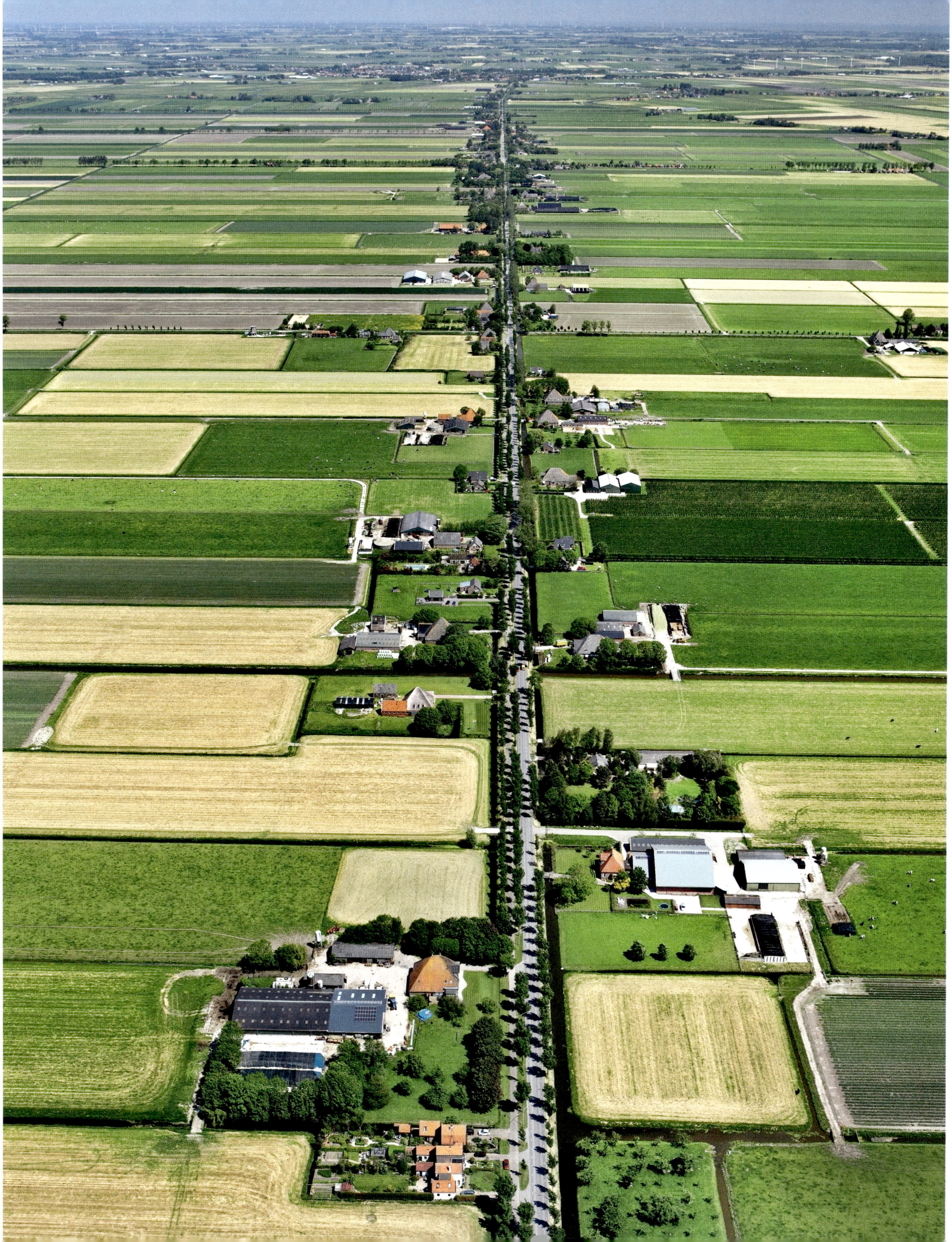

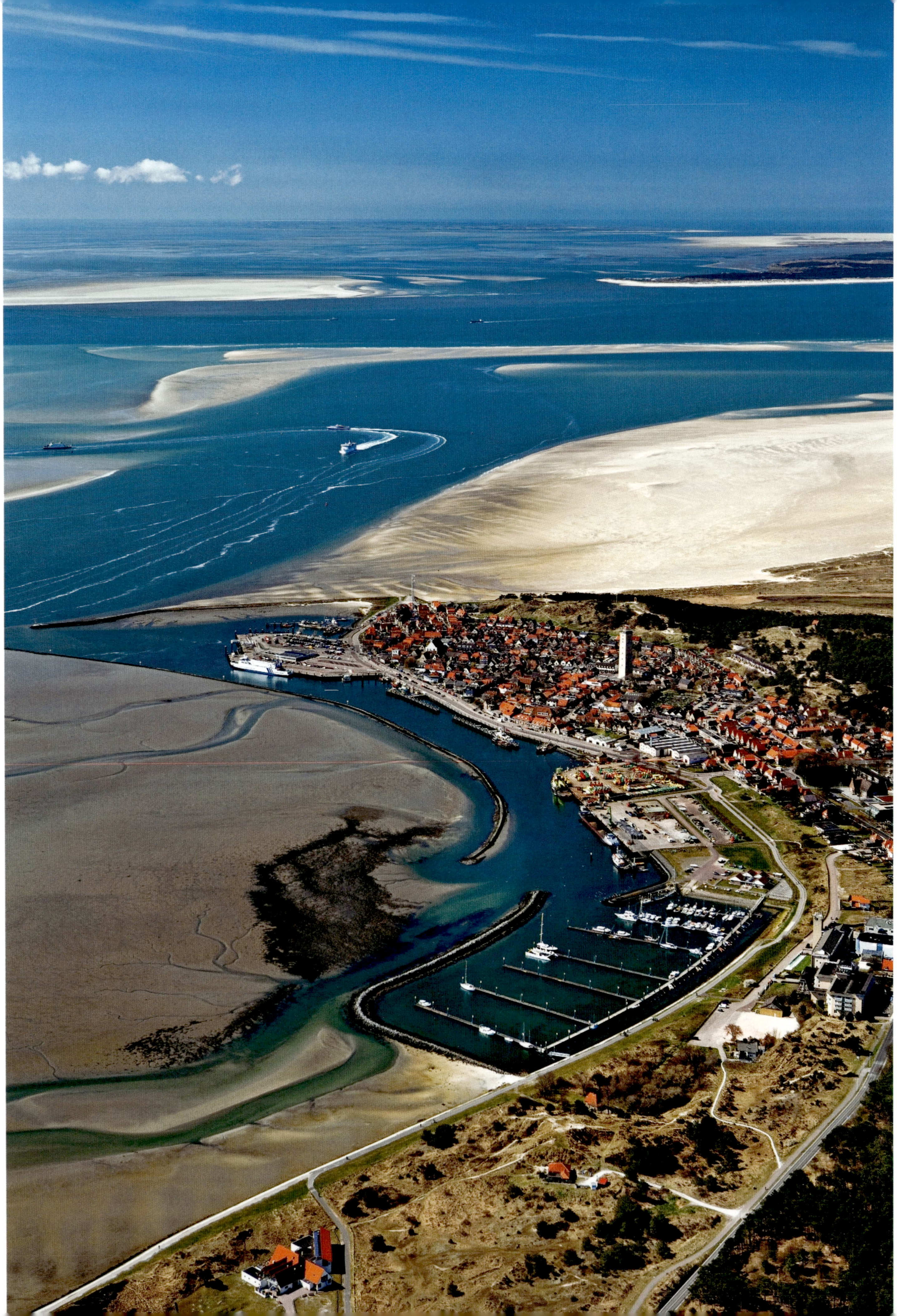

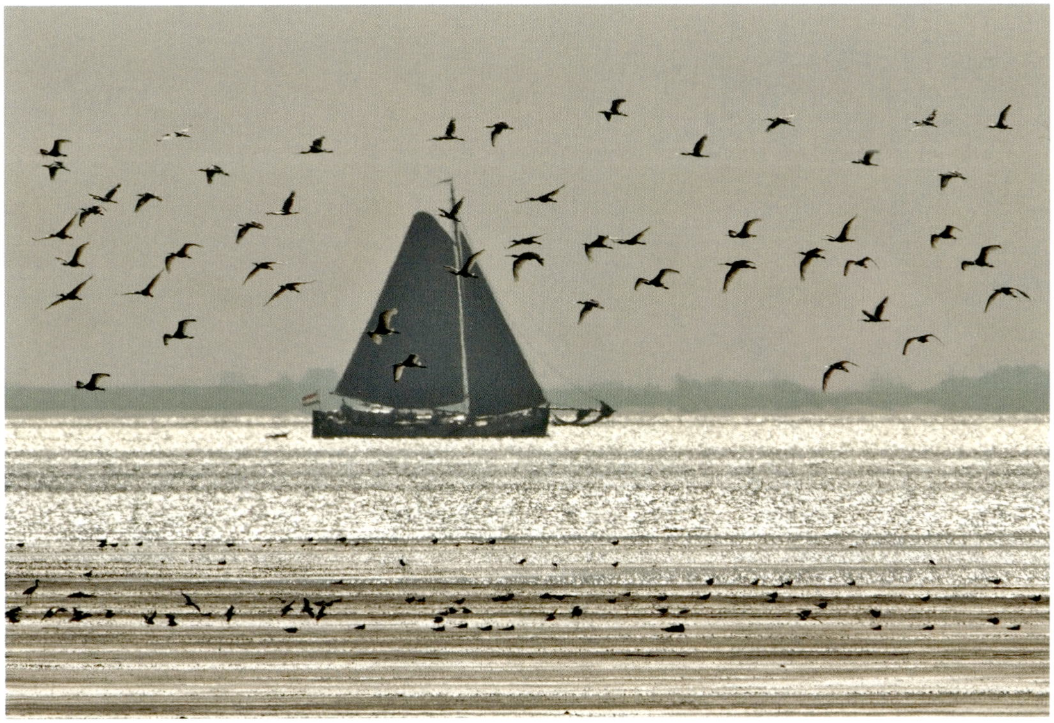

Wadden Sea

The Wadden Islands seem an oasis of peace, but in reality the archipelago bustles with all kinds of natural activities. For instance, the area provides no fewer than ten thousand terrestrial and aquatic species with their temporary or permanent habitats, and it is an annual major stopping point for some twelve million birds on their way to exotic places. Unique to the Wadden area is that it is constantly subject to change by the continuing influence of freshwater and saltwater, wind and tidal currents. The sand flats, salt marshes and channels constantly take on new forms. Animals, plants and people always manage to adapt to the shifting environment. But what always remains constant is that, rarely for the Netherlands, this is an area of expanses. This lends the Wadden area its own identity. Since 2009, the Wadden Sea has been on the UNESCO World Heritage List.

Left: The port of West-Terschelling at low tide. Ferries manoeuvring towards the harbour.

Top: A flock of spoonbills flying ahead of a sailboat off the island of Ameland.

Following pages: Not all islands are inhabited. There are a number of small islands, sandbars, which mainly serve as a breeding ground for birds and refuge for seals. They are not accessible to tourists. In the picture, the islet of Rottumerplaat, the northernmost point of the Netherlands, with a watchtower for birdwatchers and a few storage barns being the only constructions.

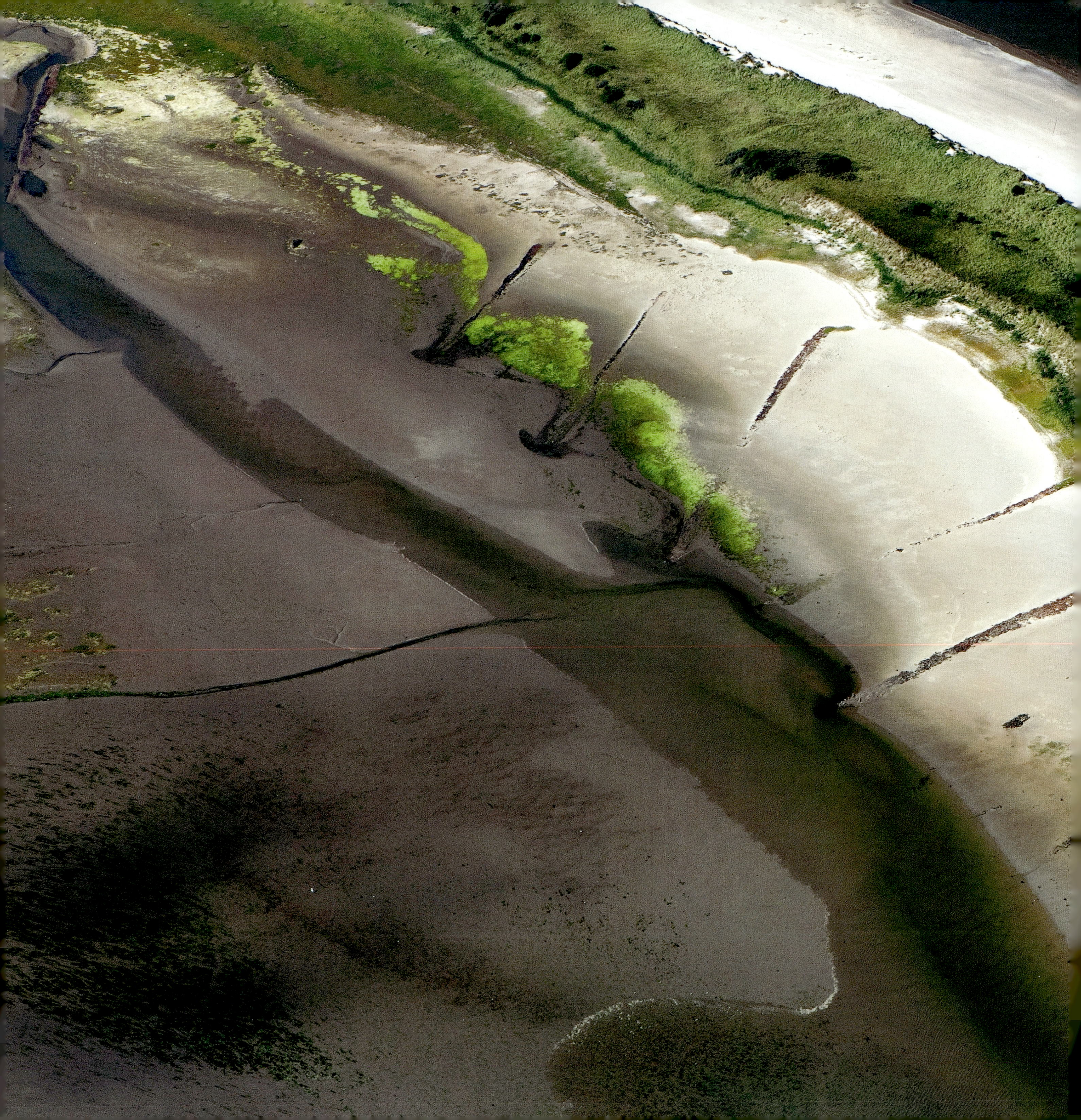

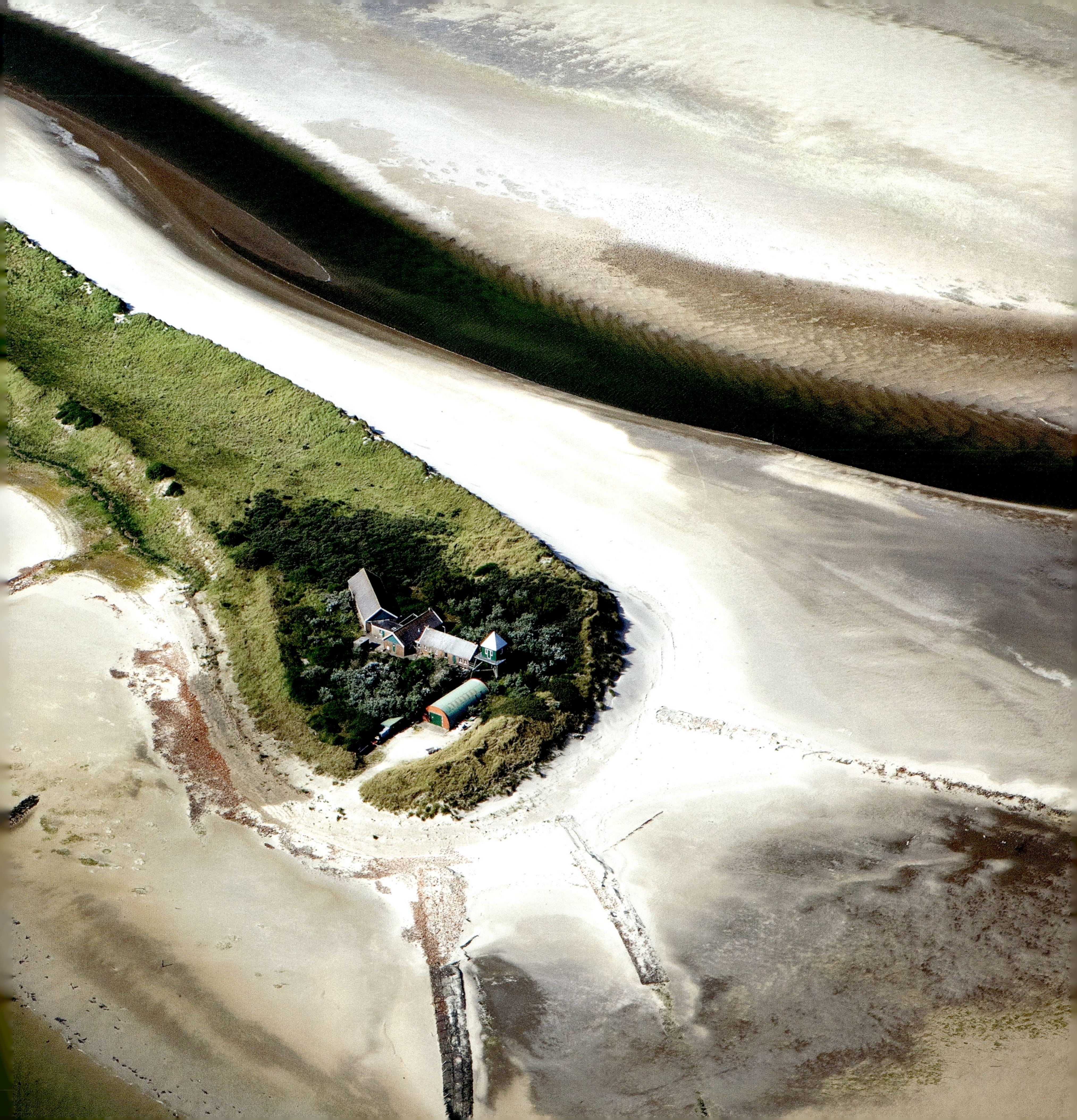

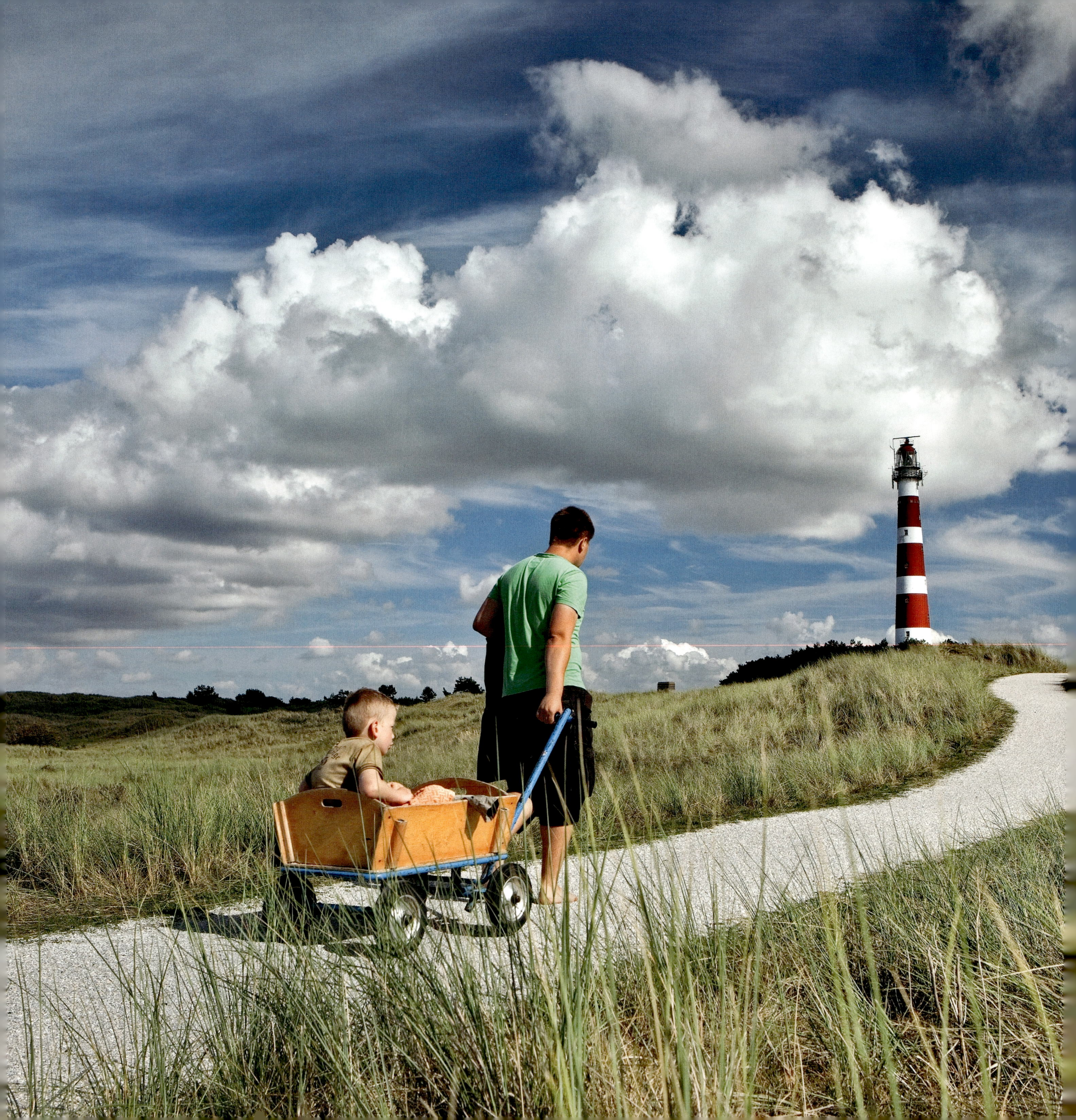

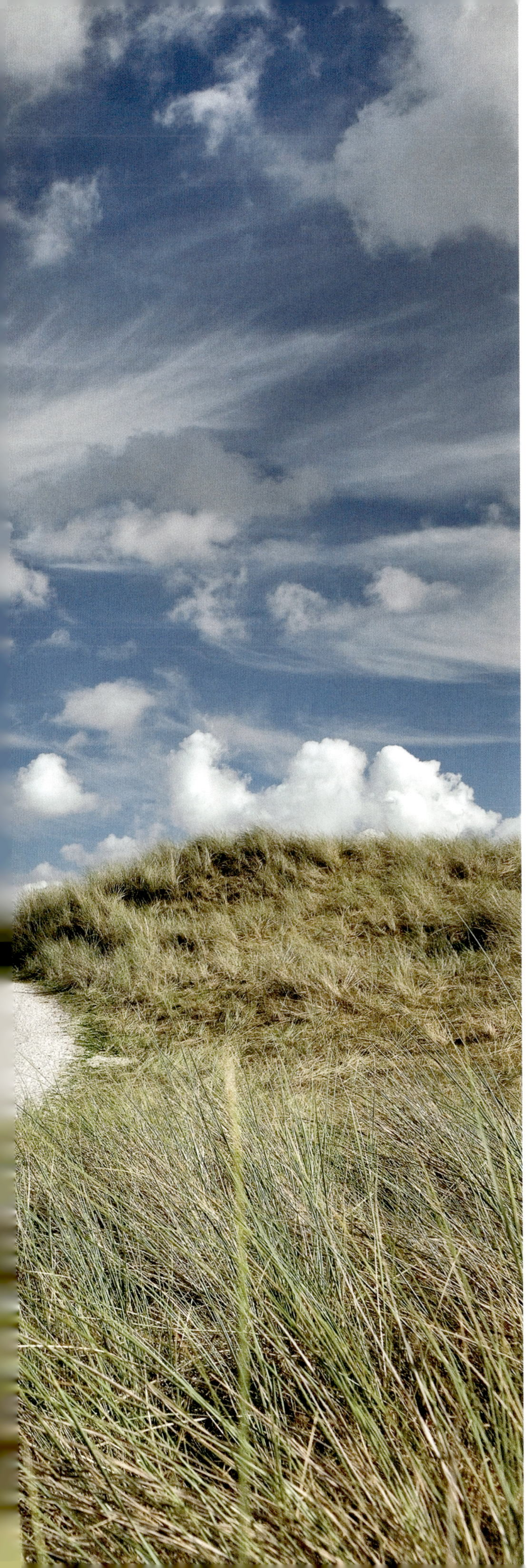

Left: The island of Ameland. A man and his son coming off the beach. In the background, the 55 metre-high, cast-iron lighthouse from 1880. The tower is open to the public.

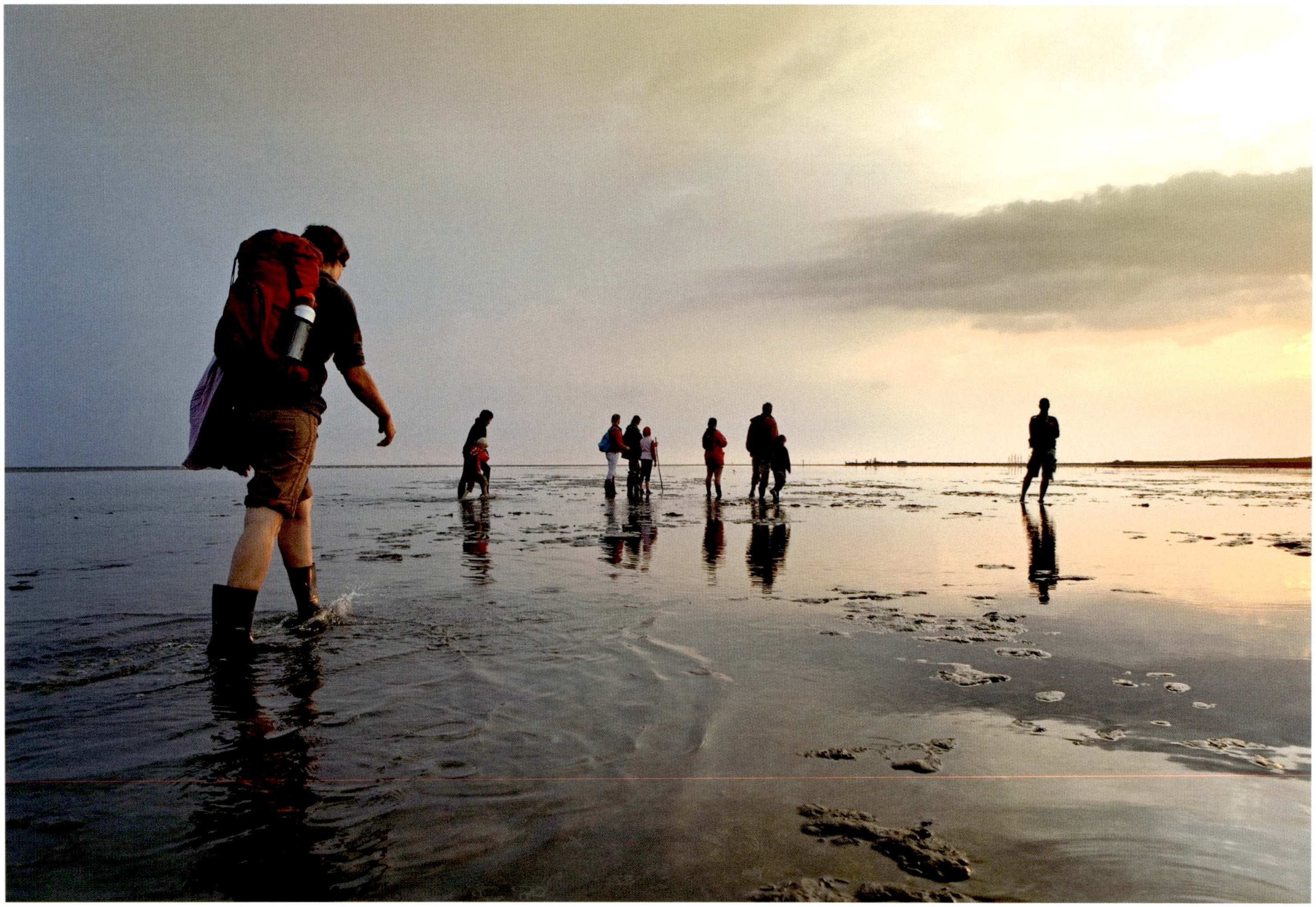

Top: It is possible to walk from the mainland to one of the Wadden islands at low tide. Some haste is advised, because if the tide comes in before the other side is reached, it will not be the first time this has happened to anyone.

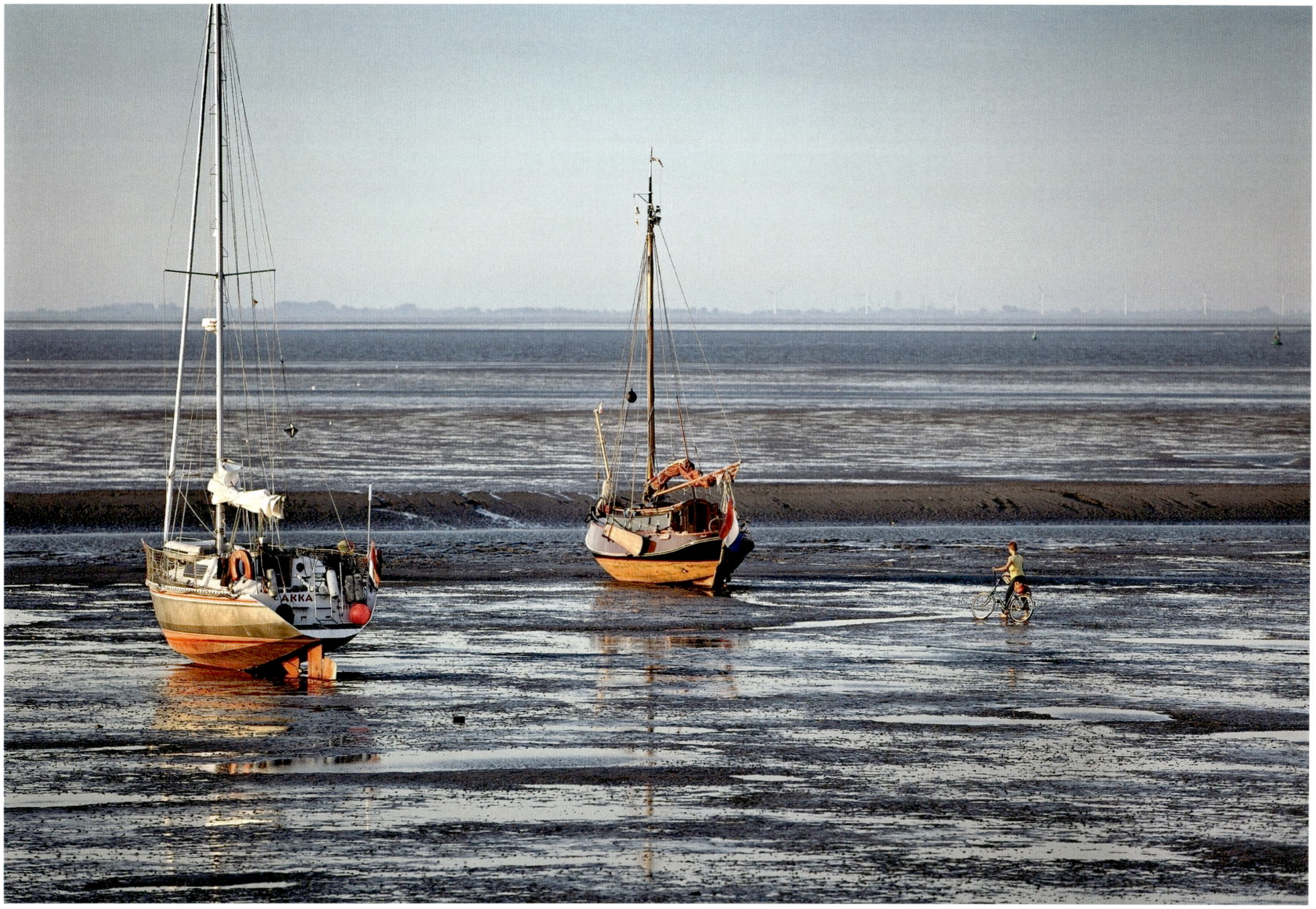

Top: Sailboats dried up on the flats in the port of Nes on Ameland. A sailor taking the opportunity to go ashore on her bike.

Following pages: Aerial view of salt marsh at Schiermonnikoog. Salt marshes are found on the border between land and sea. They are vegetation-covered salty or brackish areas, outside the dikes, that are dry at low tide and may be flooded at high water.

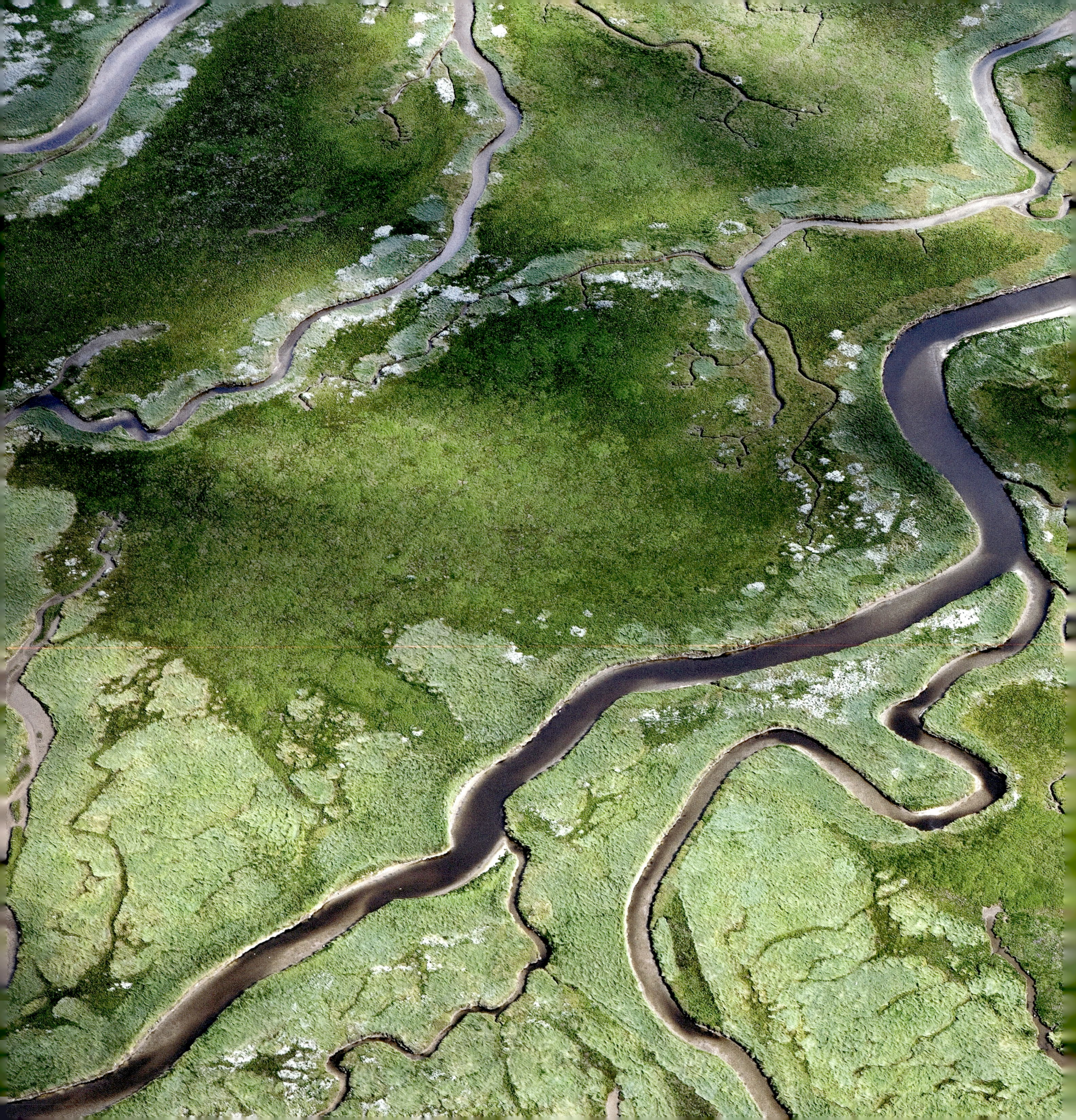

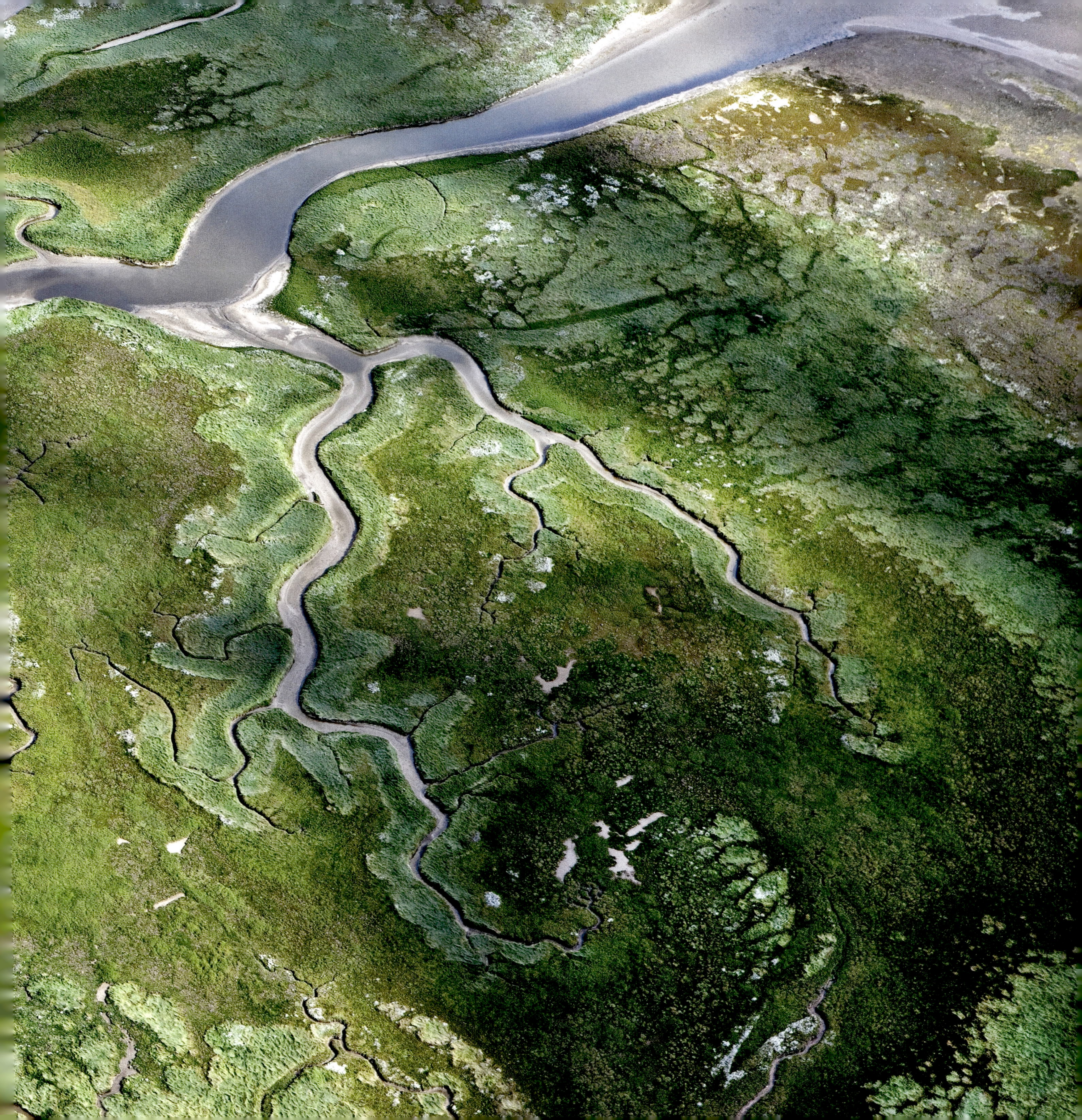

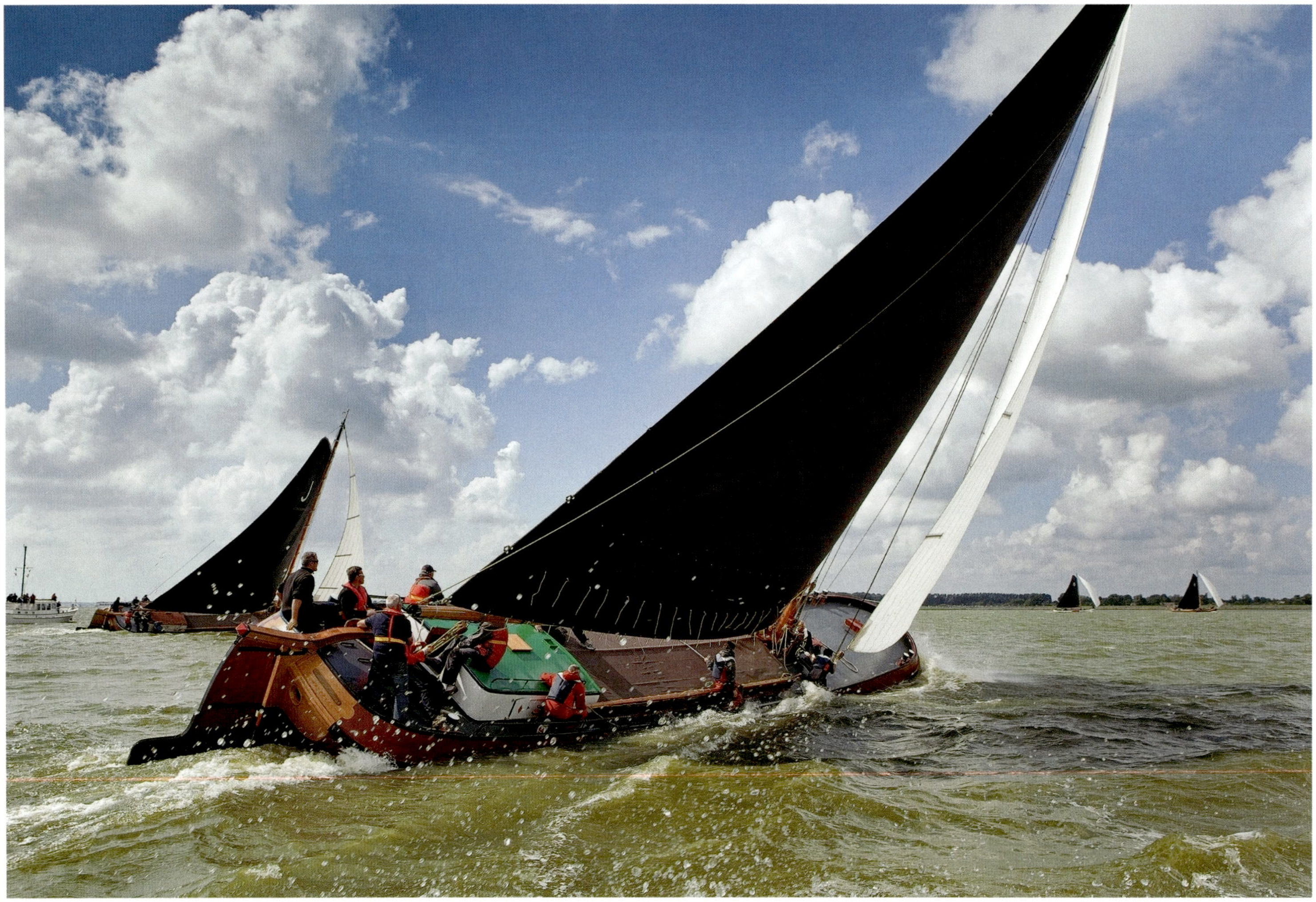

Sailing
Wind power has always been the engine that the Dutch used to tame the rivers and seas – partly out of curiosity but mainly due to economic, political and military motives. Today we sail purely for sport and relaxation. Sometimes, that recreation takes on huge proportions. For instance, each August on the Sneekermeer lake in Frisia, we have Sneekweek – the biggest sailing event on inland waters in Europe.

Top and right: Particularly famous is the Skûtsjesilen: races with traditional flat-bottomed boats. These races have been held since the early nineteenth century.

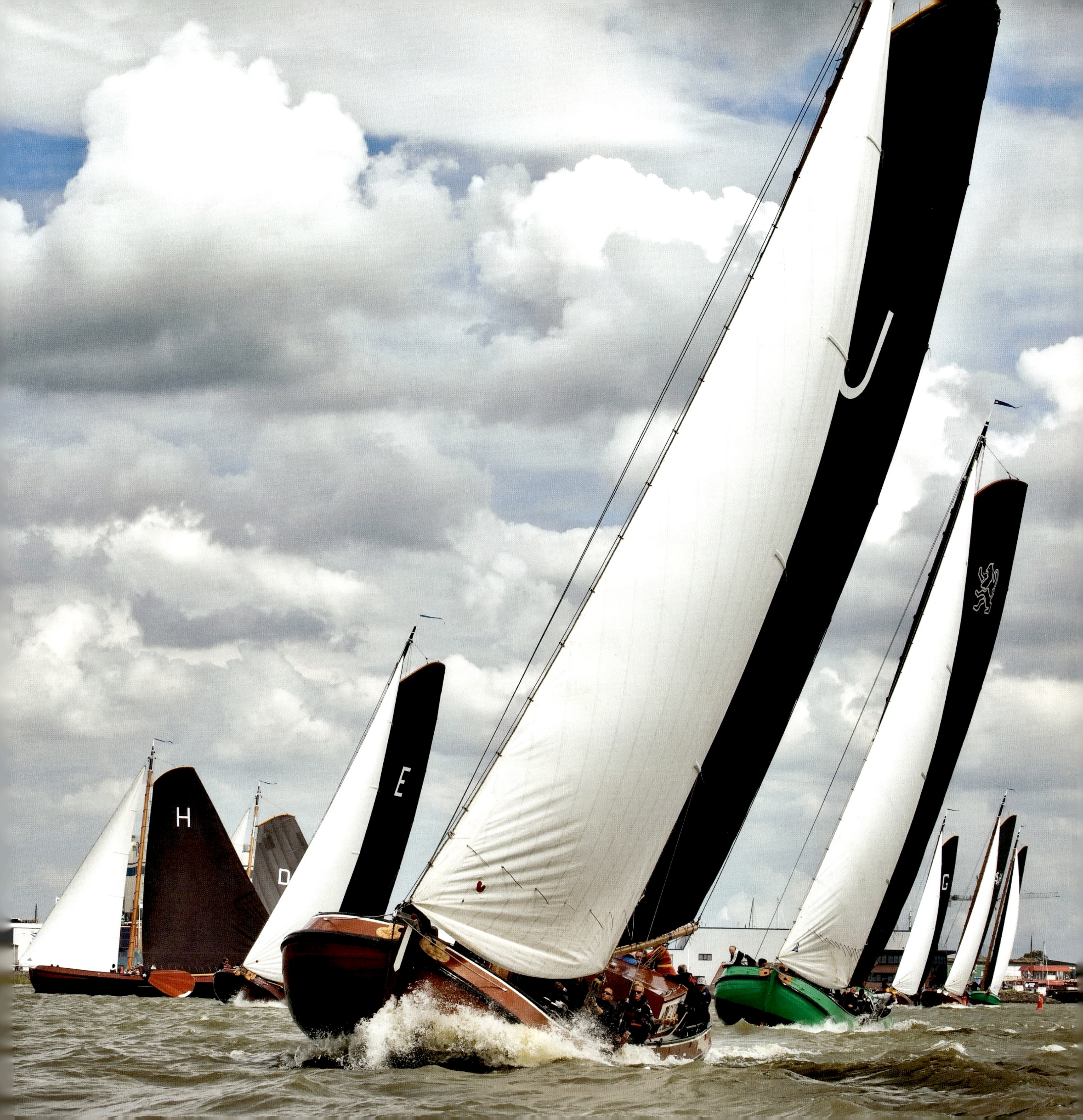
H
E
D
G

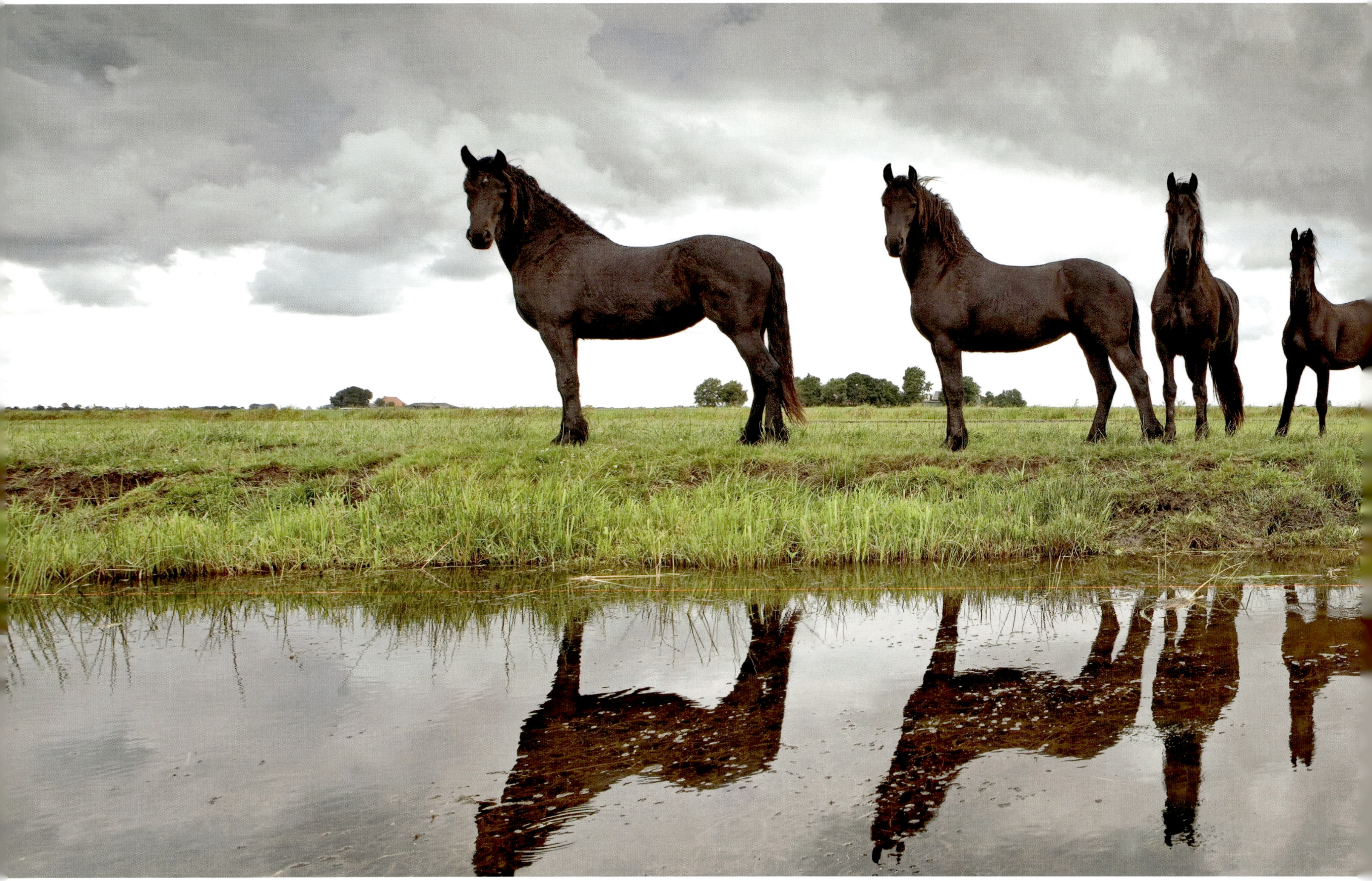

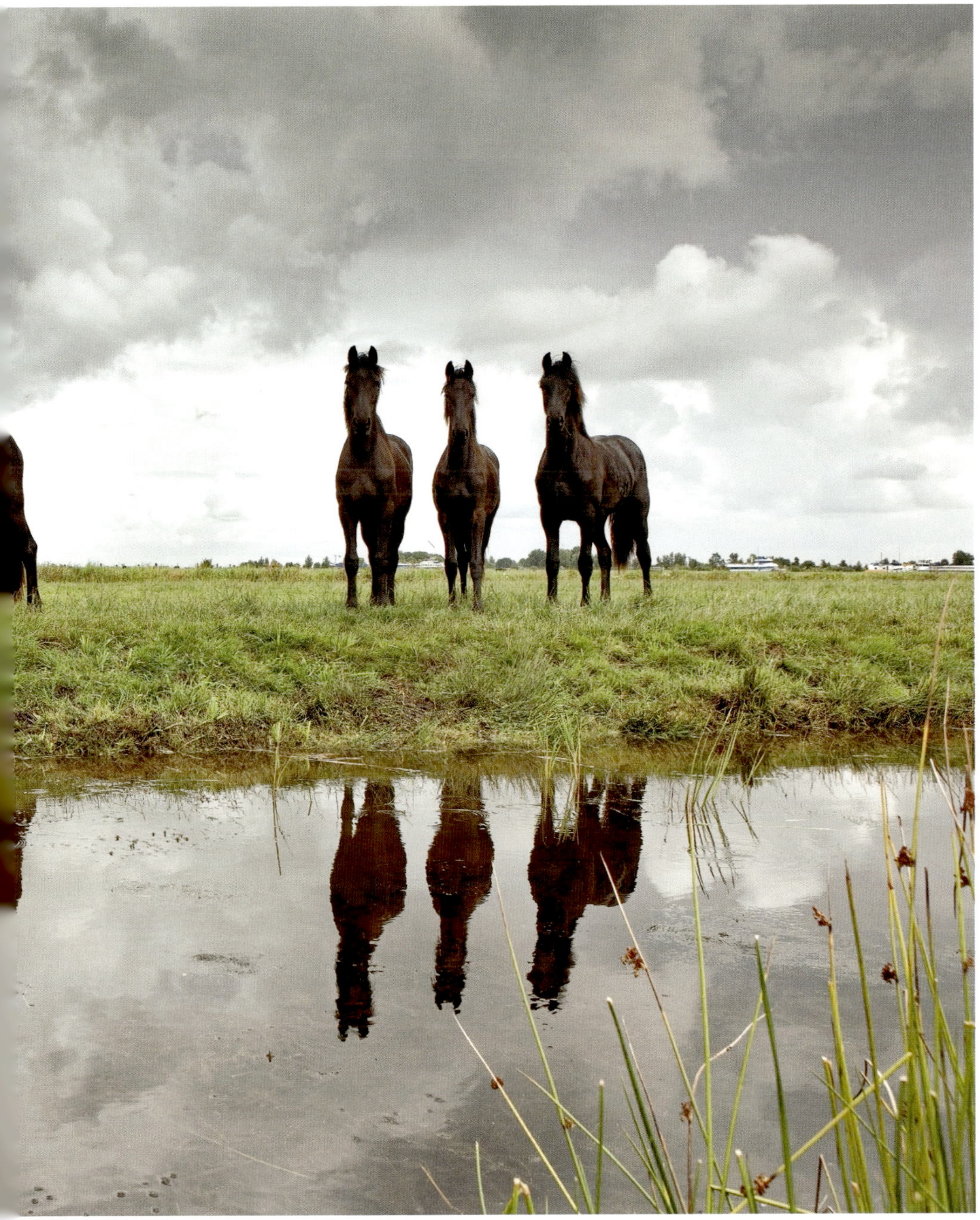

Left: The Frisian horse is an elegant-looking horse with a long mane and a proud attitude. The Frisian is strong, kind, intelligent, inquisitive and faithful – and he is a willing worker. All these features have in recent years ensured the great popularity of the Frisian horse at home and abroad.

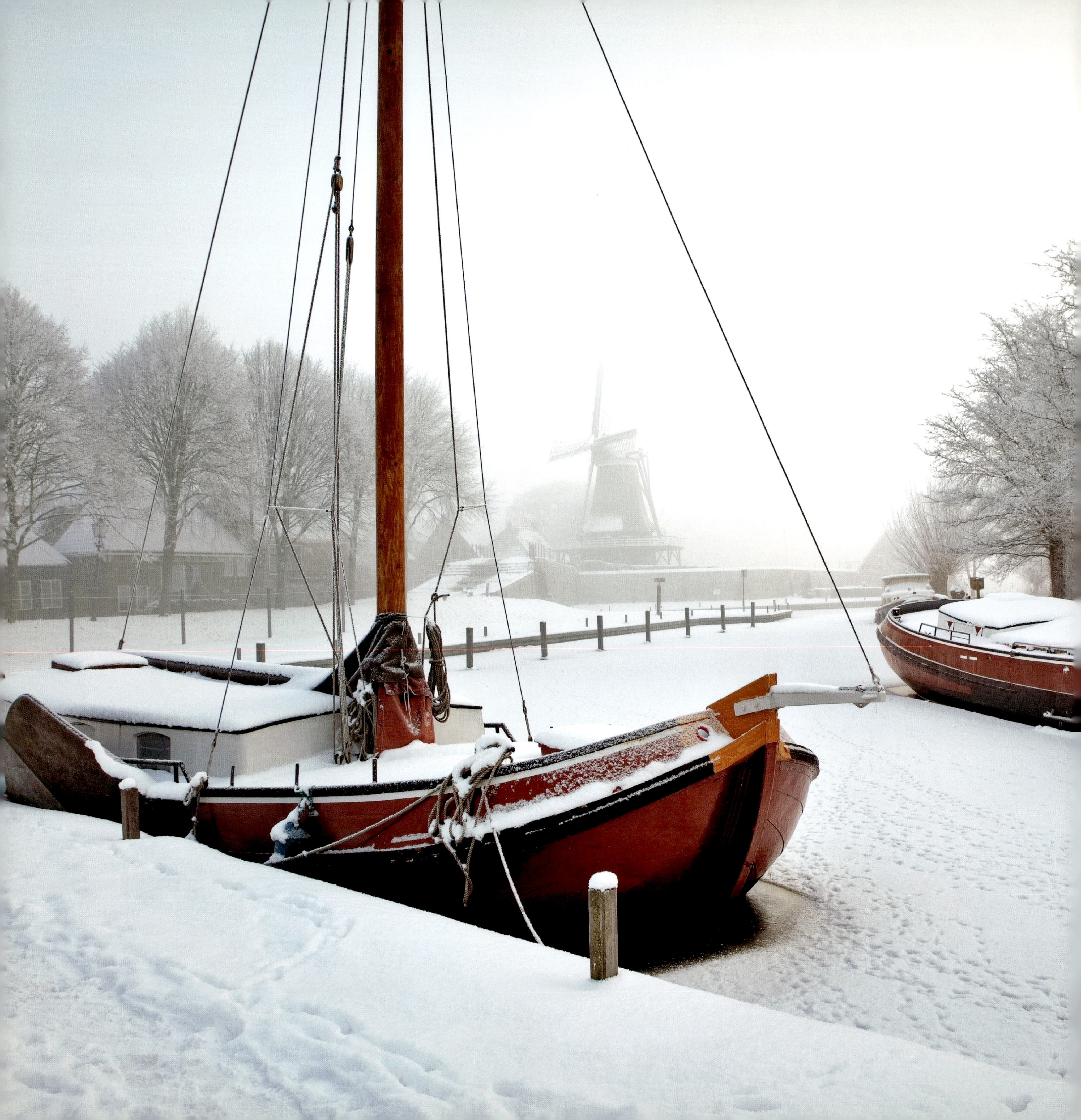

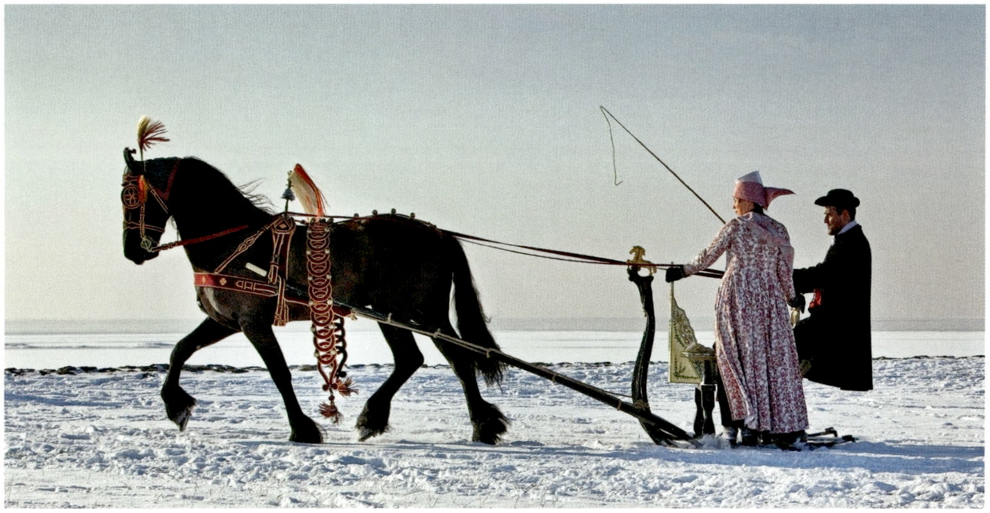

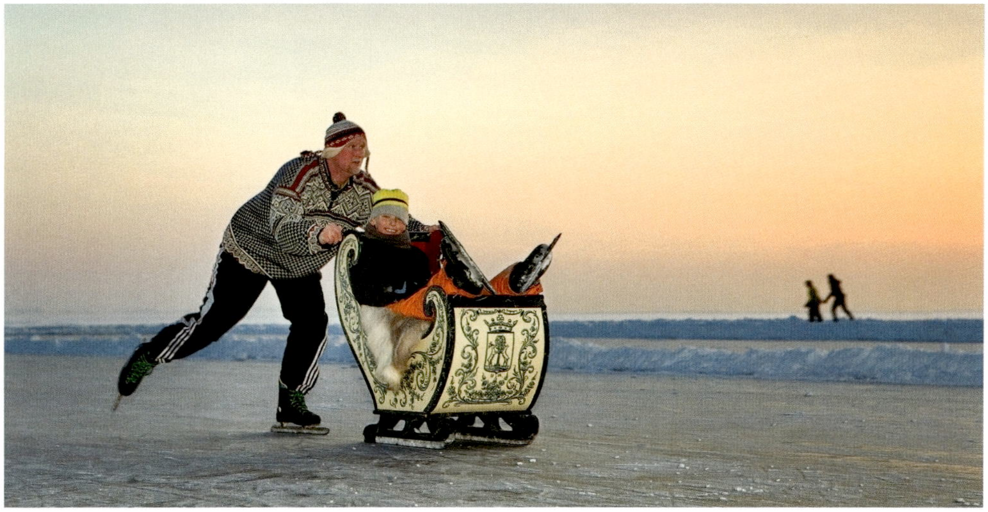

Left: Winter in Sloten.

Top: In extreme cold weather, even the IJsselmeer freezes. From that moment, the Skating Museum in Hindeloopen comes to life. Antique sleds are taken out of the attic, people have a spin in traditional costumes and sleighs come out of the barn, pulled by Frisian horses, to show off on the ice.

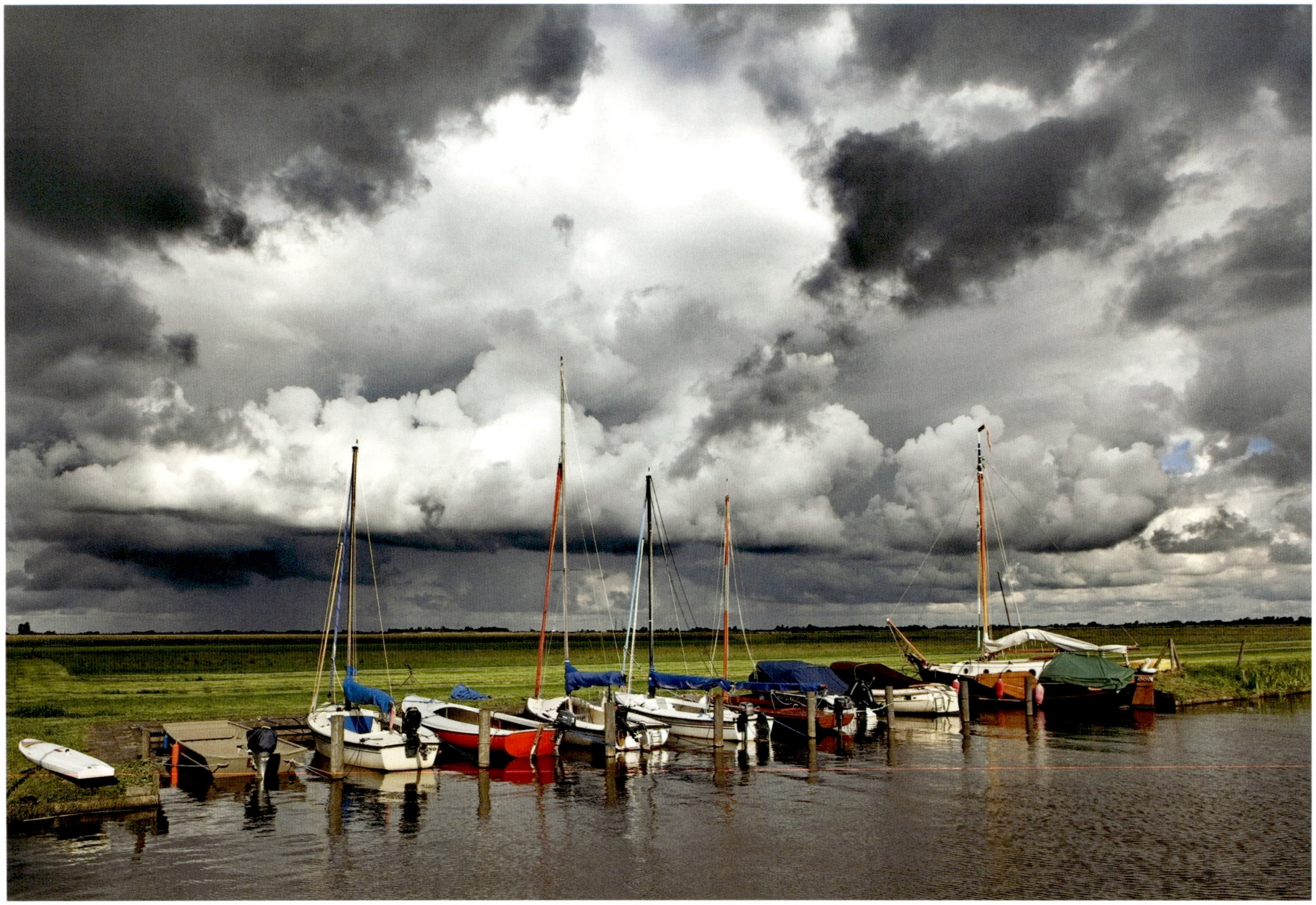

Top: The Netherlands is known for its beautiful cloudy skies. Especially renowned are thunderstorms that form in the summer and that give us spectacular images, such as here at a small marina at Elahuizen in Frisia.

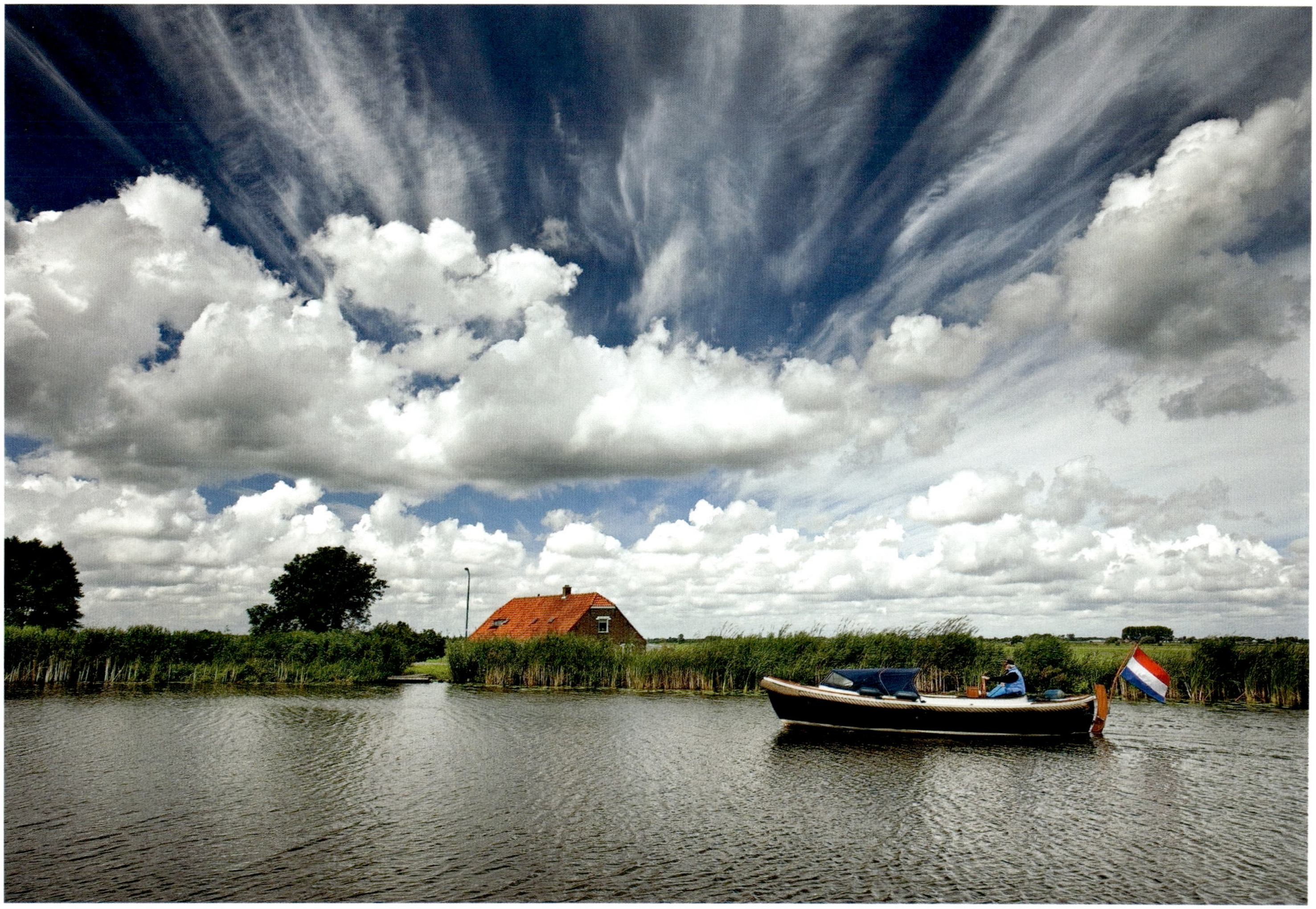

Top: Frisia may be the mecca of Dutch watersports, but the water is enjoyed all over the country, as seen by this man in a sloop on the Meije at Bodegraven in the province of Zuid-Holland.

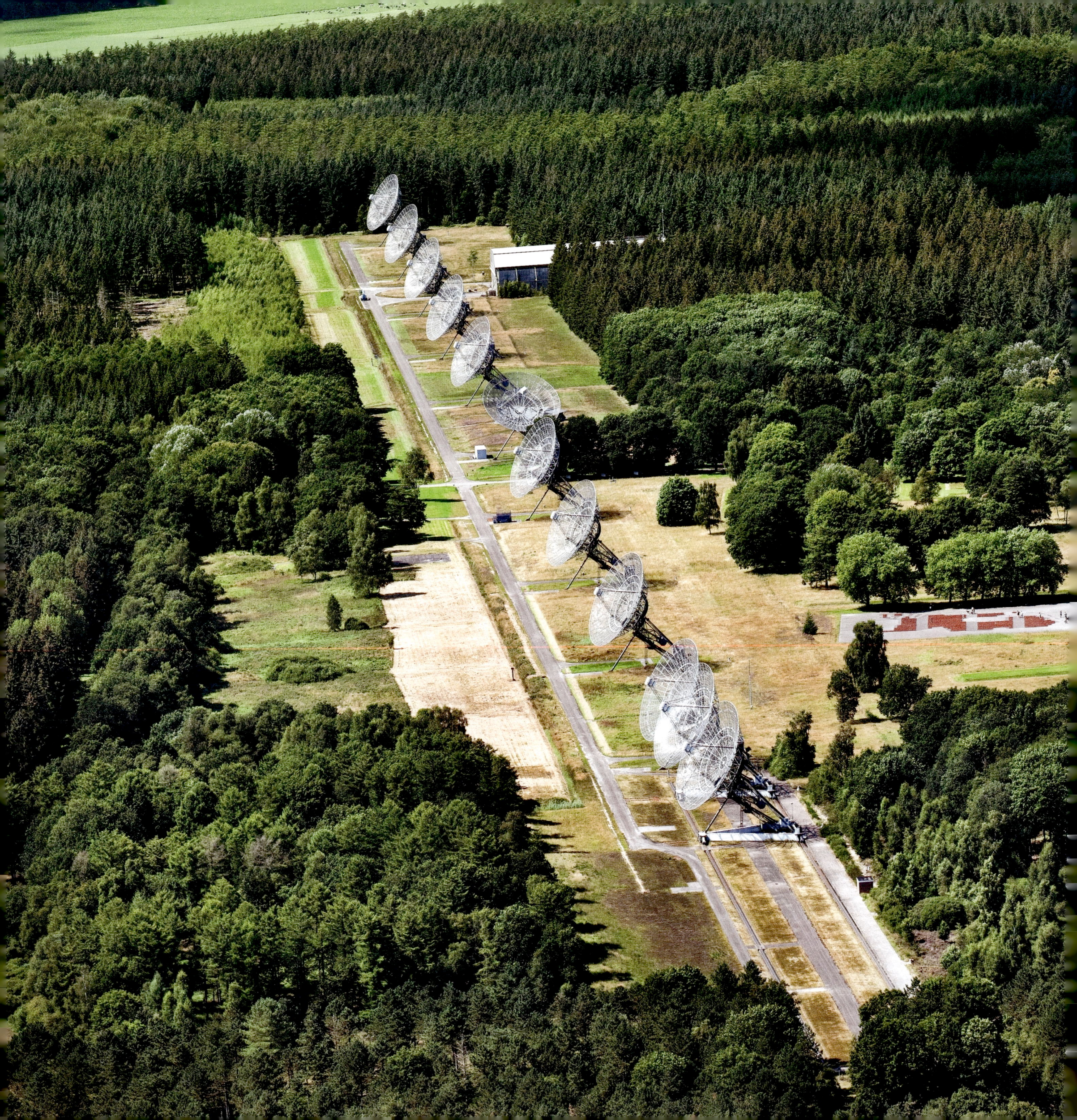

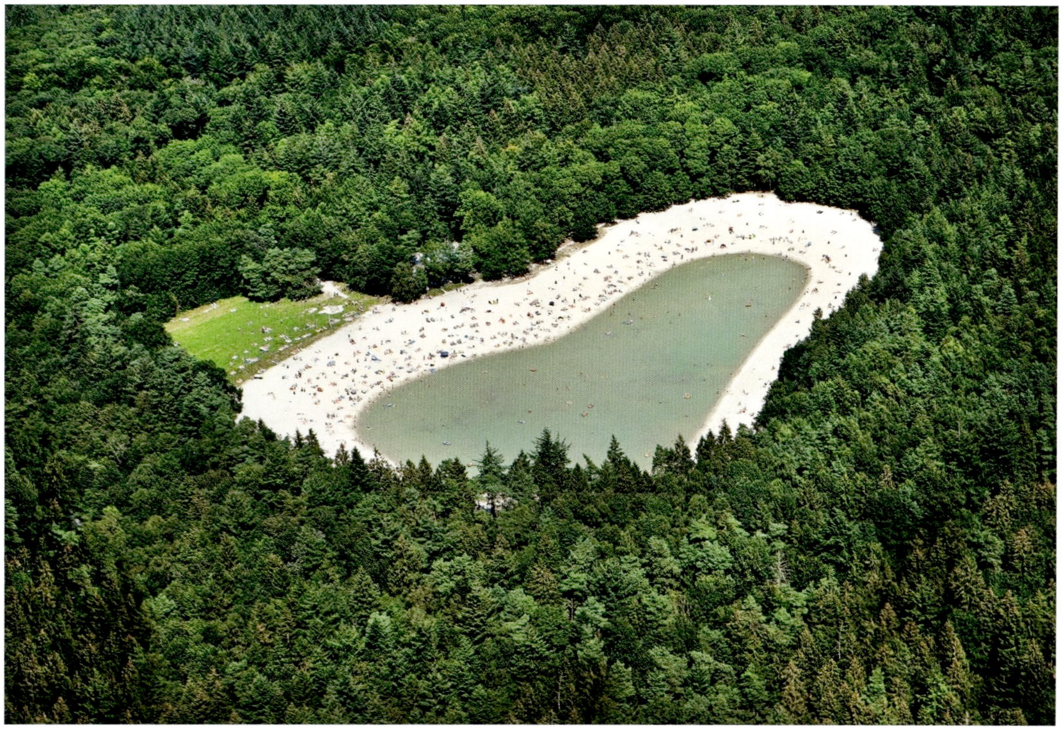

Left: The Westerbork Synthesis Radio Telescope, abbreviated WSRT, which consists of fourteen separate parabolic antennas, is a radio telescope in the woods near Hooghalen in Drenthe province. The area where the antennas are arranged is located next to the former Kamp Westerbork.

Top: Bathing and sunbathing on the beach of a fen called 't Nije Hemelriek in the woods near Gasselte in Drenthe province.

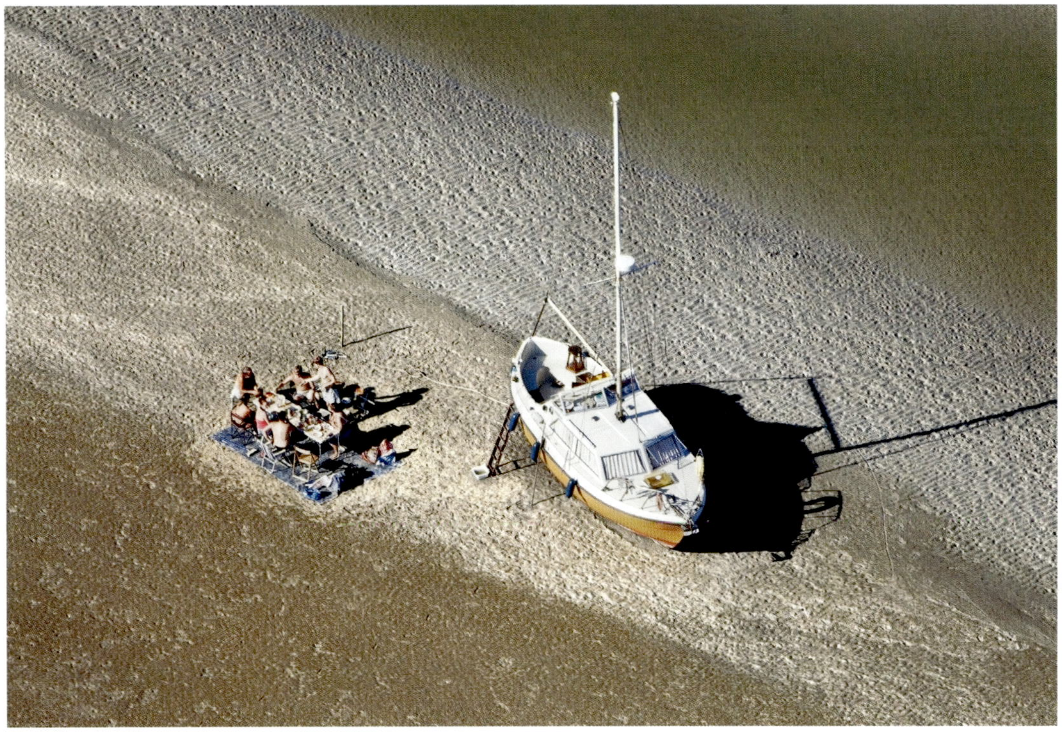

Top: People with their own yachts do not suffer from the crowds even on hot days. During low tide, lunch is spread out on the sprawling sandbanks of the Westerschelde (Western Scheldt).

Right: Whenever the thermometer rises past 25 degrees, the Dutch beaches are overrun, including this, arguably the most beautiful beach in the Netherlands: Zoutelande in Zeeland.

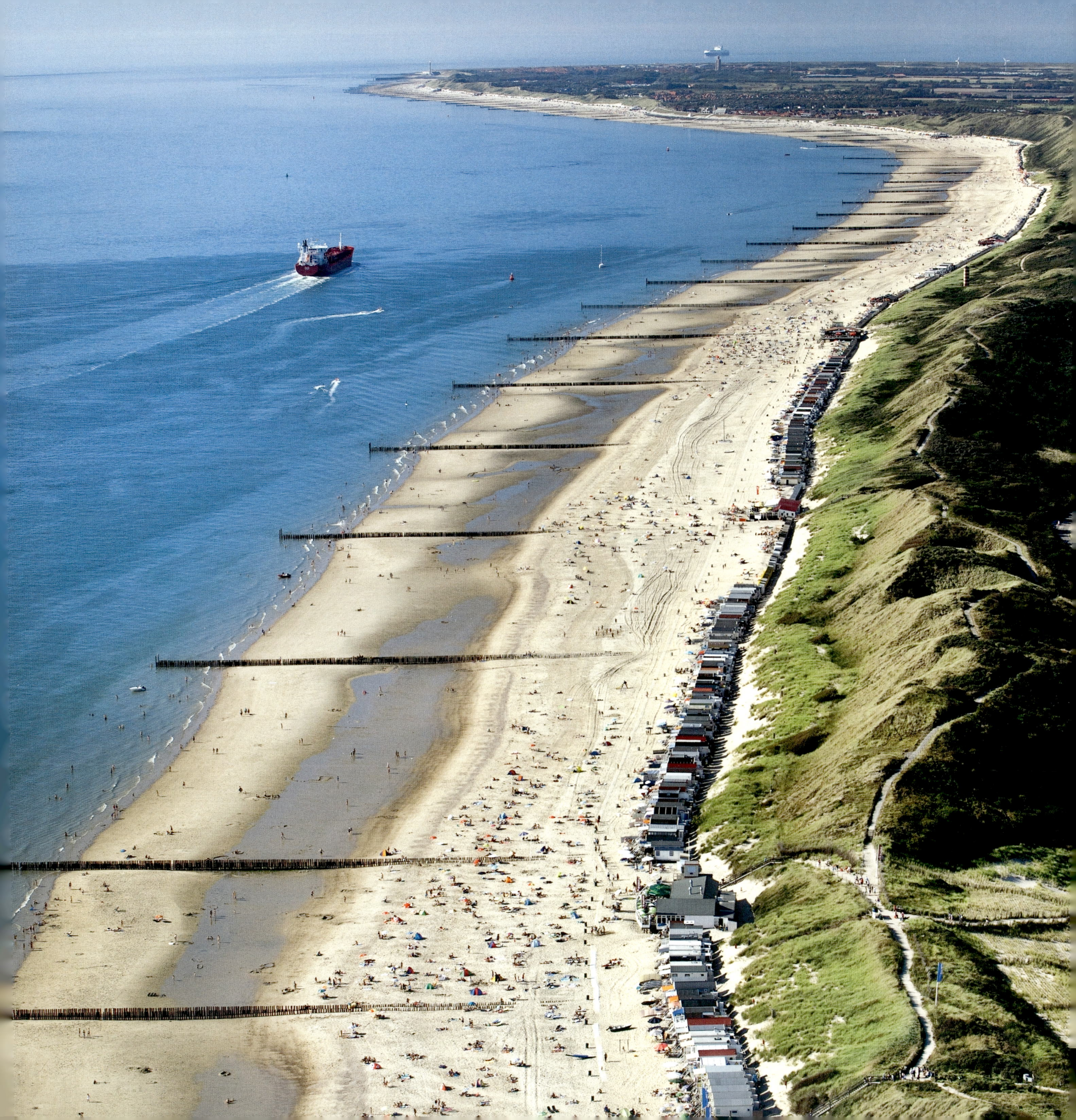

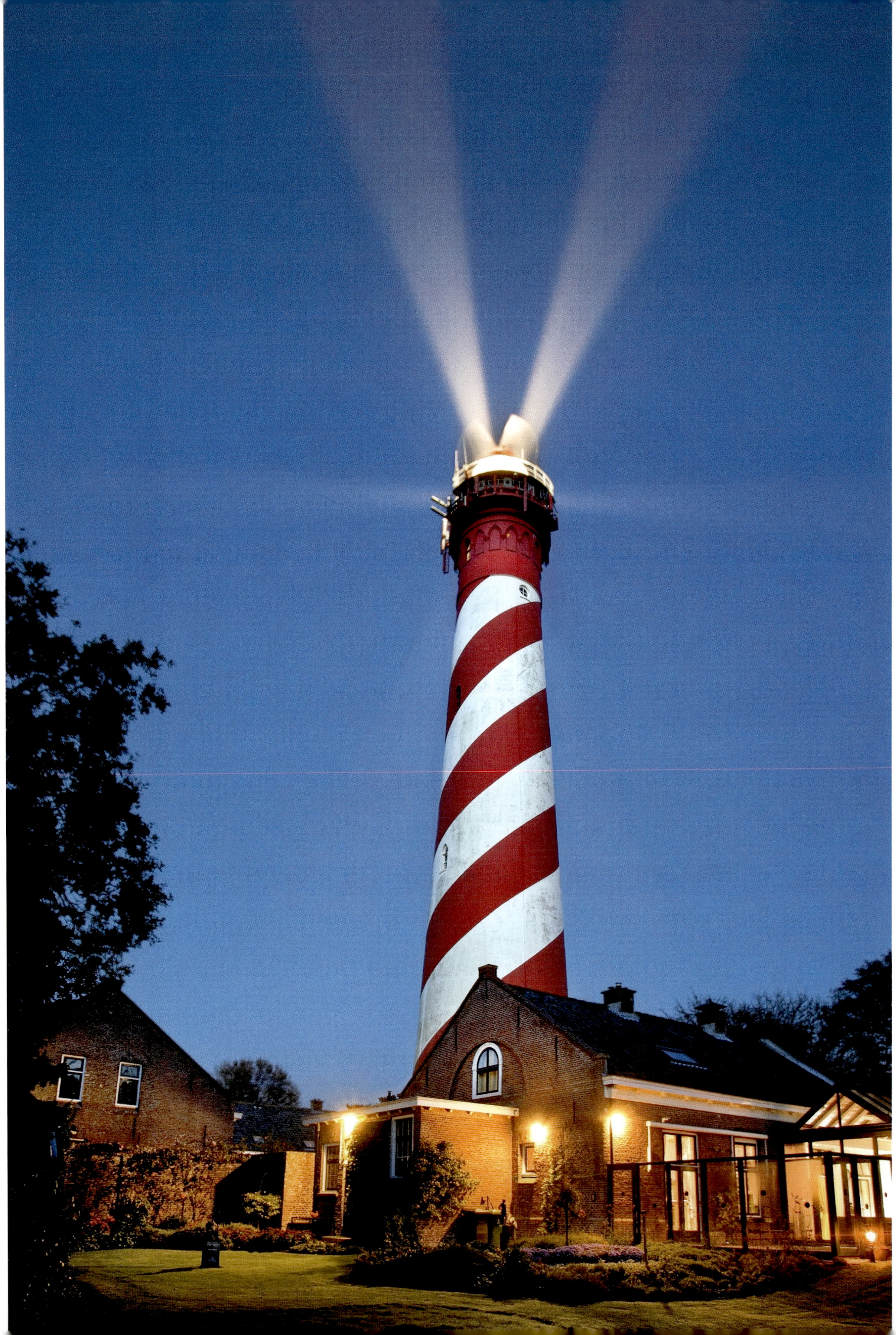

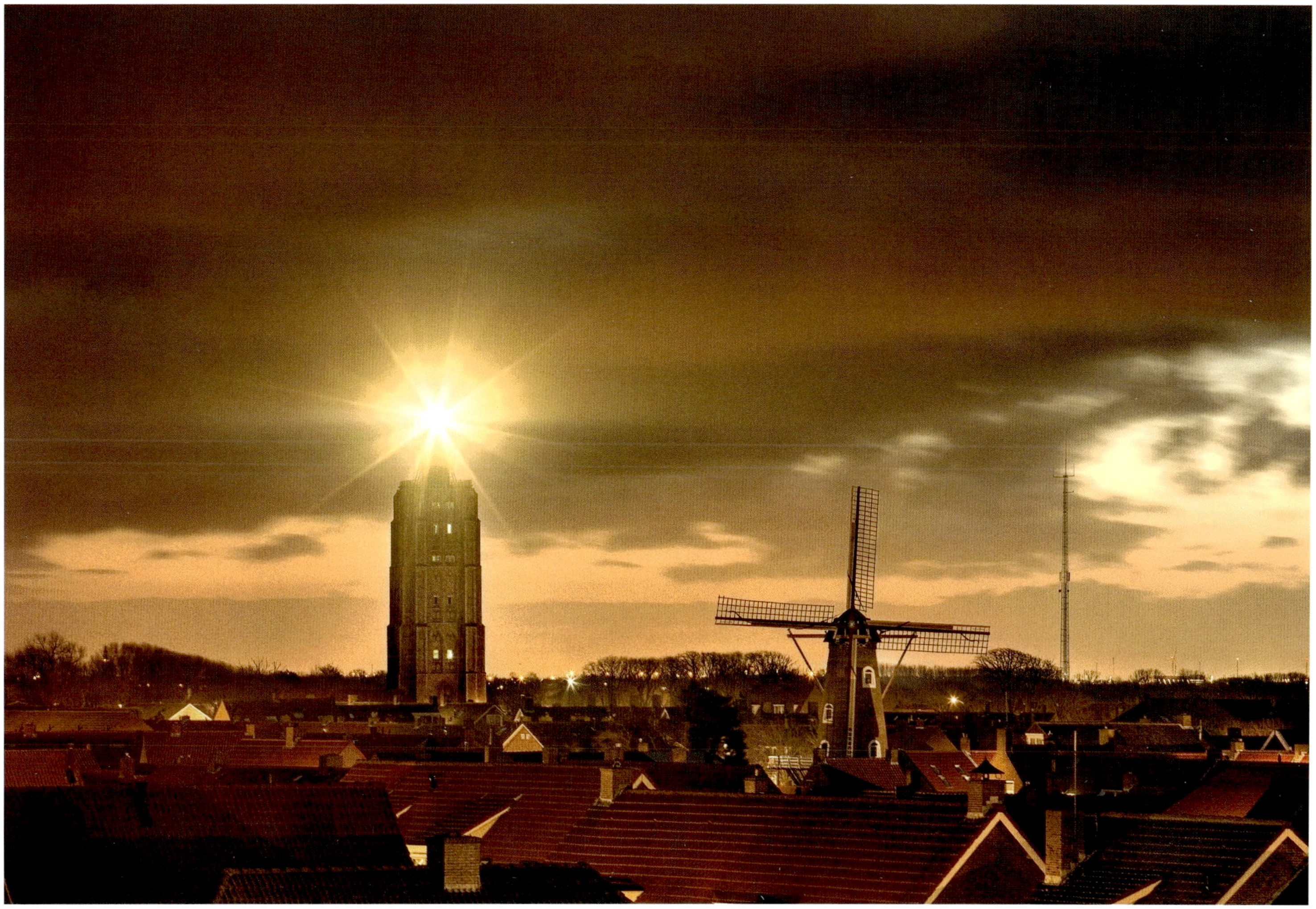

Left: The Westerlicht lighthouse at Nieuw-Haamstede in the province of Zeeland was completed in 1840. The red-and-white spiral was painted a century later as a warning to low-flying aircraft. With its 53 metres of height (above ground level) and an altitude of 58 metres above sea level, the tower is one of the tallest lighthouses in the Netherlands. The light reaches 50 km away.

Top: Westkapelle lighthouse on the island of Walcheren in Zeeland. The lighthouse was originally a stone church. Due to destruction during the Eighty Years' War and a later fire, only the tower remained. Since the early 1900s, the tower has been converted into a lighthouse. Oddly enough, it is not on the sea front, but rather on the land side of the village.

Following pages: Participants in the Frisian Eleven Cities Bicycle Tour, a yearly tour by bike past the eleven Frisian cities.

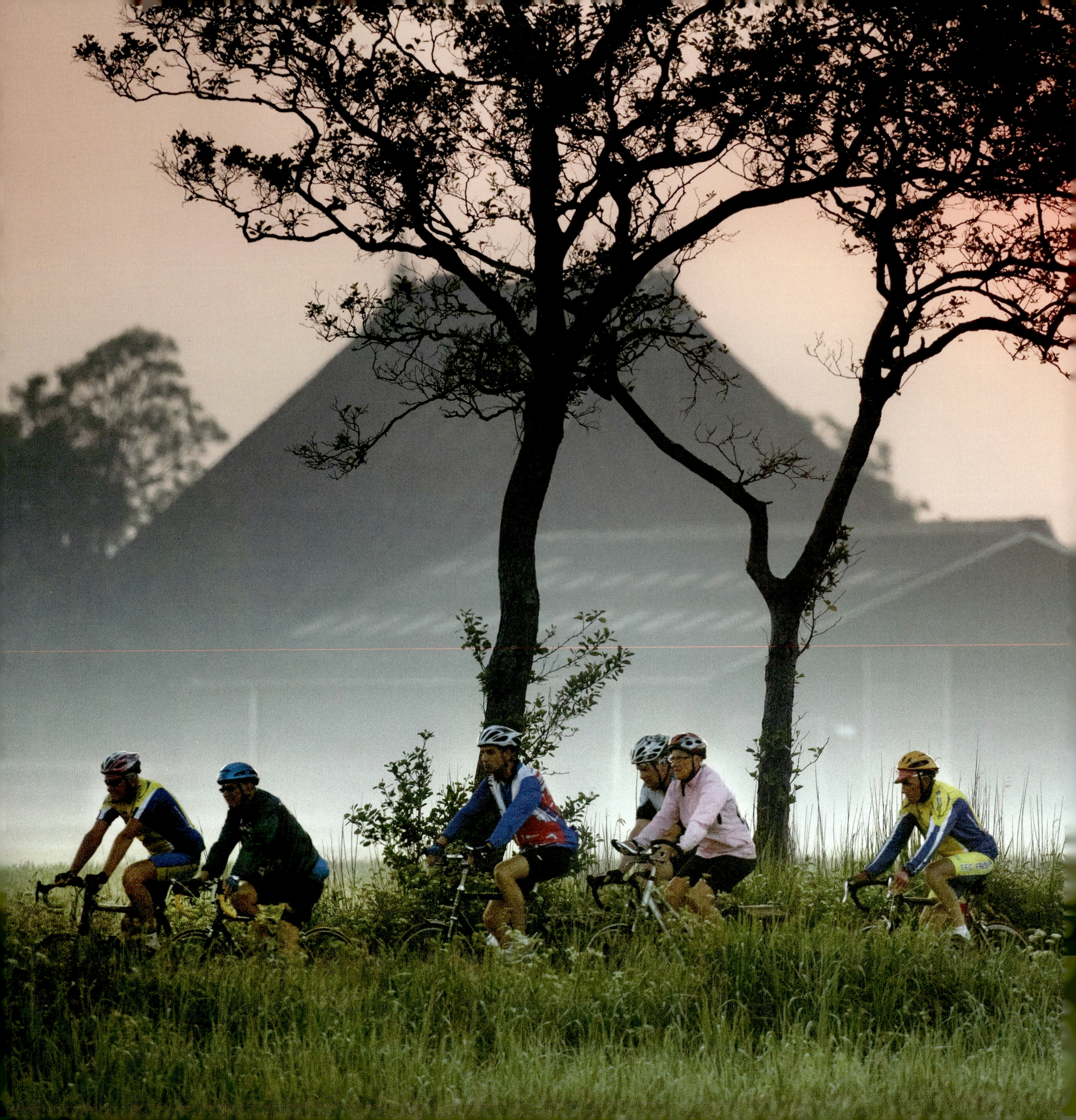

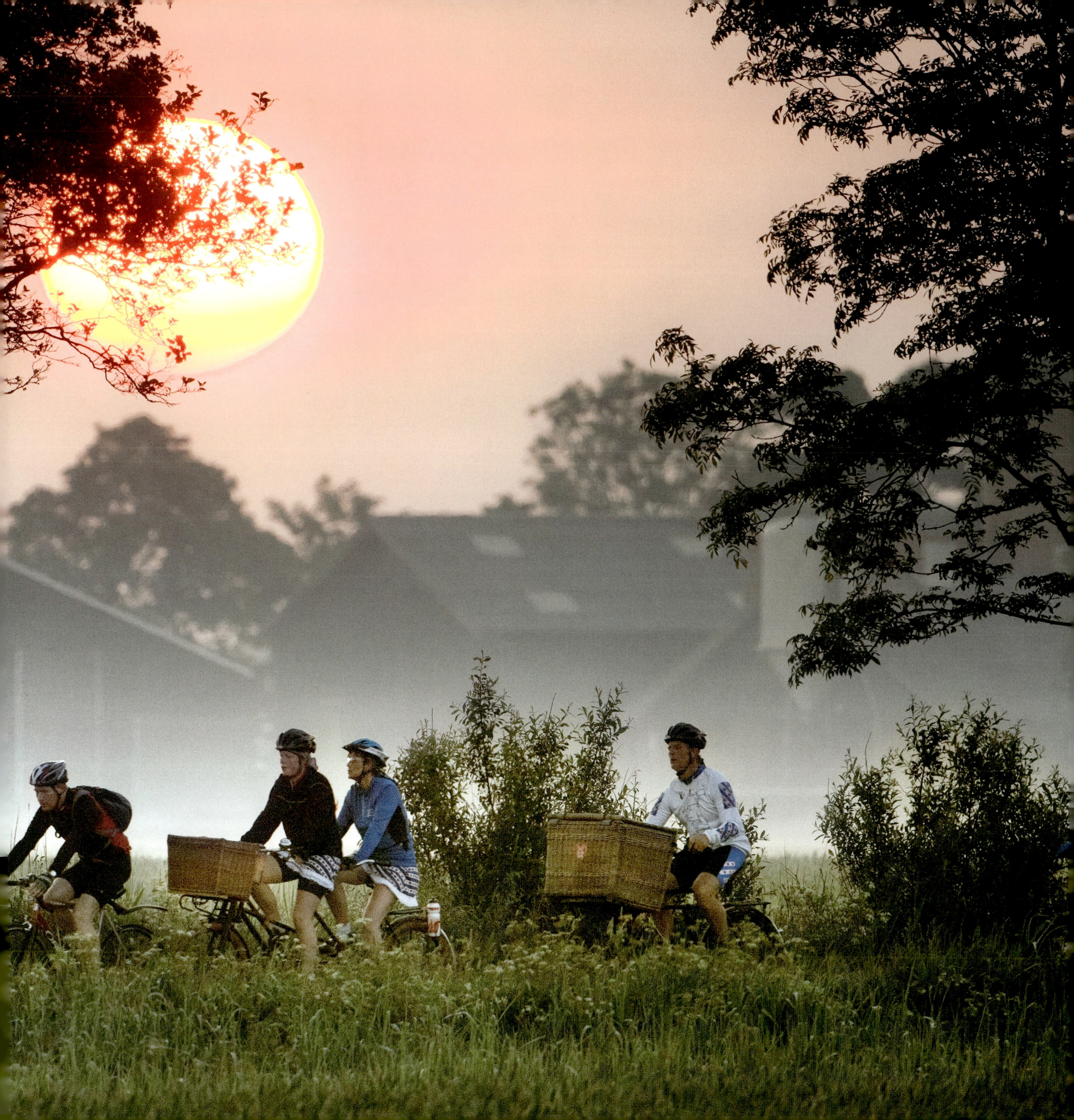

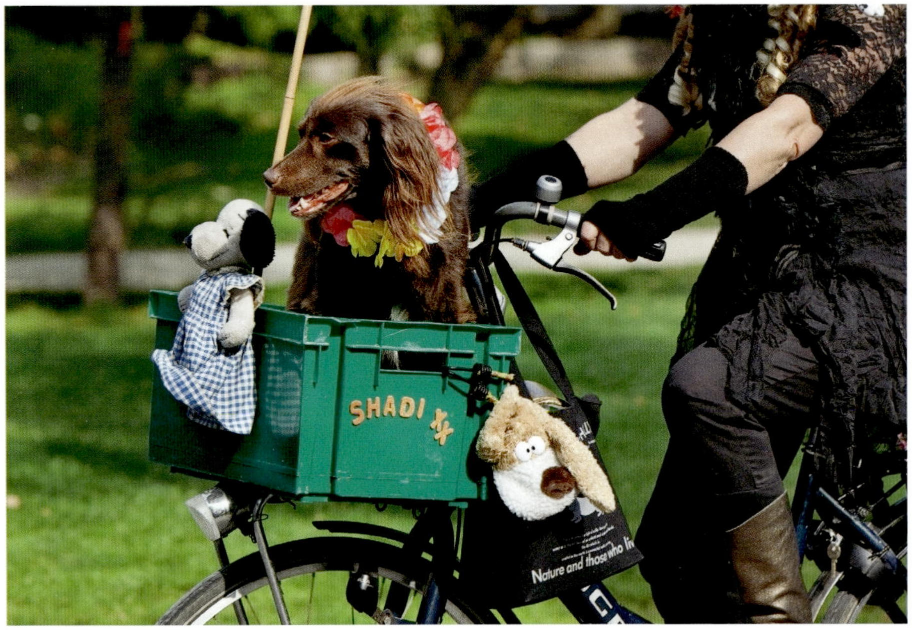

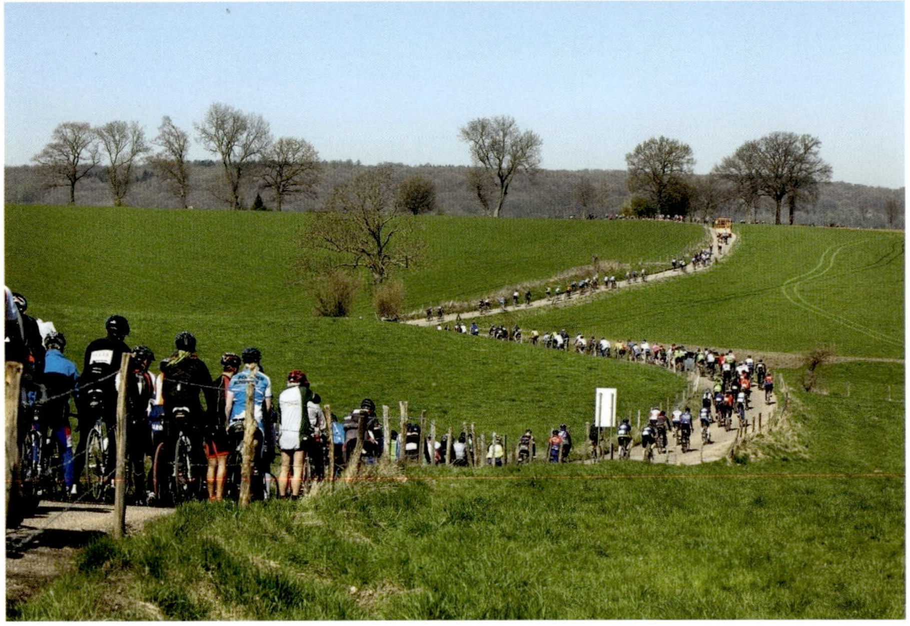

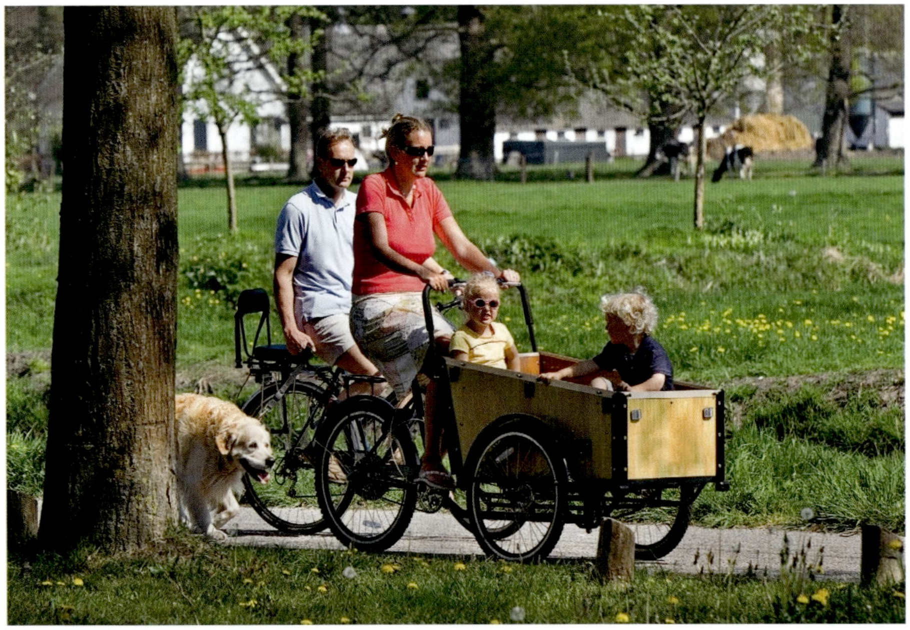

Cycling

The Netherlands is a cycling country par excellence, not surprising when you consider that we have more than 29,000 kilometres of cycle paths. In addition, nearly 5,000 kilometres of our roads are equipped with bicycle lanes. There is cycling throughout the year, but especially in the spring and summer months. Altogether, the Dutch annually travel around 18 billion kilometres by bike.

Top left: A woman cycles through the Vondelpark in Amsterdam with her dog in a basket at the front of the bike.

Centre: Traffic jams during the Amstel Gold Race cycling tour in South Limburg.

Below left: Parents and dog with children in their carrier bike, out and about in 's-Graveland.

Right: Morning rush hour of cyclists in Amsterdam, where parents take their children to school by bike and others are on their way to work.

Following pages: Festival-goers in front of their tent, having breakfast at the Lowlands music festival in Biddinghuizen, Flevoland.

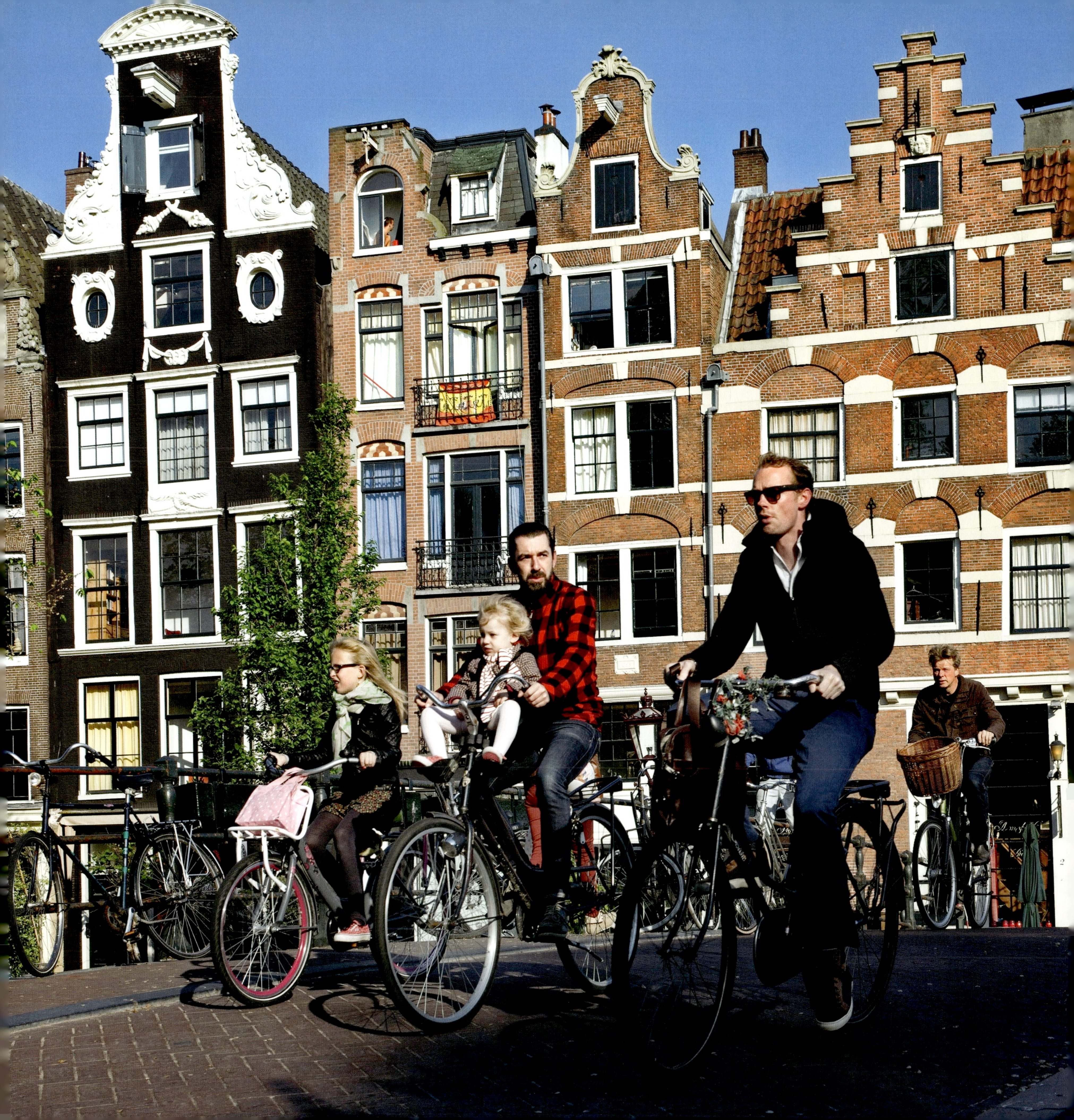

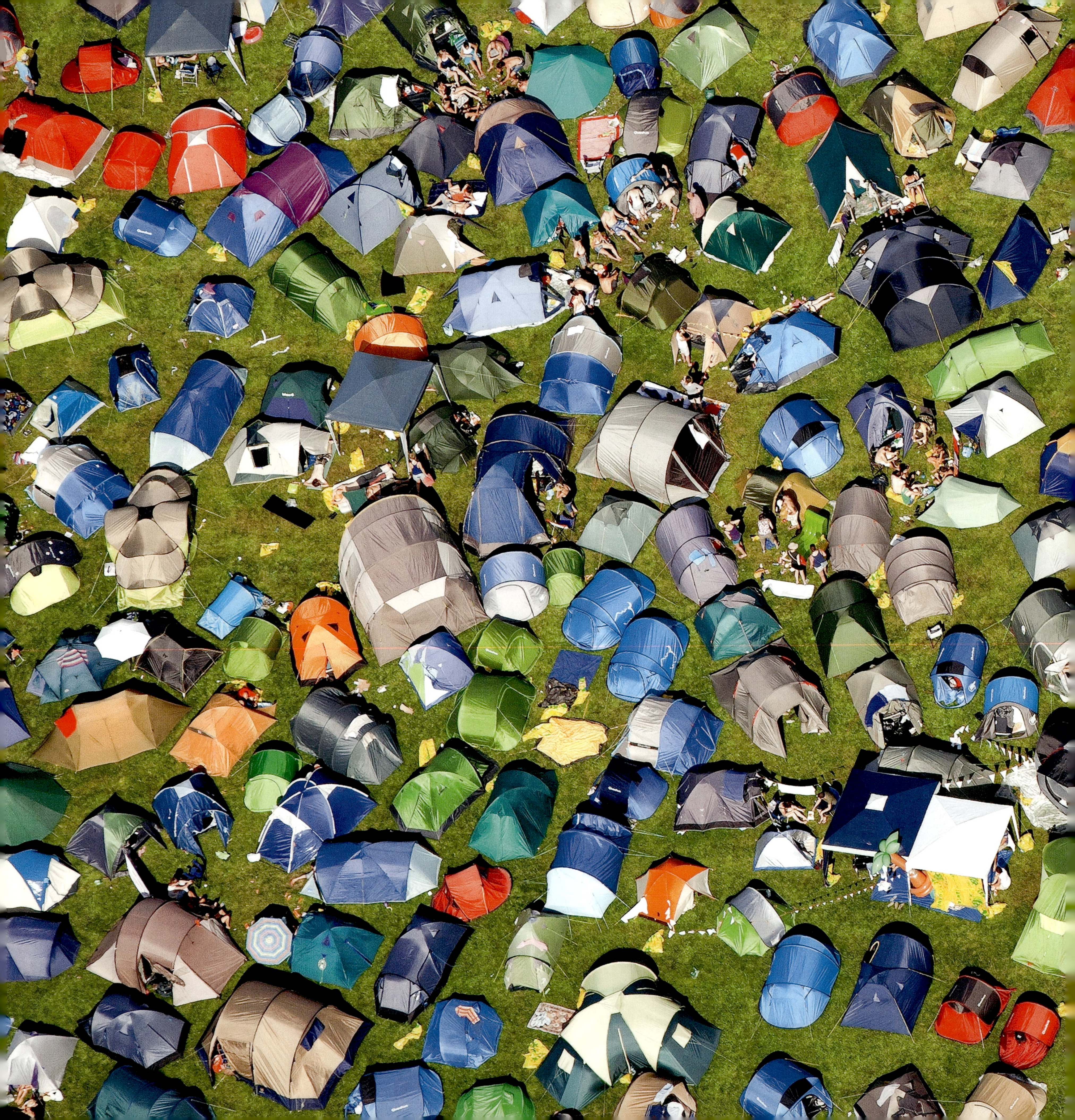

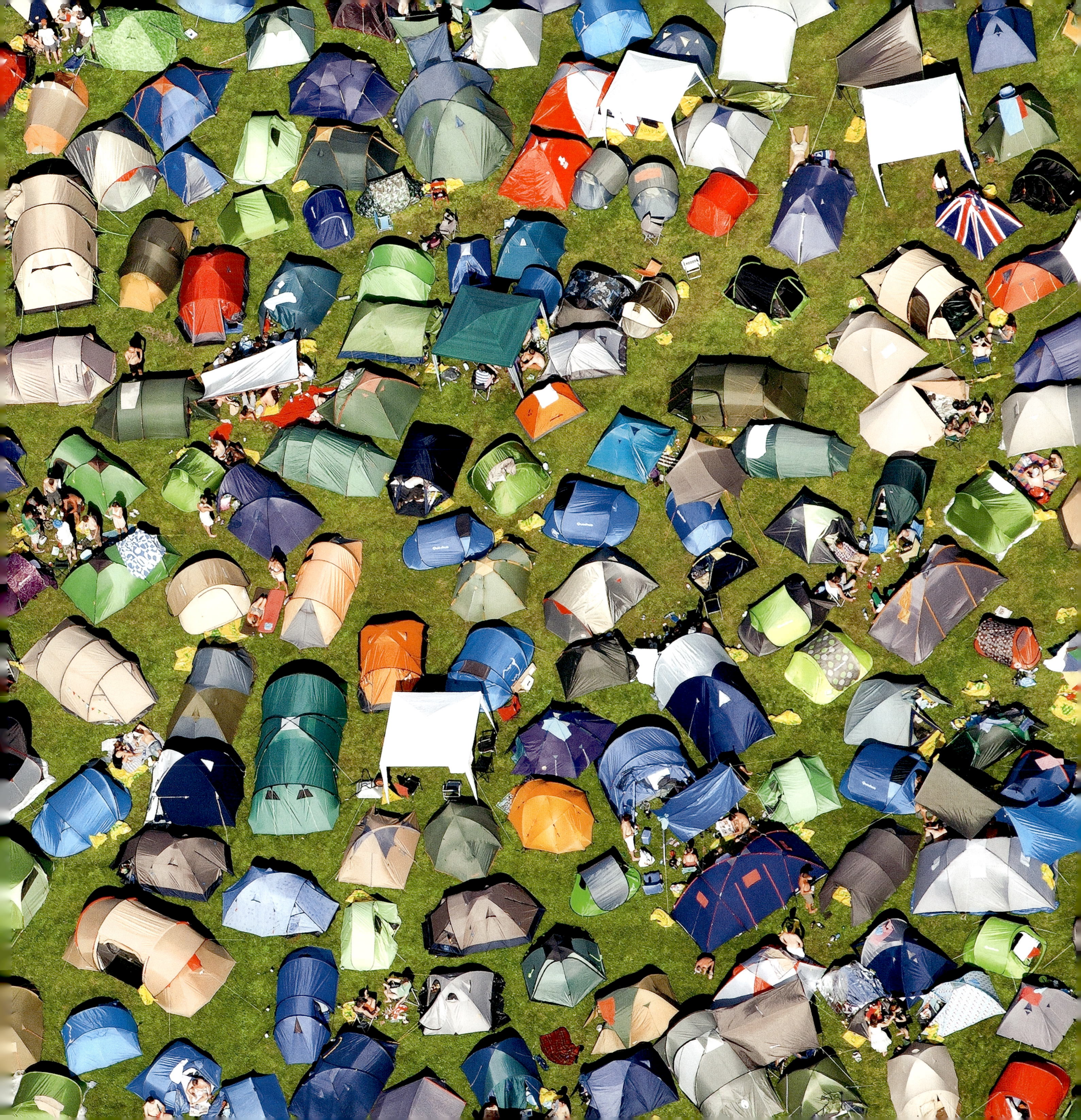

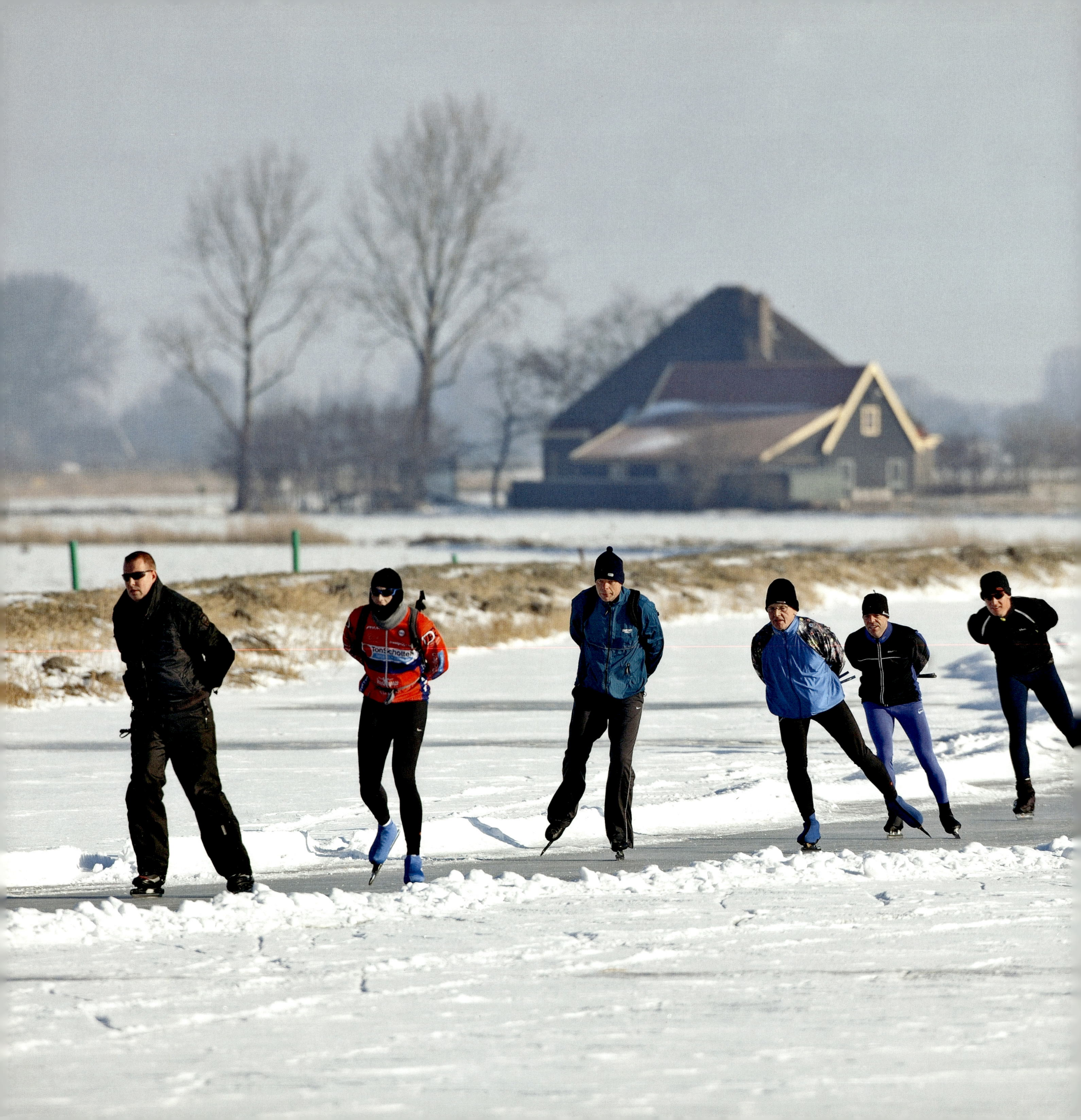

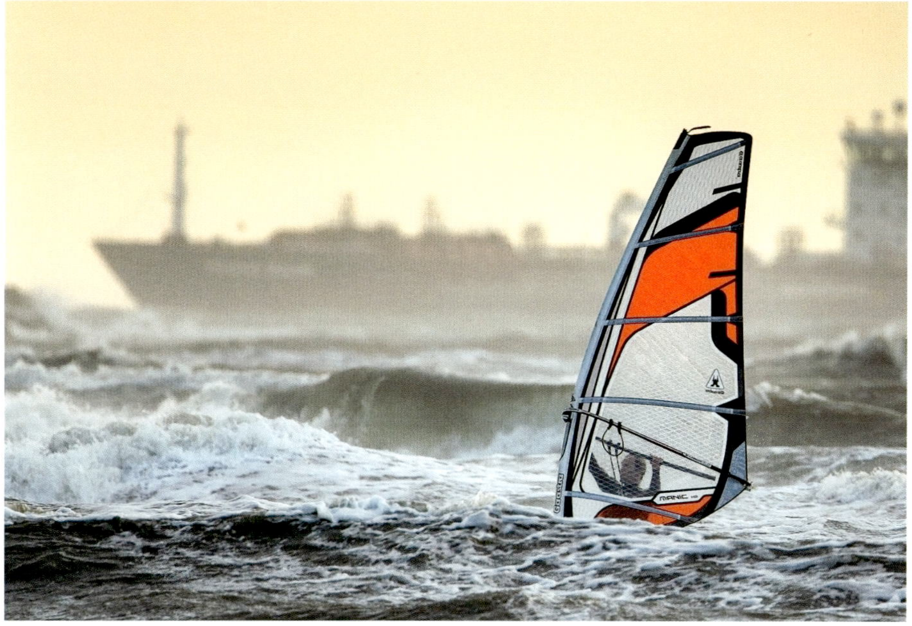

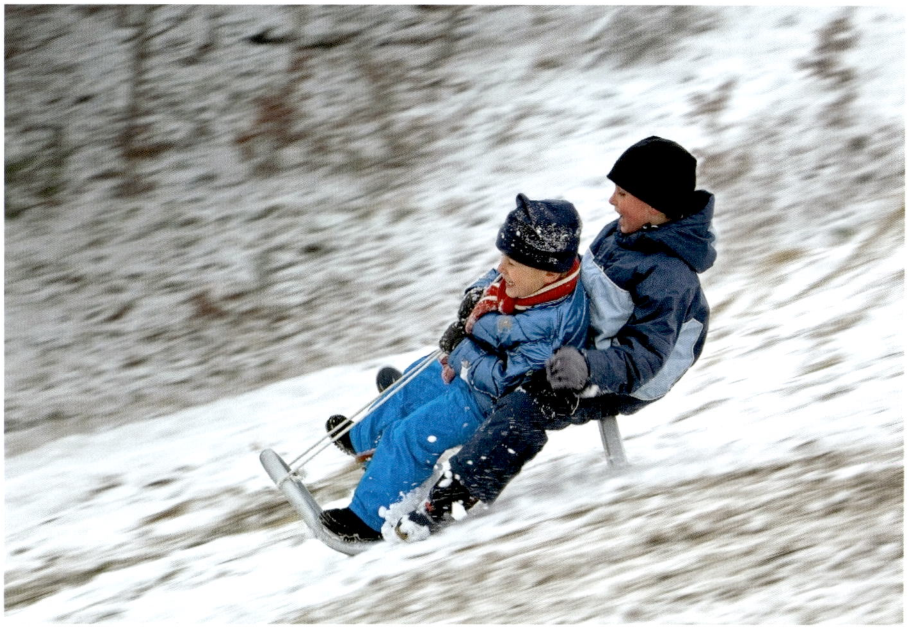

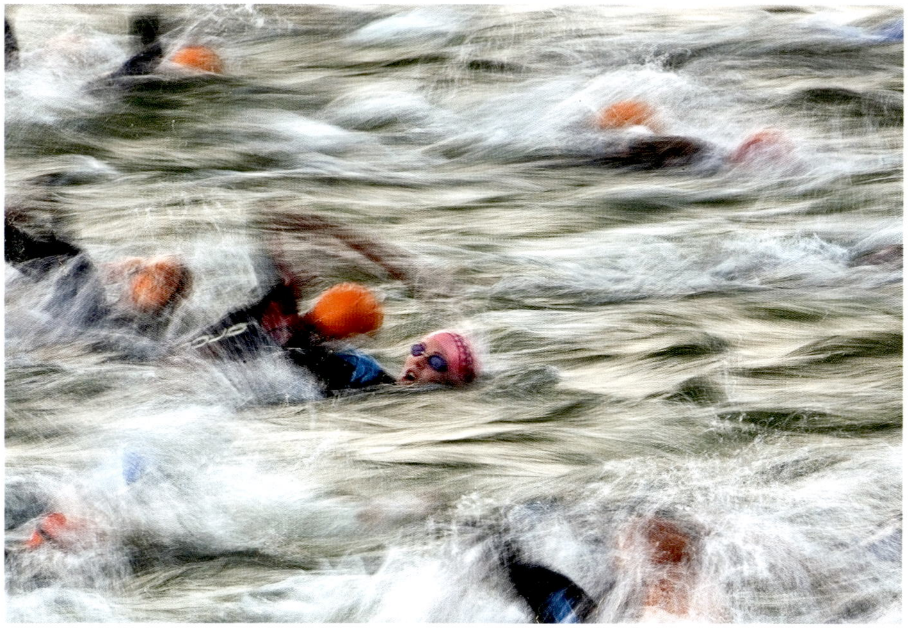

Sport

Sport is an important part of the lives of many Dutch. There are thousands of sports clubs, with a total of six million members. But outside the associations, too, many people play sports. The most popular sports are football, cycling and skating.

Left: Skaters in front of a farm near Jisp in Noord-Holland.

Top right: Windsurfer on the North Sea at the entrance to the North Sea Canal in IJmuiden.

Centre: Sledding on the dunes of Egmond aan Zee.

Below right: Swimming during the Almere Triathlon.

Following pages: Cargo ships going to and fro in the locks of the North Sea Canal at IJmuiden. At the back right, the Tata Steel plant.

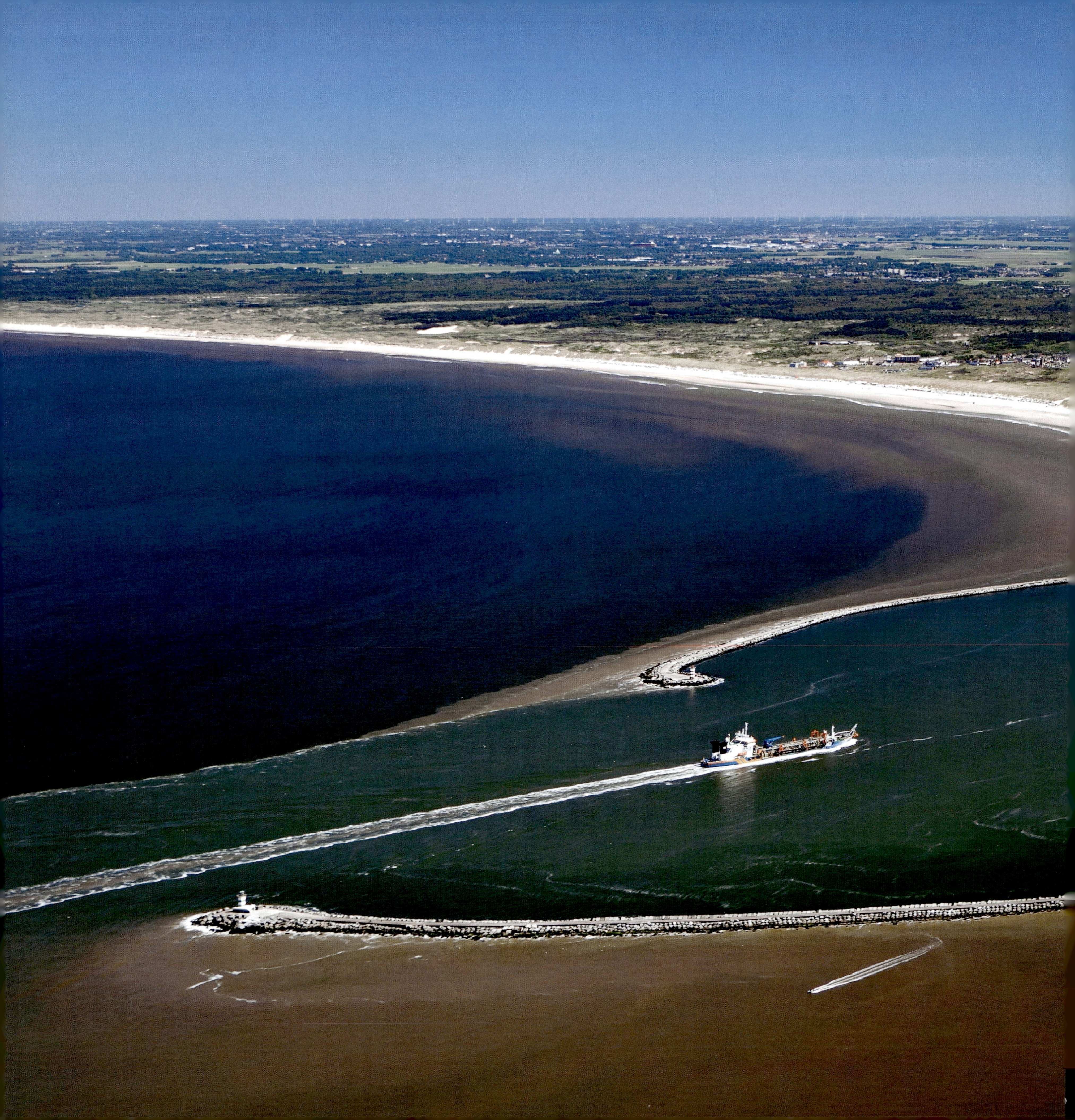

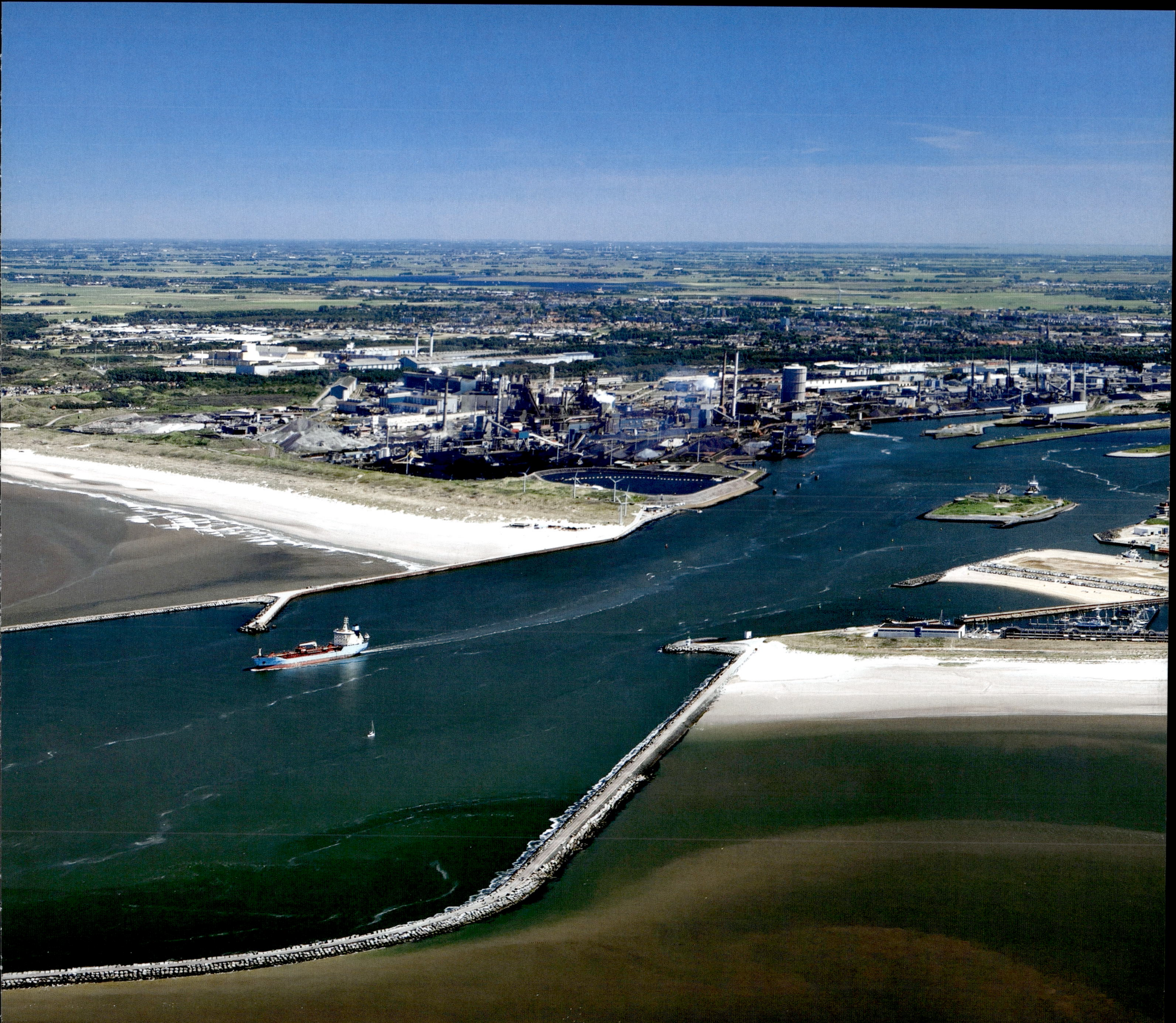

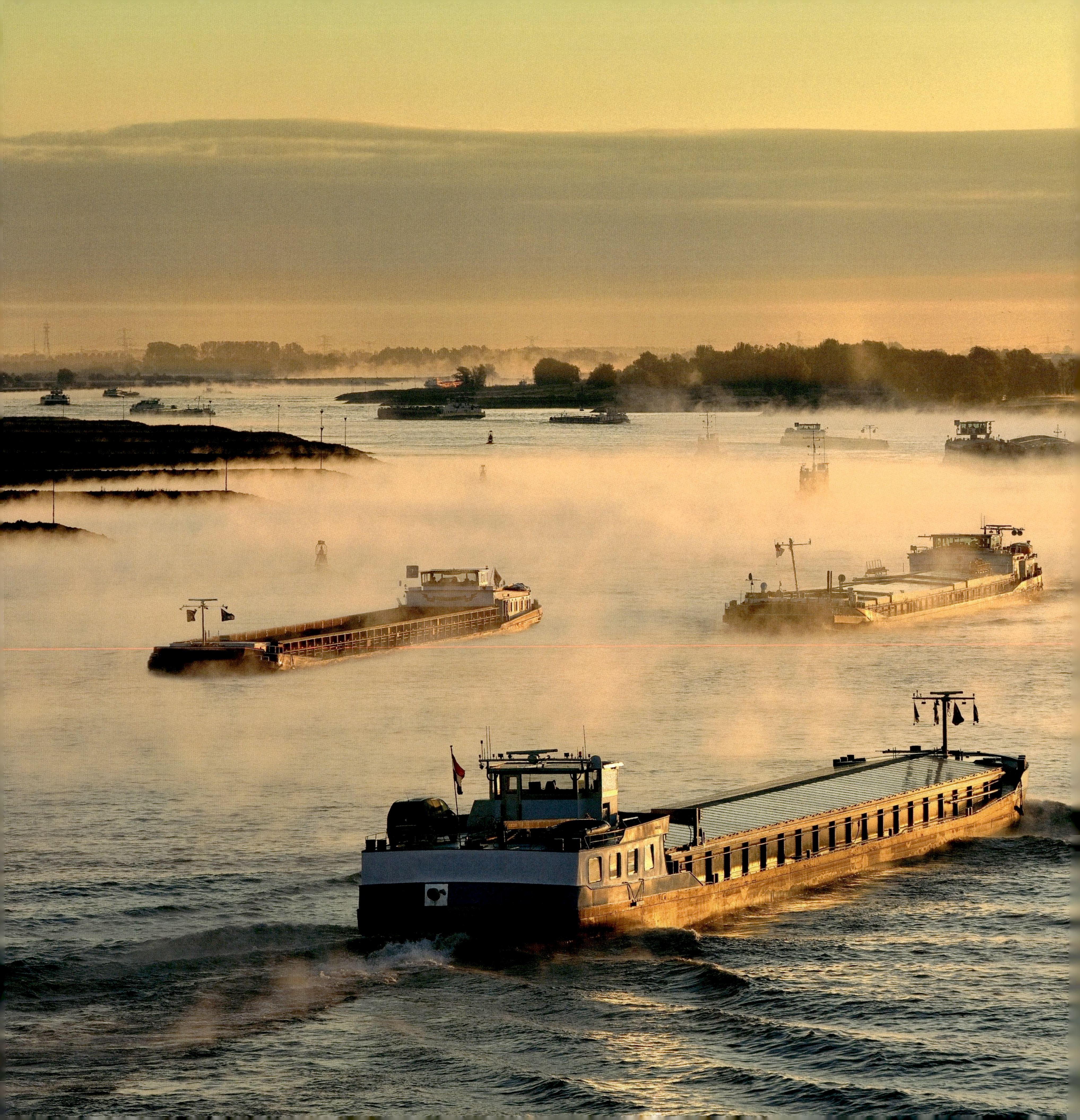

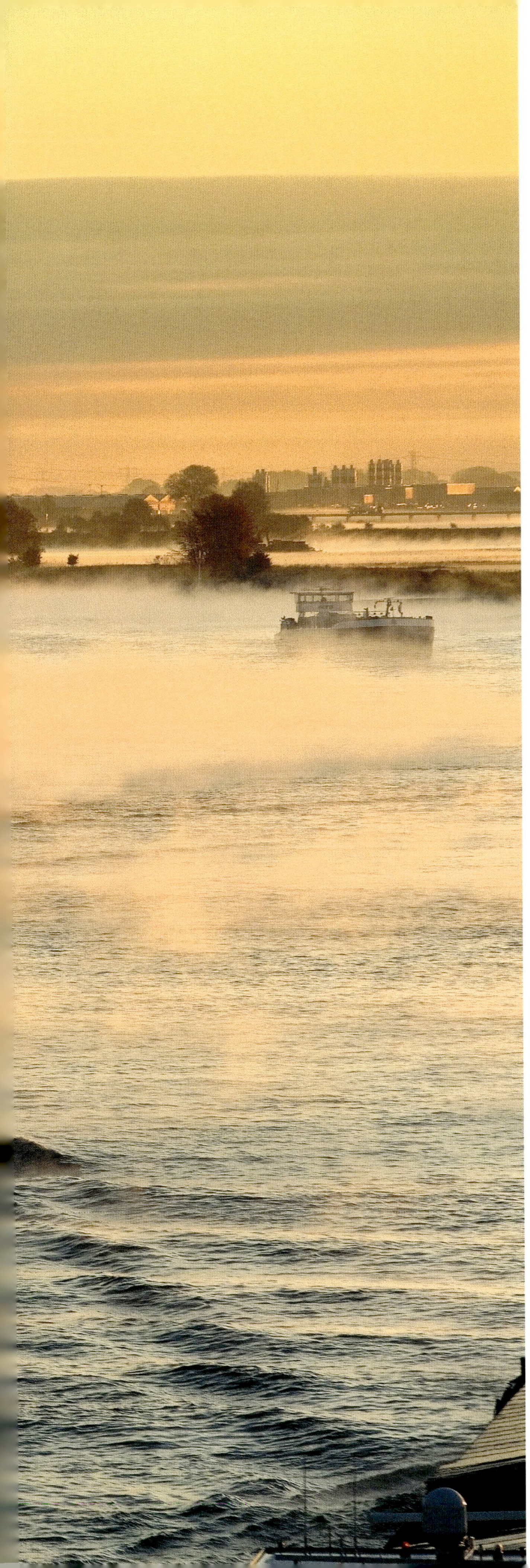

Economy

In the seventeenth century, the Netherlands was the centre of the global economy thanks to sea trade; it is even said that the Dutch Republic had the first modern economy in the world. Today, our country is still a modern economy heavily focused on waterborne commerce. Its location on the North Sea and in the delta of three major European rivers makes this an almost self-evident concentration for the country. The port of Rotterdam, the largest in Europe, is the gateway to 450 million consumers in its hinterland.

The Netherlands is one of the twenty major economies of the world. To retain this position, the government focuses on measures to benefit all companies and in particular nine 'top sectors'. These sectors are: Agri & Food, Chemistry, Creative Industry, Energy, Hi-Tech Systems and Materials, Life Sciences & Healthcare, Logistics, Horticulture / Propagation Materials, and Water. Smart collaboration between business, science and government is central to these efforts.

Left: Heavy shipping traffic on the River Waal at Nijmegen. Thirty per cent of the total freight transport is done by inland waterways. The Netherlands has the largest and most modern fleet of inland waterway vessels in Europe.

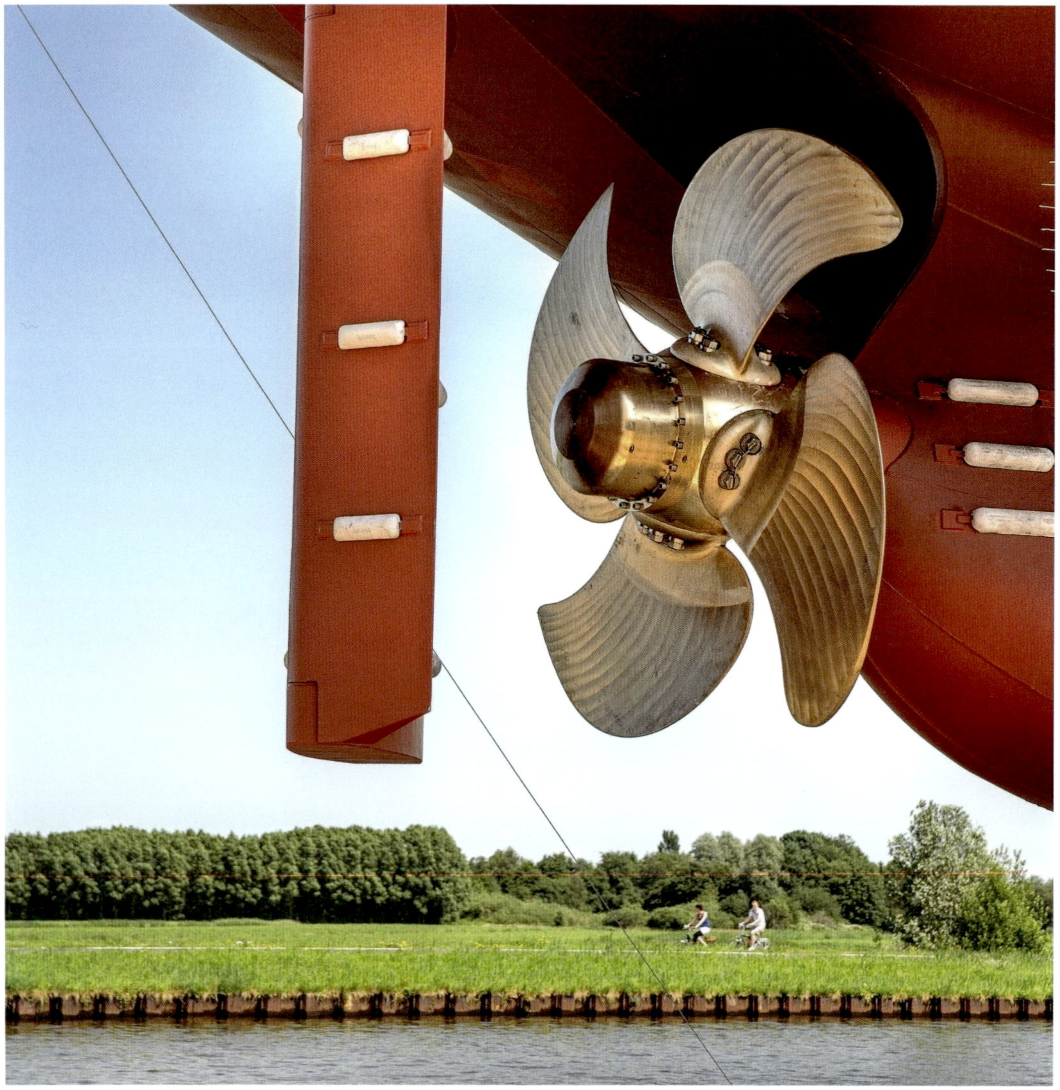

Shipbuilding

The once-thriving shipbuilding industry came to an end in the twentieth century. The cause was the increasing competition from Asian countries. A number of specialist docks have survived, however, such as builders of cargo vessels, dredgers, tugs, high-speed craft, and shipyards that focus on the construction and finishing of (very) luxury yachts.

Top: Propeller of a cargo ship at the yard of shipbuilder Ferus Smit in Westerbroek, Groningen province.

Right: Launching of the same vessel on the Winschoterdiep.

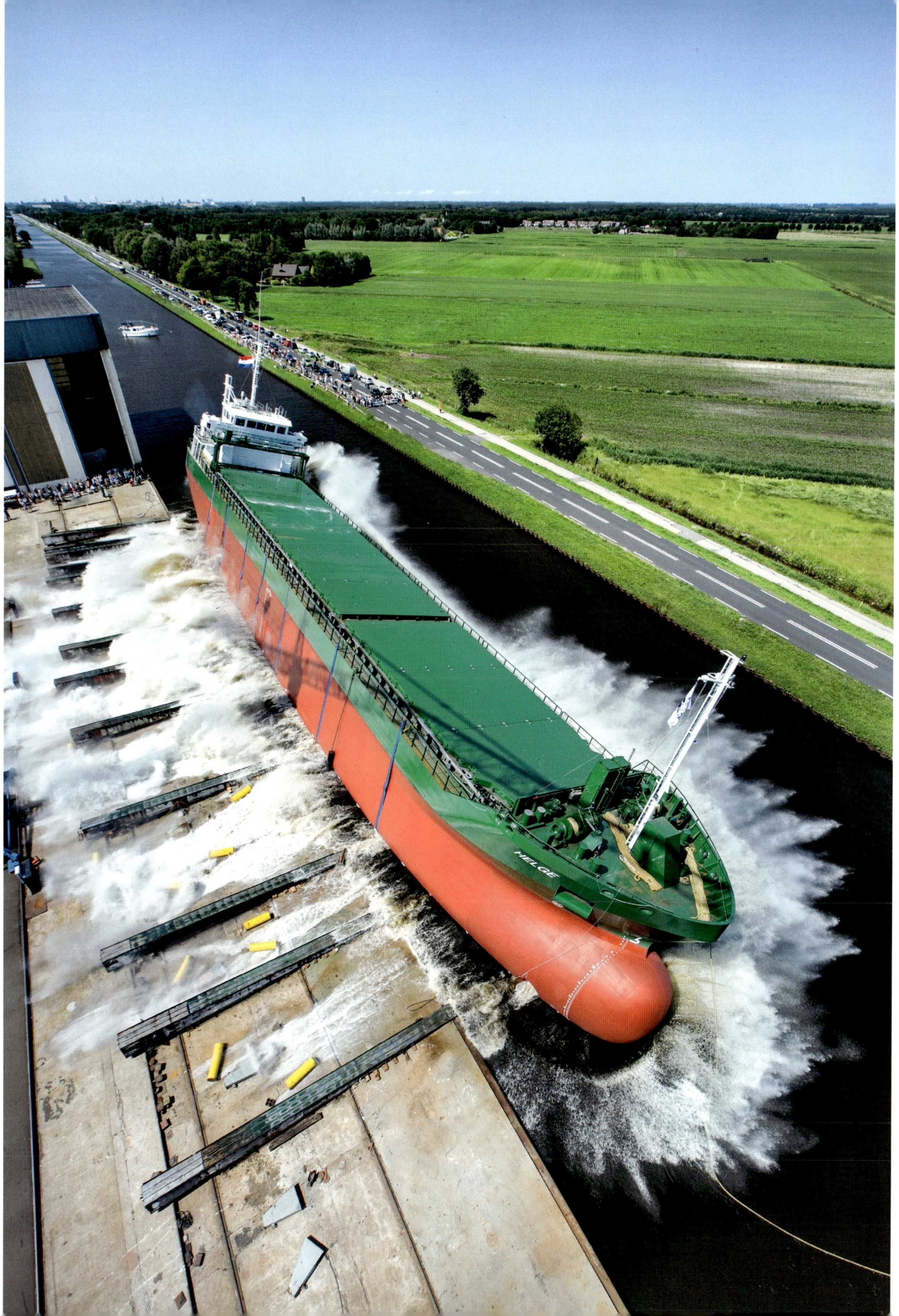
HELGE

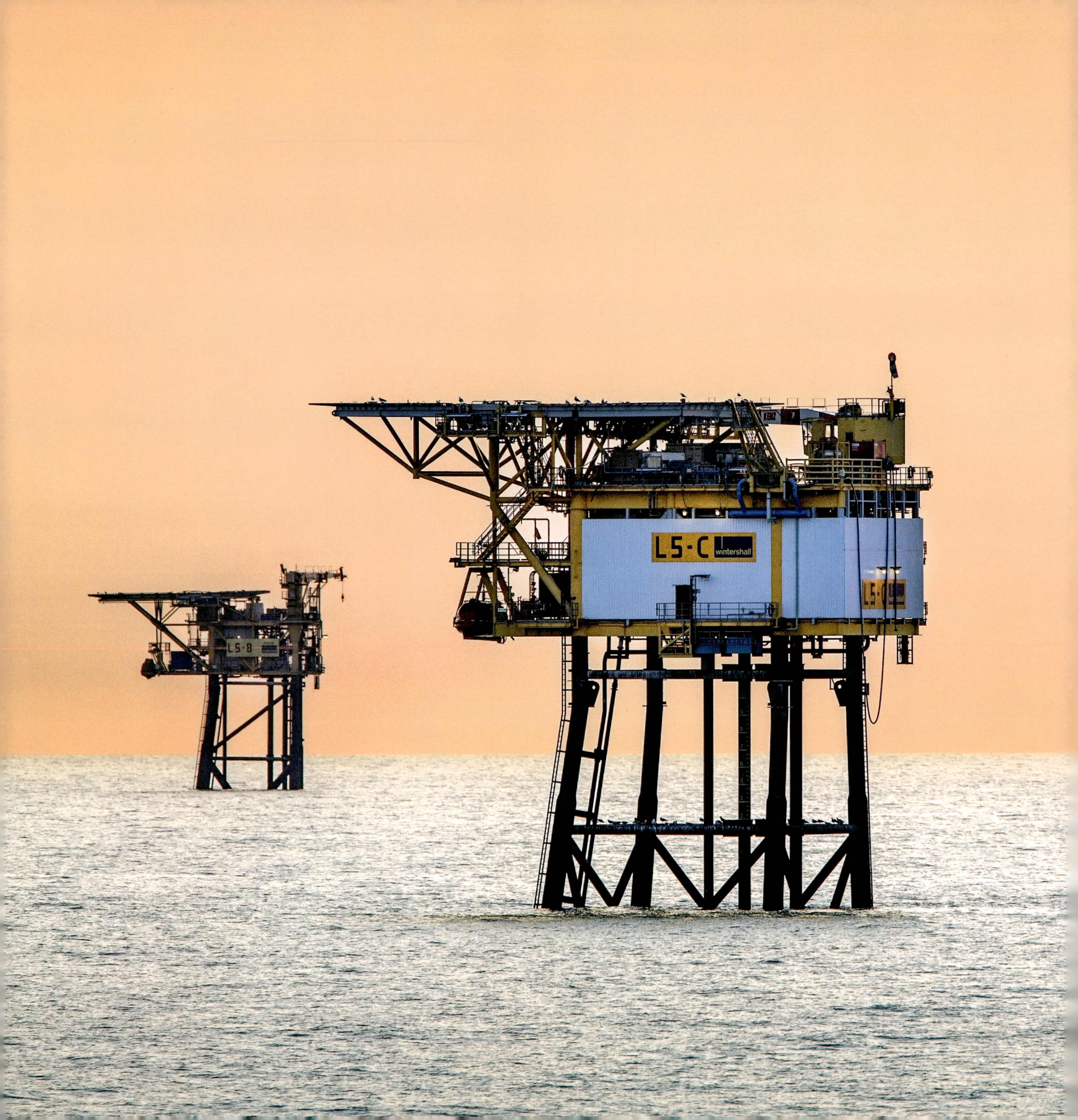
L5-C
wintershall
L5-B

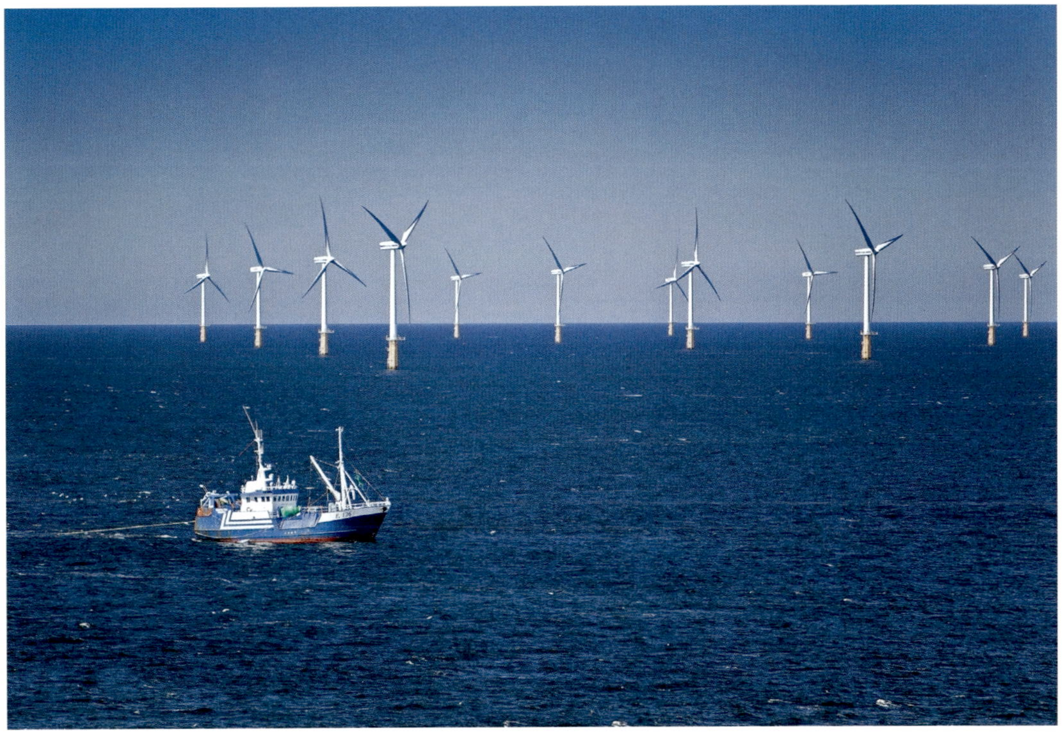

Energy
Peat was for centuries the main source of energy in the Netherlands; in the late nineteenth century, coal took over that function. Natural gas was discovered on the seabed off Groningen in 1959, and later also in the Dutch part of the continental shelf of the North Sea. And not just a little, either: it constitutes roughly 25 per cent of European gas reserves. Currently, gas provides for 50 per cent of the country's total energy needs.

Fisheries
From the seventeenth to the late nineteenth century, whaling was a good source of income. Today, the fishing sector is one with a relatively small economic share. Overfishing, and the strict catch quotas that were set in response, have caused the fleet and the processing industry to diminish.

Left: The Dutch economy does not stop at the coast. The country's exclusive economic zone, also called Dutch continental shelf, is actually larger (57,000 sq. km) than the land area itself (41,526 sq. km). In the picture: gas production platforms in the North Sea.

Top: A fishing boat passing wind turbines off the coast of Egmond aan Zee.

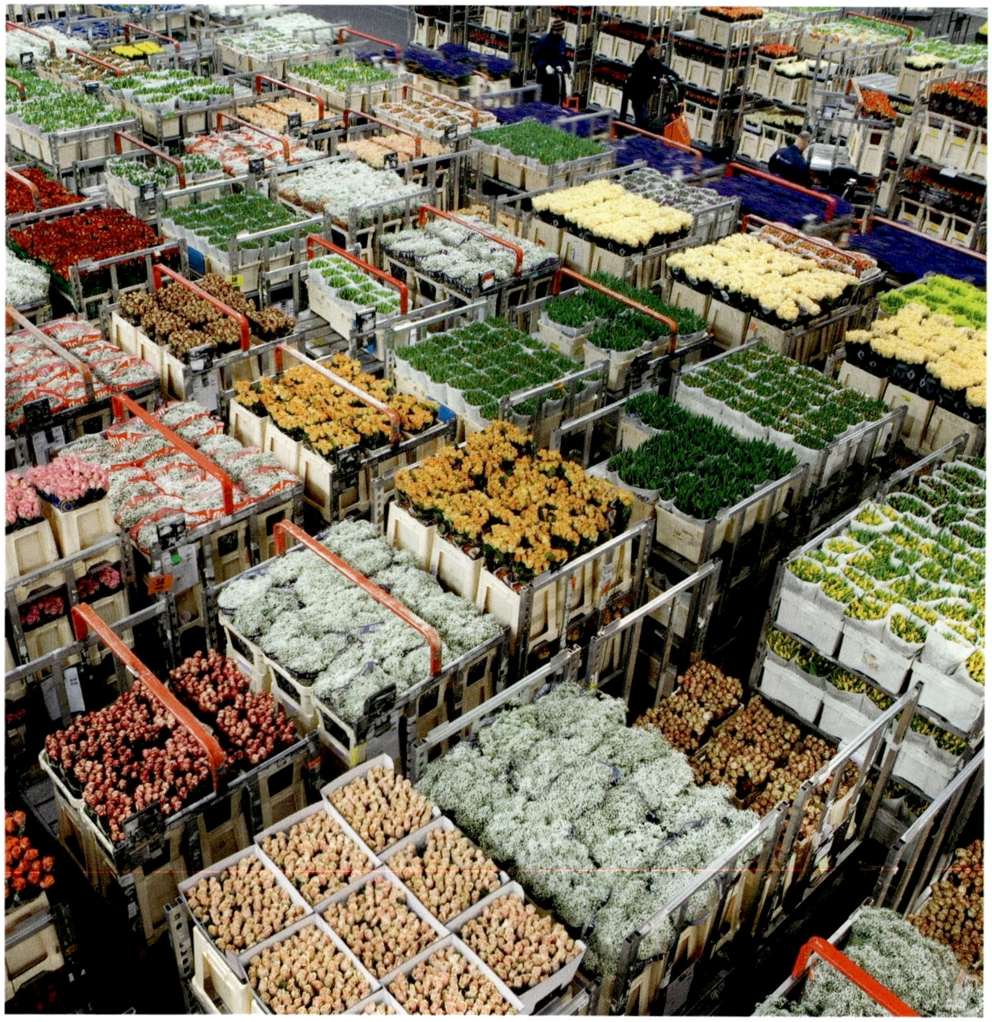

Bulbs

The flower bulb growing region, the Bollenstreek, lies along the coasts of the provinces of Noord-Holland and Zuid-Holland. Here, and now also in Flevoland, a remarkable spectacle takes place in spring as the tulips, daffodils and hyacinths come out. The colours entice tourists from around the world – every year there are about 12 million who come to the Netherlands.

Top: Aalsmeer Flower Auction, the largest commercial building in the world. The Netherlands is the world's largest floriculture exporter.

Right: Aerial view of tulip fields in Lisse.

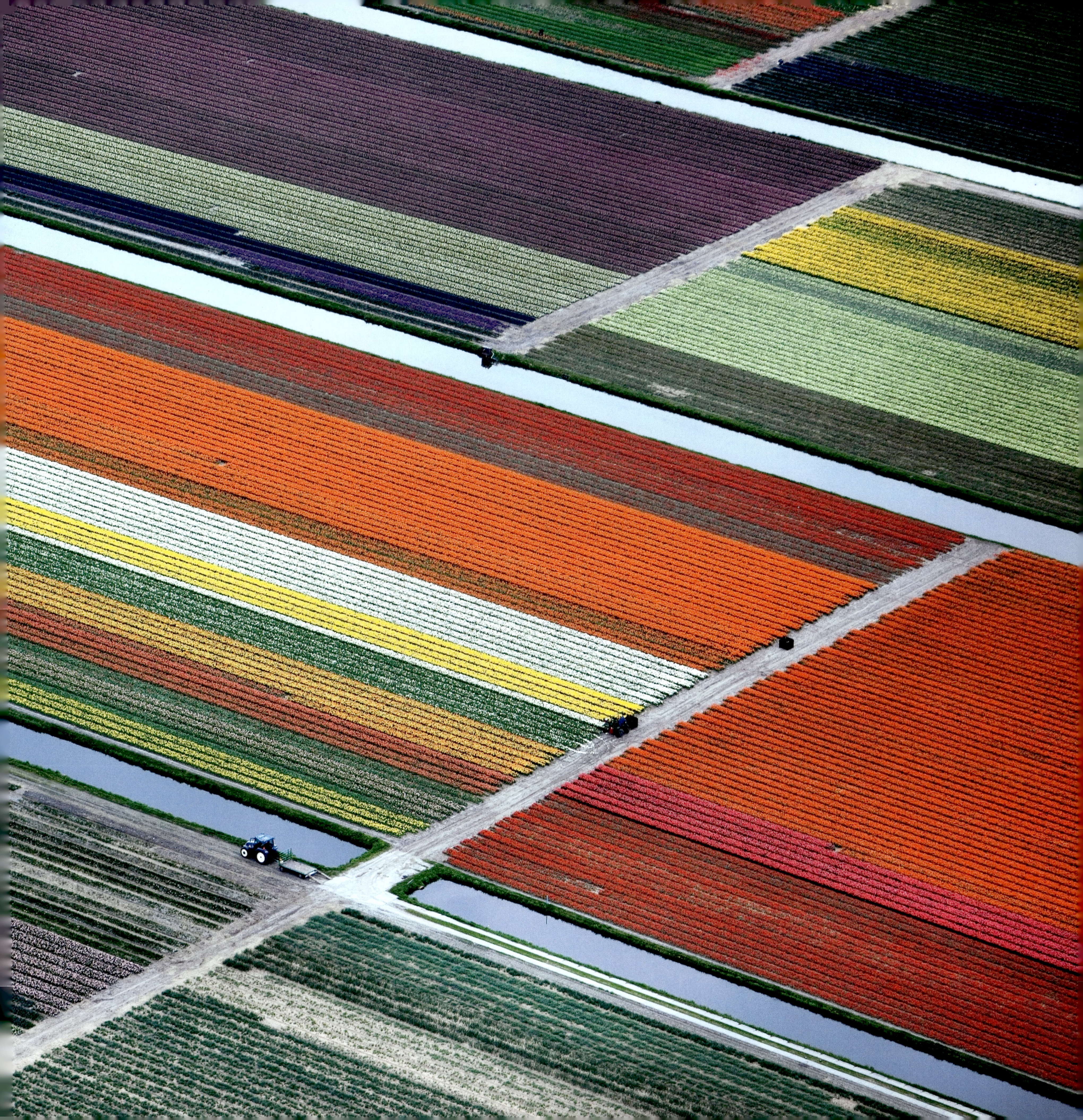

194

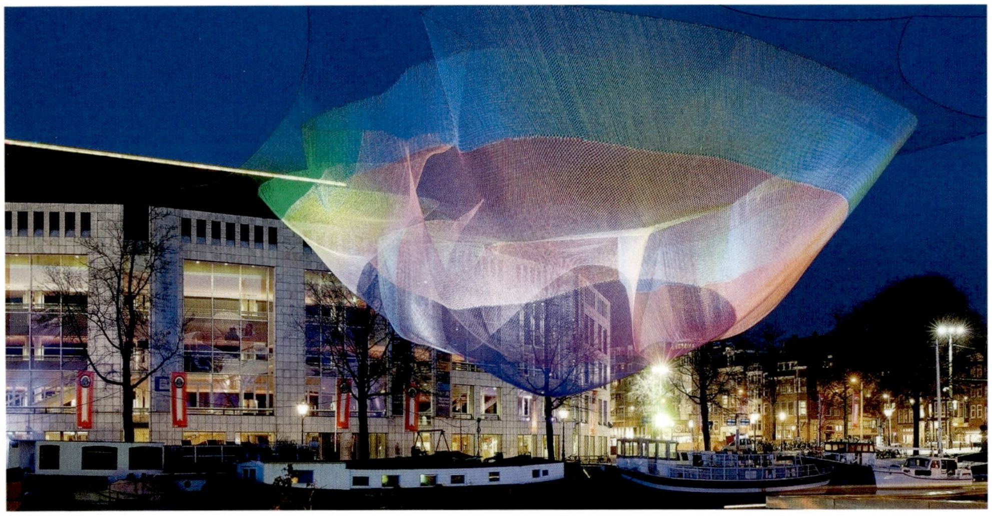

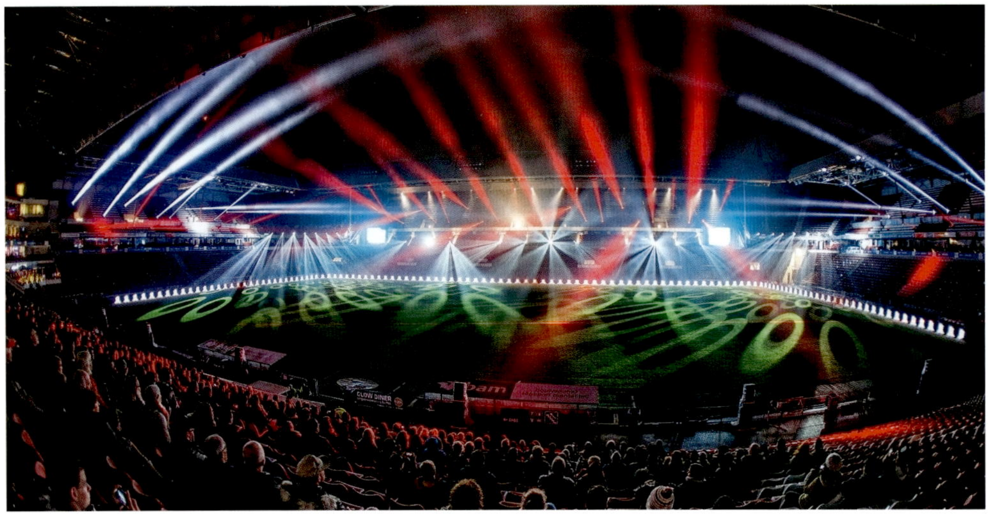

Top: The Amsterdam Light Festival. A 'net' of light by Janet Echelman stretches above the River Amstel near the Stopera.

Bottom: Clashlight, a project by Dutch artist Noralie, at the Philips Stadium during GLOW, a light festival in Eindhoven.

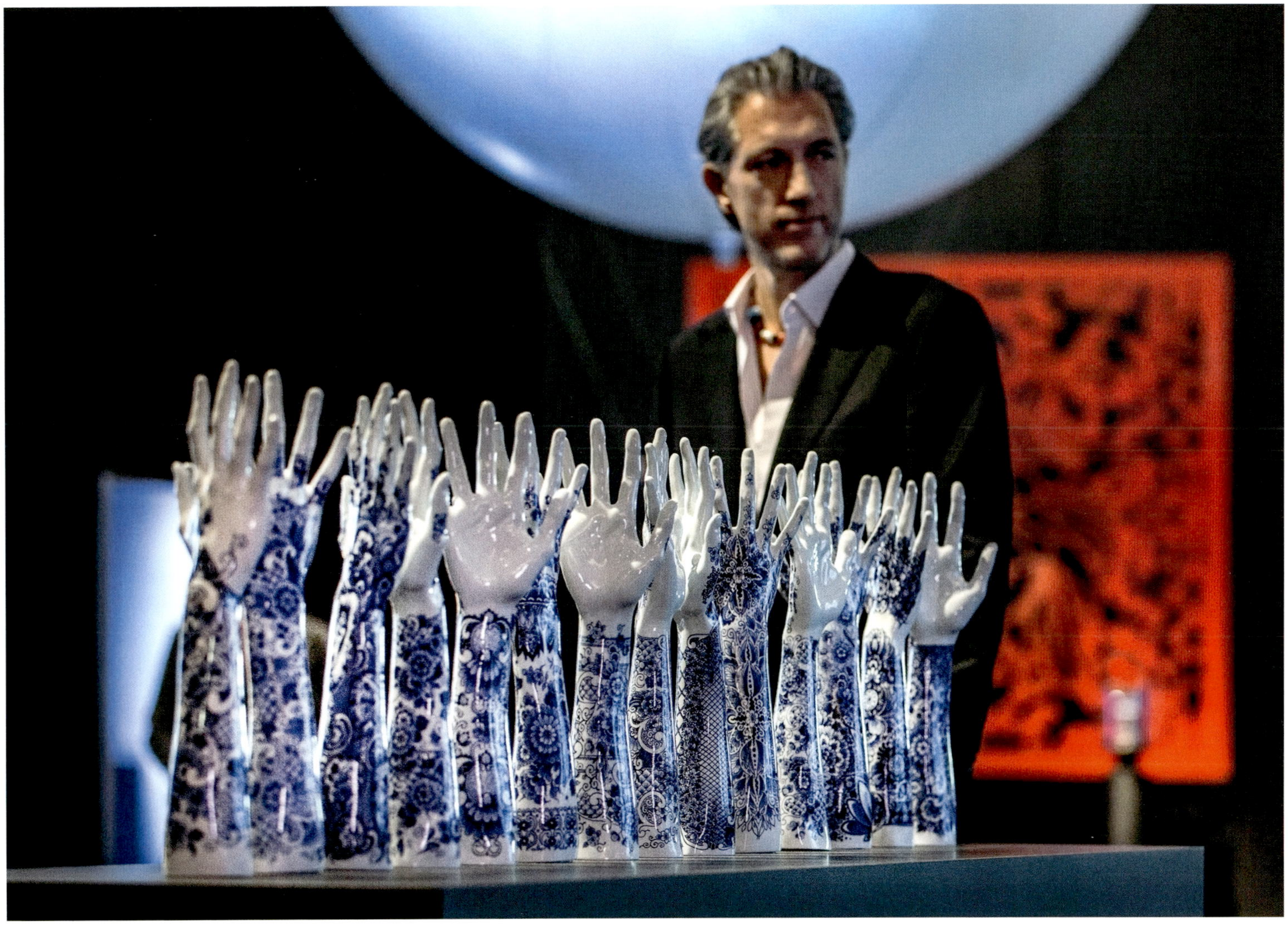

Dutch Design

The creative industry is the most dynamic sector of the Dutch economy and a top ten player internationally. The creative industries, such as design, media & entertainment, fashion, gaming, and architecture, are also innovation drivers for other sectors.

Top: The porcelain sculpture *Fragile Fingers on a Grand Piano* by Dutch designer Marcel Wanders arose from his desire to tattoo the hands and forearms of the world-renowned Dutch pianist Iris Hond. It is executed in Delft Blue colours, a symbol of Dutch tradition and beauty.

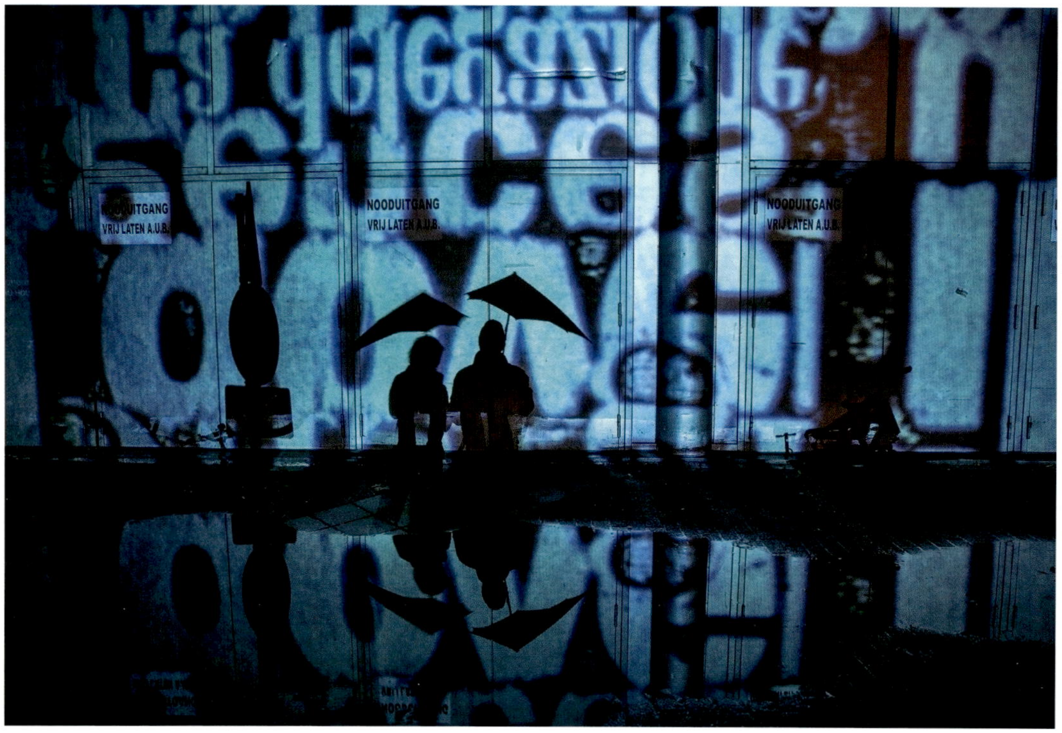

Top: Light projection on a storehouse by the Austrian artist Starsky during the GLOW light festival in Eindhoven. A couple with a Senz storm umbrella enjoying the spectacle.

Right: SENSATION – the world's leading dance event, held in the Amsterdam ArenA – a concept exported to many countries. The Amsterdam ArenA is the home of Ajax FC, but the Dutch national side also hosts its international matches at the stadium. This state-of-the-art multi-purpose stadium is internationally renowned. It is not only the setting for parties, concerts and football matches; it has also become an icon of sustainability for entertainment, sports and business. This is a concept that is now being exported worldwide.

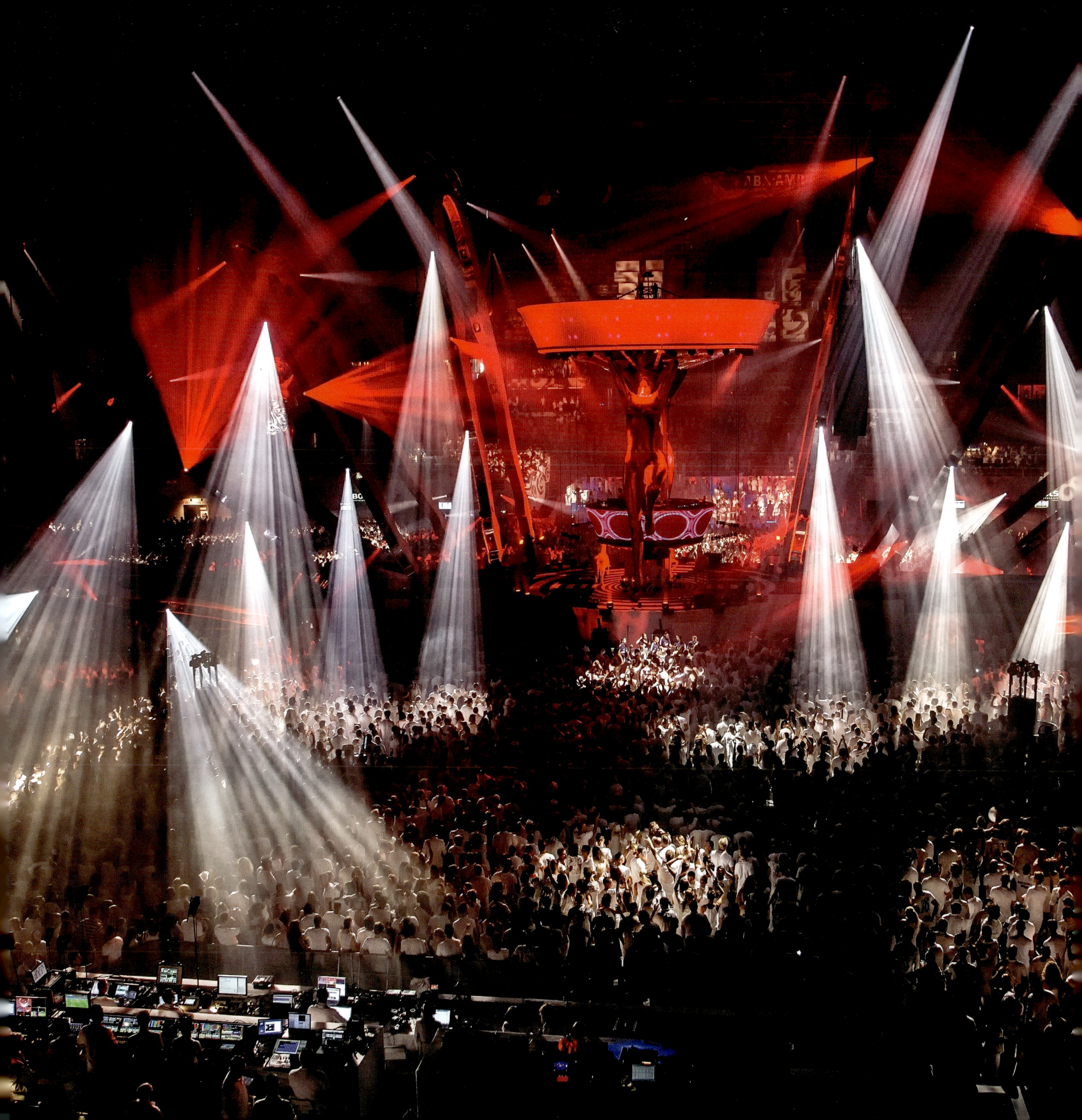

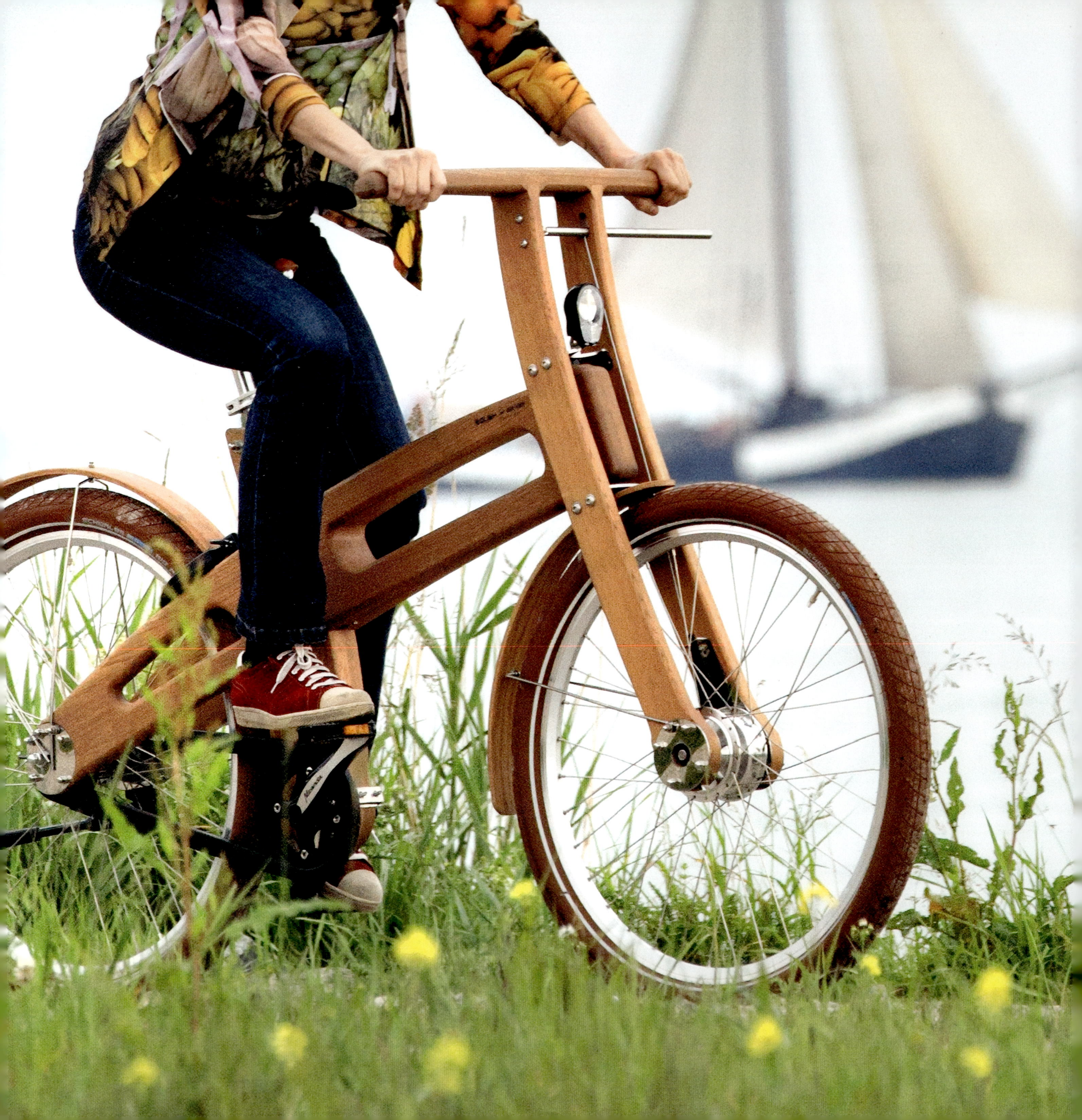

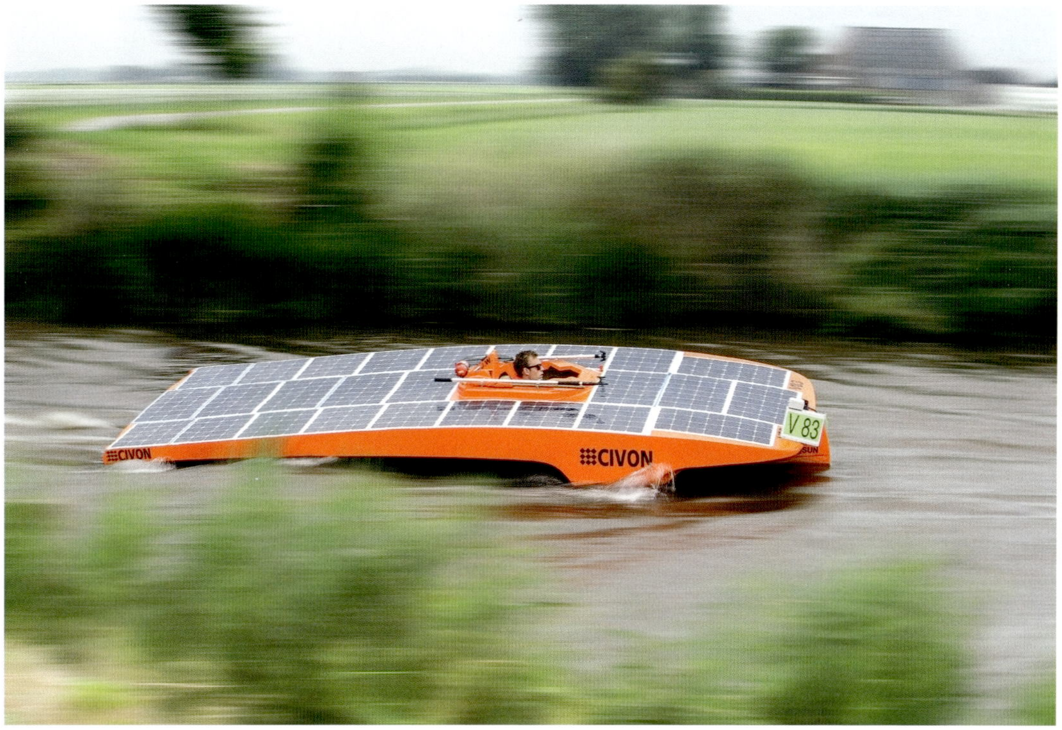

Left: The Dutch government is increasingly concentrating on design and innovation. Designer Jan Gunneweg does both. He designed a sustainable and beautiful wooden bike, for which he won a great deal of recognition worldwide.

Top: At all Dutch technical universities, students work with large companies. Dutch solar-powered cars often win prizes in international competitions. There is also much attention being paid to boats powered by solar energy, like this boat, sailed by the Achterhoek team from Doetinchem (an inland town on the German border) during the DONG Energy Solar Challenge Race in the waters of Groningen and Frisia.

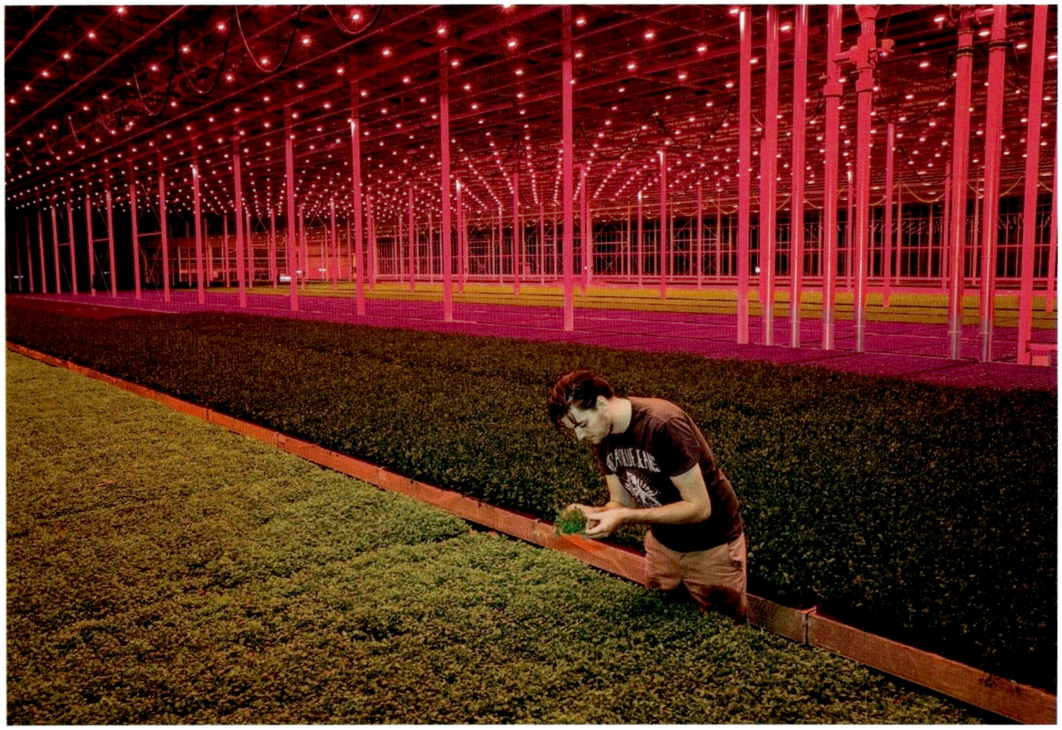

Greenhouse horticulture

The Dutch Horticulture & Propagation Materials top sector aspires to hold the position of world leader when it comes to sustainable solutions for issues including food, energy and water. Already, this is a sector that is at the forefront of the development of, for example, crops that are less sensitive to weather conditions, or that need less pesticide spraying. Tomatoes, lettuce, cucumbers, mushrooms, peppers or cauliflower – wherever in the world you eat them, chances are they came from a greenhouse in the Westland or Aalsmeer growing districts. These two regions account for the majority of the nation's total of 150,000 hectares of greenhouses where ornamental plants, fruits and vegetables are grown.

Top: One of the greenhouses in the Westland is home to the innovative company Koppert Cress. This company specialises in seedlings of unique plants, each with their own taste, smell, feel or presentation. Plants only need reddish-purple light to grow. Using only part of the light spectrum, generated by sustainable LEDlighting, leads to great energy savings.

Right: From the air, you can see why the Westland is nicknamed Glass City.

Following pages: Wheat harvest at Donderen in Drenthe province.

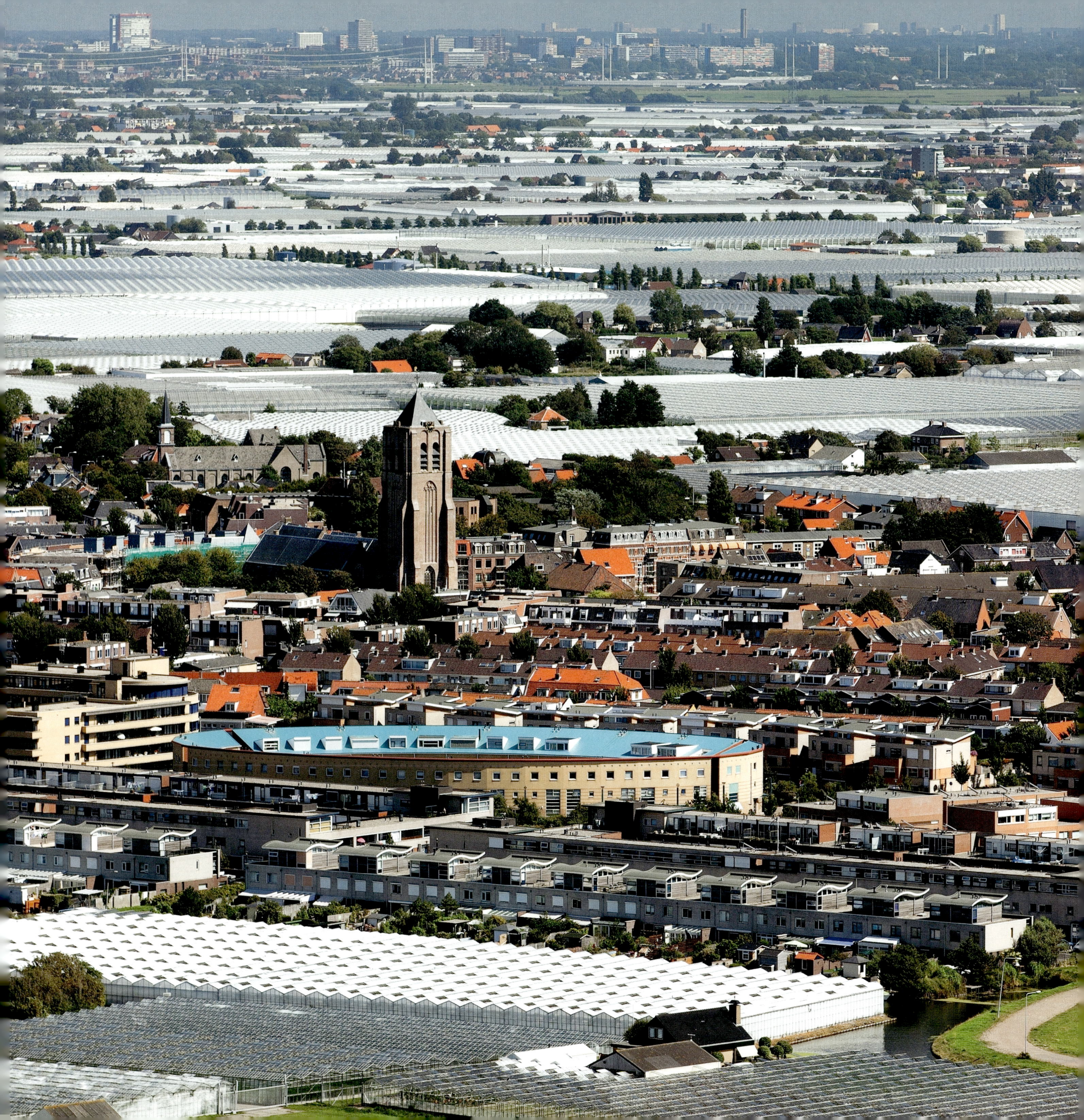

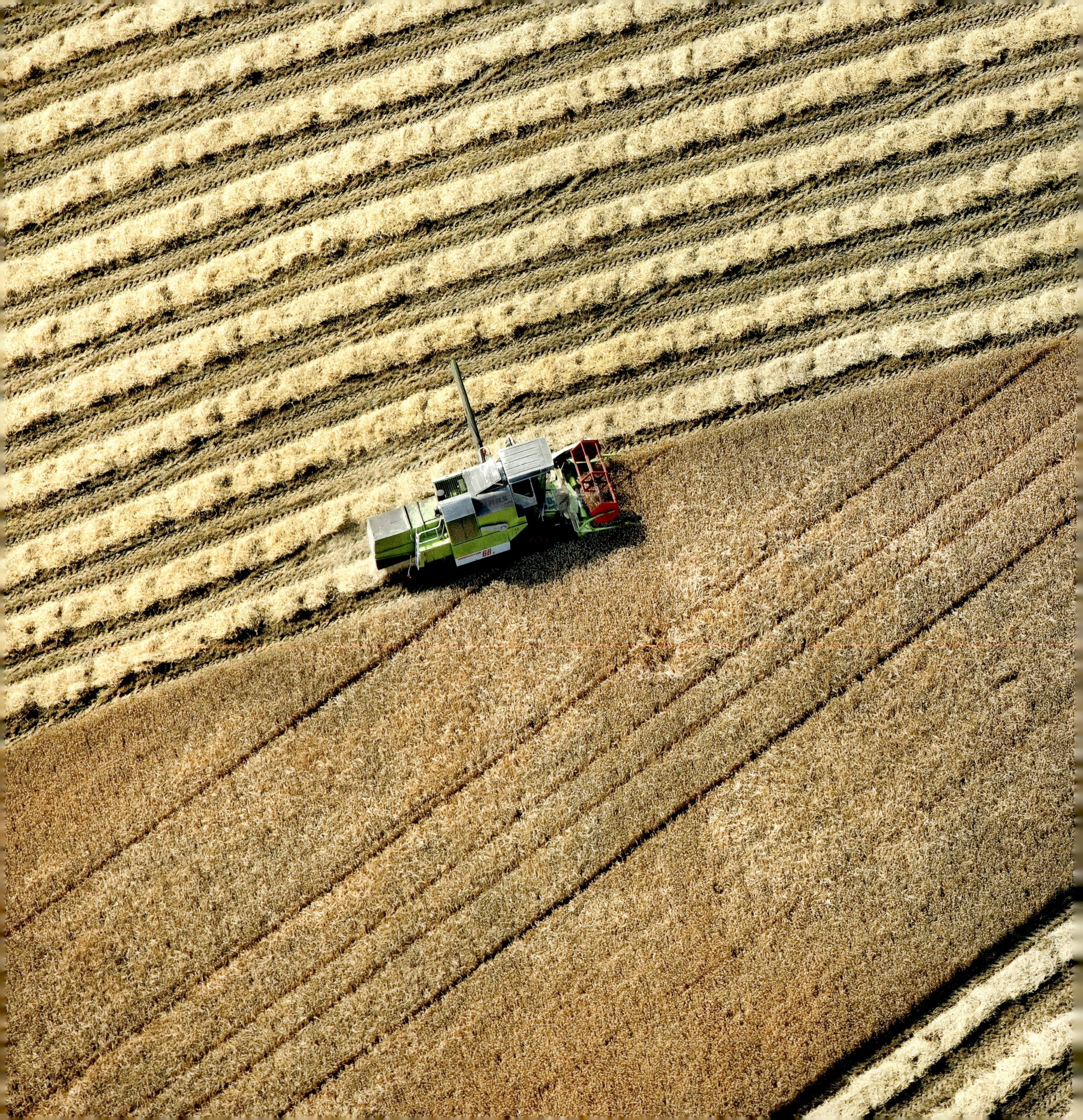

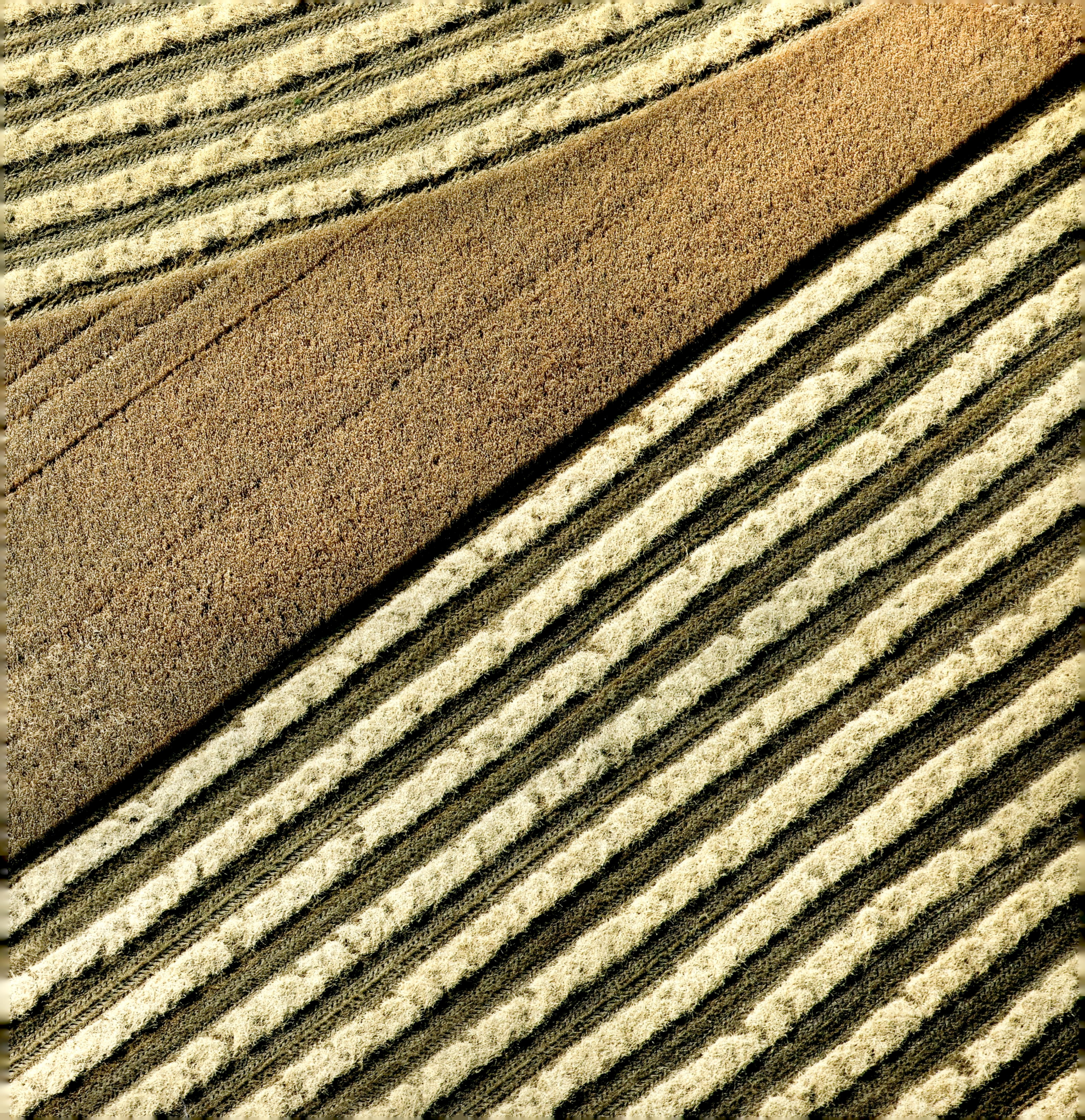

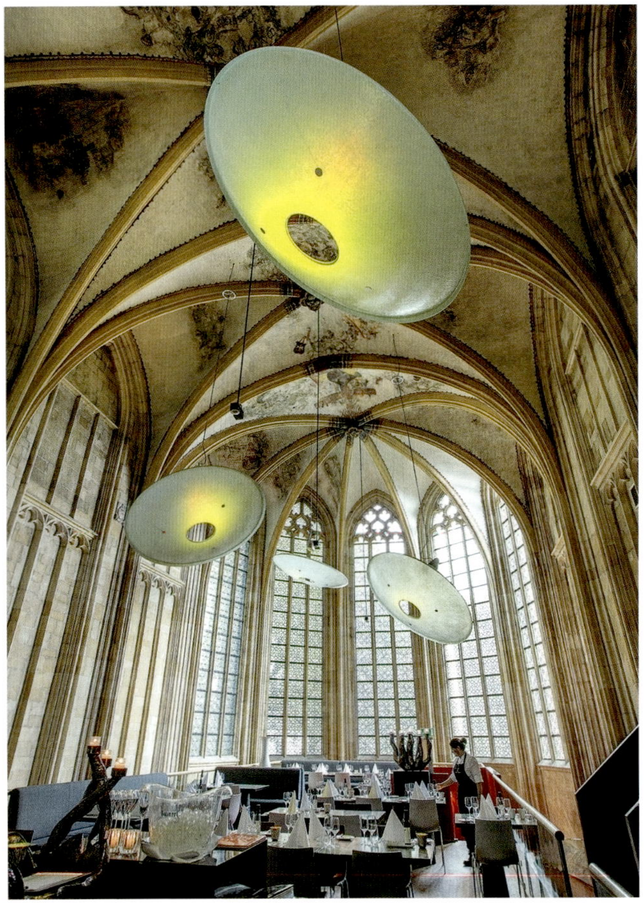

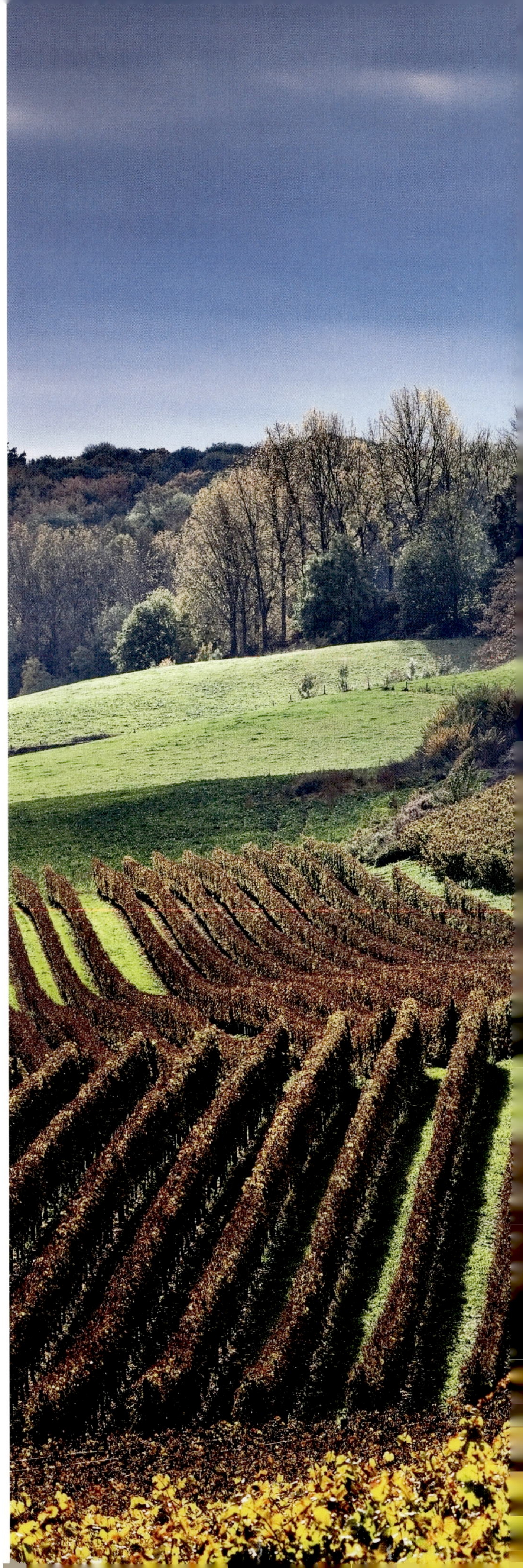

Top: Maastricht is the culinary capital of the Netherlands. In the picture: a waitress lays tables in the restaurant of the Kruisheren Hotel, a five-star design hotel located in a former Gothic monastery complex.

Right: De Apostelhoeve, the oldest vineyard in the Netherlands, on the slopes of Sint Pietersberg. Because of climate change, there are more and more vineyards to be found in the Netherlands.

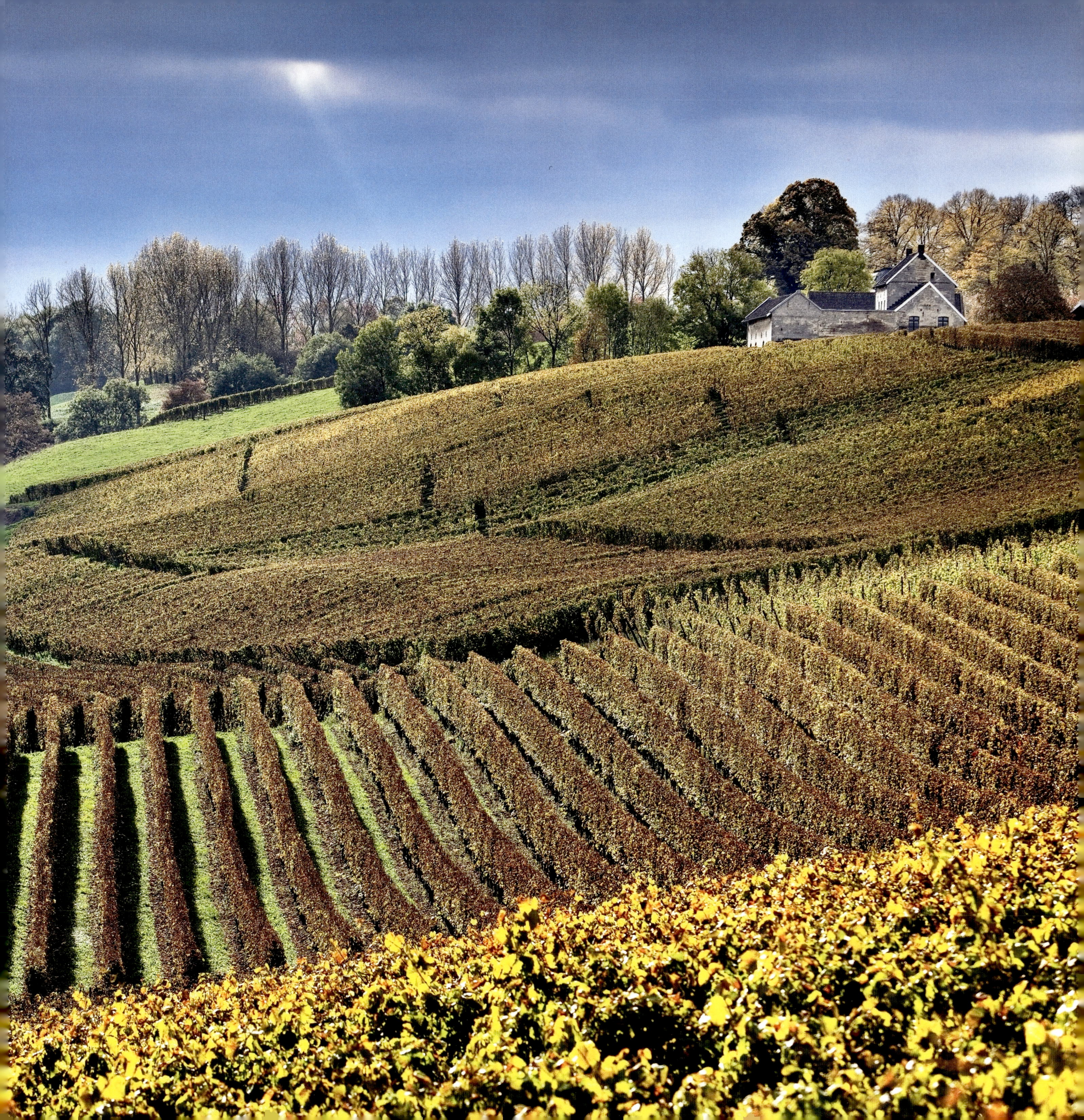

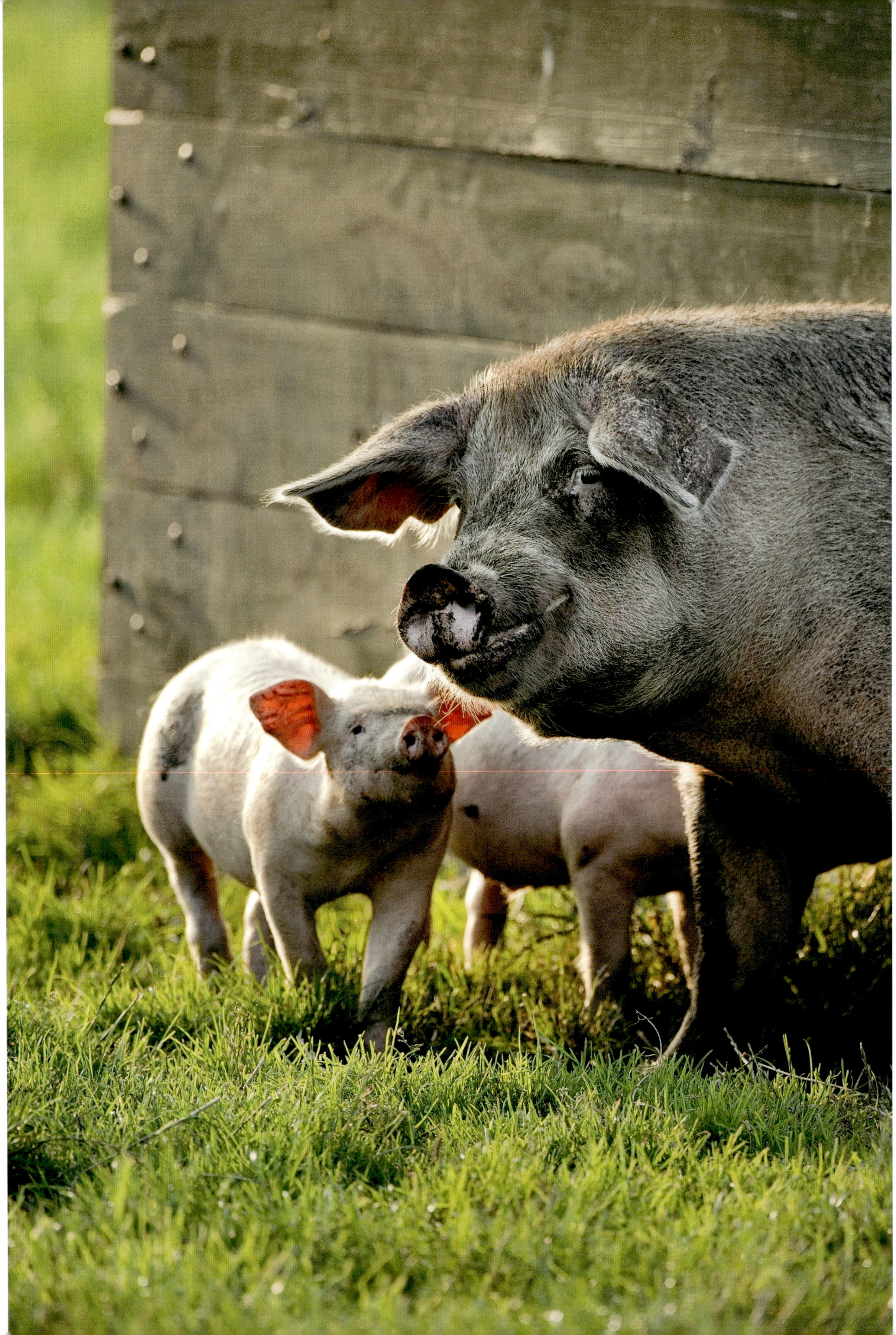

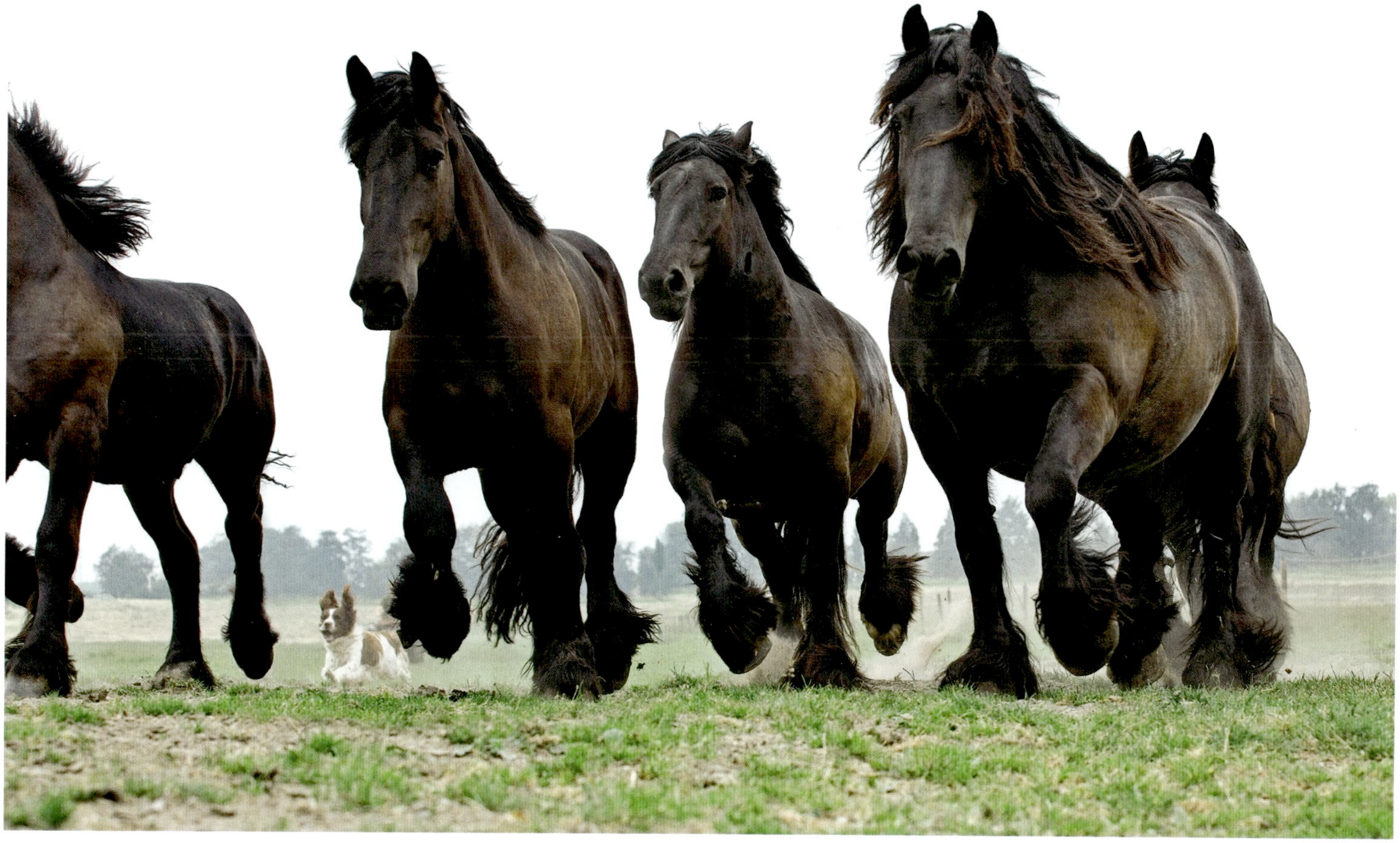

Stock farming

Grazing cows, horses, sheep and goats: they do not just form part of the Dutch landscape, they also play a part in the economy. Dutch farmers have excelled in efficiency since World War II. Mechanisation, upscaling, widespread of pesticides and veterinary medicines – add it all up and productivity has become enormous. A few examples: between 1973 and 2010, milk production per cow leaped from 4,600 to 7,900 litres. In terms of pigs and chickens, the Netherlands is the most densely populated country in the world. In 2010, for the first time, there were more than 100 million chickens, 45 million of which were chicks, in the country, and 10 billion eggs were laid. There has long been protest in the Netherlands against inhumane livestock-keeping practices, fuelled in recent decades by outbreaks of diseases such as bird flu, mad cow disease, scrapie and Q fever, not to mention the rise of resistant bacteria. Gradually, this has led to the development of alternative forms of animal husbandry.

Left: Sow with piglets in a meadow, a sight seldom seen nowadays. The large scale of pork farming means that virtually no pig sees the daylight any more.

Top: Zeeland draft horses trotting in a meadow, spurred on by the farmer's dog. Draft horses are now kept as a hobby. Their industrial function was lost once the tractor was introduced in agriculture.

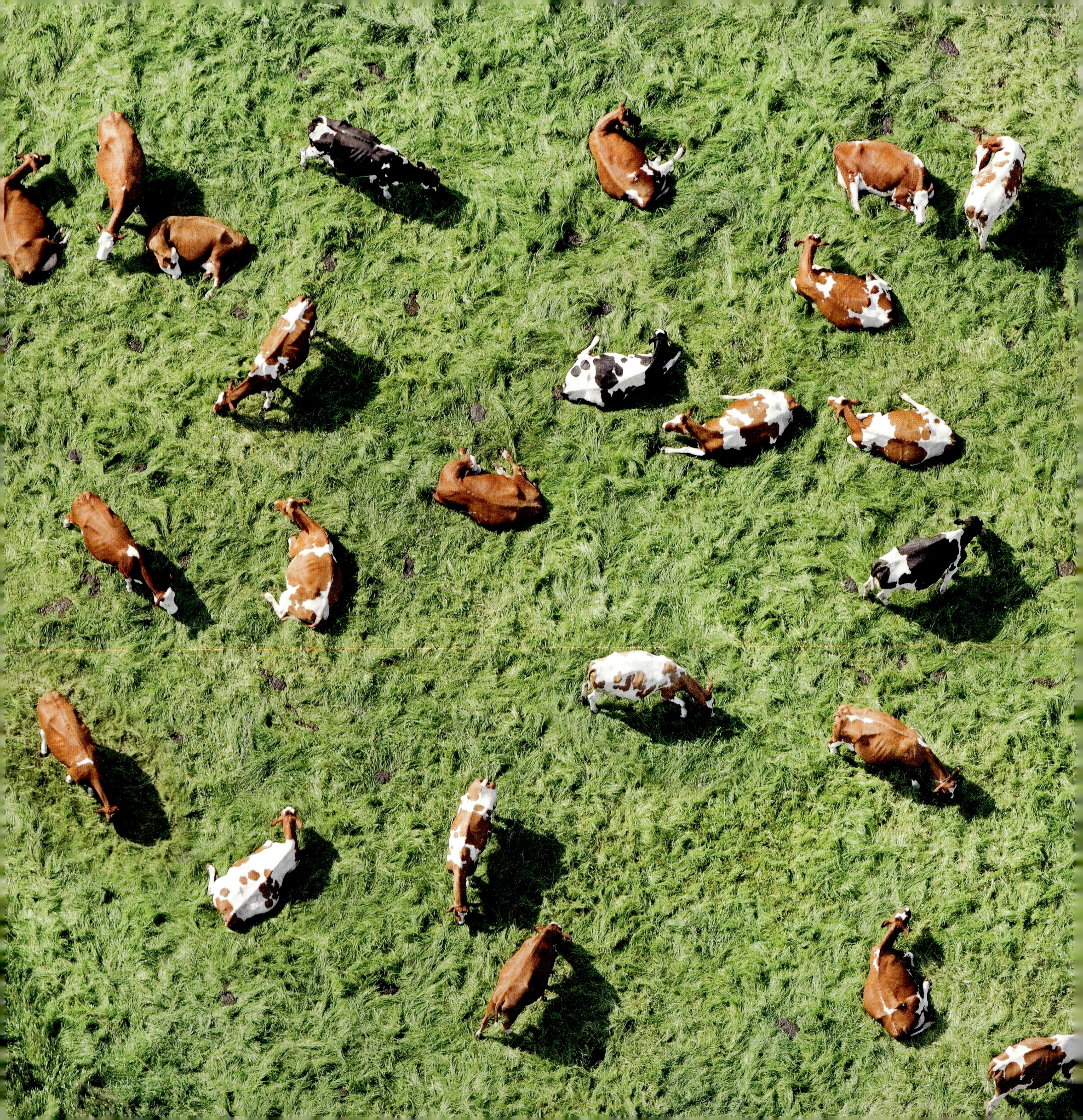

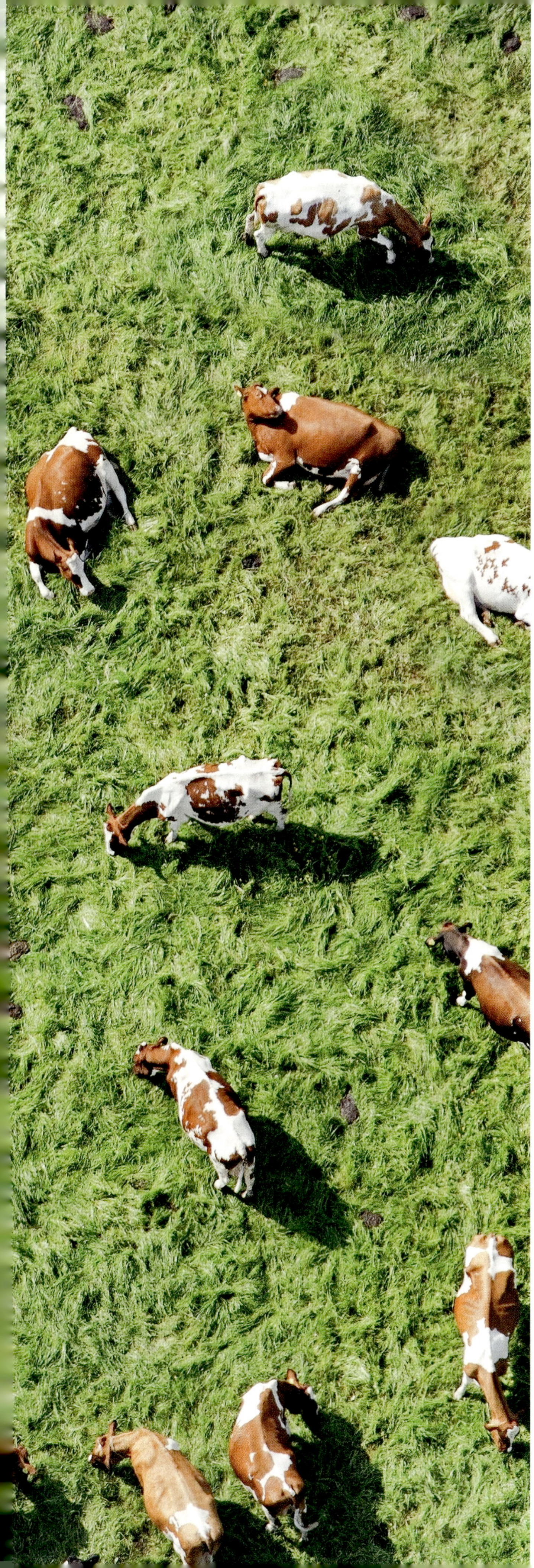

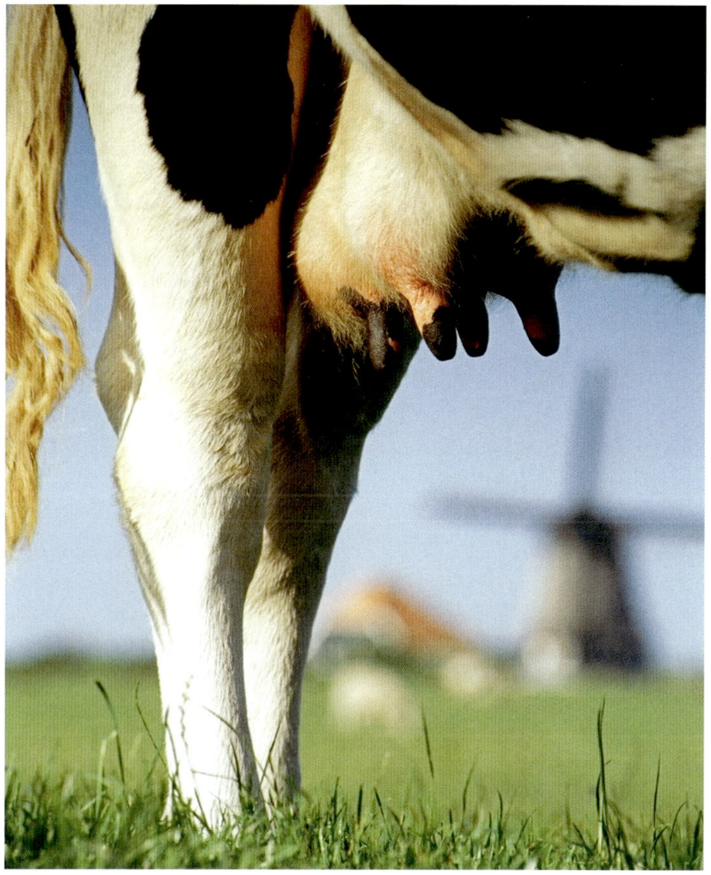

Left: Aerial view of cows chewing the cud.

Top: Iconic image: a cow, with a windmill in the background.

Following pages: Wind turbines on a wind farm near the port of Eemshaven. In the background, Goliath, a traditional drainage mill.

Page 212: A container ship entering the lock of the Zuidwillemsvaart at Heeswijk-Dinther in the province of Noord-Brabant.

Page 213: The Volkerak Locks near Willemstad, part of the Delta Works. The Volkerak Locks were constructed to enable inland vessels to cross from the Rhine to the Scheldt. They form the largest inland locks in Europe.

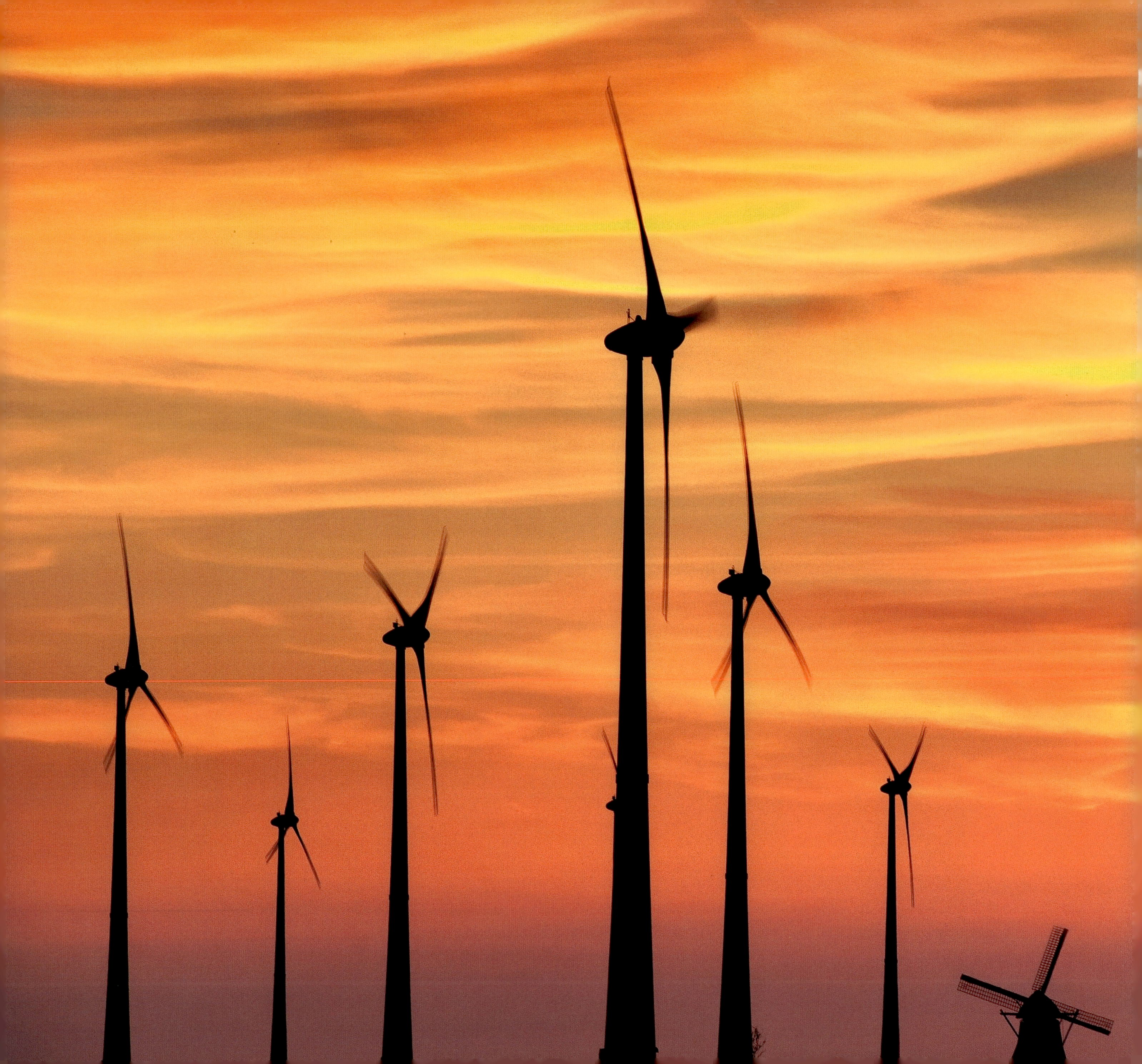

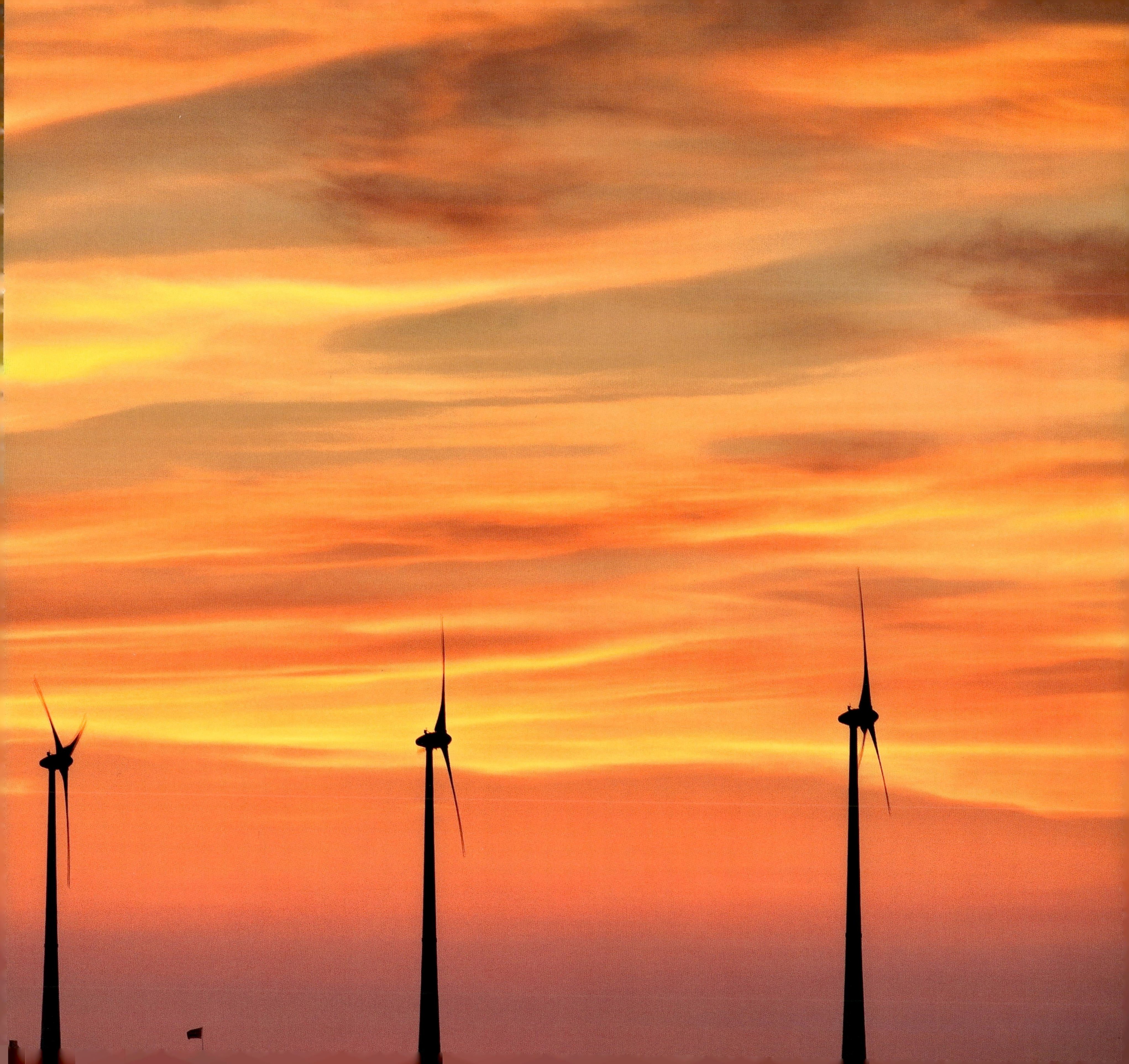

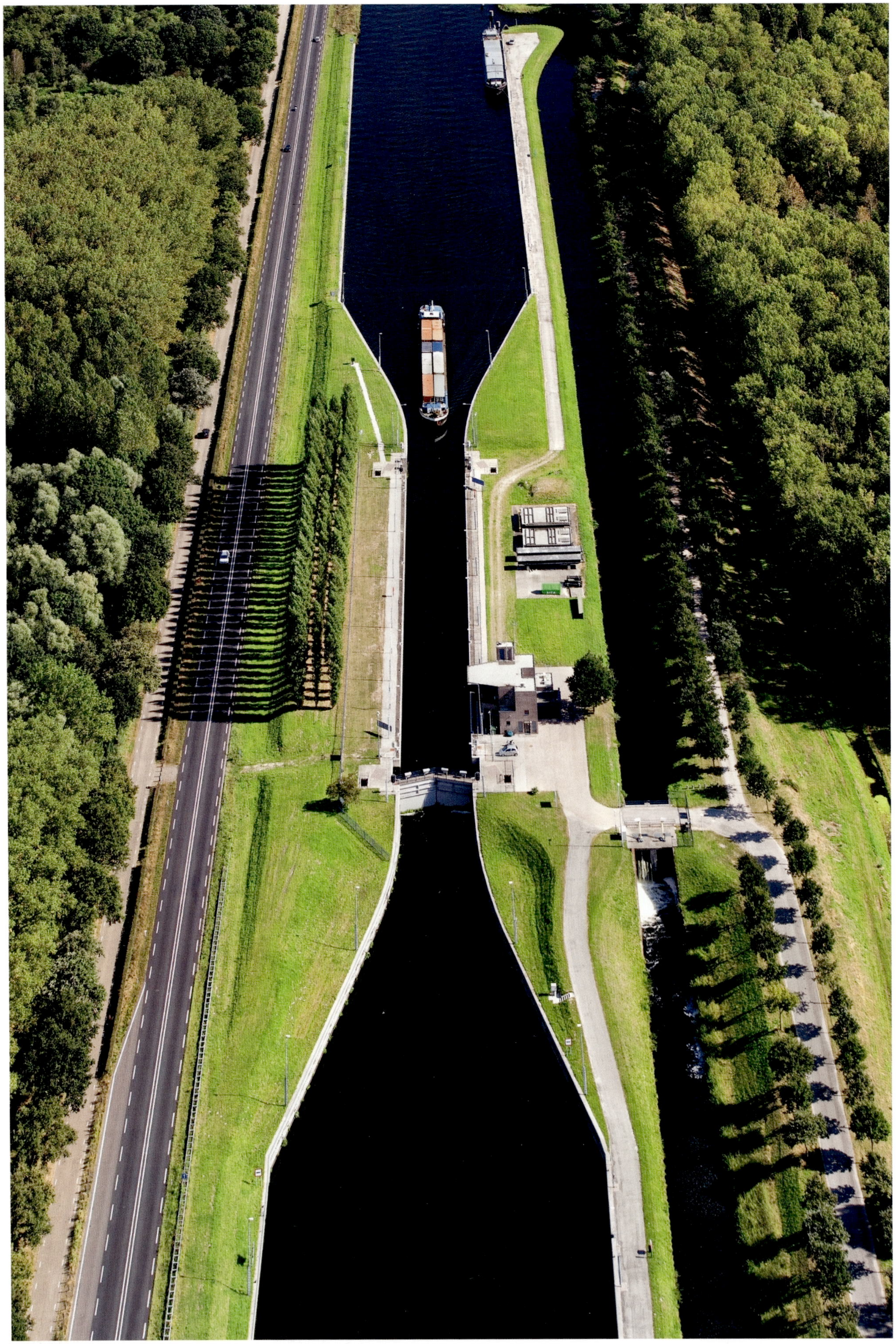

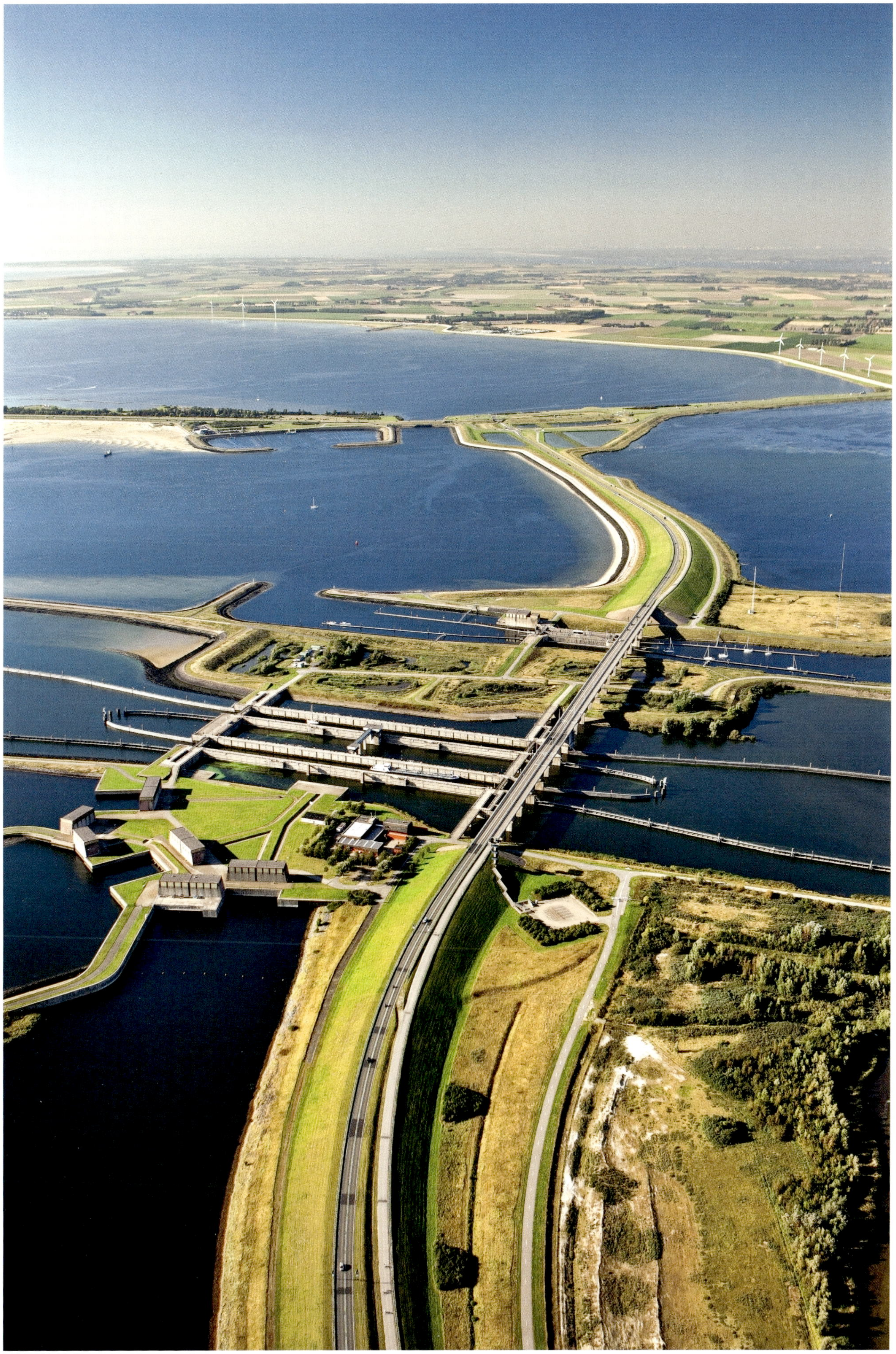

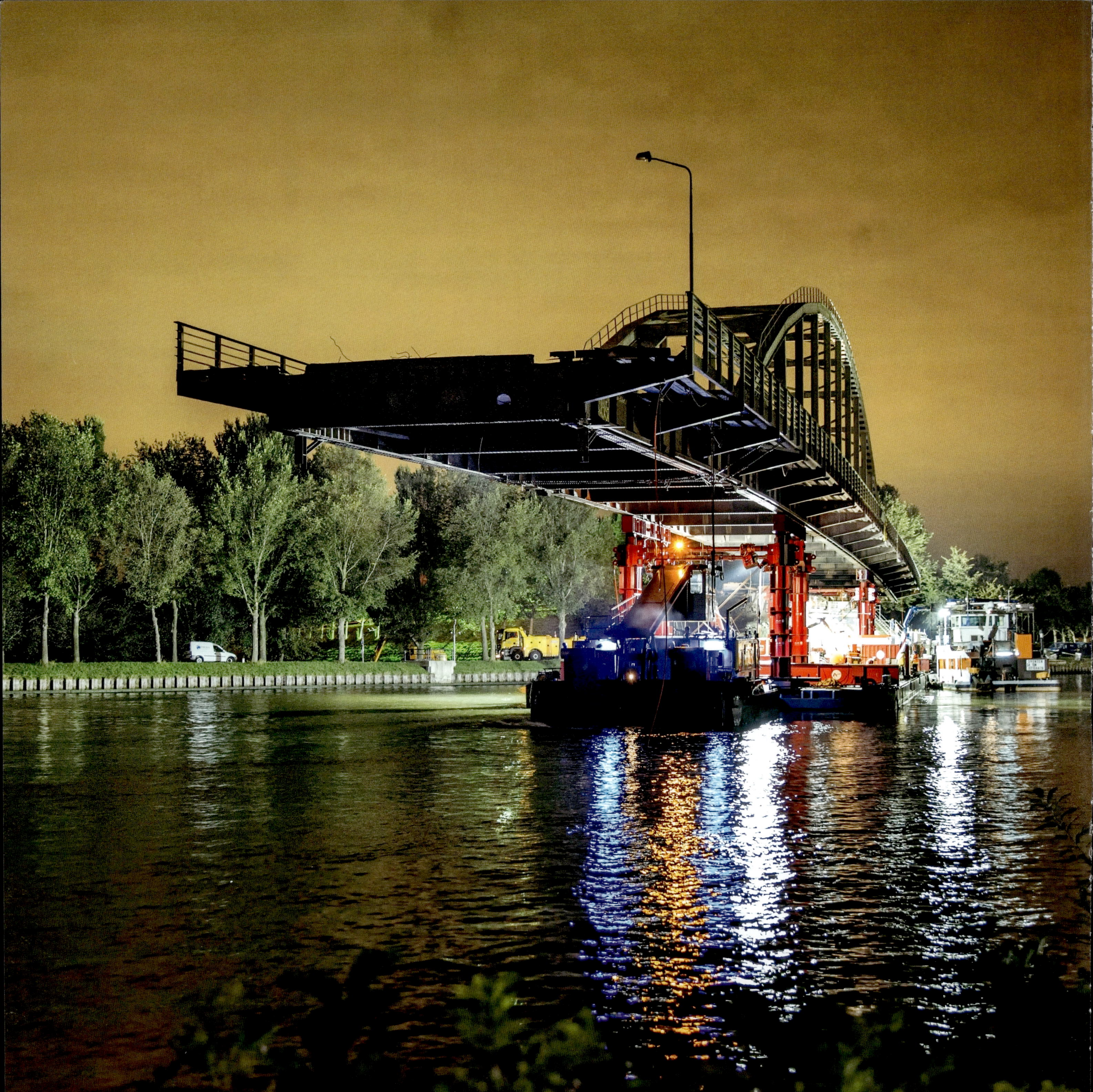

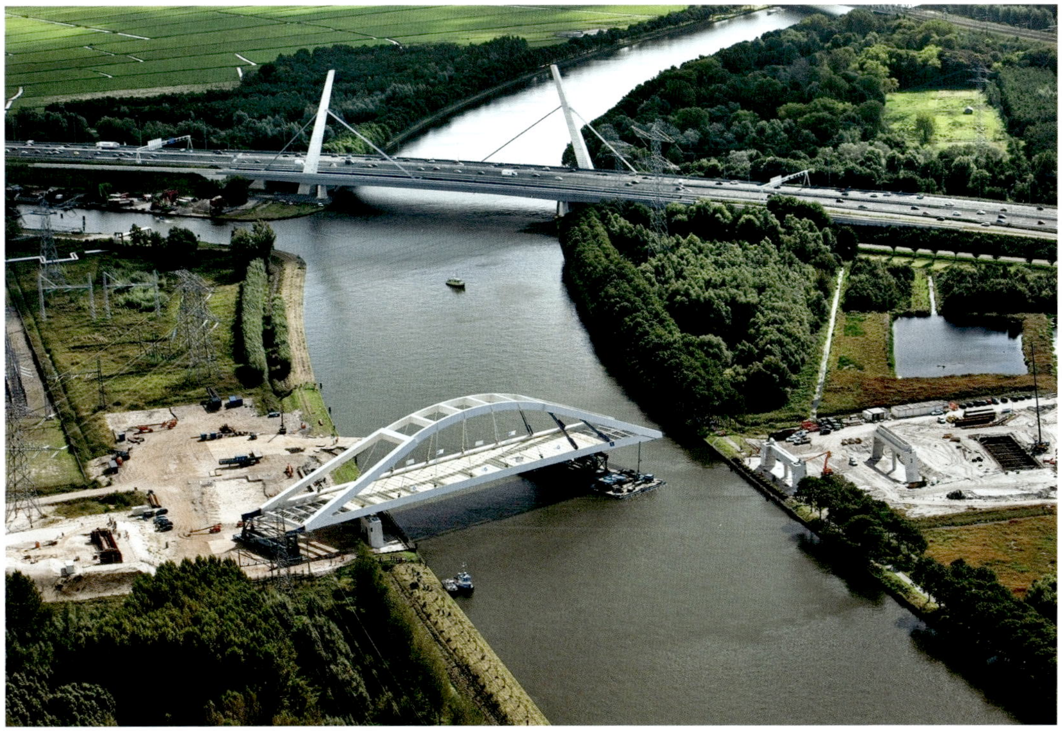

Left: Replacement of the Weesper Bridge over the Amsterdam-Rhine Canal.

Top: Placement of the Uyllanderbrug over the Amsterdam-Rhine Canal in Diemen.

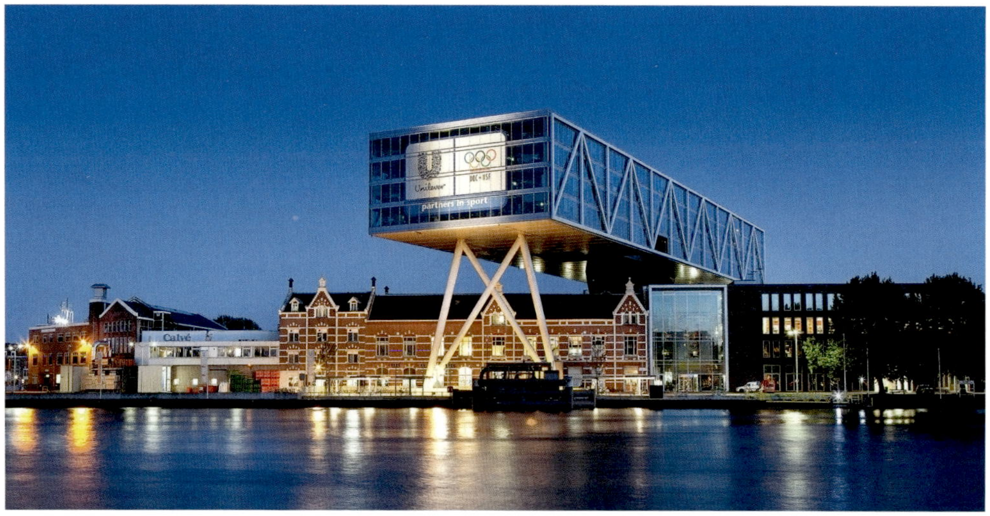

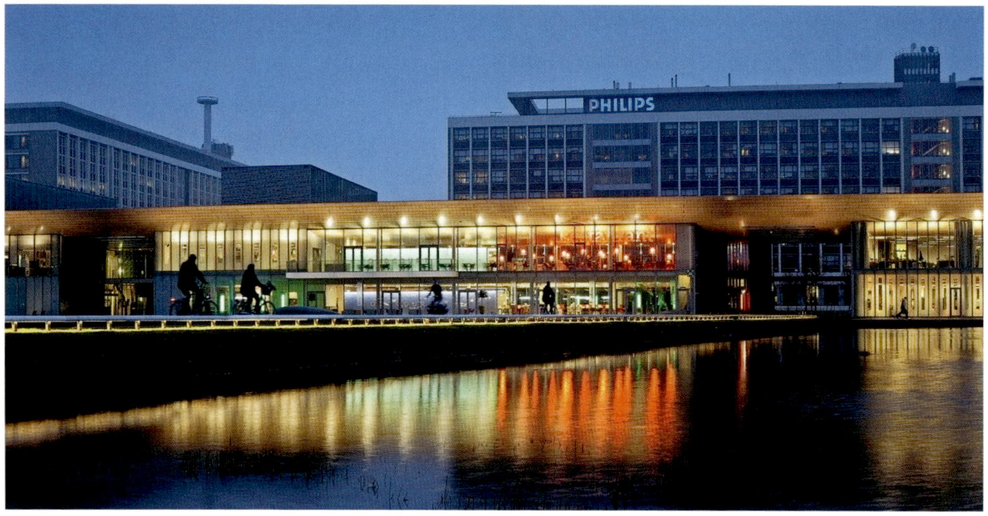

Multinational companies
Part of the (old) crown jewels of the Dutch economy are our multinationals, which – especially after the World War II – put the Netherlands on the international business map: Philips, Shell, Unilever, Heineken, Akzo, Ahold (Albert Heijn) and KLM – all names that resonate, even if some of them have partially or wholly ended up in foreign hands. Unilever continues to lead in the market for foodstuffs, personal care and cleaning products. Unilever Netherlands operates from an office in Rotterdam (top).

Industry
A particular concentration of industrial activity is located in the Eindhoven area, also known as the Brainport Region. Here, innovative companies, government and research institutions are working very closely together in the field of technology and design, such as at the Philips High Tech Campus (bottom).

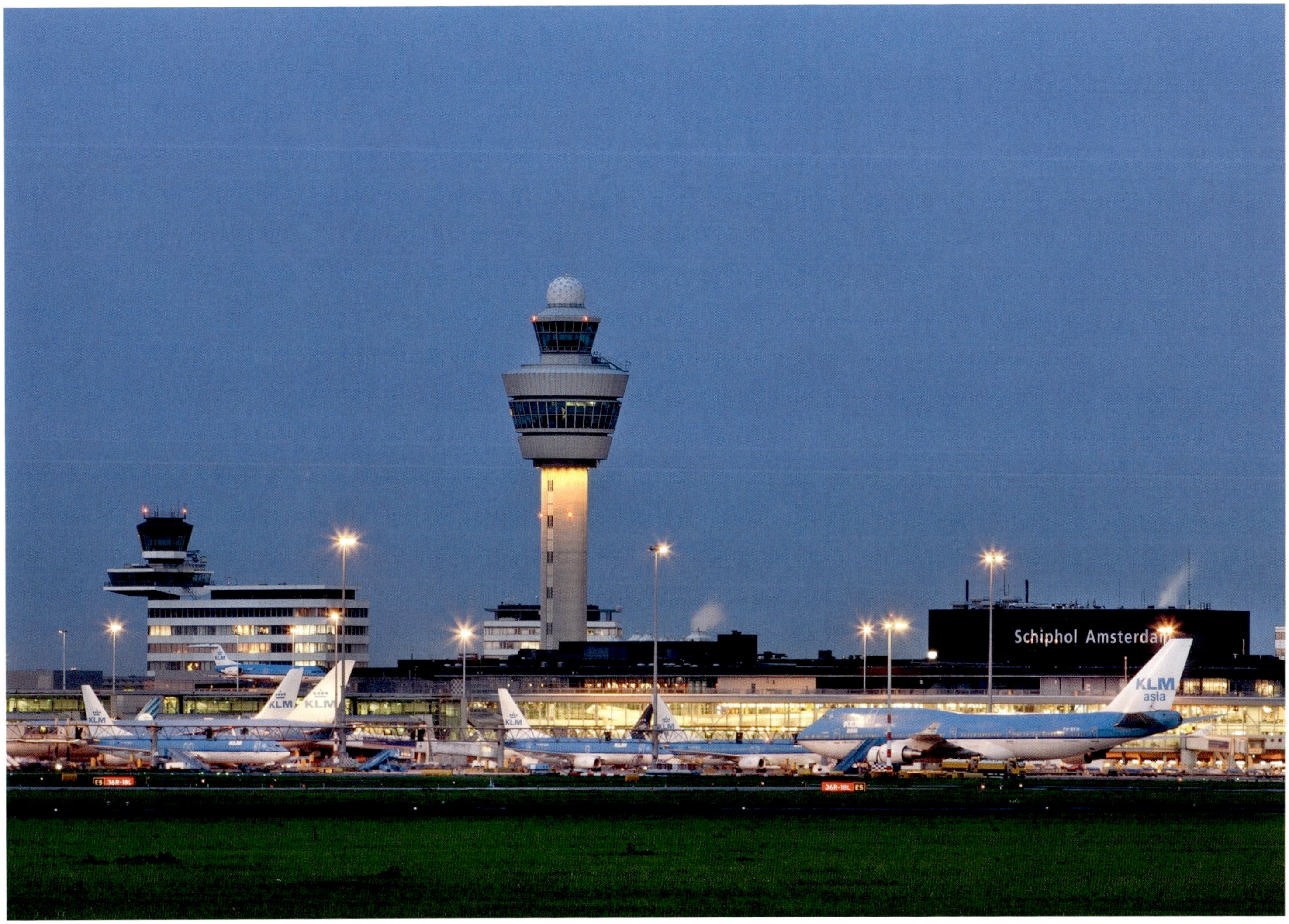

Gateway

The concept of the Netherlands as the 'Gateway to Europe' refers to more than just the port of Rotterdam. The country's other *mainport*, Schiphol Airport, plays a decisive role in the Dutch economy, too. Every year, more than 50 million passengers use this national airport and over 1.5 million tonnes of freight passes through it.

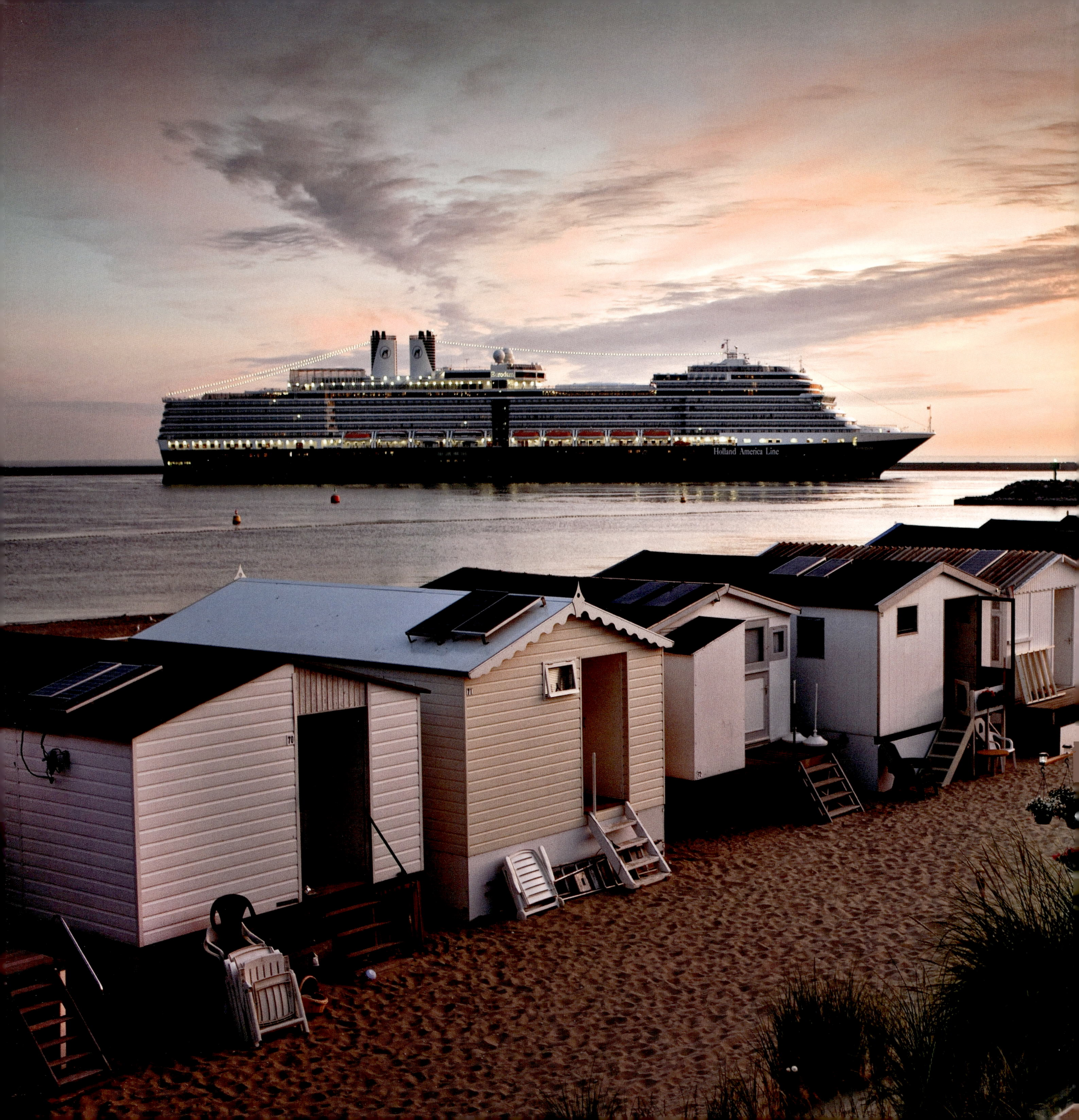
Holland America Line

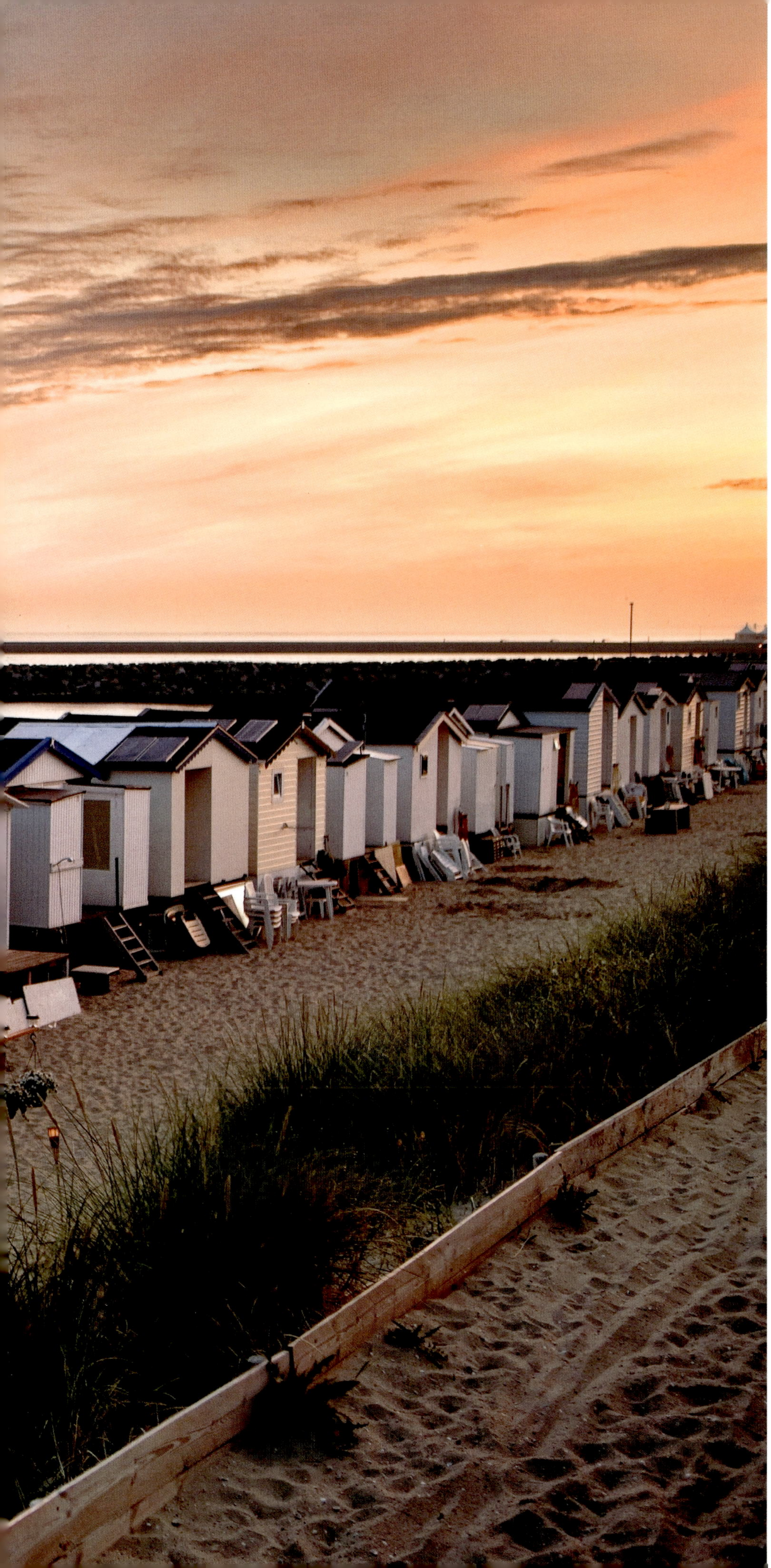

Left: The Eurodam, a cruise ship of the Holland America Line, entering the North Sea Canal at IJmuiden early in the morning. The residents of the beach houses are still asleep.

Following pages: The port of Rotterdam and its three main transshipment product groups side by side: ore, container shipping, and oil / chemical products. From the nineteenth century, the port began to benefit greatly from the industrialisation of the Ruhr area in western Germany and the construction of the Waterway. In the twentieth century, Rotterdam became a central transfer point for the whole of Western Europe for petroleum, petroleum products, coal and ore. After World War II, the port expanded out to the coast at Hook of Holland, and, with the construction of the First Maasvlakte (1973) and Second Maasvlakte (2012) reclaimed port areas, now even juts out far into the sea. From 1962 onwards, Rotterdam was the largest port in the world, until it was eclipsed by the port of Shanghai in 2004.

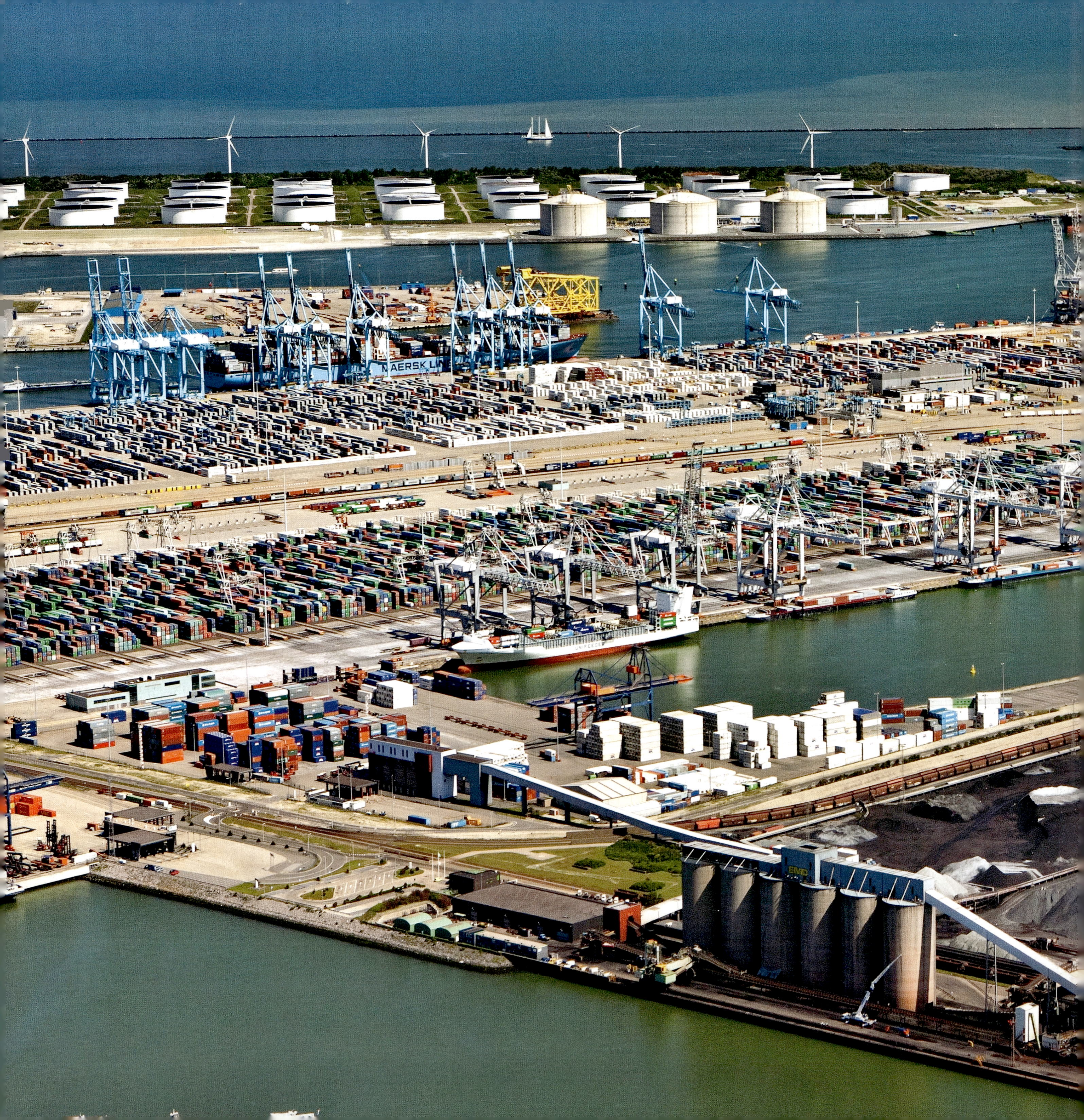

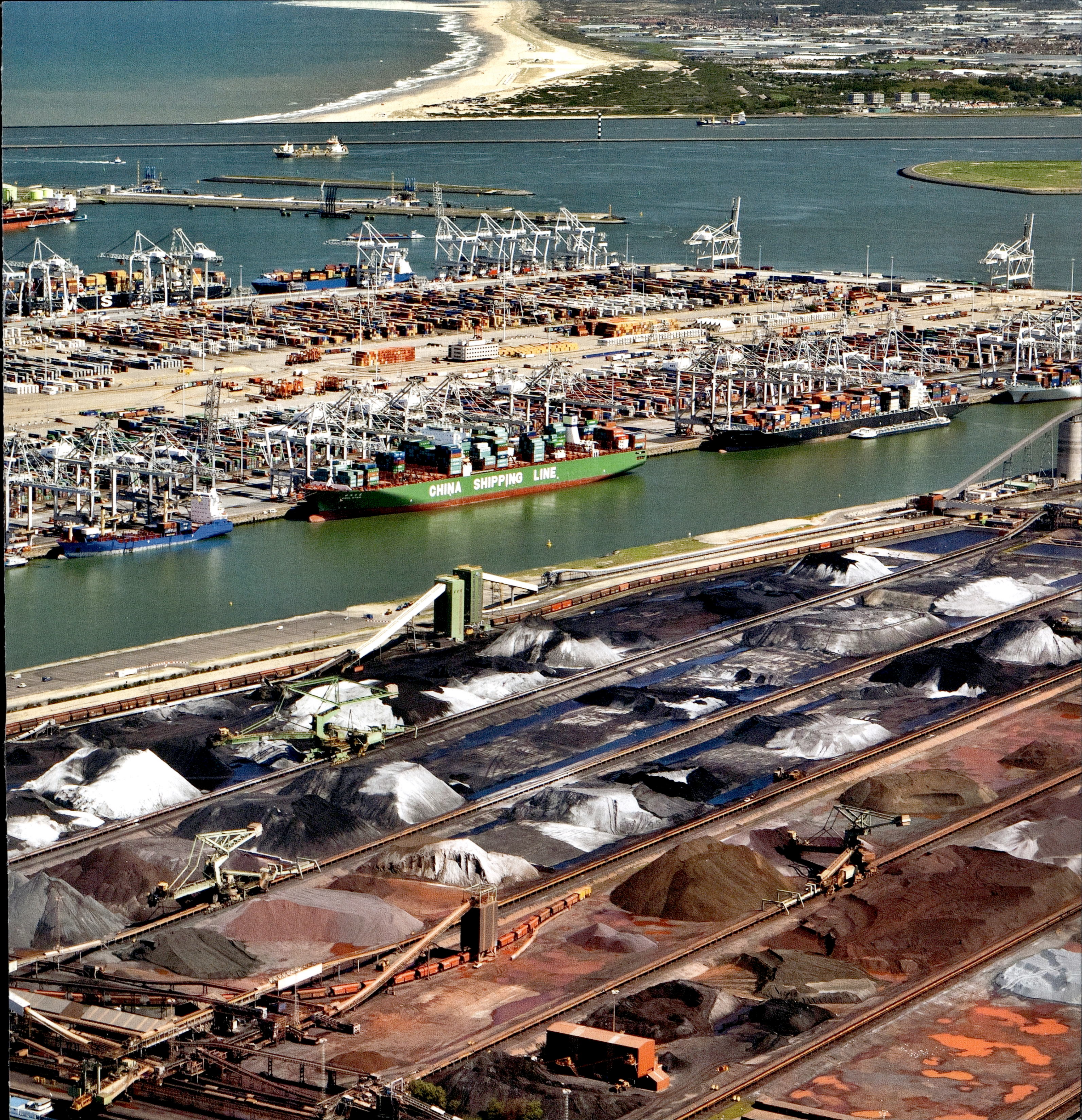
CHINA SHIPPING LINE

Frans Lemmens and Marjolijn van Steeden

After graduating from Nyenrode Business University, Frans Lemmens worked for years as a logistics expert for food aid programs in Africa and later, as a tour guide, he travelled the world. Photography has always been his passion and in 1986 Lemmens decided to become a documentary photographer, mainly concentrating on travel and nature. In that capacity he undertook a number of unique expeditions: he visited Antarctica with the Chilean Navy, he flew around the world with a Catalina flying boat, and he crossed the Sahara on foot and by camel with a traditional Tuareg salt caravan. Lemmens' desert photography of the Sahara quickly led to an international breakthrough and his first book: *The Algerian Sahara* (Focus, 1989). During an expedition in Bolivia (1989), he met his partner Marjolijn van Steeden. Since that time, they have lived and worked together. From 1993, the Netherlands became an important focus for their work. In 1997, their pictures appeared in the successful book *Visions of the Netherlands.* In 2000, Marjolijn and Frans started a new Sahara project, which in 2005 resulted in the book *Sahara, Land Beyond Imagination* – the culmination of their 'desert work'. Unilever then commissioned them for the 75th anniversary book *Unilever Matters* (2006), which illustrates the multinational's operations in fourteen countries. Then, after a few years doing travel reportage abroad, Marjolijn and Frans decided to focus once again on the Netherlands, which among other projects led in 2012 to the books *Beeld van Nederland / Icons of the Netherlands* and *The Netherlands from the Air,* both in co-operation with *National Geographic.* Their work has been published worldwide in all the media you could think of.

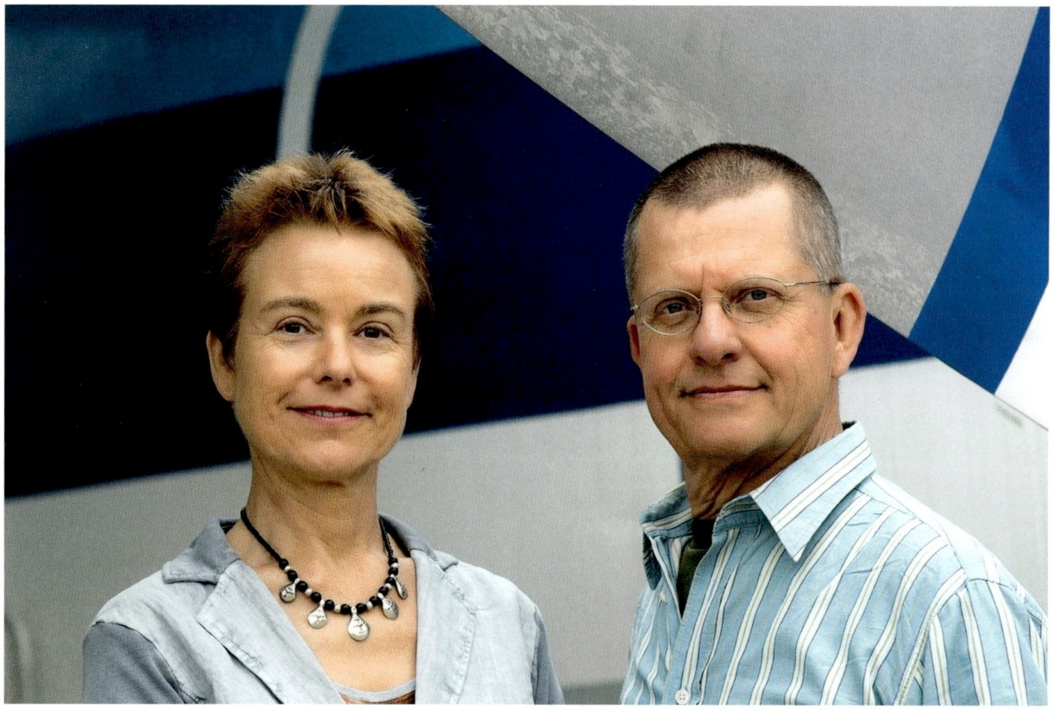

A Dutch edition of this book is also available:
Nederland op zijn mooist (ISBN 978 90 5956 577 7)

This book is a publication of G+J Publishing and Fontaine Publishers
Produced in collaboration with National Geographic Netherlands/Belgium

Fifth edition November 2017

Inside and cover photography: Frans Lemmens
Design and composition: Marjolijn van Steeden
Basic layout: Studio Jan de Boer
Text: Tjerk van Duinen / Frans Lemmens
Image licencing queries: info@franslemmens.com

ISBN 978 90 5956 580 7
NUR 652

www.fontaineuitgevers.nl
www.franslemmens.com